DATE DUE			

Money,
The Price Level,
and Interest Rates

MONEY,
THE PRICE LEVEL,
AND INTEREST RATES

An Introduction
to Monetary Theory

GAIL E. MAKINEN

Associate Professor of Economics
Wayne State University

Prentice-Hall, Inc., Englewood Cliffs, New Jersey 07632

Library of Congress Cataloging in Publication Data

MAKINEN, GAIL E
   Money, the price level, and interest rates.

   Includes bibliographies.
   1. Money. I. Title.
HG221.M334   332.4   76-42293
ISBN 0-13-600486-5

© 1977 by Prentice-Hall, Inc.,
Englewood Cliffs, New Jersey 07632

Printed in the United States of America

10 9 8 7 6 5 4 3 2 1

Prentice-Hall International, Inc., *London*
Prentice-Hall of Australia Pty. Limited, *Sydney*
Prentice-Hall of Canada, Ltd., *Toronto*
Prentice-Hall of India Private Limited, *New Delhi*
Prentice-Hall of Japan, Inc., *Tokyo*
Prentice-Hall of Southeast Asia Pte. Ltd., *Singapore*
Whitehall Books Limited, *Wellington, New Zealand*

to my mother and father

Contents

10. Modern Monetary Theory   258

The Portfolio Approach to Money Demand.
Monetary and Fiscal Policy in a Portfolio Framework.   *Monetary Policy.*
Fiscal Policy.   The Portfolio Approach—Some Additional Considerations.
The Radcliffe Report, Gurley-Shaw, and Roosa.   The Radcliffe Report.
Assessment of Prevailing Monetary Theory.
The Radcliffe View on the Effectiveness of Money.
The Importance of Banks and the Money Supply.   The Gurley-Shaw Thesis.
Secular Monetary Policy.   Cyclical Monetary Policy.   Policy Implications.
The Uniqueness of Money.   Roosa's Availability Doctrine.
The Definition of Money.   The Uniqueness of Commercial Banks.
Nonbank Financial Intermediaries and Monetary Policy.
The Availability Doctrine.   The Nominal Supply of Money.
Early Notions of the Money Supply.
An Identity as a Framework for Nominal Money Supply Analysis.
The Exogeneity of Money.
The Commercial Loan and Fisherian Theories of the Money Supply.
The Riefler-Burgess Money Supply Hypothesis.
The Academic View on the Money Supply.   Recent Academic Contributions.
Conclusion

11. Inflation   313

Inflation Defined.   The Economic Costs of Inflation.
Measuring the Social Cost of Inflation.   A Second Cost of Inflation.
The Redistributive Effects of Inflation.   *Income Redistributions.*
Wealth Redistributions.   Inflation as a Method of Taxation.
Other Problems Related to Inflation.   Causes of Inflation.
Demand-Pull Inflation.   Cost-Push Inflation.
Full Employment Reconsidered.   A Model for Analysis.
Wage-Push Inflation.   Profit-Push Inflation.
Demand-Pull and Cost-Push Discerned.   Income, or Markup, Inflation.
Sectoral-Shift Inflation.   The Phillips' Curve.
The Neo-Fisherian View of Inflation.   *The Labor Market.*
The Effect of Inflation in the Labor Market.   The Commodity Market.
The Inflationary Cycle.   Public Policy in a Neo-Fisherian Framework.
The Phillips' Curve in the Neo-Fisherian Analysis.   Conclusion

12. The Great Debate   365

Introduction.   The Essential Nature of the Debate.
Proportionality of Money and Prices.   Monetary Theory of the Price Level.
Neutrality of Money.   The Causality of Money.
The Transmission Mechanism.
The IS–LM Framework and Monetary Theory.

Preface

Since the study of economic phenomena first became of interest, people have offered various explanations for the cycles in economic activity. These explanations have ultimately come to be confined to two major hypotheses. One views variations in the supply of money as the principal cause of the cycle, whereas the other attributes such movements to factors affecting the real sector of the economy—for example, swings in investor optimism, crop failures, sunspots, oil cartels, and so forth. Closely related to the second view is a belief that a market-oriented economy is unable for some reason to generate and sustain a full-employment equilibrium but comes to rest for substantial periods with high rates of unemployed resources.

The proponents of these alternative theories of the cause of the business cycle have formulated abstract economic models to rationalize their respective observations. In each model the money supply plays a different role in determining aggregate income and employment, the rate of interest, and the general level of commodity prices. Moreover, in each model the appropriate monetary policy for economic stability is quite different. In the model which treats the business cycle as a monetary phenomenon, appropriate monetary policy centers on maintaining a stable growth rate of the money supply over time, whereas the policy suggested by the alternative interpretation of the cycle calls for adjustment of the growth rate of the money supply so that variations in market interest rates can compensate for variations in those other factors thought to initiate the cycle. Under such a policy, it is unlikely that the growth of the money supply would remain stable over time.

In this text both models will be developed, the role of the money supply in each will be analyzed, and the theoretical foundations underlying monetary policy will be discussed. The analysis draws heavily on macro theory—knowledge of such theory at about the intermediate level of sophistication should be considered a prerequisite to a full understanding of the ideas we will explore. The text itself is designed primarily for seniors and first-year graduate students who have the macro background and are familiar with the mechanics of money creation (as typically found in money and banking texts used throughout the country). Ideally, this text should be used for the second course in a two-course sequence dealing with money and monetary theory.

Unlike many contemporary texts which deal with macro theory and monetary economics, this book does not rely on the *IS–LM* mechanism as an expository device, for it conceals much of what is important in analysis, especially the operation of the labor market. However, since the framework is widely used, the problems analyzed in the chapters to follow will, when appropriate, include a discussion in which the same problem is presented using the *IS–LM* mechanism.

Most authors are aware that bias reflecting their graduate training and research interests inevitably enters into the way they view the world. My background provides no exception. My graduate training was strongly influenced by the Keynesian approach prevailing in courses on macro theory and money. Nevertheless, the works of Irving Fisher were a part of that training and the ideas of Milton Friedman have influenced much of my research. Nothing would be more pleasing than to have the readers of this text agree that the topics presented are explored in a dispassionate, objective, informative, and nonpolemical manner.

Many people have given selflessly of their time and ideas to enable me to complete this manuscript. My very deep gratitude for their invaluable assistance is given to my colleagues, Professors William Bomberger and Jay Levin, to Professor Roger Trenary of Bowling Green State University, and to Mr. Charles Schneider, a Ph.D. candidate at Wayne State, who read carefully and discussed with me the entire text. My mentor and friend, H. Peter Gray, offered many valued suggestions for improving the first third of the book. Editorial assistance was ably provided by Mrs. Margot Calarco and Dr. Theresa Vaughan, who labored to simplify my prose and make it both understandable and readable. Miss Cheri Miller devoted many long hours to typing and retyping various drafts, and offered many helpful stylistic suggestions. I wish also to thank all the individuals and institutions who so graciously consented to my requests to quote from their scholarly work. Last, but by no means least, I thank the many Wayne State students in my course in monetary theory on whom various parts of this text were tested. While I thank them all, they are absolved from any responsibility for errors contained in the pages to follow.

CLASSICAL MONETARY THEORY

Part I

Introduction

Students have become increasingly concerned with the relevance of their education to their understanding of the world about them. They have questioned the necessity of studying the works of some authors who wrote more than two hundred years ago. After all, what insights could these scholars provide into the functioning of our twentieth-century industrial state? Answering this question takes much of this text and demands the commitment of much of the student's time.

Two answers to this fundamental question are readily forthcoming. First, the classical macro model of the market economy is not something separate from the Keynesian explanation. In an article published posthumously in 1946,[1] Keynes wrote, "If we succeed in establishing an aggregate volume of output corresponding to full employment as nearly as is practicable, the classical theory comes into its own again from this point onward." This means that when full employment is achieved, the classical analysis of the forces determining the rate of interest, the volume of employment, and the general level of commodity prices is correct. We shall also see that these forces cannot be neglected even in states of less than full employment.

Second, the relevance of the classical model springs from its impact

---

[1] J. M. Keynes, "The Balance of Payments of the United States," *Economic Journal*, Vol. 56, No. 222 (June, 1946), pp. 172–87.

on today's writers: Modern monetary theory has its origins in classical writings; and classical monetary theory may be viewed as a bond linking the older writers to Keynes, and Keynes to Friedman and other contemporary scholars. For these two reasons it is important to understand the classical model of the market economy.

The model which emerges in the following pages was never developed by any single classical writer. The macro analysis of these writers was very descriptive and largely devoid of graphical treatment; however, it is both surprising and gratifying to see the extent to which they subjected their work to empirical verification. Because the classical model presented in this text represents a twentieth-century distillation from many sources, many rich insights into fundamental economic problems, which can only be gained by reading the original works, will necessarily be lost.

Before presenting the classical model and analyzing problems within its framework, its basic substance will be summarized, and the conclusions which emerge will be stated to focus attention on the most important relationships and the role of money in their determination.

The original and lasting contribution of the classical school to monetary theory lies in its formulation of what is commonly called the *quantity theory* of money. This theory provided the analytical framework for explaining the functioning of an economy; it has been used as a basis for policy recommendations and as a means for interpreting economic history.

Simply stated, the quantity theory is an hypothesis about the relationship of the stock of money to the general level of commodity prices, according to which changes in the price level are explained by prior changes in the money stock.

More substantively, the quantity theory is more than the mere conclusion that the stock of money determines prices. It consists of the set of five interrelated propositions stated below, which will form the terms of reference for the subsequent discussion of monetary theory. These five propositions are[2]:

(1) PROPORTIONALITY—The general level of commodity prices will vary directly and proportionately with the stock of money, that is, for every percentage increase in the money stock, the price level will rise by an equal percentage. This proposition will be shown to follow from an economy whose internal mechanism is capable of generating a full employment level of output, and in which individuals maintain a fixed ratio be-

[2] The organization and discussion of these propositions owes much to the work of Thomas M. Humphrey. See his "The Quantity Theory of Money: Its Historical Evolution and Role in Policy Debates," *Economic Review*, Federal Reserve Bank of Richmond (May/June 1974), pp. 2–19.

tween their money holdings and the money value of their transactions.

(2) NEUTRALITY—Changes in the stock of money will have no lasting influence on the level of real income, the real rate of interest, the rate of capital formation, and the volume of employment. The only lasting influence of a change in the money stock will be to alter the general level of prices.

(3) MONETARY THEORY OF PRICES—Propositions (1) and (2) do not preclude nonmonetary factors from influencing the price level. Therefore, proposition (3) states that the general level of prices is predominantly a monetary phenomenon and thereby precludes changes in nonmonetary variables from having a lasting impact on the general level of prices.

(4) CAUSAL ROLE OF MONEY—The series of events known as the "business cycle" can be explained exclusively by variations in the growth rate of the money supply about its long-run trend. Thus, changes in the money supply precede and cause subsequent changes in the price level.

(5) EXOGENEITY OF THE NOMINAL STOCK OF MONEY— The nominal stock of money is supply-determined, and the supply of money is under the control of the central bank. This implies that changes in the demand for money will not automatically bring forth compensatory changes in supply. It is, then, the central bank which determines the supply of money.

However, most of modern world history has been characterized by an international gold standard with fixed exchange rates. Within this institutional framework the money supply is truly exogenous and the central bank is merely the handmaiden whose function is to make national money supplies conform to the flow of gold between nations. In this context the central bank doesn't actually control the nominal money supply, but the effect is the same as if it did. Related to the exogeneity proposition are questions concerning the definition of money and the economic influence of money substitutes.

The richness of this more comprehensive statement of the quantity theory becomes clear when we note that the first four propositions were understood by the classical theorists to hold in the long run. For the short run, or period of transition (which could last for a considerable time interval), these propositions need not hold. Thus, in formulating the quantity theory, the classical theorists distinguished between static and dynamic analysis. In the dynamic context of the short run, changes in the supply of money could evoke a change in output and employment, thereby having a nonneutral effect and altering the strict proportionality between changes in the money stock and in the price level.

These five propositions were by no means universally accepted at the time they were formulated and, in the discussion of the classical school which follows, various counterarguments will be presented, for they have recognizable counterparts in modern analysis. In addition, we shall see that the denial of one or more of these propositions forms the basis of the Keynesian Revolution, and that the propositions themselves form the terms of reference for the current debate between the Monetarists and the neo-Keynesians, or Fiscalists.

From these five propositions flow some startling conclusions which run contrary to many accepted views currently held by economists interested in the short run. In particular, they imply that so long as wages and prices are flexible, the only equilibrium level of national income is that characterized by full employment. If either wage or price rigidities are encountered, only changes in the supply of money will restore full employment.

Accelerations in the rate of growth of the money supply cannot permanently lower the equilibrium rate of interest, cannot increase the rate of capital formation and growth, and cannot permanently increase the volume of employment. They can accomplish all these things in the short run, but in the longer run money will be neutral, some of the capital stock put in place during the period of transition will become redundant, and the volume of employment will fall. Quite obviously the length of the short run will be of great interest. All inflations and deflations will be interpreted as monetary affairs, ruling out cost-push explanations, and the only role for government fiscal policy will be allocative, that is, it will determine whether resources will be used by the public or the private sector.

It will be interesting to see from what mode of analysis these conclusions emerge.

chapter 1

The Classical Model

In an earlier era, no less than in contemporary times, people were interested in discovering the forces which affected the functioning of the economic system in which they lived. Much time and effort were devoted to explaining the forces determining the volume of employment and output, the composition of that output in terms of consumption and investment goods, the rate or rates of interest, the level of wages, and the general level of commodity prices. In addition to these macro questions, early economists investigated explanations of relative prices, the distribution of output among its several factor claimants, the determinants of the stability of the equilibrium, and so forth. While their insights into micro, distributional, and stability questions are invaluable, our concern is with the model the classical economists[1] constructed to explain the functioning of the market economy at the macro level.

This macro model will be discussed in three basic parts which will explain, respectively, the determination of employment and output, the rate of interest and the division of output between investment and consumption goods, and the general level of commodity prices. Our paramount concern is, of course, the role of money as a determinant of these variables.

---

[1] No distinction will be made between classical and neoclassical economists. All pre-Keynesian *General Theory* economists will be considered classical unless otherwise labeled.

THE DETERMINATION OF EMPLOYMENT AND OUTPUT

The first two sectors of the classical model can best be analyzed together, for they have a vital interdependence which arises because the demand schedule for labor is derived from the production function, which relates the level of real output to the volume of employment.

In the classical labor market, as long as the price mechanism works with reasonable promptness to adjust supply to demand, the economic system will generate continuous full employment. Departures from that desirable state must therefore be caused by certain frictions or rigidities in the system (for example, minimum-wage legislation or trade unions), or by phenomena lying outside the range of assumptions made in the classical model; for example, imperfect information about commodity and labor markets.

The volume of labor employed can be determined by the simple expedient of deriving the demand for labor and the supply of labor and by making the assumption that entrepreneurs are profit maximizers.[2]

The demand schedule for labor can be derived from the production function if it is assumed that the capital stock is held constant. Figure 1:1 shows such a production function in which total output (Y) is related to units of labor time (N) suitably measured, for example, man-years, -days or -hours.

FIGURE 1:1.   Aggregate Production Function

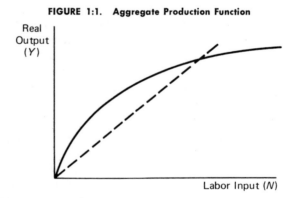

If the capital stock is allowed to vary as well, a family of real output schedules can be generated, with those lying at higher levels representing larger capital stocks.

---

[2] It is assumed throughout this analysis that both the factor markets and the commodity markets are characterized by perfect competition.

The solid line production function, graphed in Figure 1:1, depicts a situation in which additional units of labor time do not contribute equally to output. Rather, while total output rises for each added increment of labor time, it does so at a decreasing rate, and labor time is said to suffer from diminishing marginal physical productivity.

If the marginal physical product of labor as measured by the solid line is graphed, it will produce a schedule which rises initially and then declines. The declining portion is shown in Figure 1:2. How rapidly the schedule falls depends upon the extent of the decline in labor's productivity. Had we graphed the dashed line in Figure 1:1, which depicts a constant marginal product of labor, it would have produced a marginal physical product schedule parallel to the horizontal axis.

FIGURE 1:2. Marginal Physical Product of Labor

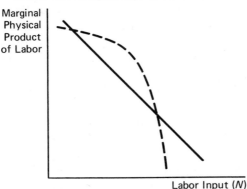

Marginal Physical Product of Labor

Labor Input (N)

Drawing upon examples from agriculture and from the manufacture of pins, classical writers suggested that the marginal product of labor could at first increase, then remain constant over some interval, and finally decline at a rate which tended to increase as more labor was added to a fixed amount of capital or land. The last two stages might be expected to produce a marginal product schedule, such as the dashed one in Figure 1:2.

In order to determine what quantity of labor will actually be demanded or whose employment will be desired, we must use the profit maximization assumption, which in perfectly competitive markets can be expressed in two ways. The first, derived from the product markets, is to alter the volume of production until the marginal revenue from selling an incremental unit is equal to the marginal cost to produce that unit.

The second, derived from the factor market viewpoint, can be expressed by altering the volume of employment until the value of labor's marginal product (which is equal to its marginal physical product multiplied by the price of the commodity being produced) is equal to the cost of labor as measured by its *money* wage.[3] Symbolically this becomes $P_Y \cdot MPP_L = W$. Rearranging the terms, the condition for profit maximization becomes $MPP_L = W/P_Y$ or where the marginal physical product of labor is equal to the *real* wage (or the money wage divided by the price of the commodity, P_Y). When an aggregation of many firms and types of labor is made, W and P must be construed as suitable weighted averages.

It should be noted that W/P is a number like MPP_L; it is not a sum of money. This similarly permits the unit of measure on the vertical axis of Figure 1:2 to be changed from MPP_L to W/P. So to increase the quantity of labor employed, the real wage must be reduced. This can be done by lowering the money wage paid for labor time, by raising the general level of commodity prices, or by some combination of both. The lowering of money wages need not be absolute, but only relative; for example, both money wages and prices can increase, but prices must rise more than money wages. In the classical model *no* direct link exists between money wages (or, more generally, production costs) and commodity prices. This implies that an increase or decrease in money wages will have no direct effect on the general level of commodity prices, which depends, as noted in the introductory remarks, on the stock of money.

The supply schedule of labor is derived from an examination of the welfare maximizing behavior of the individual who furnishes labor time to the market. If the unit of time considered is a day, the maximum amount of labor time the individual could hypothetically furnish the market is limited to 24 hours. Hours not devoted to work are hours available for leisure, and if the individual's goal is assumed to be the maximization of his welfare, the allocation of his available time between the pleasures of leisure and the blood, sweat, tears, and toil of work will depend upon the real wage. The higher the real wage becomes, the greater will become the opportunity cost of leisure and, consequently, the greater amount of labor time offered to the market. Figure 1:3 represents such a hypothetical individual.

The straight lines connecting the vertical and horizontal axes measure real income and are derived by multiplying a given money wage (prices assumed constant) by the hours devoted to work. They can be thought of as budget constraints or the objective trade-off given by the market of leisure for work. Thus, as fewer hours are spent in leisure (move toward the origin), real income rises. Higher budget lines are derived by multiplying higher real wages by the hours worked.

The indifference curves, U_1, U_2, and U_3, measure the individual's subjective welfare level, with U_3 being preferred to U_2 and U_2 to U_1,

---

[3] The specification of the money wage will depend upon the measurement of labor time used. For example, if man-years are used, the money wage will be dollars per year; if man-hours, dollars per hour, and so forth.

FIGURE 1:3.   The Allocation of Time Between Work and Leisure

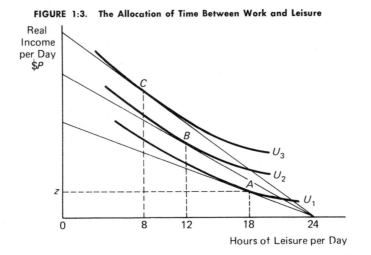

Hours of Leisure per Day

since U_3 gives every level of income given by U_2 plus an additional measure of leisure. Each individual indifference curve gives all combinations of real income and leisure affording a constant level of welfare. The slope of the curve gives the subjective rate of trade-off of leisure for real income.

A tangency of the indifference curve and the budget line represents a point of equilibrium for the subjective trade-off of real income for leisure is equal to the market or objective trade-off of the two. At point A, for example, the individual will spend 18 hours per day in leisure and work 6 hours, deriving an income of OZ equal to the product of the hourly wage and the 6 hours worked. If the hourly wage is increased, the individual will move to point B, reducing his leisure time to 12 hours and increasing his labor time offered to the market from 6 hours to 12 hours. Further increases in real wages will induce him to move to point C.

If points A, B, and C were graphed in a set of axes similar to Figure 1:2, they would show an upward rising supply schedule of labor time as the real wage rises.

This labor supply schedule embodies several very specific assumptions. First, it assumes that every worker has perfect knowledge of all opportunities in the labor market; thus, the phenomenon of frictional unemployment, which arises when labor must quit working to spend time acquiring information on alternative employment opportunities, is unknown.[4]

---

[4] In Chapter 11, a model will be constructed in which the assumption of perfect information is dropped. The relaxation of this assumption complicates the analysis considerably and requires that a distinction be made between the labor force and the supply of labor available at given expected real wages.

A second assumption is that the only way to induce individuals to furnish more labor time to the market is through paying all such labor time a higher real wage. This assumption implies that every time the real wage falls, say because of a slight rise in commodity prices, individuals will voluntarily withdraw some portion of their labor time from the market. This was the only aspect of the classical labor market that Keynes objected to, for simple observation told him that it did not occur.

The production function, the labor demand schedule derived from it, and the labor supply schedule derived from a consideration of the welfare maximizing behavior of individuals can all be combined, as in Figure 1:4, allowing the level of employment and real output to be determined.

Before examining the characteristics of the employment and output levels shown in Figure 1:4, diagram C should be noted. The intersection of the demand and supply schedules of labor produces an equilibrium real wage, $(W/P)_0$. This real wage is a number such as 5 or 300 and measures a certain physical quantity, for example, Cadillacs or ice cream cones, depending upon the items comprising the price level. It is derived by dividing a money wage or appropriate average of money wages by a commodity price or appropriate average of commodity prices. However, many possible combinations of money wages and commodity price levels may yield a given real wage. The function of diagram C is to specify all of these combinations which yield $(W/P)_0$. For example, if $(W/P)_0 = 2$, the straight line out from the origin has a slope equal to two and gives all possible combinations of money wages and price levels which have that value ($2/$1, $4/$2, $6/$3, and so forth).

After the monetary sector is added to the model, a unique price level will emerge which will then allow only one money wage rate to be consistent with equilibrium. That is, one combination such as W_0, P_0 will yield a value for $(W/P)_0$ which will ensure equilibrium in the labor, output, and monetary sectors.

The intersection of the demand and supply schedules for labor, shown in Figure 1:4, produces what is by definition full employment. Every worker who is assumed to have perfect knowledge of the labor market and who is willing to work for a real wage $(W/P)_0$ finds employment. Those individuals who would only be willing to offer their labor services for a higher real wage are of no social concern, for they can be said to be voluntarily unemployed. In addition, the real output level, Y_0, associated with employment level N_0 is also by definition full employment output.

For a more thorough comprehension of the employment/output sectors, the factors causing the labor supply and demand schedules to shift ought to be understood. Since the demand curve for labor is labor's marginal product schedule, it can shift only if the marginal product of

FIGURE 1:4.   The Labor and Output Markets

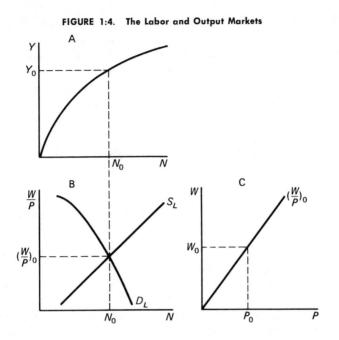

labor changes. Labor's marginal product can increase only if the total product curve shifts upward in both its position and its slope. This will occur if capital accumulates relative to labor or if some technological innovation raises the productivity of both labor and capital. Thus, the upward shift in the slope and position of the total product curve will raise the marginal product of labor and shift out the demand schedule for labor.

The supply schedule of labor can shift for any of several reasons. Labor may re-evaluate the trade-off of leisure and real income (the shape of the indifference curves in Figure 1:3 would change), thereby asking either a higher or lower real wage for the same amount of labor time. Additionally, the schedule will shift because of population growth and variations in the proportion of the population which participates in the labor force (for example, increases in working women, the abolition of child labor, and so forth). Each shift in either the supply or the demand schedule will define a new full-employment level and a new level of full-employment output and may require a new real wage for equilibrium to prevail in the labor market.

An examination of Figure 1:4 will show the equilibrium level of real output to be Y_0. What determines its composition? That is, what determines the fraction composed of capital or investment goods and that composed of consumption goods?

In the classical model the rate of interest was assigned this allocation role, which leads to a discussion of the third sector of that model—that which examines the forces determining the rate of interest. In contrast to contemporary Keynesian macro models, in the classical model the rate of interest is determined by a sector which stands apart from and is not integrated with the remainder of the model. In addition, the equilibrium interest rate is not determined in any way by the stock of money. Thus, it is often said that the classical economists had a "real" theory of the interest rate rather than a monetary theory and that the money stock had no role to play in determining the equilibrium rate of interest.

THE DETERMINATION OF THE RATE OF INTEREST

There can be little doubt that explaining the forces which determine the rate of interest has been one of the major problems facing economists. Contemporary discussion of this question draws heavily upon the early-nineteenth-century work of Henry Thornton and upon the more recent work of Knut Wicksell, Irving Fisher, and J. M. Keynes, and a great deal of it concerns whether real or monetary forces determine the rate of interest. Much of the rather violent attack on Keynes' *General Theory* was directed toward his resurrection of a monetary theory of interest rates under the name of "liquidity preference."

The following discussion of the basic forces considered by the classicals as determining the rate of interest has a strong Fisherian flavor and may be at variance with European writers in the classical tradition.[5]

For the classical economists, the interest rate which prevails in long-run equilibrium is determined exclusively by real forces—the thrift of the community as indicated by its schedule of real saving and the productivity of capital as indicated by the investment demand schedule. Figure 1:5 shows the former schedule to be positively sloped, while the latter is negatively sloped with reference to the *real* rate of interest.[6]

saving

The first task in discussing the determination of the rate of interest will be to explain the shape of the two schedules. Concerning saving, the

[5] For a discussion of other classical theories of the interest rate see F. A. Lutz, *The Theory of Interest* (Chicago: Aldine, 1968).

[6] The concept of a real rate of interest can be complex. For our purposes, it represents the money or market rate of interest less the anticipated rate of price inflation. To simplify the presentation, it is assumed that the price level is constant and everyone anticipates it will remain constant. Thus, the real and money rates of interest are equal. In Chapter 3, the classical concept of short-run disequilibrium will be analyzed and a more detailed discussion of the real rate given.

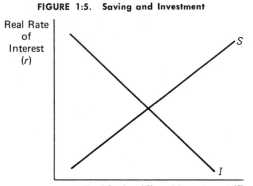

FIGURE 1:5.   Saving and Investment

Real Saving (S) and Investment (I)

classical view starts with the premise that an individual has many desires in life. Some of these require immediate gratification (freedom from hunger and pain), while others can be deferred. In deciding between immediate gratification, which calls for present consumption, and future gratification, which usually necessitates saving, the individual is concerned with the opportunity cost of each alternative, as measured by the real rate of interest. For example, if the current real rate is 6 percent, by consuming $1 of income today, the individual is foregoing the consumption of $1.06 worth of real goods and services one year from today. Thus, the higher the current real rate, the greater the opportunity cost of present as opposed to future consumption; as a result, the relative desirability of saving out of present income is enhanced. Therefore, the higher the current real rate of interest, the greater the portion of full-employment income Y_0 which is saved and available for nonconsumption purposes, which in a closed economy consists of private investment and government uses.

The preceding sentence defines the *act* of saving as not using earned or accrued income for consumption purposes; however, the *act* of saving must be distinguished from the *form* saving takes in the classical model. Later in this chapter, saving and investment will be integrated into a framework of financial markets. In that discussion, saving will take only a bond *form*, that is, the bond will represent the only store of value available to the wealth holder.

investment

The derivation of the investment demand schedule is more complicated than that of the saving schedule. As a first step, the capital stock must be distinguished from investment; the former represents a stock whereas the latter, like saving, represents a flow. However, since the level of the investment demand schedule depends upon the accumulated stock of capital, in deriving the investment demand schedule one must first specify what determines the optimum stock of capital.

As with the labor market, determining the optimum stock of capital is essentially a problem in micro economics. According to classical micro theory, at any given time there exist various combinations of capital and labor with which to produce any given output. The more capital-intensive the production process becomes, the lower will be the marginal physical product of capital. The degree of capital intensity of the production process and, hence, the optimum stock of capital, will depend upon the price of capital (which is the interest rate) relative to capital's marginal product. However, this determination of the optimum stock of capital involves comparing a physical quantity with a rate of interest, a stock concept with a flow price. In order to compare similar magnitudes, the physical productivity of capital must be converted to a percentage yield—a process accomplished in several steps. First, the supply price of capital, which represents the market price for new capital goods, must be obtained. Second, the expected revenue or profit per unit on the output of commodities produced by the capital good must be calculated and aggregated per time period, for example, profits per year designated in Equation (1:1) as R. Third, the series of annual aggregated expected profits is set equal to the supply price of capital and the equation is solved for the discount rate needed to establish the equality. This discount rate, r, is the yield on capital and was called by the classical economists the *marginal efficiency of capital,* or MEC. This discount rate, r, is compared to the market interest rate to determine how capital-intensive the production process should become and, hence, the size of the optimum capital stock.

$$\text{Supply Price of Capital} = \frac{R_1}{(1+r)^1} \quad \frac{R_2}{(1+r)^2} + \ldots + \frac{R_N}{(1+r)^N} \qquad (1:1)$$

The MEC schedule was expected to slope downward and to the right because of the diminishing marginal productivity of capital as the production process became more capital intensive. That is, as capital intensity increased, fewer and fewer commodities would be forthcoming at the margin, and, given per-unit profits, aggregate profits per time period would decline. Thus, as capital intensity increased over time, the R series of Equation (1:1) was expected to fall. Given a constant supply price of new capital goods, the rate of discount, or the MEC, must fall as capital intensity increased or the stock of capital grew relative to labor over time. Thus, because of the diminishing marginal productivity of capital, the relationship of the MEC to the size of the capital stock was expected to be negative.

The optimum or equilibrium capital stock is that at which the

MEC is equal to the market rate of interest. Should the market interest rate fall, the actual capital stock would then be less than that desired, making it profitable to add marginal increments to the existing capital stock.

Once such a disparity between the actual and desired capital stocks emerges because of a decline in the interest rate, the question arises as to how fast the gap can be closed or the actual capital stock increased. This brings us to the subject of the rate of investment, for it is net investment[7] which augments the existing capital stock and moves it toward its new optimum level.

Net investment will only be undertaken in a given time period if its yield is equal to or greater than the market rate of interest. In computing the yield on new investment, the formulation is the same as that used to compute the yield on the capital stock—that is, the supply price of new capital goods is set equal to the expected future profits from that capital. The classical analysis held that as the rate of investment rose, the expected yield on investment (which can be called the *marginal efficiency of investment,* or MEI) would fall, thus producing a negative relationship between the quantity of investment per unit of time and its expected yield, r. This relationship is shown in Figure 1:6.

FIGURE 1:6.   **The Investment Demand Schedule**

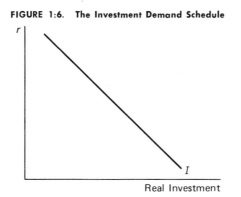

Real Investment

However, the reason for the decline in the marginal efficiency of investment, as the rate of investment per unit of time increased, was thought to be different from that which caused the MEC to decline. Since additions to the capital stock through net investment were small in relation to the size of the capital stock, diminishing returns could not explain the short-run decline in expected yield on new investment.

---

[7] Gross investment must be distinguished from net investment. In equilibrium, the capital stock will wear out at a given rate per year. To maintain the stock intact will require investment. However, to the extent that all investment merely replenishes the depreciated capital stock, we have gross investment but no net investment.

Rather, the decline was attributed to a rising supply price of capital as greater demands for capital goods were placed upon the capital-goods industry in the short run. In terms of Equation (1:1), the decline in r, which is now taken to be the MEI, is due to a rising supply price of capital, not to a decline in expected profits or the R's. However, nothing excludes diminishing returns from serving as a supplementary explanation for the decline in the MEI, or r.

Equilibrium and the Natural Rate of Interest

The intersection of the saving and investment schedules produces the equilibrium real rate of interest. This unique real rate will be designated the *natural rate of interest*, for it among all the real interest rates produces the equilibrium condition in which desired saving from a full employment income is exactly equal to desired investment. Thus, the volume of resources not needed for consumption purposes at full employment is exactly equal to the volume of resources that society desires to use for investment purposes. So long as that portion of income not being returned to the circular flow through consumption is being returned by way of private investment, the rate of circular flow will remain constant and the economic system will remain in a state of equilibrium.

The classical economists imposed one implicit requirement upon those two schedules—that they intersect at a positive real rate of interest, that is, that the natural rate be positive. Consider for a moment what lack of intersection, as shown in Figure 1:7, implies. It is that more is saved out of a full employment income in terms of goods and services available for nonconsumption purposes than others wish to use for non-consumption or investment purposes. We thus have an excess supply of

FIGURE 1:7.   Nonintersection of Saving and Investment

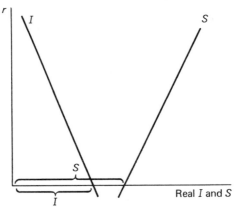

goods available for nonconsumption purposes at a zero real rate of interest. Classical economists might have called this situation a "general glut,"
and it implies that equilibrium is inconsistent with full employment.

The Financial Markets and the Equality
of Money and Real Interest Rates

We have frequently been using the term *real rate of interest*. However,
the real rate is unseen and is neither reported in the financial press nor
discussed by the leading bankers or businessmen. What *is* reported and
discussed is the money rate of interest. In this section, our analysis will
show why in equilibrium the money rate must conform to the real rate,
and thus why the interest rate was regarded by the classical economists
as a nonmonetary, or real, phenomenon.

To see why in equilibrium the real and money rates must be equal,
we must specify the *form* taken by saving and the *form* through which
businessmen raise the money needed to acquire additions to their real
capital stock. That form will be the *bond*. That is, all saving or income
earned but not used for consumption will be used to purchase bonds
and all desired investment projects will be financed by firms borrowing
through the medium of a bond. This assumption does, of course, limit
the scope of the financial sector of the market.

For the time being, the act of hoarding or holding savings in a
money form is excluded as representing supposedly irrational behavior.
Would any rational person give up the positive interest yield of a bond
to hold money which yields nothing? Obviously not, thought the classical
economists.

Now that the bond has been introduced as the form in which savings are held and investment financed, a financial sector corresponding
to Figure 1:5 can be constructed (shown in Figure 1:8). Part A represents
the real magnitude of saving and investment. The money value of desired
saving is supplied to the financial market as loanable funds and is shown
in Part B as $S_m(S)$. These funds are supplied in demand for bonds as
shown in Part C as $D_B(S)$. Thus, loanable funds representing real saving
are supplied to the financial markets in return for bonds which they
demand.

Corresponding to the real value of desired investment in Part A is
a demand for loanable funds shown in Part B as $D_m(I)$. These loanable
funds are obtained in exchange for bonds which are supplied to the
financial markets and are shown in Part C by the supply schedule $S_B(I)$.
Since Part B is merely the money counterpart of Part A, the slope and
position of its two schedules are identical to their corresponding counterparts in Part A, and hence the money rate of interest will equal the real
rate.

FIGURE 1:8.   **Financial Markets**

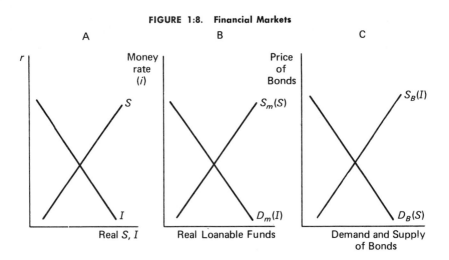

If either I or S or both shift, their corresponding counterparts in Parts B and C will also shift, producing changes in money interest rates and bond prices. So long as the banking system neither creates nor destroys money and we exclude hoarding, the money rate will always be equal to the real rate of interest.

THE DETERMINATION OF THE GENERAL LEVEL OF COMMODITY PRICES

To explain the determination of the general level of commodity prices, the classical writers formulated what we have called the crude quantity theory of money.

This influence of money on prices was deduced from an analysis of historical experience. Its first formalized statement is attributed to the French writer Jean Bodin, who linked the two together when he attempted to explain the price revolution which swept Europe for almost a century after the Spanish introduced great quantities of gold and silver into Europe from their American colonies in the sixteenth century. Bodin's rudimentary analysis was subsequently refined, formalized, and made more rigorous by others in the classical tradition. Interestingly enough, the quantity theory can alternatively be viewed as a theory of aggregate demand and as a theory of the demand for money. As a theory of money demand, it represents what has come to be called the *Cambridge* (England), or *cash-balance*, approach to the quantity theory formulated by Alfred Marshall, A. C. Pigou, and J. M. Keynes.

When explaining the price level with the quantity theory, it is both easier and more direct to use the American, or *income-velocity*, approach formulated by Irving Fisher.

Fisher's conclusion regarding the effect of money on commodity prices was deduced from a simple identity which arises when the act of exchange is examined. In a closed economy, nothing can be purchased by one person which is not simultaneously sold by another, since the act of sale or exchange must encompass both purchase and sale, these being the two parts of a transaction. The total value of all purchases made with money can be viewed as equaling the average stock of money then in existence multiplied by the average number of times that money stock was turned over, or spent for goods and services. Fisher let M stand for the average stock of money and V for its turnover rate, or velocity. Thus, MV represents total purchases made during a given time period, or aggregate money demand.

Since total money purchases must equal total money sales, Fisher set about to symbolize the total money value of sales, or the money value of aggregate supply. Every item sold represents a physical quantity multiplied by its price and the sum of all these can be expressed mathematically as $\sum_{i=1}^{N} p_i q_i$. In order to simplify this notation, Fisher let $\sum_{i=1}^{N} p_i$, or the sum of all the prices, be represented by a suitable commodity price index called P. He let the value of $\sum_{i=1}^{N} q_i$ be represented by one of two symbols; if the quantity referred to all goods and services sold in a given time period, it became T, symbolizing total transactions, whereas if it referred only to new goods and services sold (those which would enter the GNP accounts), it was symbolized by Y. Similarly, the price index must be revised to reflect the quantity being used.

Thus, Fisher's identity becomes:

$$MV_T \equiv PT$$
or
$$MV_Y \equiv PY$$

where V_T and V_Y measure, respectively, money's turnover against all goods and services sold or its turnover against new goods and services. Unless otherwise specified, all references to velocity will be to the V_Y, or income-velocity, concept rather than to the V_T, or transactions-velocity.

This identity is often called the *Equation of Exchange,* and is used to formulate the quantity theory of money. It expresses the truism that the total value of purchases must be identically equal to the total value of sales or that the total value of goods demanded must be identically equal to the total value of goods supplied.

Fisher did not end his analysis merely by formulating an identity. His ultimate contribution was to turn the identity into a theory which explained how and why changes in the stock of money produced proportional changes in the price level. For example, from past data we might find that during 1970, United States national income was $800 billion and the average stock of money was $200 billion. This would produce an income velocity of 4. Fisher realized that the real output component of the $800 billion had to be explained by economic forces and that while mathematically the velocity was 4, the turnover rate of money was something behaviorally determined. Therefore, what made its value 4 rather than something else? Perhaps one of the greatest misuses of the quantity theory by classical economists was their assumption that velocity was a virtual constant—a value which was necessary to preserve an equality in an equation.

It should also be noted that the proposition that the level of prices varies directly and proportionately with the stock of money is essentially one which holds in a long-run, full-employment equilibrium, if we assume that velocity and real output are constant.

Before investigating the relationship of money and prices in depth, we must note that MV is merely an additional way to specify aggregate demand. As such, it consists of the spending for consumption and investment and could also include government expenditures and net purchases by foreigners. However, in a closed economy, MV is equal to the familiar $C + I + G$. Most classical writers chose to ignore the components of aggregate demand with the possible exception of Wicksell, whose work constituted the first serious approach to what is now called Income–Expenditure Analysis.

Fisher's Equation of Exchange, $MV = PY$, can be used to examine the impact of a change in the money supply. If the level of real output, Y, is fixed at full employment, and velocity, V, is assumed to be relatively constant, any increase in the stock of money, M, must result in a proportionate increase in the general level of prices.[8] Thus, if aggregate demand increases, MV rises and the money value of aggregate supply must also change in exact proportion to preserve the macro equality $MV = PY$. Since V and Y are constants, the change in M must induce a proportionate change in P. Moreover, under these assumptions, all changes in P must originate from a change in M. Thus, increasing the level of workers' money wages or raising interest rates or rents will not result in a rise in the general level of commodity prices. The level of

---

[8] As a simple example of what causes demand to rise, consider the case of a Spanish explorer returning to Spain from Mexico with a shipload of silver. His wealth having risen, he seeks to convert what will become money into other assets, thereby increasing his spending rate, MV.

prices is a purely monetary phenomenon. However, if M remains constant and either V or Y changes, the level of P will change as well. This can be seen by simply rearranging Fisher's identity $MV = PY$ to $MV/Y = P$. Any change in M, V, or Y can produce a change in P, but under the assumption of a constant V and Y, P changes only in response to prior changes in M.

Once the equation of exchange is graphed, the classical model will be complete; this is shown in Figure 1:9.

FIGURE 1:9.   **The Equation of Exchange**

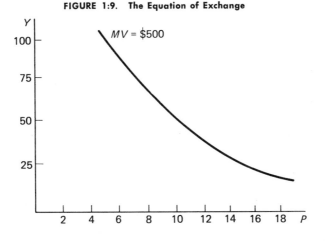

In order to fix an initial position in the set of axes, the level of real output will be assumed to be given at $Y = 100$. Then, if the value of MV is equal to $500, the general level of prices must be equal to 5 to preserve equality between aggregate demand and aggregate supply. This combination of 100, $500, and 5 gives us one point in Figure 1:9, where $MV = $500. Now, let the value of real output decline to one-half its previous value, or 50, while MV continues to equal $500. To preserve equality, P must double to 10. Similarly, let Y again fall by one-half to 25, while MV remains at $500. P must again double to a value of 20. The resulting schedule traces out all combinations of Y and P consistent with a given value for MV, and will have the geometric properties of a rectangular hyperbola.[9]

This schedule will shift with any change in M or V. For example, let Y remain at 100 and let MV be increased to $1,000. For equality to

[9] From an economic viewpoint, the rectangular hyperbola is a unit elastic schedule throughout its range. Thus, a rectangle inscribed beneath any point on the schedule will be equal to any other rectangle inscribed beneath any other point. Since each rectangle measures total spending, and all rectangles are equal, total spending remains unchanged for each price-level–output combination given by the schedule.

be maintained, P must now increase to 10. Using the same method as above, a new MV schedule can be traced out which lies to the right of $MV = \$500$. Conversely, a schedule for $MV = \$250$ could be traced out which would be to the left of $MV = \$500$.

As a preview of Chapter 4, the quantity theory can be developed as a theory of the demand for money; this is frequently called the Cambridge, or cash-balance, approach to distinguish it from the Fisherian, or income-velocity, approach.

As an example, assume that during the past year national income was $1,000 and that the average stock of money during this period was $100. These facts can be interpreted to mean that during that time period people held an average of one-tenth of their annual income in cash balances. If these average money holdings represent their demand for money, the quantity theory then states that on the average, people demand cash balances equal to one-tenth of their income. Why are these cash balances held? A principal reason is to make transactions in the marketplace, because an economic unit's (consumer or business) income and expenditures are not perfectly synchronized. Before this relationship is graphed, a simple example may help to clarify the idea.

Suppose an individual's money income is $6 and is paid at the beginning of a given week. He then spends his income uniformly during the week. What are his average money holdings, or his demand for money, during this time span? His average money holdings were $3 per

$$\frac{\$6 + \$5 + \$4 + \$3 + \$2 + \$1 + \$0}{7 \text{ days}} = \frac{\$21}{7} = \$3$$

day, or his demand for money was equal to one-half his weekly income. He held cash balances in order to make daily transactions because his income and expenditure flows were not related.

This demand-for-money relationship can be represented by the following formula:

$$M_D = k(PY)$$

where PY represents money income and k represents the portion of that income the public desires to hold in a money form. In the examples above, k was equal to either one-tenth or one-half. Of interest are why k equals those particular values and what causes the value of k to change over time. The answer is the same as the answers to similar questions posed earlier about why velocity had a certain value and what caused it to change over time. This equivalence is most easily seen by noting the relationship between k and V.

Velocity   Demand for Money

$MV = PY$ $M = k(PY)$

$M = \dfrac{1}{V} PY$ $M/PY = k$

$M/PY = \dfrac{1}{V}$

Thus, $k = 1/V$. This is an important equality, for it means that every behavioral, technological, or institutional force which explains the velocity of money also explains the demand for money. So statements about velocity are also statements about the demand for money, or the value of k. Chapter 4 will explore this relationship in greater depth. Figure 1:10 is used to graph the demand for money. The value of the slope of the line which divides the quadrant is the value of $1/k$, or V, for it is equal to PY/M, which the above formulation establishes as the value of V.

Figure 1:10 is the familiar transactions demand for money found in Keynesian models, and it was to this purpose that Keynes relegated the quantity theory of money.

The Cambridge approach to the quantity theory can also be considered as a theory of price-level determination. All that is required is a manipulation of the Cambridge equation from $M = kPY$ to $M/kY = P$. Thus, the price level will vary if either the money stock, the level of real output, or the fraction of money income held in a money form varies.

FIGURE 1:10.   The Transactions Demand for Money

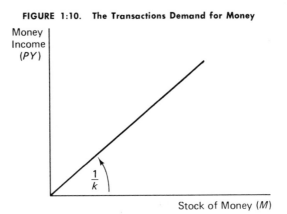

THE FULL CLASSICAL SYSTEM

Figure 1:11 integrates all sectors of the classical model.

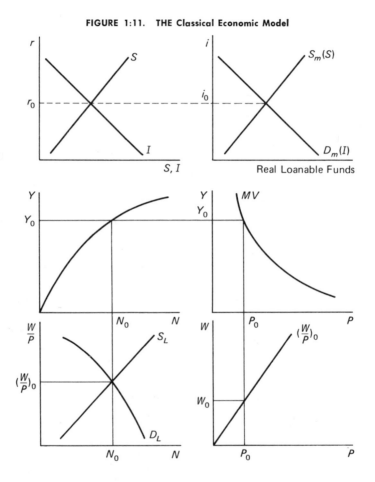

FIGURE 1:11.   THE Classical Economic Model

The lower portion of the diagram determines the level of real output, the real wage, the general level of prices, and the level of money wages, while the upper portion determines how Y_0 will be allocated among consumption and investment uses, which is the function of the interest rate.

Since each diagram in Figure 1:11 represents a separate equation in the general-equilibrium framework, the classical model can be expressed by a system of equations which will allow us to compare it with the

Keynesian model to be developed in a subsequent chapter. The system in functional form is:

$$I = f(r) \qquad (1{:}3)$$

$$S = f(r) \qquad (1{:}4)$$

$$I = S \qquad (1{:}5)$$

$$M_D = \frac{1}{V}\, PY \qquad (1{:}6)$$

$$M_D = M_S \qquad (1{:}7)$$

$$Y = f(N) \qquad (1{:}8)$$

$$D_L = f(\frac{W}{P}) \qquad (1{:}9)$$

$$S_L = f(\frac{W}{P}) \qquad (1{:}10)$$

$$D_L = S_L = N \qquad (1{:}11)$$

Equations (1:5), (1:7), and (1:11) express the conditions for equilibrium, that is, investment = saving clears the commodity markets, money demand = money supply clears the money market, and the demand for labor = supply of labor clears the labor market.

CONCLUSION

The objective of this chapter has been to construct the basic classical model within which a variety of economic problems will be analyzed. Later, this model will be contrasted with a Keynesian model and a detailed comparison undertaken in order to capture the essence of the Keynesian Revolution.

Of ultimate interest, of course, is the role money plays in the classical model as a determinant of employment, output, interest rates, and the level of prices. Our preliminary discussion has indicated that the only role of money is to determine the level of commodity prices. However, in a subsequent discussion of the period of transition, or short run, it will be shown that money can exert a temporary influence on all the variables in the Equation of Exchange—P, V, and Y. Its dominant influence on the price level will be found to be characteristic of the longer run.

This chapter has also laid the groundwork for a detailed analysis on the two ways of viewing the quantity theory: The Cambridge cash-balance approach and the Fisherian income-velocity approach.

Selected References and Readings

ACKLEY, GARDNER, *Macroeconomic Theory* (New York: Macmillan, 1961).

BLAUG, MARK, *Economic Theory in Retrospect,* rev. ed. (Homewood, Ill.: Irwin, 1968).

COCHRANE, JAMES, *Macroeconomics Before Keynes* (Glenview, Ill.: Scott, Foresman, 1970).

CONARD, JOSEPH, *An Introduction to the Theory of Interest* (Berkeley: University of California Press, 1959).

HUMPHREY, THOMAS, "The Quantity Theory of Money: Its Historical Evolution and Role in Policy Debates," in *Economic Review,* Federal Reserve Bank of Richmond (May/June 1974).

LUTZ, F. A., *The Theory of Interest* (Chicago: Aldine, 1968).

SHAPIRO, EDWARD, *Macroeconomic Analysis* (New York: Harcourt, Brace & World, 1966).

chapter 2

The Classical Model
in the Long Run

In order to appreciate the full range of insights held by the classical school on the functioning of the market economy, chapters 2 and 3 must be read as an integrated whole. Chapter 2 presents classical monetary theory as expounded by those writers of the Ricardian tradition with its concentration on long-run equilibrium and its relative disdain for analysis of the short run, which it regarded as a mere "period of transition" linking sequential states of equilibrium. But to conclude that the Ricardians represented the total state of classical monetary theory is to miss the essence of their great theoretical contribution in examining the role of money as the cause of the period of transition. It is this analysis, presented in Chapter 3, which serves as the basic theoretical underpinning for the current monetary doctrine known as *Monetarism*.

To understand how the classical writers could reach certain conclusions concerning cause and effect, and their policy prescriptions, several economic problems will be analyzed according to their model. The range of problems will include an increase in the supply of money, an increase in the supply of labor, an increase in the demand for labor, a rise in money hoarding, a change in the habits of thrift, wage-and-price rigidities, and the role of fiscal policy.

AN INCREASE IN THE SUPPLY OF MONEY

The first problem is designed to demonstrate one of the core propositions of the quantity theory of money—namely, that money is neutral in its impact on the economy. That is, a change in the nominal money stock can have no long-run effects on real output, the level of employment, the real rate of interest, or the composition of final output. The factors affecting the secular changes in these real magnitudes were thought to be determined by such basic phenomena as the kind of economic system, the qualities of its people, their habits of thrift, the state of technology, the availability of natural resources, and so forth. These factors, rather than money or monetary institutions, ultimately determined the "wealth of nations."

The increase in the money supply discussed here is assumed to come about through the commercial banking system. Given an increase in their excess reserves, the banks proceed to lend out the reserves by buying bonds and supplying new money to the market for loanable funds.[1] In Figure 2:1, this is shown as an outward shift in the demand for bonds in Part C and as an outward shift in the supply of loanable funds from $S_m(S)$ to $S_m(S + CB)$ in Part B (the difference between the two schedules representing new money creation).

The increase in the supply of loanable funds will drive down the money rate of interest from i_0 to i_1. Both lenders and savers will respond to this lower money, or market, rate of interest. The lower rate will make it profitable to undertake additional investment previously unprofitable

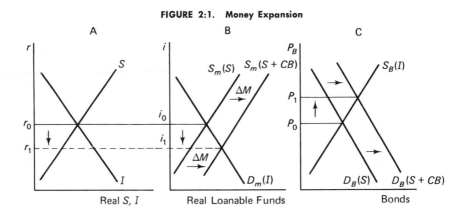

FIGURE 2:1. Money Expansion

[1] This analysis was first formulated in the nineteenth century by Henry Thornton, whose work will be analyzed in depth in Chapter 3.

at interest rate i_0, and it will persuade individuals to save less and consume more of their income, leading to an excess of intended investment over intended saving. This disequilibrium is reflected in the commodity market by a rise in effective demand from MV to $M'V$, as shown in Figure 2:2. This rise is made possible by additional money creation to finance the rise in desired investment spending and consumption spending. The combined effect of a rise in C and I is to force up commodity prices in proportion to the rise in M, since real output, Y, is fixed. To maintain equilibrium elsewhere in the system, money wages will have to rise as rapidly as prices in order to keep the real wage, W/P, unchanged. As long as the banks create money, the inflation will continue and MV will shift out; however, once money creation halts, the money rate of interest will again be equal to the natural rate and the system will be back in equilibrium. None of the real variables will have changed. Output will again be at Y_0, the level of employment at N_0, the real wage at $(W/P)_0$, the real interest rate at its natural level r_0, and the composition of output between consumption goods and investment goods as it was before the inflation. Only nominal magnitudes will have changed. The general level of prices will have increased in proportion to the change in the money stock, and it follows from the constancy of $(W/P)_0$ that money wages must also have risen in the same proportion to the rise in

FIGURE 2:2.   The Response of the System to an Increase in Money

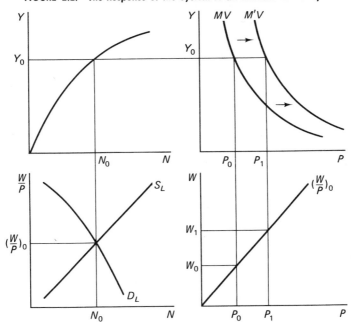

the money stock. Lastly, while the nominal money stock rose, the real money stock, M/P, remained constant, since the price level, P, rose in proportion to the change in M.

According to this analysis, when the two states of equilibria are compared, money is neutral.

However, certain strict conditions implicit in the analyses must be met to produce neutrality. The first is that wages and prices must be flexible. If rigidities exist, it is possible for changes in the real wage and the level of real output to occur; in addition, the price level need not rise. These possibilities are demonstrated below. Second, the participants in economic activity must be free of *money illusion,* which means that their behavior must depend on the real and not the nominal value of such variables as income, wages, and interest rates. If this condition is not met, inflations which raise the money value of income might induce shifts in the saving schedule, leading to variations in the natural rate of interest. Other alterations in behavior can also be specified. Third, changes in the supply of money must not alter the distribution of income in the society. Since the society consists of individuals whose tastes are different and for whom the relative attractiveness of saving versus consumption is different, income redistributions can lead to shifts in the saving schedule and alter the composition of real output, that is, change relative prices. Fourth, and last, the participants in economic activity must have perfect information about the conditions of supply and demand under which they participate in various markets. If such information is imperfect or is obtained in different ways by different factor groups, changes in the money supply which change the price level can alter such real magnitudes as saving, investment, the supply and demand for loanable funds, and the supply and demand for labor. The possibility of nonneutral money will be explored at greater length in the chapters 3, 11, and 12.

A deflation will present just the opposite problem, in which the banks contract the supply of money by selling bonds from their portfolios. This increases the supply of bonds in Part C of Figure 2:3 from $S_B(I)$ to $S_B(I + CB)$, and in Part B increases the demand for loanable funds from $D_m(I)$ to $D_m(I + CB)$. The contraction of the money supply will raise the money interest rate relative to the natural rate, inducing a larger quantity of saving and a smaller quantity of investment. Since saving exceeds investment, aggregate demand, MV, will fall, its decrease derived from falls in both C and I. The deflation will continue as long as banks contract the nominal money stock. However, when the contraction ends, all the real variables, including the real money stock, ought to be at the levels which prevailed before the deflation.

Correct countercyclical monetary policy would be to expand bank reserves by the amount the banks desire to hold, thereby avoiding the

FIGURE 2:3. Monetary Contraction

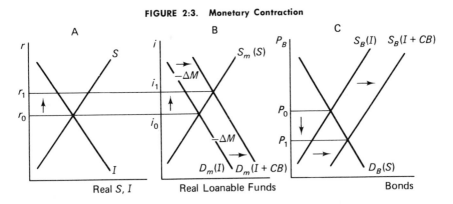

necessity of building them up through monetary contraction. If counter-cyclical policy were called for, it would be signaled by changes in the price level, as it is the price level which adjusts to any disparity between the money interest rate and the natural rate of interest.

WAGE AND PRICE RIGIDITIES

Two quite different rigidities will be examined in this section. First, the government will be permitted to impose wage-and-price controls during an ongoing inflation; in the second example, labor will be allowed, through collective action, to force up money wages.

Price and Wage Controls

Continuing the problem above, the ongoing inflation can be assumed to result from commercial banks creating new money in a full-employment environment. In this set of circumstances, the government decrees a freeze on commodity prices and wages at the P_1 and W_1 levels shown in Figure 2:2. Since the supply of money continues to increase, but prices and wages are frozen, neither P nor Y in the equation of exchange can adjust; the only possible variable left to restore equality between aggregate demand and supply is velocity. Thus it becomes necessary for velocity to fall as fast as the supply of money increases. This fall is unnatural and would not occur if it were not for the controls. The cause of the fall in velocity can best be explained if the quantity theory is viewed in its Cambridge, or cash-balance, form. The banking system, in the process of money creation, is converting bonds into money. However, this excess purchasing power has been temporarily immobilized by the wage-and-price freeze and cannot be used to buy anything. It represents a rise in unwanted idle balances relative to the money income of society. This rise in money balances will be reflected in a rising value of the Cambridge k, which links the money supply, M, to the value of aggregate supply, PY.

As soon as the controls are lifted, the accumulation of idle balances will be liquidated, returning the value of k, or V, to its previous level, forcing up prices in proportion to the rise in M, and returning the value of real balances, M/P, to their preinflation level.

In the situation presented above, the only effect of the controls is to delay the inflationary surge. They in no way restore equilibrium to the system and, in fact, delay movement toward that state.

Money Wage Increases Due to Collective Action by Labor[2]

The action by labor raises the money wage from W_0 to W_1 in Figure 2:4, thereby raising the real wage from $\dfrac{W_0}{P_0}$ to $\dfrac{W_1}{P_0}$. The effect is to create an excess supply of labor, for at $\dfrac{W_1}{P_0}$ the quantity of labor supplied exceeds that demanded. Since the quantity of labor demanded falls to N_1, output declines to Y_1, and given the value of aggregate demand, MV, the price level must rise to P_1 to maintain equilibrium between aggregate demand and aggregate supply. The rise will reduce the real wage somewhat and necessitate further adjustments before the new equilibrium can be known. (These secondary adjustments will not be considered in this analyses.) In addition, the decline in real income, Y, will shift the saving schedule to the left, raising the natural rate of interest.[3] Since the supply of loanable funds will also decline, the money rate of interest will rise to maintain equality with the new higher natural rate.

This problem demonstrates the classical belief that the price level is a monetary phenomenon, for the rise in money wages did not directly cause the price level to rise. The only link between factor payments and the price level is the level of real output. Hence, the rise in money wages, by increasing the real wage, reduces the volume of employment and the level of real output. Since fewer real goods are available at a constant level of money demand, prices are forced upward. The new equilibrium

---

[2] The classical writers might disagree that this situation can arise, for it implies that the currently employed, N_0, suddenly decide that they want "more," a higher real wage for the same amount of work, knowing that their behavior will result in unemployment for some members. The factors causing this change in behavior are left unspecified.

[3] As specified for the model in Chapter 1, saving is a function only of the rate of interest. However, it was assumed that full employment would prevail. If, for some reason, real income declines below its full-employment level, the saving schedule will shift leftward unless all the decline in real income is matched by an equal decline in consumption.

FIGURE 2:4. Response of the System to Trade Union Pressure

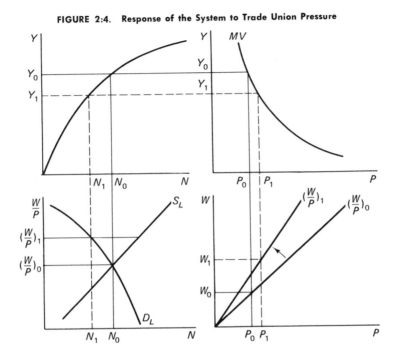

will be characterized by an excess supply of labor which cannot effectively be eliminated because money wages cannot be reduced.[4]

A possible monetary policy would be for the central bank to expand the money stock until the price level is inflated by as much as money wages increased, lowering the real wage to $(W/P)_0$, the level of employment to N_0, and output to Y_0. Such a policy would, however, serve to drive down the real wage to its previous full-employment level. If labor desires a higher real wage and exercises market power to achieve higher money wages, the danger of a wage–price–wage spiral is introduced.

AN INCREASE IN THE SUPPLY OF LABOR

An increase in the supply of labor is characteristic of a growing and changing economy. As long as the birth rate exceeds the death rate, the size of the population will grow and the size of the labor force should

---

[4] To the extent that this model had both a unionized and nonunionized sector, the unemployment in the unionized sector, resulting from the increase in real wages, could seek employment in the nonunionized sector by depressing money and real wages. Output could expand in that sector, thereby making it unnecessary for prices to rise in general. Over time a growing disparity might arise between wages in each sector. However, whether it would occur or not would depend, in part, on the possibility of capital/labor substitutions.

also expand. From time to time, the participation of certain segments of the population in the labor force might also be expected to change, as with the abolition of child labor, the introduction of the housewife into the organized labor market, and so forth.

Any increase in the supply of labor is seen in Figure 2:5 as an outward shift in the supply schedule of labor from S_L to S'_L. At the prevailing real wage $(W/P)_0$, there emerges an excess supply of labor, that is, involuntary unemployment. In the perfectly competitive market situation, labor begins to bid down the money wage. The fall in money wages decreases the real wage, which in turn increases the quantity of labor time demanded and decreases the quantity of labor time supplied. As a larger quantity of labor time is employed, the level of real output rises from Y_0 to Y_1. Since total nominal aggregate demand, MV, has not increased, the rise in real output can only be disposed of by selling it at a lower price, thus preserving the equality between aggregate demand and the value of aggregate supply. The fall in prices raises real aggregate demand, MV/P. It is necessary that money prices fall only if the money supply is held constant.

Keynes, among other classical economists, objected to any long-run monetary policy whose goal was to keep the supply of money constant,

FIGURE 2:5. Response of the System to an Increase in Labor Supply

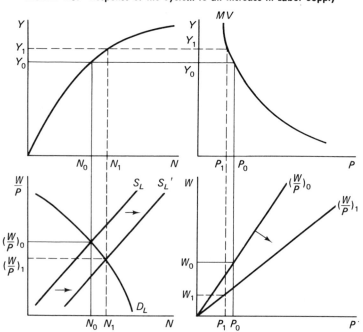

thereby forcing commodity prices to fall over time. He felt that a long-run deflation would create unfavorable expectations. Several American economists of similar views were led to advocate a simple monetary rule designed to achieve long-run price stability: That on the average the rate of money spending, MV, be allowed to grow as fast as real output.[5] If the value of velocity, V, were reasonably constant over time, the monetary rule would call for allowing the supply of money, M, to grow, on the average, at the same rate as Y, thus preserving the stability of the price level in the long run. If V were subject to some long-run trend, the rule would call for the money supply to be adjusted to counter that trend as well as to match the growth of Y. If this course of action were followed, unfavorable expectations caused by a sagging price level would be minimized.

Interestingly, a demonstration of this simple rule of monetary growth is a good deal more complicated than one might expect and is properly carried out in the context of a carefully specified growth model. Depending on how the model is specified and how the money supply is increased (whether by the monetization of bonds or by merely printing and spending it), it is possible to show that any constant growth rate of money may in the long run exert nonneutral effects, that is, change permanently the natural rate of interest, the equilibrium capital stock, the real wage, and so forth. While such an analysis will not be made here, Chapter 12 contains a more extensive discussion of the long-run nonneutrality of money in the classical model.

AN INCREASE IN THE DEMAND FOR LABOR

In most developed economies the capital stock, through saving, accumulates relative to labor, thereby increasing the marginal product of labor. Also, it is possible for technological innovation to raise the productivity of both labor and capital. Whichever occurs, the total product curve in Figure 2:6 will shift upward, and if the upward shift does not move by some constant amount, the marginal product of labor will increase, shifting out the demand curve for labor. If wages do not immediately adjust, excess demand will occur in the labor market. Competition among employers will force up money wages, which, given prices, will force up real wages and lead to an increase in the quantity of labor time supplied. The increase in employment and in labor productivity will increase real

---

[5] For a discussion of the origin of this idea among American economists, see Thomas M. Humphrey, "Role of Non-Chicago Economists in the Evolution of the Quantity Theory in America, 1930–1950," *Southern Economic Journal*, Vol. 38, No. 1 (July 1971), pp. 12–18.

FIGURE 2:6.   Response of the System to an Increase in Labor Demand

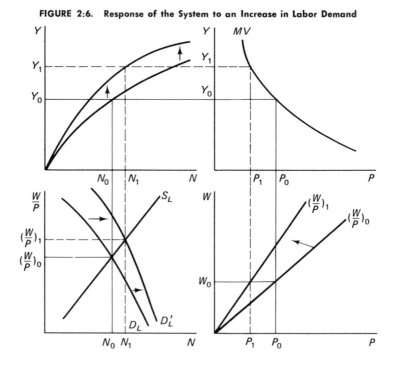

output. So long as aggregate money demand, MV, remains constant, the price level will fall (real aggregate demand, MV/P, will of course rise).

As with the case of an increase in the supply of labor, the above result will prevail only if the money stock is held constant. If, however, a constant price level is desired, the money supply ought to be increased at roughly the same average rate as the level of real output increases, necessitating a long-run policy of keeping the money rate of interest below the natural rate as in our first problem.

The new equilibrium will be characterized by a higher real wage consisting of a higher money wage and either a constant or a lower price level, a higher volume of employment and real output, and a lower level of interest rates. The decline in interest rates is the result of both an increase in saving and a decline in the marginal productivity of capital, which shifts the investment schedule leftward.

The case analyzed above produces the seeming anomaly of a higher real wage and higher employment. The two go together in this example because of the rising productivity of labor, which, indeed, accounts for the increase in material prosperity and the rising standard of living experienced by most developed countries.

Again, for a smooth adjustment, flexible wages, prices, and interest rates are a necessity.

A RISE IN THE LEVEL OF THRIFT

As a consequence of placing a higher value on future consumption than on present consumption, individuals will save more out of a given income at each interest rate, thereby shifting out the saving schedule in Figure 2:7 from S to S', and the supply of loanable funds schedule from $S_m(S)$ to $S_m(S')$. This will decrease the natural rate from r_0 to r_1 and the money rate from i_0 to i_1. The decline in the interest rate makes additional marginal increments of investment profitable, and the additional supply of loanable funds provides the financial wherewithal to make the additional investment possible. Full-employment aggregate demand, MV, remains unchanged, but its composition is altered. The rise in thrift causes consumption to decrease, freeing the resources required for the rise in investment. While C falls, the quantity of I rises and $C + I$ remains constant.

In the longer run, the increase in the rate of investment will augment the capital stock, decreasing the marginal productivity of capital, raising that of labor, increasing the real wage, and so forth.

A decrease in thrift has the opposite effect. To the extent that the interest rate quickly adjusts, MV will remain unchanged—however, its composition will be altered.

MONEY HOARDING

When the basic building blocks of the classical model were introduced in Chapter 1, both the *act* of saving and its *form* were discussed. The classi-

FIGURE 2:7.   A Rise in the Level of Thrift

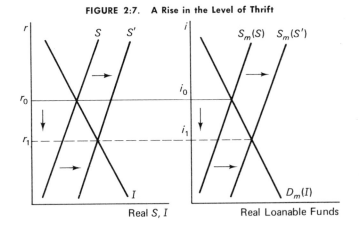

cal writers assumed that saving would always be in the bond form, for no rational man would forego a positive return for the zero return earned on hoarded money; thus, hoarding was viewed as an irrational act. Disregarding the question of rationality, we will analyze its effects in the classical model.

Hoarding is defined as the act of accumulating one's wealth in a money form. Money previously in active circulation is withdrawn and held rather than spent on goods, services, or bonds. As a result, in the money market shown in Figure 2:8 the demand for loanable funds increases from $D_m(I)$ to $D_m(I + H)$, the difference between the two schedules representing the amount of desired hoards.

FIGURE 2:8.   A Rise in Hoarding

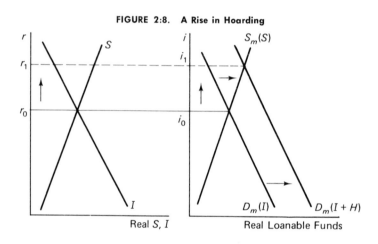

The increase in the money interest rate from i_0 to i_1 causes the real rate to rise above its natural level, r_0. This increases the quantity of desired saving and decreases the quantity of desired investment, thereby making intended saving greater than intended investment.

The rise in hoarding which produces the excess of intended saving is reflected in the commodity market (shown in Figure 2:9) by a decrease in aggregate demand, MV. Aggregate demand falls because V falls (or the Cambridge k rises). So long as the commodity price level falls in response to the decrease in aggregate demand, and money wages fall accordingly, the real wage is maintained and the volume of employment remains stable. The effect of the rise in hoarding will be a deflation in the economy. As long as individuals withdraw active balances into hoards, velocity will continue to fall, and the price and wage structure will gradually sag. If the adjustment of wages to prices is relatively quick, employment will be maintained.

Once the hoarding ceases, $D_m(I + H)$ will recede to $D_m(I)$, the money rate of interest will decline to i_0, which is equal to the natural rate, r_0, saving and investment will again be equal, inventory accumulation will cease, and prices and wages will no longer fall.

FIGURE 2:9. System Response to a Rise in Hoarding

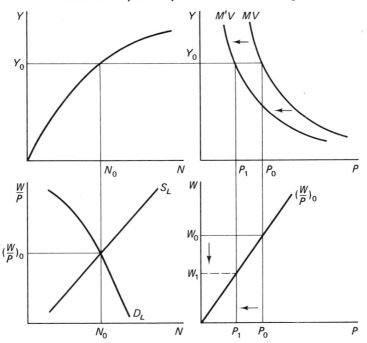

When the hoarded money balances are returned to active circulation, the reverse will take place and the economy will be reinflated.

An appropriate monetary policy to prevent falling prices when there is widespread hoarding would be for the central bank to expand the money supply by the amount which the public wished to hoard. This action, shown in Figure 2:10, will prevent the money rate from rising and saving from exceeding investment, so that hoarding will not deflate the economy.

FISCAL POLICY IN THE CLASSICAL MODEL

Some may think that a discussion of fiscal policy in a text devoted to monetary theory is misplaced, but an examination of the issue of fiscal policy will clarify its role and what it might be expected to accomplish.

Classical economists were aware of lapses from full employment, but believed them to be temporary in nature; so long as wages, prices,

FIGURE 2:10.   Monetary Policy in the Face of Hoarding

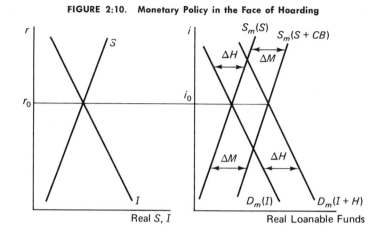

Real S, I   Real Loanable Funds

and interest rates were reasonably flexible, the market economy would generate full employment. Government expenditure programs were therefore usually analyzed in a full-employment context, as we will do for a rise in government expenditures relative to tax receipts. Such a rise in government expenditures can be likened to a rise in private investment expenditures.

Thus, in terms of Figure 2:11, real sector investment shifts from I to $I + G$, where the difference in the two schedules represents the new expenditures by the government not covered by tax receipts. Since these expenditures are not financed by taxes, the government will be forced to borrow the money by selling bonds. This action will shift outward the demand for loanable funds in Figure 2:11 from $D_m(I)$ to $D_m(I + G)$. The rise in the money rate to i_1 induces an equivalent rise in the real rate to r_1, which increases the quantity of saving and reduces the quan-

FIGURE 2:11.   A Government Budget Deficit

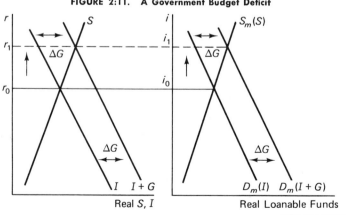

Real S, I   Real Loanable Funds

tity of investment. The concomitant decrease in consumption furnishes the resources for the higher level of government expenditures; the only function, then, of fiscal policy has been to reallocate resources: Less are used by the private sector and more are available for use by the public sector. The transfer of resources is now commonly called the *crowding-out effect*—that is, government expenditures have crowded out an equivalent amount of private expenditures (although the crowd-out was of course voluntary). While the composition of aggregate demand has changed from $C + I$ to $C + I + G$, its total value remains unchanged.

Had the expenditures been financed, not by borrowing from the private sector, but by creating new money, the situation would be quite different and would represent the response of the banking system to a rise in loan demand on the part of the government. In effect, the banking system monetizes government bond debt. This is shown in Figure 2:12 as an outward shift in the supply of loanable funds from $S_m(S)$ to $S_m(S + CB)$.

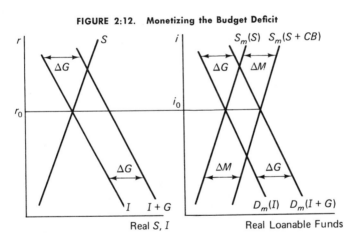

FIGURE 2:12.   Monetizing the Budget Deficit

Careful analysis of this example reveals that fiscal policy merely becomes the means for carrying out monetary policy and should not really be called fiscal policy at all.

By financing the rise in government expenditures through money creation, the money rate of interest is prevented from rising to equal the new equilibrium natural rate. The consequence is that investment plus government spending now exceeds saving, or the value of aggregate demand exceeds that of aggregate supply, forcing up the commodity price level to restore equilibrium. The inflation of prices will persist as long as the government expenditures are financed by new money.[6]

---

[6] The full implications of this problem are deeper than the preceding analysis suggests. Given a steady budget deficit and an equal rate of money creation, the analysis implies that

In summary, since the classical economy always tended toward full employment, fiscal policy had no real stabilization role to play. Its only role was allocative—deciding whether the public or private sector used the available resources. When fiscal policy plays this role, government expenditures crowd out private expenditures dollar for dollar; there is no multiplier process working in the classical economy.

When government expenditures are financed in money-creating ways, they serve as the means for carrying out monetary policy and their consequences are identical to those previously shown to result when the banking system expanded the money stock by buying up evidences of private indebtedness, that is, by monetizing private bonds.

CONCLUSION

The purpose of this chapter has been to analyze a number of problems within a model which might have been used by a classical economist in the Ricardian tradition, focusing on the long run and neglecting the short run, or period of transition. Thus it could be assumed that the participants in the labor market had perfect knowledge of all alternatives open to them and that the wage rate, the price level, and the rate of interest all adjusted to allow a tolerably smooth transition from one equilibrium to another.

As a matter of fact, many counterparts to the foregoing analysis could be found in both the writings of the classical economists and in their policy recommendations. However, it would be a serious error to conclude that they never analyzed the short run—their many theories of the business cycle stand as testimony to their interest in the period of transition. Chapter 3 will investigate, among other topics, the classical economists' interest in and exploration of the short run, in which substantial ignorance of labor market opportunities, unequal perceptions of changes in the price level on the part of savers and lenders, and the activities of commercial banks all interact to produce periods of disequilibrium which may last a decade or more.

---

the rise in government spending yields no additional resources allocated to the public sector. If the purpose of the rise in expenditures and the consequent deficit is merely to expand the money supply, the lack of new resources flowing to the public sector is irrelevant. If, however, the public sector wants the resources, it will be forced to accelerate the rate of inflation in order, by deceiving the public, to acquire the requisite goods and services. The means of acquiring resources through deception is discussed in Chapter 3 when Fisher's period of transition is considered.

APPENDIX 2:1

While each of the problems considered in this chapter has been analyzed within the confines of a classical model, each could also be viewed in terms of the conventional *IS–LM* framework.

The *IS* schedule, derived in Figure 2:13, combines all the points of equality between desired saving and desired investment; it therefore gives all points in which the commodity market is in equilibrium. As presented in this chapter, the saving schedule depends upon both the level of income and the rate of interest. In Figure 2:13, Panel *A*, a family of saving schedules for each income level is given.

FIGURE 2:13. Derivation of the IS Schedule

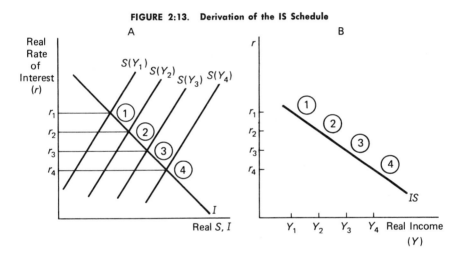

The investment schedule was assumed to depend only on the rate of interest and to be negatively sloped. When all the points of equality between desired saving and investment are plotted—designated as points (1), (2), (3), etc.—they will trace out all combinations of the real interest rate and level of real income compatible with commodity market equilibrium. Such a construction is shown in Panel *B*, which is the conventional *IS* schedule.

Since in the classical model there is no asset demand for money linked to the interest rate, construction of the *LM* schedule showing all points of equilibrium between the demand for money and the supply of money is relatively easy. If we assume that the supply of money or the lending policy of commercial banks is not influenced by the market, or money, rate of interest, the *LM* schedule is a vertical line. If, however, the lending policies of banks do depend upon market interest rates, the *LM* schedule is likely to be positively sloped. Figure 2:14 shows the classical *LM* schedule. Note that the vertical axis measures the money rate of interest, not the real rate. However, since the long run is the period under analysis, it can be assumed that both rates are equal.

FIGURE 2:14.   The LM Schedule

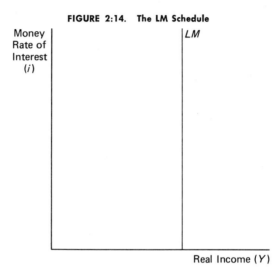

Combining both the *IS* and *LM* schedules in Figure 2:15 yields the equilibrium level of the interest rate (r_0, i_0) consistent with full-employment income (Y_{FE}).

FIGURE 2:15.   Equilibrium in the Economic System

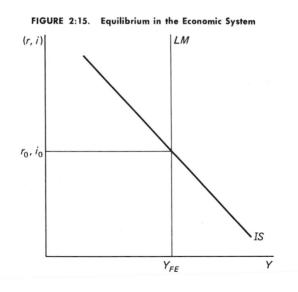

An Increase in the Supply of Money

An increase in the supply of money will, in Figure 2:16, shift the LM schedule to the right of the full-employment level of income from LM_0 to LM_1, reducing the market interest rate below the equilibrium rate, r_0, i_0.

FIGURE 2:16.   An Increase in the Supply of Money

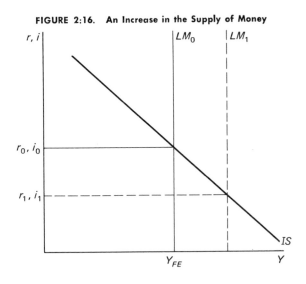

The excess demand, $Y_0 - Y_{FE}$, will force the price level to rise, reducing the real money stock, M/P, and shifting the LM schedule to the left. When equilibrium is again restored, the LM schedule will center on Y_{FE}. At any income level other than Y_{FE}, changes in the level of prices will shift the LM schedule in the direction of full-employment income.

Wage and Price Rigidities

wage and price controls

In the case of an ongoing inflation created by the banking system which is dealt with by imposing wage- and price-controls, nothing happens in the IS–LM framework because the force expanding the money supply, which shifts the LM curve to the right, is exactly counterbalanced by the force which artificially increases the demand for money and shifts the LM schedule to the left.

money wages forced upward by the collective action of labor

The initial effort by labor to force up money wages results in a leftward shift (in Figure 2:17) in the level of real income from Y_{FE} to Y_0 as the real wage is raised above its full-employment level. Interest rate r_0, i_0 is then too low for equilibrium with income level Y_0, which results in price inflation just as though the money supply had been increased when the real income level was Y_{FE}.

FIGURE 2:17.   A Rise in the Money Wage Thru Union Pressure

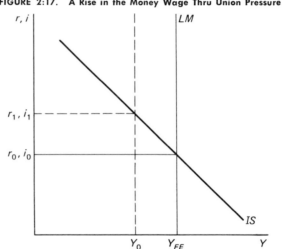

The result of the rise in prices is to reduce the value of real money balances, M/P, shifting the LM schedule leftward. However, as the price level rises, the real wage falls and the level of income consistent with the new lower real wage moves toward Y_{FE}. The rise in interest rates produced by the decline in real balances ultimately produces an equilibrium combination of real income, real wage, and interest rates. The new equilibrium should be less than Y_{FE}, but greater than Y_0.

Any expansion of the nominal money supply which serves to inflate the price level and reduce the real wage should move the system toward Y_{FE}, unless further attempts are made by organized labor to raise the money wage. In that case, the adjustment to reach Y_{FE} should be more protracted.

Increase in the Supply of Labor

An increase in the supply of labor has the effect of raising the full-employment level of real income from Y_{FE_0} to Y_{FE_1}. In Figure 2:18, the

rise in the level of full-employment income produces an *IS–LM* equilibrium at less than full employment. However, the expansion in real output will, in the classical model, cause the price level to fall, increasing
the value of real balances, M/P. Thus LM_0 shifts to the right toward
LM_1 and the new full-employment equilibrium. The same effect could
be produced by monetary expansion geared to the growth in full-employment income.

FIGURE 2:18.   An Increase in the Supply of Labor

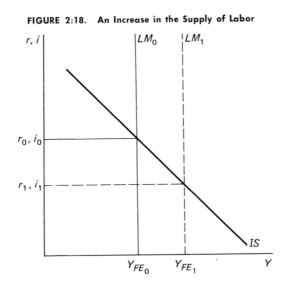

Unfortunately, the nonneutral effects produced by money expansion geared to maintaining a long-run stable price level cannot be shown
in Figure 2:18.

An increase in the demand for labor will produce essentially the
same results as an increase in the supply.

Whenever the labor market forms the center of analysis, the shortcoming of the *IS–LM* framework is obvious: It hides the adjustment of
the labor market and requires the analyses to be descriptive.

A Rise in Thrift

A rise in the level of thrift (a greater amount saved out of a given income at each interest rate) will shift the *IS* schedule to the left from IS_0
to IS_1. However, since the *LM* schedule in Figure 2:19 is vertical, the
shift in the *IS* curve will have no effect whatsoever on the level of income, producing only a decrease in the equilibrium level of the interest
rate from r_0, i_0 to r_1, i_1.

The results produced in this example are of great potential interest for they indicate that no matter what happens to the IS schedule, it will have no effect whatsoever on the equilibrium value of real income and employment; it will only change the level of the rate of interest consistent with full-employment income, Y_{FE}. Thus the only forces in the classical model capable of causing a change in the level of income are those underlying the *LM* schedule. This means that the business cycle will generally be monetary in origin for the classical economists and its major cause will be irregular variations in the supply of money. In Chapter 3, this conclusion will be verified.

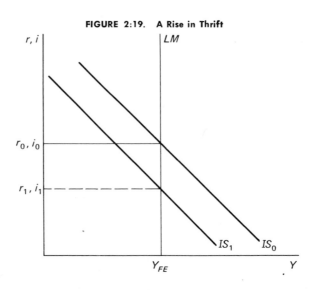

FIGURE 2:19.   A Rise in Thrift

This potency of monetary policy is easily seen when fiscal policy is analyzed.

Fiscal Policy in the Classical Model

The effect of a rise in government expenditures relative to tax receipts is to shift to the right the *IS* curve in Figure 2:20 from IS_0 to IS_1. This raises the equilibrium level of the interest rate from r_0, i_0 to r_1, i_1, but has no effect on the level of real income and employment. Thus government expenditures must have displaced, or crowded out, an equal amount of private expenditures. The amount of the crowd-out can be obtained by comparing the level of income associated with r_1, i_1 and IS_0 (the *IS* curve without government expenditures), Y_0, with Y_{FE}. The difference is the amount of real income or output previously used by the private sector which now goes to the public sector. Thus government expenditures have simply displaced, or crowded out, an equivalent private use

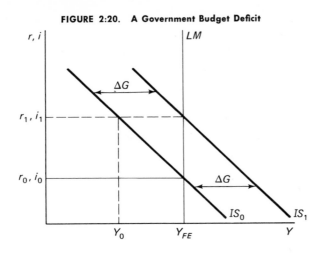

FIGURE 2:20.   A Government Budget Deficit

of resources. So long as the *LM* curve is vertical, fiscal policy cannot change real income—it merely alters its allocation.

Money Hoarding

A rise in money hoarding represents a rise in the demand for money, which other things equal will shift the *LM* schedule in Figure 2:21 to the left from LM_0 to LM_1.

If money hoarding induces price deflation, the level of real cash

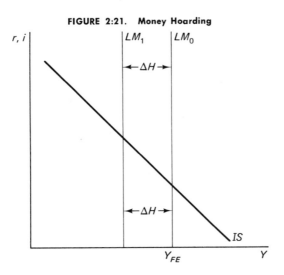

FIGURE 2:21.   Money Hoarding

balances, $M/P,$ will rise and shift the LM schedule to the right, back to the level consistent with full employment.

Alternatively, the monetary authority could simply supply enough new money to satisfy the desire to hoard, thereby maintaining the LM schedule at LM_0.

Selected References and Readings

See Those at the End of Chapter 1.

chapter 3

The Classical Model
in the Short Run

Periods of great economic stress—inflation, deflation, depression, widespread bank failures, balance-of-payments problems, suspension of both the internal and external convertibility of currencies, and so forth—are frequently the source for analytical inspiration. The desire to discover the cause of these events has motivated both contemporary and ancient scholars, for history spares no one the agony of these circumstances.

The suspension of the gold convertibility of the British pound in 1797 during the Napoleonic Wars, and the subsequent period of economic distress, stimulated many economic analyses, which on the whole appear of surprisingly high quality. The great issues in this debate were remarkably similar to those raised during the American inflation associated with our involvement in Vietnam from 1965 to 1975. For this reason a review of the British experience is of interest, for it will provide insight into the classical view of the cause of the business cycle and into the modification which cyclical activity introduces to the core propositions constituting the quantity theory of money.

The principal issues in the British debate were whether inflation, caused by an overissue of Bank of England notes, forced suspension of convertibility, and if it did, the means by which such an overissue might be avoided in the future.

In its later stages, the debate became famous as the controversy between the Currency and the Banking schools, while in its initial stage the debate was between the Bullionists and the Antibullionists.[1] The Currency School triumphed ultimately in the sense that their policy recommendations were embodied in both the unofficial rules of conduct of the Bank of England and in the Bank Charter Act of 1844. In addition, the theoretical bases of their recommendations came to form the foundation for classical monetary theory.

While this chapter will not concentrate heavily on the debate *per se,* it will begin with a summary of the initial position of each side. The summary will then be developed at greater length, for the topics of this debate illustrate the classical view of the nonneutrality and exogeneity of money, and the uniqueness of the definition of any group of assets as money—issues currently under debate by monetary theorists.

THE CURRENCY SCHOOL–BANKING SCHOOL CONTROVERSY

The central economic goal of this nineteenth-century era was the preservation of the gold standard and the free convertibility of the pound sterling for gold. A country's internal level of prices was of concern only because of its effect on foreign-exchange rates and the gold stocks.

In 1797, when the convertibility of the pound into specie was suspended (until 1821), the pound depreciated relative to gold and to other convertible currencies. The question then arose of whether the depreciation was evidence of inflation and, if so, if it had been caused by an overissue of the notes of the Bank of England. The question might have been resolved by reference to price indices—but these were largely nonexistent at the time.

The position of the Bullionists (and later of the Currency School) was that the paper pound had indeed been issued to excess. Their reasoning was based on a monetary theory of the price level which held that a close link existed between the stock of money and the level of internal prices. Whenever the stock of money increased at a faster rate than real output, internal prices would rise. The rise in internal prices would make foreign goods an attractive alternative to domestic substitutes, leading to an increase in imports. Similarly, exportable domestic goods would find it increasingly harder to compete with foreign substitutes, leading to a decline in exports. Under a convertible currency, the rise in imports and decline in exports would lead to an outflow of gold;

---

[1] For a discussion of the issues, see Jacob Viner, *Studies in the Theory of International Trade* (London: Allen & Unwin, 1935), chapters 3, 4 and 5; Lloyd Mints, *A History of Banking Theory* (Chicago: University of Chicago Press, 1945), chapters 2, 3, 4, 6 and 7; Thomas Humphries, "The Quantity Theory of Money: Its Historical Evolution and Role in Policy Debates," *Economic Review,* Federal Reserve Bank of Richmond (May/June 1974), pp. 2–19; A. B. Cramp, "Two Views on Money," *Lloyds Bank Review,* No. 65 (July 1962), pp. 1–15.

under an inconvertible currency, it would lead to a depreciation of the currency in the foreign-exchange market. Thus, the heavy outflow of gold which forced suspension in 1797, the subsequent depreciation of the pound, and the premium on gold bullion were all taken as evidence of an overissue of Bank of England notes, the major form of domestic money. The cure was to curtail the issue of these notes and, in the future, to issue them in amounts corresponding exactly to the amount of gold that theoretically could be circulated as coins.[2] In this way, the gold convertibility of the pound could be ensured.

The Banking School argued, as did their Antibullionist predecessors, that suspension of gold convertibility in 1797 and the subsequent depreciation of the paper pound were not caused by an overissue of paper money. Quite the contrary, paper money could never be overissued, so long as gold convertibility was maintained. The suspension and depreciation, they argued, were caused by the necessity of making huge outlays abroad to support the British military in a war with France that started in 1793, and by the necessity of making extraordinary imports of grain following several years of bad harvests in England.

In addition, they held that control of Bank of England notes would not guarantee control of the price level, for at least four reasons. First, they believed that large sums of money were hoarded and did not actively circulate; additions to the money supply might simply be added to the hoards, while contractions of bank notes might bring forth compensatory dishoarding. Second, in addition to Bank of England notes, there existed a number of other money substitutes which circulated and which could exert an impact on prices. The Banking School believed the volume of these substitutes (demand deposits, open book credit, and commercial bills of exchange) to be independent of the note issue of the Bank of England. Thus control of one asset, arbitrarily defined as money, would not guarantee control of the price level and the external convertibility of the pound. Third, and most important, they argued that the supply of money is demand-determined, so that an excess supply of money which would serve to drive up the price level can never occur. Fourth and last, they argued that the price level is governed by the relationship of aggregate demand to aggregate supply; only by influencing demand could Bank of England notes affect the price level.

The two schools appear to differ on a number of fundamental issues: The cause of economic disturbances, the determination of the price

---

[2] This was to be achieved by permitting the Bank of England to monopolize the note issue of the country and by imposing a 100 percent reserve requirement on those notes. Thus their issue could rise only if the Bank received or had on hand an equivalent amount of free gold. In the United States a similar plan for 100 percent reserve banking was advanced in the 1930's by Henry Simons and Irving Fisher as a means of minimizing the influence of monetary fluctuations on economic activity.

level, the power of money, the definition of money, and the policy to be pursued to ensure economic stability.

CHANGES IN THE STOCK OF MONEY

Having summarized the two contending explanations for England's economic problems in the first half of the nineteenth century, we will now explore in greater depth the position of the Bullionist–Currency School, which became the most widely accepted monetary theory. Since in their view an overissue of the money stock, by raising internal prices relative to those abroad, was the cause of the suspension of convertibility, an analysis of how the money stock is changed and how it causes prices to rise should be our first order of business. As this is tied in with their analysis of the cause of economic disturbances, the following discussion will link the two. It will show that the classical writers believed money to be nonneutral in the short run, that is, that variations in the money stock could cause changes—transitory ones to be sure—in real variables.

The classical writers, associated with the Currency School, specified two distinct mechanisms through which changes in the money supply were linked or transmitted to the price level.

The first and simplest has been termed the *direct mechanism;* the second, more complex linkage, which involves the commercial banking system, has been called the *indirect mechanism.*

The Direct Mechanism

Formulated by David Hume and Richard Cantillon in the eighteenth century, the operation of the direct mechanism can most easily be seen in a country which uses only gold and silver money. In such a country, any individual who owns a gold mine or who imports gold from abroad, owns or possesses a money machine. When the amount of money in his possession increases, the relationship between his actual money holdings and those balances he desires to hold, relative to his wealth or income, is no longer in equilibrium. Since his actual money holdings now exceed those he desires to hold, he seeks to get rid of the excess money supply by buying a wide range of assets, thereby increasing the demand for goods and services.

In Figure 3:1, this attempt to get rid of the excess money balances will shift MV to $M'V$ and produce, ultimately, a proportional rise in the price level from P_0 to P_1.

The essence of the direct mechanism is that a stable relationship exists between an individual's money holding and his rate of expendi-

FIGURE 3:1. The Direct Mechanism

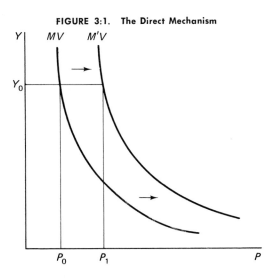

tures and, possibly, his level of wealth. Thus, when his actual money balances are increased, they exceed those he desires to hold relative to his expenditures and wealth. He corrects the disparity by spending the excess balances. The rise in the price level serves to reduce the real value of the money stock until actual money balances are again equal to those the individual desires to hold.[3] Thus, while nominal magnitudes are initially larger, the subsequent rise in prices reduces real values to what they were before the new money was injected into the system.

It must not be supposed that the direct mechanism is inoperative in our contemporary society. Quite the contrary, foreign-trade activity, domestic mining, and direct issues of paper money to finance government activities are all ways to directly change the money stock.

The Indirect Mechanism

The indirect mechanism involves the commercial banking system and was first expounded in 1802 by a remarkable Englishman, Henry Thornton, in his book, *An Enquiry into the Nature and Effects of the Paper*

---

[3] The direct mechanism is more complicated than a first glance would suggest. In the example, the nominal wealth of society rose and the operation of the direct mechanism can be viewed as a wealth adjustment, that is, the desire of individuals who "feel wealthier" to consume more of everything.

However, what happens in the case where one asset is given up in exchange for money, for example, a Treasury bill is purchased by the Federal Reserve for money? Will the direct mechanism operate? In chapters 11 and 12 it will be shown that for neo-Keynesians the answer is generally no (except for the fact that portfolio composition has been altered), while for those in the Friedman tradition, the answer is yes.

Credit of Great Britain. Thornton, a banker by profession, was foremost among the Bullionists and like his colleague, David Ricardo, died too soon to participate in the later monetary debates of the mid-nineteenth century. Thornton believed that the main shortcoming of the direct mechanism was that it could not adequately explain how bank notes came into circulation and was an inadequate explanation for money creation in advanced societies with commercial banks.

Let the commercial banking system come into possession of additional excess reserves and it will proceed to lend them out by lowering the money rate of interest relative to what Thornton called *the rate of mercantile profit,* or the expected yield on new capital projects (the marginal efficiency of capital). This reduction in the money rate of interest, by making the desired capital stock greater than the actual stock, would induce businessmen to increase the rate of investment. The banking system would provide businessmen with the financial resources to expand their holding of assets. This would in turn lead to a rise in aggregate money demand and ultimately to a proportional rise in the general level of prices.

In terms of the classical model developed in Chapter 1, Figure 3:2 explains the sequence of events. In the initial equilibrium, the natural rate of interest, r_0, is equal to the money rate i_0. The commercial banks,

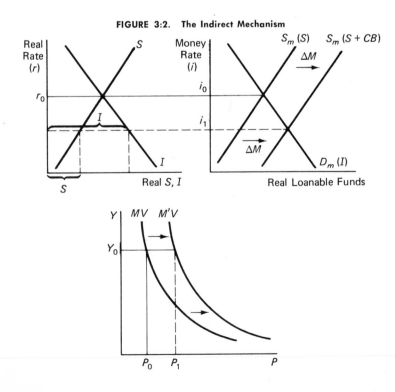

FIGURE 3:2.   The Indirect Mechanism

with their increased free reserves, now enter the bond market, buying bonds and expanding the supply of loanable funds. This drives down the money rate of interest from i_0 to i_1 and makes desired investment greater than desired saving.

The rise in investment and consumption (the counterpart of the fall in saving), or aggregate demand, is financed by new money creation. This expands MV to $M'V$, forcing up the level of commodity prices. Thus the existence of changes in the general level of commodity prices is a sign that the natural and money rates of interest are not in equilibrium. The money creation will come to an end when the banks no longer have lendable reserves. The central bank can hasten this move toward equilibrium by raising reserve requirements or by selling government securities from its portfolio.

Since Thornton was attempting to describe the world he lived in, his analysis has an interesting implication. The fundamental cause of economic disturbances such as inflation or deflation will usually be monetary in nature, arising from a divergence between a relatively flexible money interest rate and a highly stable natural rate (the rate which equates desired saving and investment). The stability of the natural rate was assumed to result from the ingrained behavior of the population relating to the desirability of thrift vs. consumption, and from the stability of the productivity of capital. Of course, economists such as Thornton were aware that the natural rate could change and cause the economy to fluctuate, but they believed that such changes were clearly overshadowed by movements in the money rate of interest. The villain in the classical model is the commercial banker, and as he can be controlled by the central bank, the latter becomes the devil incarnate.

It is a great tribute to Henry Thornton that his "indirect mechanism" was assimilated into the works of Ricardo, John Stuart Mill, and Alfred Marshall, thus becoming an integral part of classical analysis. It is also to be found in the works of Wicksell and has distinct similarities to the liquidity preference theory of Lord Keynes. It is the forerunner of what is today called a *stock-adjustment*, or *portfolio-adjustment*, mechanism. A decline in the money interest rate leads the wealth holder to rearrange his portfolio of assets. Physical capital is now substituted for bonds in the portfolio and the wealth holder is more likely to increase his liabilities by borrowing to enable him to expand his stock of physical assets. Thus changes in the money supply lead to substitution effects in the portfolios of wealth holders.

THE NONNEUTRALITY OF MONEY

Figures 3:1 and 3:2 both suggest that changes in the stock of money produce changes in the level of prices. However, it would be in error to believe that these changes were instantaneous. Rather, the classical writers believed that changes in the supply of money could change real variables in the process of producing changes in the price level.

Perhaps the earliest statement of nonneutrality is given by David Hume[4] in his essay "Of Money":

> In my opinion, it is only in the interval or intermediate situation, between the acquisition of money and the rise in prices, that the increasing quantity of gold and silver is favourable to industry. . . . The farmer or gardener, finding that all their commodities are taken off, apply themselves with alacrity to the raising of more. . . . It is easy to trace the money in its progress through the whole commonwealth; where we shall find that it must first quicken the diligence of every individual, before it increases the price of labour. [Changes in the quantity of money, therefore,] are not immediately attended with proportionable alterations in the price of commodities. There is always an interval before matters can be adjusted to their new situation; and this interval is as pernicious to industry when gold and silver are diminishing as it is advantageous when these metals are increasing. [But in the end] prices of commodities are always proportional to the plenty of money. . . .

Henry Thornton had similar views on nonneutrality, as illustrated in the following reference to a decrease in the supply of money:

> It is true that if we could suppose the diminution of bank paper to produce permanently a diminution in the value of all articles whatsoever, and a diminution . . . in the rate of wages, also, the encouragement to future manufacture would be the same. . . . The tendency, however, of a very great and sudden reduction of the accustomed number of bank notes is to create an *unusual* and *temporary* distress, and a fall of prices arising from that distress. But a fall arising from that distress, will be attended probably

---

[4] A contemporary of Hume, Richard Cantillon, discussed nonneutrality in terms of the way new money is introduced into the system. Usually, the new money would not be distributed in proportion to the existing money holdings, but would accrue to one or a few groups. With their money holding augmented, these individuals now play a much more important role in determining the composition of aggregate output. See his *Essay on the Nature of Trade*, reprinted in part in Edwin Dean, ed., *The Controversy Over the Quantity Theory of Money* (Lexington, Mass.: D. C. Heath 1968), pp. 2–8.

In a glowing tribute to the work of Hume, Milton Friedman, following a more extensive version of the quote cited above, states that recent monetary theory has gone beyond Hume's analysis by but one derivative. That is, to produce the nonneutral effects Hume discusses may require not a mere change in the money supply, but an alteration in the rate of change because the public builds expectations into its behavior. Apparently in Hume's time stable prices were the expected norm, and thus he had good reason to neglect anticipated changes as an assumption of his analysis. See Milton Friedman, "25 Years after the Rediscovery of Money: What Have We Learned?" *Papers and Proceedings of the American Economic Association*, Vol. 65, No. 2 (May 1975), p. 177.

with no corresponding fall in the rate of wages; . . . [for] the rate of wages, we know is not so variable as the price of goods. There is reason, therefore, to fear that . . . the sort of distress of which we now speak, would occasion much discouragement of the fabrication of manufactures.[5]

Viner[6] provides an extensive discussion of nonneutrality, as viewed by the writers of the first half of the nineteenth century. Basically, nonneutrality was produced for reasons such as various contractual rigidities which prevented costs from changing as rapidly as prices or from an inability to forecast the future accurately. In the interim, while contracts were being adjusted and forecasts revised, real wages—and thus output—could change. Thus a monetary expansion could induce inflation, lowering the real wage and expanding output. When wage adjustments were made, the real wage would be restored to its previous level and output would fall. Second, price-level changes would cause wealth redistributions. If these were in favor of debtors, the classical economists felt that the more productive members of society gained, thereby leading to a rise in capital formation and output. Third, inflation could lower the real interest rate if nominal interest rates failed to keep pace with prices, thereby stimulating investment. Fourth, if prices rose relative to wages, the level of real consumption enjoyed by wage earners supposedly would fall and resources available for investment would increase along with profits, thereby altering the distribution of income and the subsequent composition of output. The last of these effects producing nonneutrality is the so-called *doctrine of forced saving*, attributed in England to Henry Thornton.[7]

It is of interest, in the light of his great influence on the analytical method of the classical school, to note the view of Ricardo on nonneutrality. Viner tells us:

It is not surprising that Ricardo, with his loyalty to the metallic standard and his temperamental reluctance to explore the short run and intermediate phases of economic process, also did not take kindly to these doctrines. His references to them are few, and tend to be obscurantist in nature. As in other cases, he alternated between outright denial of their validity, on the one hand, and qualified admission of their correctness for the short run, but with minimization of their importance, on the other hand.[8]

In summary, their mechanisms for explaining how money affects

---

[5] Lloyd Mints, *A History of Banking Theory*, pp. 55–56, footnote 51.

[6] Jacob Viner, *Studies in the Theory of International Trade*, pp. 185–200.

[7] F. A. Von Hayek, "A Note on the Development of the Doctrine of 'Forced Saving'," *Quarterly Journal of Economics*, Vol. 47 (1932), pp. 123–33.

[8] Jacob Viner, *Studies in the Theory of International Trade*, pp. 195–196.

the level of prices, rather than their theories of nonneutrality, constitute the lasting influence of the Currency School.

THE MONEY SUPPLY AND THE BANKING SCHOOL

It was the argument of the Banking School that the rise in prices could not have been caused by an overissue or relative increase in the supply of notes by the Bank of England, because money can never be over-issued. While their view of the money supply is wrong, it is of interest because it represents the origin of an idea that the banking system passively supplies money only in response to a demand for it. Thus the stock of money is demand-determined and money *per se* cannot cause economic disturbances; the origin of the disturbances must lie elsewhere. Bankers or central bankers are therefore blameless when it comes to inflations, deflations, balance-of-payments disequilibria, and so forth.

The reasoning of the Banking School was based upon the real bills doctrine and the Law of Reflux.

The real bills doctrine, first formulated by Adam Smith, held that so long as paper bank notes or money (the two schools disagreed on a common definition of money—see below, "The Uniqueness of Money") was advanced in discount of "sound" (nonspeculative) short-term commercial paper, they could never be issued in excess of the "needs of business," as no one would borrow, at interest, funds which he did not need.

Thus if bank lending were restricted to self-liquidating commercial paper based upon goods in process, the volume of notes or money in an economy would necessarily expand in pace with the volume of transactions.

If for some reason the banks forced additional notes on the public, the Law of Reflux was appealed to, which stated simply that the excess notes (those not needed in the course of business) would be returned to the banks to repay loans, as a deposit, or in redemption for gold coin.

These ideas advanced by the Banking School have several interesting implications. First, they deny that the central bank can control the money stocks, since money is a demand-determined variable. Second, they imply that the supply of money is, in essence, infinitely elastic. Third, they deny the validity of both the direct and indirect mechanisms expounded by the Currency School, which linked money to prices; since the money stock is demand-determined, an oversupply can never develop to act on prices. Fourth, they imply that the origin of the business cycle is nonmonetary in nature. Fifth, they imply that since the stock of money is demand-determined, price-level changes, produced by nonmonetary stimuli, ought to precede and cause subsequent changes in the money stock. This fifth point, which opens the possibility of cost-push inflations, will be explored more extensively below, when the work of Thomas Tooke is examined.

It is little wonder that the propositions of the Banking School were embraced by the directors of the Bank of England, for they made that majestic institution a constitutional monarch: One that reigns, but does not rule.

Of crucial importance to the real bills doctrine was a theory about what determined the "needs of trade" and what would happen if the banks refused to advance the necessary funds to finance those needs.

As to the term *needs of trade,* Mints tells us: ". . . I know of no attempt by any of them to state precisely what they mean by these expressions."[9] Additionally, he relates that if the volume of bank notes failed to keep pace with these needs, the analysis of the Banking School implied that it would lead to a reduction of output, but they did not specify how this would happen.

The fallacy of the real bills doctrine was very early exposed by Henry Thornton (1797). If the "needs of trade" are governed by the real yield on capital, and the bank, or money, rate of interest is held below the yield on capital, the demand for loans will be insatiable and the corresponding supply of bank notes (money) infinite. Thus, confining loans or discounts to "sound" commercial paper does not furnish a check to the overissue of bank notes, even if they are convertible into gold. Thornton, in *An Enquiry,* also advances at least three other reasons why adherence to the discounting of sound short-term commercial paper would be no bar to overissue. Nevertheless, the compelling simplicity of the real bills doctrine of commercial banking was so powerful that it was enshrined in the Federal Reserve Act of 1913, which limited central bank advances to commercial banks to sound, short-term commercial and agricultural paper.

Despite the fallacy of the real bills doctrine, it advanced the idea, accepted even today, that the central bank cannot control the supply of money, for it is a purely demand-determined variable. Put quite simply, at stake in this issue is whether the supply of money is exogenous (controllable by the central bank) or endogenous (determined by the individuals in the economic system). To the Currency School, the stock of money was exogenous, whereas to the Banking School, it was clearly endogenous.

THE RICARDO–TOOKE CONUNDRUM

Empirical evidence has frequently been introduced to verify or disprove theoretical work, for one test of the validity of a theory is its ability to

---

[9] Lloyd Mints, *A History of Banking Theory,* p. 94.

predict. Thus Thomas Tooke, a leading member of the Banking School and pioneer of the statistical investigation of economic phenomena, introduced data on the relationship between interest rates and the price level which conflicted with the predictions of Thornton's indirect mechanism.

Tooke's work, reconfirmed some 100 years later by A. H. Gibson and again in the period 1965–1975 in the United States, is interesting because it raises doubts about the correctness of the liquidity preference theory of interest rates formulated by Keynes and renews interest in the theoretical work of Irving Fisher, which is quite at variance with that of Keynes. Tooke's work is therefore worthy of careful consideration.

Tooke pointed out that if the indirect mechanism expounded by Henry Thornton were correct, a certain pattern ought to be observed in the actual data accumulated during the business cycle on interest rates and the general level of commodity prices. In particular, the data ought to show a strong negative correlation between the money interest rate and the level of commodity prices, as can easily be seen by reference to Figure 3:2. While money is being created, which serves to drive up the price level, the interest rate will be continuously below its equilibrium level, i_0. Thus, rising prices ought to be consistent or correlated with low market interest rates.

However, in his *History of Prices,* the first volume of which was published in 1838 and successive volumes until 1857, Tooke showed that movements in the general level of commodity prices and interest rates were positively correlated; that is, high price levels and high interest rates (those above i_0 in Figure 3:2) go together as do low price levels and low interest rates. In addition, by taking first differences of successive years, it can be shown that rising price levels and rising interest rates go together, as do falling price levels and falling interest rates.

Tooke rationalized this positive correlation between the level of prices and the level of interest rates in terms of an embryonic income–expenditure theory under which costs of production governed aggregate supply. The relationship between aggregate demand and aggregate supply therefore determined the level of prices, much as they do in a modern Keynesian-type model.

Because Tooke regarded the interest rate as an element in production costs, when it rose it forced up prices, thereby yielding the positive correlation he found between movements in interest rates and the price level.[10] Whenever the price level comes to depend upon factor costs,

[10] In micro theory, the interest rate represents the cost of capital and is thus a part of fixed costs, since it does not vary with output in the short run. As an element of fixed costs, it does not enter the marginal cost or short-run supply schedule. Hence, it does not determine prices.

In the United States, this view that rising interest rates cause rising prices has been

models which embody such ideas lend themselves to cost-push interpretations of inflation. Thus, Tooke's exposition[11] can be regarded not only as an early statement of the income–expenditure approach to monetary theory, but as one of the very early interpretations of inflation as cost-push in origin.

As an additional attack on the Currency School position, Tooke's work also tended to show that changes in the level of prices precede changes in the stock of money, not the other way around.

Nevertheless, in the intellectual battle the Currency School was successful and Thornton's indirect mechanism became the accepted channel by which the money stock was linked to the price level. But Wicksell comments that whenever Tooke's empirical findings were offered as proof that the theory of the Currency School was incorrect, they were passed over in silence.[12]

THE GIBSON PARADOX

Tooke's finding of a positive correlation between commodity price levels and the money rate of interest was reconfirmed by an empirical study conducted by the English banker A. H. Gibson, first published in 1923 and in an expanded version in 1926.[13] Keynes, in Volume II of his 1930 *Treatise on Money,* was quite impressed by Gibson's work, exclaiming:

> For the extraordinary thing is that the "Gibson Paradox"—as we may fairly call it—is one of the most completely established empirical facts within the whole field of quantitative economics, though theoretical economists have mostly ignored it.[14]

So successful had the Ricardians been, that not only was Tooke's theory rejected—because it was at variance with the quantity theory—but his empirical work was ignored as well. Classical monetary theory continued to teach a mechanism for money creation developed from the work of Henry Thornton—a mechanism whose operation would generate ex-

---

associated with the former Chairman of the Joint Economic Committee, Wright Patman of Texas. In a recent paper, using a full-cost model where interest costs would affect prices, Steven Seelig was unable to uncover evidence to support the Congressman's claim. See his "Rising Interest Rates and Cost Push Inflation," *Journal of Finance,* No. 4, Vol. 29 (Sept. 1974), 1049–61.

11 Thomas Tooke, *An Inquiry into the Currency Principle* (London: 1844).

12 Knut Wicksell, *Lectures on Political Economy,* Vol. II, *Money,* L. Robbins, ed. (London: Routledge and Kegan Paul 1935), p. 202.

13 *Bankers' Magazine* (Jan. 1923 and Nov. 1926).

14 J. M. Keynes, *A Treatise on Money,* Vol. II, *The Applied Theory of Money* (London: Macmillan, 1930), p. 198.

pected data on prices and interest rates at variance with almost all empirical observations from at least 1790 through 1928.

In order to correct this major oversight, Keynes proceeded to resolve what he called *Gibson's Paradox*. He did so within the framework of the indirect mechanism. By a rather remarkable coincidence, the great Swedish economist Knut Wicksell, aware of the controversy between the Ricardians and Tooke, had provided a virtually identical explanation for the phenomenon some 30 years earlier. Henceforth, it will be called the Keynes–Wicksell explanation. Remember that at this time both authors were working within the framework of the quantity theory, even though both eventually moved in other directions. But an important, direct implication of their analyses is to reverse the major cause of the business cycle, by attributing the major source of cyclical disturbances to the saving–investment sector rather than to the monetary sector. Thus erratic fluctuations in the natural rate, relative to the money rate, create an inequality between desired saving and investment and result in either inflations or deflations. Equally interesting, in their analyses, the stock of money becomes a passive element largely supplied to "meet the needs of the trade." This does not mean that they believe the central bank cannot control the supply of money; it only means that for some reason, it does not choose to do so. Thus for Keynes–Wicksell, the money supply could be exogenous in the sense that the central bank could control it if it wished to do so.

Figure 3:3 presents the Keynes–Wicksell explanation for Gibson's finding. The analyses start from equilibrium in which the natural rate, r_0, is equal to the money rate of interest, i_0. Then they assume that some major technological innovation occurs which increases the productivity of capital and causes both the MEC and MEI to increase. The investment demand curve then shifts out, as does the demand for loanable funds. If nothing changes, the money rate ought to rise to i_1 and be equal to the new higher natural rate, r_1. No other changes would occur in the economic system other than a reallocation of full-employment income from consumption to investment uses. However, according to Keynes–Wicksell, bankers are slow to perceive the rise in the natural rate, and possessing free reserves which they had not previously been willing or able to lend out, they now meet the increased demand for loanable funds by discounting loans at the prevailing money rate of interest. This action expands the supply of loanable funds from $S_m(S)$ to $S_m(S + CB)$. As a result, ΔM of new money is created, which serves to finance the excess of desired investment over desired saving, that is, the excess demand. As aggregate money demand expands, the commodity price level is forced up to preserve equilibrium between aggregate demand and the value of aggregate supply. The inflation will continue as long as the commercial banks keep the money rate below the natural rate. Both Keynes and

FIGURE 3:3.   System Adjustment to an Increase in the Natural Rate

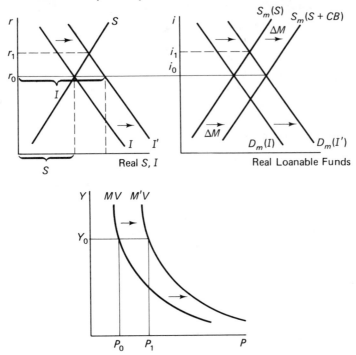

Wicksell assert that the rise in the deposit/reserve ratio, or alternatively, the decline in the level of free reserves, will force banks to curtail new lending. This will cause $S_m(S + CB)$ to shift back toward $S_m(S)$ and the money rate of interest to rise to the natural rate. Once the money creation process stops, both the price level and the interest rate will be high and stable.

Thus, the Keynes–Wicksell analyses are able to explain rising commodity prices and rising interest rates, and high, stable commodity prices and stable interest rates; they are also able to explain the deflationary side of the cycle. All these findings are consistent with the empirical results of Tooke and Gibson.

Both Keynes and Wicksell neglect two factors which seem especially relevant to their analysis. First, they do not consider what variables, if any, induce commercial banks as profit maximizers to hold free reserves which they were either not willing or not able to lend out prior to the change in the demand for loanable funds. Second, although both are aware that the disparity between natural and money interest rates causes changes in commodity prices, they do not spell out the implication of these price changes on the lending behavior of savers and commercial banks, even though such changes in the price level affect the value of the principal lent and interest received. This implies either irrationality on the part of lenders, that is, that they may be lending at negative real interest rates (money rate less the inflation rate), or a slow adjustment process which can be neglected for the short-run period under analysis. This is not to say that the classical writers were unaware of the implications of commodity price changes on the behavior of lenders. Henry Thornton attributed the high money rates of interest in Russia[15] to price inflation, and Alfred Marshall[16] notes specifically that commodity price changes can alter the real rate of interest and that such changes have cyclical implications. However, it was Irving Fisher who first systematically formulated a theory of the business cycle which involved money stock changes, commodity price changes, and a disparity between money interest rates and real interest rates induced by the commodity price changes which then caused the cycle to evolve. Fisher's contribution will be examined in great depth, for he provided the most sophisticated statement by the classical writers on the nonneutrality of money, and is currently undergoing a modern revival.

FISHER'S ANALYSIS

Paul Samuelson,[17] echoing the prediction of Joseph Schumpeter, calls Fisher America's greatest analytical economist. The ideas of Fisher were revived during the mid-1960's, when the United States experienced a period of rising commodity prices and rising interest rates, for his work provides an alternative to that of Keynes–Wicksell in which the monetary cause of the business cycle is preserved. In 1895, at the request of the American Economic Association, Fisher began what was to become a rather lengthy study of the effect of commodity price changes on the rate of interest. His preliminary analysis, published in 1896 as *Appreciation and Interest,* was followed in 1907 by *The Rate of Interest,* in 1911 by *The Purchasing Power of Money,* and the series culminated in 1930 with *The Theory of Interest.* In these four volumes, Fisher reported empirical findings and developed a monetary theory of the business cycle consistent with his findings. In order to understand his contribution fully, our first task will be to explore the supposed effect of commodity price movements on the rate of interest. Then we can analyze Fisher's theory of the

---

[15] H. Thornton, *The Paper Credit of Great Britain,* F. A. Hayek, ed. (New York: Augustus Kelly, 1965), pp. 335–36.

[16] A. Marshall, *Principles of Economics,* 8th ed. (London: Macmillan, 1962), pp. 492–94. See also, Keynes' descriptions of the effects of inflation on interest rates in his *Monetary Reform* (New York: Harcourt, Brace and Co., 1924), pp. 23–31.

[17] *Ten Economic Studies in the Tradition of Irving Fisher* (New York: John Wiley, 1967), pp. 17–18.

business cycle, which involves the relationship between money, commodity prices, and interest rates. Remember that Fisher's purpose is to provide a theoretical explanation for the findings of Tooke and Gibson.

Commodity Prices and Interest Rates

Fisher starts with the assumption that people who lend money always realize that what is lent is command over goods in general. Thus, when a sum of money is lent for a fixed time period, the lender wishes to receive in payment purchasing power equal to that lent plus an interest payment, also with equal purchasing power. For example, assume that in an environment of stable prices, in which neither lender nor borrower expects any commodity price changes, the lender is willing to lend $100 at 3 percent interest. He expects to be paid, one year hence, a sum whose purchasing power at that time would be 3 percent greater than $100 is today. Now, suppose that both lender and borrower know with perfect certainty that one year hence prices will be 5 percent higher than today. How will this affect lending behavior? In order to keep the purchasing power of his principal intact, the lender must be repaid $105, one year hence. To maintain the purchasing power of the interest payment, he must be repaid $3.15. Thus, to maintain constant purchasing power of both principal and interest will require repayment of $108.15 for a loan of $100. To accomplish this, the lender will ask an interest rate of 8.15 percent. In addition, the borrower will be willing to pay the higher rate, for he knows that the goods he buys today will be worth 5 percent more at the end of the year than they are worth today. So when both lender and borrower know with perfect certainty the future course of commodity prices, the money rate of interst, i, will be equal to the natural rate (or that rate prevailing during price stability which requires the $I = S$), r, plus the expected rate of inflation, p^e, and the product of rp^e. Thus $i = r + p^e + rp^e$. In conditions of perfect certainty, the natural rate, r, will be equal to $i - (p^e + rp^e)$. This relationship is of some importance, for it shows that if both lenders and borrowers anticipate the same rate of inflation, desired saving will be equal to desired investment, even though there is an ongoing inflation; and that such an equilibrium relationship can prevail in the long run, as long as both anticipations are unchanged. It also implies that a high money rate of interest can be consistent with a low natural rate and that to judge the latter from the former is apt to be very misleading.

Under conditions of perfect foresight, *rising* commodity prices ought to go hand in hand with *high* but stable money interest rates, and *falling* commodity prices with *low* but stable money interest rates. In addition, if either high or low but stable commodity prices prevail with no further anticipations of change, the money rate of interest ought to return to its natural level, that is, the level prior to the inflationary cycle, given that neither the S nor I schedule has shifted. These conclusions can be deduced from the analysis above, in which both lender and borrower knew with certainty that commodity prices would increase by 5 percent during the year ahead. With this knowledge, the money rate rose immediately from 3 percent to 8.15 percent. But this predicted relationship between commodity prices and money interest rates is not in accord with the empirical findings of Tooke and Gibson and would, in addition, imply a good deal more fluctuation in the money rate of interest than is usually observed in financial markets.

Before continuing, two points should be made. First, under conditions of perfect foresight, the natural rate of interest which set $S = I$ did not change. Thus, a 3 percent natural rate with price stability is equivalent to an 8.15 percent money rate with a 5 percent expected inflation, and high money or nominal rates can be associated with low real rates. Second, Fisher's analysis could violate one of the explicit assumptions pertaining to the form which savings can take—that is, that it must be a bond. But instead of an inflation, consider the case of a deflation. Let commodity prices be expected to fall by 5 percent. Does this imply that a negative money rate of interest of 2.15 percent would be observed, that is, that lenders would be willing to pay borrowers to make loans? A simple application of the formula $i = r + p^e + rp^e$ might lead to that expectation; however, this situation will not occur, for the lender has the option of either making loans or holding his wealth in a money form. If he opts for the latter course, his money will earn 5 percent in terms of increased purchasing power. Thus, a deflation should not lead to negative money interest rates.

Why, according to Fisher, do we get the results reported by Tooke and Gibson? Because people do not have perfect foresight. According to Fisher:

> . . . we are so accustomed in our business dealings to consider money as the one thing stable——to think of a "dollar as a dollar" regardless of the passage of time, that we reluctantly yield to this process of readjustment, thus rendering it very slow and imperfect. This inadequacy and tardiness of adjustment are fostered, moreover, by law and custom, which arbitrarily tend to keep down the [money] rate of interest.[18]

Expectations about future changes in prices, then, are governed by past experiences. Exactly how does the past influence expectations about the

    [18] I. Fisher, *The Purchasing Power of Money* Reprints of Economic Classics (New York: Augustus Kelley Publishers, 1971), pp. 57–58.

future? Fisher believed that people do not equally weigh all past experiences, that their most recent experiences are most influential in the formation of their expectations about the future. In addition, in Fisher's discussion of the business cycle (analyzed below), he gave the distinct impression that borrowers and lenders form different expectations. Borrowers, being primarily the businessmen of the day, are strongly influenced by contemporary events which directly affect their current profit position, while lenders or savers are more strongly influenced by the past and are slower to adjust to current events.

In *The Theory of Interest,* Fisher set out to estimate the length of the period over which expectations are, in fact, formed. His first task was to decide how to weight the past. Drawing upon previous work, he conf.ned himself to one form of weighting system—the simple straight-line function, or arithmetic progression. As an example, how much did the population expect prices to change in 1890? Fisher's estimation technique would first require choosing the number of years considered important for the formation of expectations. Suppose this "time horizon" to be eight years. Thus, 1889 price changes would be assigned a weight of $\frac{8}{36}$; 1888, $\frac{7}{36}$; 1887, $\frac{6}{36}$; . . . 1882, $\frac{1}{36}$. The denominator, 36, is simply the sum of the eight arithmetic progression weights $(8 + 7 + 6 \ldots + 1)$; the sum of all the weights is equal to unity. By using this method, an entire time series of expected price changes can be constructed, assuming that expectations are formed over an eight-year period; for example, to obtain expected prices in 1891, simply move the weighting distribution forward one year. The eight-year horizon is but one of an infinite number of possibilities—which is to be chosen? Fisher constructed several alternative time series of expected prices by assuming different horizons. He then correlated these alternative series of expected prices, one at a time, with a series of money interest rates; the series of expected prices which gave him the highest correlation coefficient was selected as the best. He could then tell which weighting horizon was the best. In his work, the horizon proved to be from 20 to 30 years, depending upon whether American or British data were considered and whether long-term or short-term interest rates were used. His results imply that rates of commodity price change occurring as long as 30 years ago can influence contemporary views on the future course of price inflation, although, to be sure, this influence is slight.

So when prices are rising, interest rates will rise, but with a lag. The length of the lag is determined by the particular time horizon of the population. The longer that horizon, the smaller will be the effect of contemporary price changes on market interest rates; for example, an eight-year time horizon will yield a current-period weight of .22, whereas a twenty-year horizon will yield a current-period weight of .095.

Fisher's analysis of commodity price movements and interest rates presents one problem which does not arise with the Keynes–Wicksell analysis. If the price level remains high and stable, that is, the rate of price change becomes zero, the money interest rate will not remain high and stable, but will return to the preinflation rate. Thus we would get high, stable prices and low interest rates—low relative to those prevailing during the inflationary period.

Table 1 presents, in a highly simplified form, the Fisherian analysis of the relationship of commodity price movements and the money rate of interest under the assumption that saver and investor have identical expectations about the future course of prices. A stable price level will be assumed first, then a rise in prices, an increase in the rate of inflation, and finally stable prices. We will also assume that in forming their expectations about future price movements in period t, the population has a three-year time horizon, that is, that they weight equally the actual rate of price inflation in periods $t - 1, t - 2, t - 3$.

The following conclusions are taken from Table 1 and may be sensitive to the assumptions made:

a. When prices are rising, money interest rates will be rising, but the response will lag. In the example, it takes at least one period of inflation to produce a rise in the money rate of interest.

b. As long as commodity prices are rising, the money rate of interest will be rising. When the rate of inflation diminishes, the market rate of interest will rise at a diminishing, but lagging, rate. The interest rate will rise until period 13, even though the rate of inflation diminished in period 9 and went to zero in period 12.

c. Once prices are high and stable, the interest rate will be (1) high and stable for a brief period (only because of the assumption of a short lag), then (2) it will fall back to the natural rate which prevailed prior to the start of the inflationary cycle.

d. If the rate of inflation is rapid enough and if price expectations lag behind to a considerable degree, the real rate of interest can be negative where the real rate is the nominal rate less the actual rate of inflation. History is replete with examples of negative real rates.

Fisher's Theory of the Business Cycle

Fisher's theory of the business cycle, which explains the relationship between money, commodity prices, and interest rates, will now be examined. A great deal of Fisher's work dealt with the analysis of equilibrium conditions. However, in *The Purchasing Power of Money,* he

TABLE 1. The Fisherian Hypothesis Under Conditions of Identical Price Expectations

Time	1	2	3	4	5	6	7	8	9	10	11	12	13	14	15	16	17	18
Price Index	100	100	102	104	106	111	117	123	130	138	146	155	155	155	155	155	155	155
Actual Rate of Inflation	0	0	2	2	2	5	5	5	6	6	6	6	0	0	0	0	0	0
Expected Rate of Inflation	0	0	0	⅔	1⅓	2	3	4	5	5⅓	5⅔	6	6	4	2	0	0	0
Natural[1] Rate	3	3	3	3	3	3	3	3	3	3	3	3	3	3	3	3	3	3
Money[2] Rate	3	3	3	3⅔	4⅓	5	6	7	8	8⅓	8⅔	9	9	7	5	3	3	3
Real[3] Rate	3	3	1	1⅔	2⅓	0	1	2	2	2⅓	2⅔	3	9	7	5	3	3	3

[1] This is the interest rate which, during the period of price stability and zero expectations about future price changes, will produce a long-run equilibrium between intended saving and investment.

[2] This is not the true money rate, for we have neglected the product of the natural rate and the expected rate of change in prices. Thus the data show $r + p^e$, not $r + p^e + rp^e$.

[3] This is the money rate less the actual rate of inflation. It is not perceived by either lender or borrower, who see as their estimate of the real rate the money rate less the rate of inflation they expect.

devoted one chapter exclusively to the business cycle, which he called the "period of transition." This chapter was devoted to a discussion of the nonneutrality of money. It is ironic that toward the end of this chapter he tells us, ". . . periods of transition are the rule and those of equilibrium the exception . . . ,"[19] yet he devoted a scant 18 pages out of 515 exclusively to this subject. Had the emphasis been reversed, one wonders what Fisher's ultimate influence might have been. However, his analysis of the business cycle is also elaborated upon in several other articles.[20]

Fisher's description of the business cycle will first be presented in verbal form, then diagrammatically. The latter description will be necessarily incomplete—putting a dynamic theory into a static form presents some problems. However, to the extent it is successful, it should develop additional appreciation for Fisher's contribution.

[19] *The Purchasing Power of Money*, p. 71.

[20] Among many speeches, letters to the press, articles, and books devoted to the subject, the following are of special merit: "A Statistical Relationship Between Unemployment and Price Change," *International Labor Review* (June 1926), pp. 785–92; "The Business Cycle Largely a 'Dance of the Dollar'," *Journal of the American Statistical Association* (December 1923), pp. 1024–28; and "Our Unstable Dollar and the So-Called Business Cycle," *Journal of the American Statistical Association* (June 1925), pp. 179–202. Patinkin observes ". . . that over his lifetime Irving Fisher devoted far more attention to the problem of the 'transition period' . . . than to his famous long-run proposition about the proportionate relationship between the quantity of money and the price level." See Don Patinkin, "On the Short-Run Non-Neutrality of Money in the Quantity Theory," *Banca Nazionale Del Lavoro Quarterly Review*, No. 100 (March 1972), pp. 3–22. This extensively researched reference provides an extended discussion on the non-neutrality views of both American and English economists in the pre-Keynesian twentieth century. He concludes his summary with two observations of interest:

". . . the analysis of the short-run impact of monetary changes on real output was presented by quantity theorists . . . not as casual minor afterthoughts of a basic long-run analysis of the neutrality of money, but as major subjects of discussion. Indeed, in most cases, quantity-theorists devoted far more attention to these short-run effects than to the long-run one.

". . . it also appears that a common feature of the quantity-theorists' short-run analyses was the role, not of the level of prices, but of their rate of change. For some writers, the anticipation of a changing price level affected economic activity through its effect on 'business confidence.' Others explained this effect more concretely—and more systematically—in terms of the lag of wages and other costs behind prices, and of the consequent effect of such a lag on profits. And, for still others . . . this effect was formally integrated into a general theoretical framework that distinguished between the nominal and real rate of interest. . . . Besides these effects, many of the quantity-theorists also referred to the effect of a changing price level in changing the distribution of real income and wealth."

In addition, J. Ronnie Davis has presented an extensive discussion of the views of Chicago economists in the early 1930's, calling for compensatory fiscal policy to stabilize the business cycle. See his "Chicago Economists, Deficit Budgets, and the Early 1930's," *The American Economic Review*, Vol. 58, No. 3 (June 1968), pp. 476–81.

In light of the current interest in the work of Irving Fisher, it is worth noting that in his later work on economic disturbances, the divergence between the money and natural rates of interest came to play a much more subsidiary role. He shifted attention to the effect of the absolute level of prices on the burden of debt and its implications for business bankruptcies and collapses. See Fisher's *Booms and Depressions* (New York: Adelphi Co., 1932) and "The Debt-Deflation Theory of Great Depressions," *Econometrica*, Vol. I (1933), pp. 337–57. His later views are nicely summarized in Joseph E. Reeve, *Monetary Reform Movements* (Washington, D.C.: American Council on Public Affairs, 1943), Chapter 11.

In his original work, Fisher made a distinction between money proper and bank deposits (somewhat as the earlier Banking School had done), the latter being imperfect substitutes for the former. Similarly, he differentiated the velocity of circulation of money from that of bank deposits. These distinctions will not be considered further in this presentation, as they are no longer relevant.

The inflationary phase of the cycle is initiated by an increase in the stock of money via the direct mechanism. This increase in the money stock accomplishes two things initially. First, it causes aggregate demand, MV, to expand, forcing the commodity price level to rise. Second, some of the increase in high-powered money (that capable of serving as bank reserves) finds its way to the banking system, where it expands free reserves and serves as the basis for subsequent expansions of bank deposits. This second factor is not a necessary condition for the subsequent cyclical upswing, however.

The initial increase in prices is the cause of a cumulative upward spiral, for it catches savers and labor unprepared for the inflation. Having experienced price stability, they have made no provisions for rising prices in their lending and their contractual relationships. Businessmen then find themselves in the advantageous position of having their sales receipts rise relative to their production costs, thereby increasing the amount and rate of profit.[21] This increase in profits leads to a desire to increase the quantity of investments, which banks are willing to finance from their newly acquired free reserves or by drawing down their reserve/deposit ratio; such an increase leads to secondary expansions in the stock of money and further rises in the price level, thereby increasing profits even further. It is this secondary expansion in the stock of money which causes desired investment to exceed desired saving for while the real rate of return of the investor has increased, the real rate of the saver has declined, for he either does not perceive or does not adjust to the inflation. However, the increase in prices will eventually cause both lenders and labor to anticipate further price increases, and these anticipations will be reflected in both money interest rates and wages, as both factor groups try to preserve the real value of their capital and income.

So far, the cycle appears to support the previously stated contention that borrowers and lenders do not form their expectations over the same time period. Businessmen borrowers are more strongly influenced by their current profit position in making investment decisions, whereas savers and lenders are governed by historical, institutional, and various

---

[21] In *The Purchasing Power of Money*, Fisher scarcely mentions the position of labor. However, it does occupy an important part of his analysis in the *International Labor Review* article. The graphical analysis to follow presenting Fisher's view of the cycle can be found in an expanded version in W. A. Bomberger and G. E. Makinen, "The Fisher Effect: A Graphical Treatment and Some Econometric Implications," *Journal of Finance* (in press).

legal considerations (for example, usury laws) and are relatively slow to adjust. This distinction is made rather sharply in Fisher's work; however, it should not be pushed too far, for in most developed economies a large amount of saving is done by businessmen and institutions through financial intermediaries, such as pension funds and insurance companies.

Lest Fisher be slighted, we should note that he mentioned the effects of inflation on output and the velocity of circulation, thereby discussing all the elements in the equation of exchange. Thus inflation, to the extent that it is unanticipated by labor, will lower the real wage and lead to an expansion of output; this effect is only transitory, however, and its extent depends on the length of time it takes labor to accurately forecast the future course of prices. During the period of adjustment, however, money is nonneutral.

Inflation, since it depreciates the purchasing power of money, will also accelerate its circulation, or turnover. Fisher tells us that "we all hasten to get rid of any commodity which, like ripe fruit, is spoiling on our hands. Money is no exception; when it is depreciating, holders get rid of it as fast as possible."[22] This, of course, causes prices to rise at an even faster rate. But like output, this rise in velocity is transitory and caused by the extraordinary conditions associated with the initial increase in prices.

As long as the banks continue to expand the stock of money, investment will be greater than saving and prices will rise. As long as actual price increases are greater than those expected by lenders, profit margins will be above normal and the inflation will continue, assuming the banks accommodate the increased demand for loanable funds. The situation may become explosive. It is here that Fisher imposes an institutional constraint to bring the inflation to a halt. The constraint is the reserve requirement imposed either by law or custom on commercial banks. As their reserve/deposit position deteriorates, the banks are forced to curtail their lending, thereby adding less and less to the supply of loanable funds. Thus, reduction in the rate of growth of loans correspondingly reduces the growth rate of the money stock and with it the growth of commodity prices. As the supply of loanable funds from this source is reduced, the market rate of interest rises. When this rate (and the rate of rise of money wages) is equal to the actual rate of increase in prices, profit margins will be reduced to their previous level and the demand for loanable funds will cease to expand. If, however, money interest rates and wages continue to rise because inflationary expectations now exceed actual price changes, the demand for loanable funds will contract because profit margins will start to fall. This will not, however, contract or deflate the economy so long as the banks do not allow monetary contraction.

22 *The Purchasing Power of Money*, p. 63.

A contraction would take place, according to Fisher, in the final stages of the inflationary cycle, when costs start to exceed the actual rate of change of prices and a crisis of confidence occurs, usually because of a higher-than-normal rate of business failures. Such bankruptcies raise doubts about the value of commercial paper held by banks, precipitating a currency drain from the banks. Having an abnormally low reserve/ deposit ratio, their only recourse to meet the drain is to call in loans. Interest rates rise to fantastic levels, and the calling of loans contracts the stock of money. It is this contraction which makes the level of intended saving greater than intended investment, for it pushes up the real rate of interest to which savers respond and lowers the yield on investment by further raising costs relative to prices. Since saving now exceeds investment and the money stock is reduced, aggregate demand, MV, falls. The economy now enters the downswing—the price paid for the profligacy of the unhealthy upswing.

Now that the verbal explanation of the cycle has been completed, it will be recast in diagrammatic form, step by step. To keep the presentation manageable, only the financial sector will be examined; we will assume that labor and lender adjust in a similar fashion.

The only factor complicating the following analysis is that savers and borrowers do not respond in the same way to inflation. After Fisher, we will assume that borrowers respond to the *current* rate of inflation. Thus the real rate of interest which they realize on any investment project will be equal to the money rate, i, less the actual rate of inflation, p^A. Savers, on the other hand, respond to an *expected* rate of inflation, and for them the real rate is equal to the money rate, i, less the expected rate of inflation, p^e. When $p^A = p^e$, the real rate for both borrowers and savers is equal; this is called the *natural rate* (Fisher calls it the *normal rate*), for it ensures that $I = S$ at full employment, and that the economic system is in long-run equilibrium. Thus, it will be possible to have equilibrium during an ongoing inflation so long as $p^A = p^e$.

Because savers and investors do not respond in the same way to an ongoing inflation, graphical illustration of their behavior becomes more complicated. The following digression is designed to aid in interpreting the diagrammatic exposition given below. In these diagrams the actual real rate, $r = i - p^A$, is measured on the ordinate rather than the expected real rate, $r = i - p^e$, to which savers respond. Whenever the two inflation rates, p^A and p^e, are unequal, the saving supply schedule will shift. For example, suppose prices start to rise after an initial period of stability. If the rise in prices is unperceived by savers, they furnish the same real volume of saving as before, but at a lower real interest rate $(i - p^A)$. Thus, the saving schedule must be shifted downward in a diagram whose ordinate measures the actual real rate, $i - p^A$.

If the expected rate of inflation, p^e, exceeds the actual rate, p^A, savers will furnish the same real volume of saving only at higher nominal interest rates which are designed to compensate for the expected rise in prices. Thus, in a diagram which measures $i - p^A$ on the ordinate, the saving schedule will shift upward by the amount of the excess of p^e over p^A.

The analysis begins by assuming that a state of equilibrium prevails in which neither lender nor borrower expects the level of prices to change.

Step 1.   The stock of money is increased via a foreign-trade surplus or the activities of domestic miners. This causes MV to increase and the commodity price level to rise. It also serves to expand the free reserves of commercial banks. To make the initial parts of the analysis easier, assume that the total money supply and the price level increases are 2 percent.[23]

Step 2.   The rise in the price level, given the prevailing money interest rate, reduces the real rate of interest of the investor, $i - p^A$, thereby making profitable marginal additions to the capital stock which prior to the inflation were unprofitable. Since the real rate of interest of investors has decreased, it can be represented by a movement down the investment demand schedule to point B, which is equal to $i - p^A$ or $3\% - 2\% = 1\%$. This is consistent with the earlier presentation of classical theory, for the greater the capital intensity of the production process, the lower at the margin will be the yield on investment, here called the real rate. Thus in Figure 3:4 the inflation moves investors from A to B in the left-hand diagram.

Since the saving schedule is graphed in the $i - p^A$ plane and not the $i - p^e$ plane, it will appear to shift downward so long as the inflation goes unexpected by lenders. Savers, then, furnish at an $i - p^A$ rate of 1 percent the same quantity of real saving that they furnished during price stability at 3 percent; at the 3 percent rate they provide what they did during price stability at 5 percent, and so on. The saving function is seen to shift down and the volume of real saving to rise. The downward shift is equal to $p^A - p^e$, or 2 percent. However, the downward shift in the saving function is to a point such as C, which lies above point B, the point desired by investors (it would move to point B only if I were a vertical line). At real rate $i - p^A$, desired investment exceeds desired saving. This excess is eliminated by a rise in the money rate to C', which occurs when borrowers must raise additional real balances to finance their investment plans. The demand schedule for loanable funds shifts

---

[23] This increase in the money stock is to be regarded as a change in its rate of growth relative to its long-run trend. In order to keep the level of prices constant over time, the money stock would have to grow at a rate about equal to the rate of growth of real output. Short-run oscillations in the rate of growth of the money stock about this long-run trend could set in motion a period of transition.

FIGURE 3:4

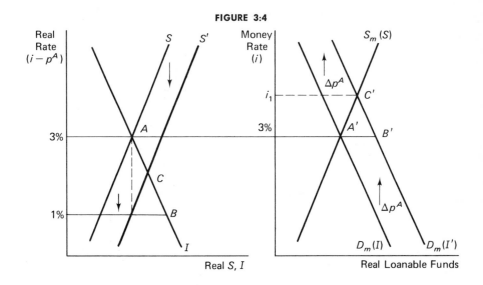

up by the increase in the rate of profit, which can be approximated by p^A. As the supply schedule of loanable funds does not change, because of expectations of constant commodity prices, the money rate will rise by less than the rate of inflation, p^A.

The rise in the money rate will increase the real rate, moving investors from point B to point C, restoring equilibrium between saving and investment. Even though the real rate, $i - p^A$, has declined, savers will assume it has risen. This occurs because the combination of a rise in the nominal rate of interest and a constant level of expected prices, p^e, is regarded by savers as an equivalent rise in their expected real rate of interest, $i - p^e$. Thus they will furnish a larger volume of real saving and loanable funds.

Of importance is the fact that the money interest rate will embody not just the price expectations of the lender, but the weighted average of both lender and borrower. In addition, a transitory increase in both real saving and investment is produced. It is this transitory increase that demonstrates the nonneutrality of money, and different perceptions of inflation by savers and lenders are necessary to produce it.

Before moving to Step 3, let us consider what would have happened if both lenders and borrowers had the same price expectations, so that for both the real rate would be $r = i - p^A$. Let it again be assumed that the money stock and associated spending are increased by 2 percent, pushing up commodity prices at that rate. This will reduce the real rate of borrowers, as shown in Figure 3:5, from 3 percent to 1 percent, making profitable additional increments of investment and shifting up the demand schedule for real loanable funds by 2 percent. However, savers

FIGURE 3:5

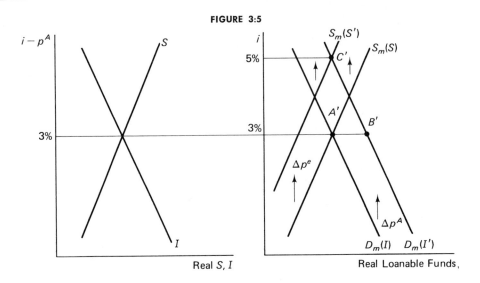

also perceive the same rate of inflation, and in order to keep the value of their principal intact, demand that a 2 percent premium be added to the previous money rate of 3 percent. As a result, the supply schedule of real loanable funds is shifted up by 2 percent. The effect of the activities of both borrowers and lenders is to raise the money rate by a full 2 percent to 5 percent; this 5 percent money rate corresponds to the natural rate of 3 percent. Equilibrium is thus preserved between I and S at the old natural rate of 3 percent, only if both parties have equal expectations of the rate of commodity price changes. In this case of equal perception, changes in the money supply are neutral since the level of S and I remains unchanged. Thus, as shown above, unequal perception of inflation is necessary to produce nonneutrality. Again, money interest rates embody the weighted average of expectations of both lenders and borrowers.

Step 3. As a variation on Step 2, the commercial banks will be allowed to create new money by reducing their reserve/deposit ratio in response to the increased demand for loanable funds (savers are still assumed to expect commodity prices to remain constant, that is, $p^e = 0$).[24] This situation is shown in Figure 3:6.

As in Step 2, the initial inflation is not perceived by savers, and in the $i - p^A$ plane, the saving schedule will shift down. The inflation will also make more profitable marginal increments of investment, for the

---

[24] In Fisher's description of the cycle, the expansion of bank money is likely to occur when the nominal interest rate rises as shown in Figure 3:4. The expansion in bank money arises, according to Fisher, because lenders "including banks are led to become more enterprising. Beguiled by the higher nominal rates into a belief that fairly-high interest is being realized, they extend their loans, and with the resulting expansion of bank loans, deposit currency . . . expands." See *The Purchasing Power of Money*, p. 60.

real rate of borrowers, $r = i - p^A$, will fall. As in Figure 3:4, this decrease will produce an initial excess of desired investment over desired saving. However, the rise in the demand for loanable funds is now met by an increase on the supply side equal to the new money created by banks. The action of the banks shifts out the supply of loanable funds from $S_m(S)$ to $S_m(S + CB)$. This shift will prevent the money rate from rising to C', the level which will produce equality between I and S (C' being the nominal rate corresponding to the real rate C). The excess of investment over saving, equal to the distance DB, is financed by new money creation and shows up as a rise in MV, or aggregate money demand. This so-called *secondary increase* in the stock of money by commercial banks forces prices to higher levels. As long as the commercial banks create money, the money rate will be prevented from rising, and investment will exceed saving.

FIGURE 3:6

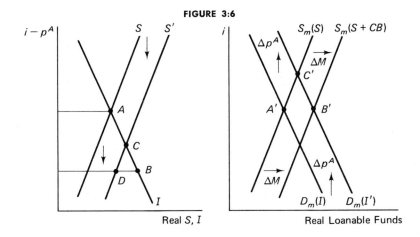

Real S, I

Real Loanable Funds

In this step, the additional new money, or liquidity, provided by the commercial banks prevents the money interest rate from reflecting the price or profit expectations of lenders and borrowers.

Step 4. At this stage in the explanation, we will assume that savers have positive inflationary expectations. In Fisher's theory, this will occur after the lender experiences a period of actual inflation. Initially, it is assumed that these expectations are less than the actual rate of inflation ($p^A > p^c$). In order to give continuity to this presentation, Figure 3:7 represents an extension of the diagrams shown in Figure 3:6. The initial position of the diagram is one showing an excess of investment over saving (equal to the distance DB) and money creation equal to $A'B'$ (where $A'B' = DB$).

In order to keep their real rate constant, savers now ask a higher money rate equal to the inflation they expect to prevail over the period

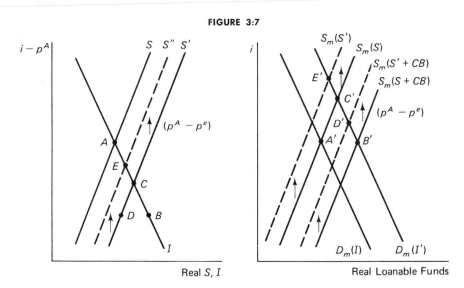

Real S, I   Real Loanable Funds

of the loan. This shifts the $S_m(S)$ and the $S_m(S + CB)$ schedules up by the amount of the inflation expected by savers, p^e, raising the money rate from B' to possibly D'. However, since $D_m(I)$ does not have zero elasticity, the money rate of interest will rise by less than the inflation expected by savers. Thus, the real rate of savers, $r = i - p^e$, declines, and they save less in real terms. In the left-hand diagram, the perception of inflation by savers will shift up the saving schedule by the amount of the expected inflation, and S'' will be above S' by an amount equal to p^e and below S by an amount equal to $p^A - p^e$.

In addition, the rise in the money rate of interest increases the real rate of interest of the investor, $i - p^A$, making unprofitable marginal additions to capital which had been profitable at the lower money rate. The quantity of investment then declines, and a move along the investment demand schedule to a point above B is made. It is at this point in the cycle that observers are apt to blame overinvestment as the cause of the downswing to follow. Since the real rate for investors rose and that for savers declined, the real quantity of saving and investment declined, and the money rate of interest rose. However, since the rate of money creation by banks has not changed, the gap between investment and saving remains unchanged.

Had savers' expectations of inflation been equal to those of investors ($p^e = p^A$) the saving schedule would have shifted back to S and the money rate of interest would have been pushed above D'.

Step 5. Here the end of the rising portion of the cycle is approached. This happens when the banking system ceases to create money, which is likely to occur as their reserve/deposit ratio declines to abnormally low levels. The actual rate of inflation then drops to zero, but savers, guided by the past, expect a positive rate of inflation to continue. Again, for continuity, the graphs in Figure 3:8 are assumed to represent an extension of those shown in Figure 3:7.

FIGURE 3:8

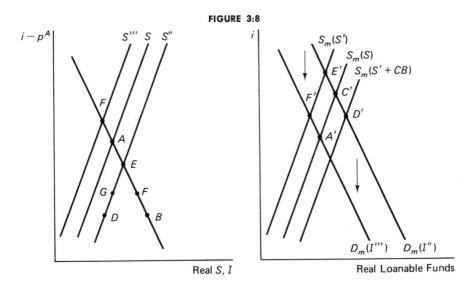

Real S, I   Real Loanable Funds

The end of money creation will cause the supply schedule of loanable funds, $S_m(S' + CB)$, to rise and be coincident with $S_m(S')$. This will force up the money rate of interest to E'. It will also cause the actual rate of inflation, p^A, to fall to zero. The rise in i and the fall in p^A will raise the real rate of interest to the lender and make unprofitable additional marginal increments of investment. The fall in the inflation rate, by reducing the profitability of investment, will cause the demand curve for loanable funds to shift down by the amount of decrease in profitability—approximated by p^A. This is just the reverse of Step 2. The money rate of interest will decline to F'.

Since money creation has ceased, the gap between saving and investment is eliminated. However, whether the new equilibrium point remains at E depends upon the state of expectations of savers. If they expect prices to rise by the same amount as last period, the position of S'' and $S_m(S')$ will remain unchanged. If they expect a higher rate of inflation, S'' and $S_m(S')$ will move up by the amount they expect the rate to increase. If, on the other hand, they expect the rate of inflation to decrease, S'' and $S_m(S')$ will shift down by the expected rate of decrease.

Even if their expectations of inflation accelerate, producing upward shifts in the saving and supply of loanable funds schedules, they will not produce an economic contraction in Fisher's model. While the real value of saving and investment will fall, nothing has caused MV, or aggregate demand, to change. Thus, the decrease in real investment is being matched by a rise in consumption expenditure, the consequence of a fall in saving.

It is important to note that the rise in money interest rates will again reflect the joint expectations of both lenders and borrowers.

Step 6.   In order to get the deflation which in Fisher's moral language is the retribution paid for the profligacy of the expansion, we must have a contraction of deposit money by the banking system. This contraction would occur as p^e overtakes p^A, forcing a drop in the nominal interest rate from E' to F' in Figure 3:8. As the nominal rate falls, banks will observe a lower real rate of return $(i - p^e)$ on their portfolio. This lower rate of return will provide the incentive to restore their reserve/deposit ratio to a more normal level. This they do by issuing fewer loans and failing to renew others. This action produces a contraction in the supply of money, shifting the demand for loanable funds schedule to $D_m(I + C)$ in Figure 3:9 and raising the nominal interest rate to I'.

FIGURE 3:9

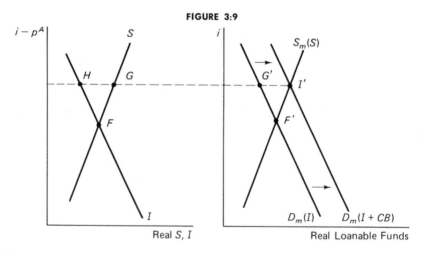

If, for convenience, it is assumed that savers and lenders have expectations of constant prices, they will regard this rise in the money rate as an equivalent rise in the real rate. The quantity of saving will increase to perhaps G. The rise in the money rate will also raise the real rate of interest of borrowers, making unprofitable increments of investment which were profitable before the rise in the money rate. Thus, a gap opens between saving and investment equal to the amount of real balances destroyed $(HG = G'I')$. In this environment of stable prices and expectations of stable prices, changes in the money rate are regarded as inducing equal changes in the real rates for both savers and investors. At this point, the Fisherian analysis is identical to those of Keynes–Wicksell and Thornton, presented earlier.

As the cycle continues, high real interest payments on previously accumulated debt and the unavailability of credit send marginal firms into bankruptcy. This causes banks to call in loans (for they fear that more business firms will fail), contributing to more bankruptcies and a further contraction of the money supply. As conditions worsen, confidence in the banking system declines, leading to runs on the banks and a further contraction of money and credit as the cycle accelerates downward.

The contraction of the money stock shown in Figure 3:9, by reducing aggregate demand, MV, will cause the general level of prices to fall. The deflation will affect the real rate of lenders, thereby inducing shifts in the demand schedule for loanable funds. It will also lead to expectations of price changes by savers, thereby affecting the saving and supply of loanable funds schedules. As an exercise, the student should work out a typical deflationary episode.

Throughout this step-by-step explanation of the business cycle, care has been taken to note the changes, if any, in the real rate and the degree to which the money rate embodies the price expectations of borrowers and lenders. This was done because many of the empirical tests made of Fisher's theory have assumed that the real rate remains invariant and that the money rate embodies "price expectations," with the implicit assumption that those of borrower and lender are the same. The analysis above ought to cast doubt on the validity of such estimating procedures, for they neglect changes in the real rate, liquidity effects originating in the banking system, and possible differences in the expectations of lenders and borrowers.

ALTERNATIVE THEORIES OF THE BUSINESS CYCLE

In any comparison of the monetary theory of the business cycle developed by Fisher with the nonmonetary, or real, theory as presented by Keynes–Wicksell, it may well be an impossible task to determine which is valid. However, there are factors which one ought to expect to observe if either explanation is the correct one and, in order to understand each approach more fully, some problems connected with each explanation might be noted.

Since Keynes–Wicksell postulate a rising natural rate of interest due to increases in the productivity of capital, new capital equipment should be more productive than the existing stock of capital equipment.

Since it is more productive, new capital goods ought to sell at a higher price than existing capital goods. However, technological improvements in the capital goods industries, by reducing costs, may prevent the price of new capital goods from rising over time as their productivity increases.

The Keynes–Wicksell explanation is beset with three difficulties that appear to limit its relevance to the short run, though it was developed as an explanation for the long run. First, their presentation does not explain the long-run source of bank reserves which are required to accommodate the long-run rise in the demand for loanable funds, which follows from the long-run rise in the natural rate. Second, the Keynes–Wicksell explanation implies a completely passive banking system which willingly accommodates the needs of business and is itself, seldom, if ever, the cause of the cycle. Yet even the most extreme adherent of this view must acknowledge that the work of Friedman and Schwartz,[25] and Cagan,[26] presents compelling evidence that autonomous changes in the stock of money have played a major role in the business cycle. Third, since their theory is based upon lags in the lending behavior of banks (they fail to perceive immediate changes in the natural rate), it is inappropriate for the long run, where such lags are insignificant.[27]

Concerning Fisher, an ideal test would be to observe a country which issues two types of bonds: One with constant purchasing power due to a built-in cost-of-living index and the other without such a feature. The difference in the yields between the two ought to measure the expected rate of change of commodity prices and permit calculation of the time horizon over which expectations are formed. In addition, any change in the yield on the constant purchasing power alternative could be attributed to changes in the natural rate, subject to certain exceptions. However, such ideal states are not available, and one is left with the type of test that Fisher proposed and which is explained above.

From the tests made by Fisher using both British and American data, it would appear that expectations of commodity price changes are formed over relatively long time periods, making Fisher's explanation relevant to the long run. However, Fisher was, in a sense, resurrected to explain the very rapid and almost coincident rise in interest rates and commodity prices in the 1965–1969 period. This would imply a very rapid rate of expectation formation—that is, expectations formed over a very short time period, quite contrary to the indications of previous empirical tests. Unless one makes some *ad hoc* special assumptions,

[25] M. Friedman and A. Schwartz, *A Monetary History of the United States, 1867–1960* (Princeton, N.J.: Princeton University Press, 1963).

[26] P. Cagan, *Determinants and Effects of Changes in the Stock of Money, 1875–1960* (New York: National Bureau of Economic Research, 1965).

[27] R. A. Mundell, *Monetary Theory* (Pacific Palisades, Cal.: Goodyear, 1971), pp. 18–19.

Fisher's explanation cannot be made applicable to the 1965–1969 period.[28]

However, this does not imply that expectations of commodity price changes are always formed over long periods. In societies which have experienced hyperinflations and in those with more or less chronic inflations—many Latin American countries, for instance—expectations of commodity price changes are probably formed over extremely short periods. Institutional practices such as price-indexed bonds, insurance contracts, and wage rates serve to reinforce this conjecture. Under these inflationary conditions, the Fisherian analysis seems most appropriate. To urge policies which neglect the effect of inflation on lending, investing, and cash-balance holding, or to assume that it has no effect, may lead to policies which seriously threaten economic stability. However, an important question concerns the threshold inflation rate, which makes the Fisherian explanation relevant to the short run. Thus far, empirical studies have not provided the answer.

We have discussed two alternative theories of the business cycle; however, their implications for monetary policy have yet to be examined. It may come as a surprise to see that their policy implications are remarkably similar: The central bank's monetary policy should be geared to ensure a constant price level. However, in the Keynes–Wicksell model, this policy may not be successful in the downswing phase of the cycle.

The existence of inflation in the Keynes–Wicksell analysis arises

---

[28] An extensive empirical literature of recent origin uses both quarterly and annual United States data to test whether anticipations of price-level changes enter the nominal interest rate structure. Studies by Thomas Sargent in 1969 and by William Gibson in 1970 reveal long lags similar in length to those originally estimated by Fisher. See Thomas Sargent, "Commodity Price Expectations and the Interest Rate," *Quarterly Journal of Economics*, Vol. 83, No. 330 (Feb. 1969), pp. 127–40; William Gibson, "Price Expectations Effects on Interest Rates," *Journal of Finance*, Vol. 25, No. 1 (March 1970), pp. 19–34. Later work by William Gibson and Yohe and Karnovsky suggests the lags are quite short. However, the conclusion of the Yohe–Karnovsky study is very sensitive to the procedure used to estimate the lags. See William Gibson, "The Lag in the Effect of Monetary Policy on Income and Interest Rates," *Quarterly Journal of Economics*, Vol. 84, No. 335 (May 1970), pp. 288–300; "Interest Rates and Monetary Policy," *Journal of Political Economy*, Vol. 78, No. 3 (May/June 1970), pp. 431–54; and "Interest Rates and Inflationary Expectations: New Evidence," *American Economic Review*, Vol. 61, No. 5 (Dec. 1971), pp. 854–65; William Yohe, and Denis Karnovsky, "Interest Rates and Price Level Changes, 1952–1969," *Review*, Federal Reserve Bank of St. Louis, Vol. 51, No. 12 (Dec. 1969), pp. 18–38. In an intriguing paper, Sargent has argued that the reason for the implausibly long lags found in some studies may be the inability of econometric estimation techniques to separate what are, in fact, two lags. In a model in which nominal interest rates are determined by both real (saving and investment) and monetary (real money balances) forces, Sargent argues that while individuals may come quickly to anticipate inflation and embody such expectations in their saving and investment behavior in the manner specified by Fisher, actual changes in the price level may be slow to respond whenever income diverges from the full-employment level. This slow response of prices means that real money balances are also slow to change, thereby preventing the nominal interest rate from fully and promptly reflecting inflationary expectations. See Thomas Sargent, "Anticipated Inflation and the Nominal Rate of Interest," *Quarterly Journal of Economics*, Vol. 86, No. 343 (May 1972), pp. 212–25.

because the commercial banks are tardy in recognizing a rise in the natural rate. They therefore expand the stock of money by accommodating the increased demand by business for loanable funds at the existing money interest rate. The obvious policy for the central bank is to force up the money rate by reducing the volume of reserves available to the banks. This policy will be pursued automatically if the central bank stabilizes the price level. However, in the downswing, the decreased demand for loanable funds by business will be met by a decrease in the supply of such funds, for the banks in the Keynes–Wicksell world merely accommodate the "needs of trade." Central bank increases in bank reserves (for the purpose of persuading banks to avoid deflating the money stock) appear ruled out by the assumed behavior of the banks. Thus, the effectiveness of a central bank policy designed to iron out the business cycle by ensuring a constant commodity price level may be asymmetric: It will work on the upswing of the cycle, but not on the downswing. In addition, the existence of lags may further complicate the stabilization objectives of the central bank.

For the Fisherian, a sustained inflation implies that commercial banks are holding down the money rate of interest by creating additional deposit money, which allows intended investment to exceed intended saving. Again, the obvious central bank policy is to reduce bank reserves through open market operations or through increases in reserve requirements.

Thus, whichever analysis one believes correctly describes the origins of the business cycle, the monetary policy for stabilization is much the same.

THE UNIQUENESS OF MONEY

In order to maintain the external convertibility of the British pound, the Currency School advocated control of the supply of Bank of England notes and that, by the imposition of 100 percent reserves, they be made to fluctuate in exact accordance with the external movement of specie. It was their concentration on these notes, to the exclusion of other assets which served as mediums of exchange, that raised the issue of what is and is not money. The arguments of this question were largely sidetracked on irrelevant issues and never resolved.[29] Some 100 years later in the late 1950's an English monetary commission known as the Radcliffe Committee again debated the issue of what is money and agreed that a narrow range of assets was an inappropriate variable for policy

---

[29] For a discussion of the contending positions, see Viner, *Studies in the Theory of International Trade*, pp. 243–254 and Mints, *A History of Banking Theory*, pp. 95–100.

purposes. Their conclusion followed from their view that many assets could serve as stores of value.

Since the characteristic properties of any asset called *money* have been of such interest, the views of the Currency and Banking schools on this issue ought to be summarized so that they may later be contrasted with their twentieth-century counterpart.

Familiar with the policy prescriptions of the Currency School, the Banking School pointed to the obvious fact that other assets were equally as acceptable as notes of the Bank of England in serving as mediums of exchange. These other assets—demand deposits, notes of so-called "country banks,"[30] commercial bills of exchange, and open-book credit—were used often in transactions, and while quantatively much smaller than Bank of England notes, they were of increasing importance as the nineteenth century progressed. Thus any watertight distinction between money and near-money was of little importance.

Moreover, the Banking School could see no link existing between the stock of money narrowly defined and the volume of credit or of money substitutes. Hence, the latter could vary independently of the former, and since the substitutes, by influencing aggregate demand, could influence prices, control of only bank notes was self-defeating. Thus in their view the volume of credit which could be erected on the base of any asset called "money" was large, variable, and unpredictable.

The Currency School recognized that these substitutes, or *auxiliary media,* existed, but, in rebuttal to the Banking School, contended that the substitutes could not exert an independent influence on the level of prices; they merely magnified the influence of the Bank of England notes. However, substantial differences of opinion are to be found among the ranks of the Currency School regarding this view and why the Bank of England notes ought to be singled out for discriminatory treatment.

First among their reasons was a belief that payments in specie and notes bore a constant proportion to payments by the substitutes; thus they could not vary and exert an independent influence on prices.

Second, some believed that since the turnover rate, or velocity of circulation, of the substitutes was much lower than that of notes and coin, the influence on the price level of these "economizing expedients" was only "trifling or transient."

Third, the supply of some substitutes was linked directly to Bank of England notes. This was the case with country bank notes, because the issuing banks held their reserves in notes of the Bank of England. Henry Thornton went so far as to explain why the country banks could not overissue their notes even if they wanted to follow such a course.[31]

---

[30] These notes were taxed out of existence when the Bank Charter Act of 1844 concentrated a monopoly of the note issue in the Bank of England.

[31] This argument rested upon a regional balance-of-payments analysis. For example, if

Fourth, many viewed bank demand deposits as arising from the deposit by a customer of notes or specie, which the banker would merely pass on in return for a loan. Taking the view that all deposits are derivative, it was easy for them to argue that the volume of deposits depended upon the availability of notes and specie. A reduction in the latter would therefore, produce a reduction in the former. Hence, bankers did not have the power to expand deposits to fill the gap caused by a reduced supply of notes or specie.

Fifth, in times of crisis, Bank of England Notes were always demanded for final payments. Thus one could ignore other circulating media for they were not used in really crucial situations.

By concentrating attention on a definition of money which centered on its properties as a medium of exchange, the essential question in the discussion was overlooked. No matter which group of assets is defined to be money, the influence of money substitutes operates mainly to accentuate variations in the velocity of those assets defined to be money.

Using the equation of exchange, $MV = PY$, the influence of country bank notes, open-book credit, and commercial bills of exchange is to vary the value of V, given that M is defined as Bank of England notes. The relevant question then becomes, by controlling M, as defined by the Currency School, can the value of PY be controlled as well, or do variations in V systematically offset variations in M? This issue was totally ignored by the participants in the debate and by those of the Radcliffe Committee.

Related to the issue of the control of PY by controlling M is the proposition that no matter how money is defined, variations in velocity should not dominate variations in the money stock as a cause of variations in PY. If velocity variations do dominate, the potential is very great for serious errors in policy to arise. For example, a desire to alter PY by a given percentage may call for a certain change in the money stock. However, if variations in velocity are relatively large, any slight error in estimating their change could have serious consequences for PY. Thus, rather than expanding PY by a given percentage, the change in M could, when combined with an inaccurately predicted V, cause a much larger increase in PY. Rather than stabilizing the economy, it may cause serious inflation. The possibility of such serious errors makes it important how money is defined or what group of assets is included in a definition.

---

the banks in Lancaster expanded their notes, they would serve to drive up prices in that region, increasing their imports from London and decreasing their exports to the urban center. Their notes would then accumulate in London banks and be presented for redemption in specie or Bank of England notes. Such redemptions would decrease the reserves of the country banks and force a contraction of their issue.

OTHER FACTORS AND THEIR INFLUENCE ON THE PRICE LEVEL

The orthodox monetary theory which emerged from the analysis of the Currency School was from time to time confronted with the charge that nonmonetary factors could exert an effect upon the price level. For example, if the government imposed an excise tax on some commodities, this ought to have an influence on the domestic price level. Similarly, increases in the prices of imported commodities ought to make domestic commodities which embody them as an input more expensive, or, if such commodities are consumed directly, they ought to raise the cost of living. Additionally, it was suggested that the industrial structure of the country, that is, the degree to which its markets for productive services and commodities departed from atomistic competition, could be a source of inflation.

Orthodox theorists agreed that each of these factors might exert a transitory, or short-run, influence on the price level, but in the longer run the influence was held to be largely negligible unless and to the degree that each factor forced inefficient production options upon the country.

As to the ability of excise taxes and changes in the price of imports to raise the price level permanently, the orthodox conclusion that this was impossible followed from the view that individuals maintain a more or less constant relationship between real money balances and the level of real income; thus the transitory rise in the price level following the imposition of selective excise taxes or the rise in the price of imports would reduce real money balances below their desired level. In an attempt to restore equilibrium between actual and desired magnitudes, the rate of money spending would decline, leading to a decline in the prices of goods in general. Thus it was the decline in the price of other goods which would offset the rise in the prices of the goods subject to the excise tax or imported from abroad. The price level remains a monetary phenomenon.

However, this conclusion is subject to a potentially serious qualification. The excise tax or the rise in the prices of imported goods could cause the factors of production to be combined in less efficient ways than before, leading to a decline in real income and a higher price level. If the imposition of the tax or the rise in the price of imports is a once-and-for-all occurrence, the related decline in real output would cause a similar once-and-for-all rise in the level of prices and would not generate continuous inflation. Other things equal, subsequent changes in the price level would then depend on the growth rate of the money stock.

To the extent that the industrial structure of a country was characterized by monopolistic or oligopolistic sellers of products and factor services, orthodox micro-analysis would explain that prices and wages would be *higher* in those sectors than if their markets were atomistically competitive. However, such an industrial structure could not account for *rising* prices unless monopolists were holding reserves of unexploited power (that is, unless they were not maximizing their net returns, be they profits or wages) or unless markets previously competitive were to become monopolistic. The general view of orthodox theorists was that individuals who argued that labor unions and oligopolistic business firms were responsible for inflation simply confused levels and rates of change of prices. This does not deny that increasing monopolization may lead to less efficient production, causing a decline in the rate of growth of real output.

CONCLUSION

The purpose of this chapter has been to explore the classical analyses of the short run, or period of transition, to see whether the essential propositions of the quantity theory of money need hold. For this reason, one of the greatest controversies in economics was selected for analysis.

Our assessment of the theoretical propositions advanced by the more influential of the two groups of protagonists, the Currency School, reveals that they regarded variations in the stock of money as the basic cause of economic disturbances. These variations were communicated to the real sector of the economy by a direct wealth-adjustment mechanism and by an indirect mechanism involving the banking system, interest rates, and variations in the desired stock of capital.

For several reasons they believed that variations in the money supply would not result in an instantaneous and proportional adjustment in the price level. Rather, the variations could have an effect on real output, employment, capital formation, and velocity, because of transitory changes in real wages, real interest rates, expectations of price changes, and the distribution of wealth and income. These changes were brought about because of lack of accurate foresight or inability to recontract immediately. Thus, money was clearly nonneutral in the short run, estimated to last upwards of a decade by Fisher, whose work on the period of transition is generally considered to be the most sophisticated theoretical treatment of the quantity theory.

Since money was the fundamental cause of the cycle, the central bank was to play a leading role in the minimization of economic disturbances.

This required that money be sharply defined and that control of it, and consequently of economic activity, not be hindered by the availability of money substitutes or credit, in general. Thus, money came to be defined as Bank of England notes and tight regulation was achieved by imposing a requirement of 100 percent specie reserves. This is the forerunner of a contemporary quantity theory proposition that control of the monetary base gives the central bank control of the supply of money and of economic activity.

However, both empirically and theoretically, few of these propositions went unchallenged. The Banking School advanced a number of propositions designed to counter what became the accepted orthodoxy in monetary theory. These included:

(1) That the business cycle was nonmonetary in nature. The work of Keynes and Wicksell implied that it depended upon the expectations of entrepreneurs.

(2) That the central bank could not control the money stock because it was determined by the needs of trade, or demand-determined. Thus, money was an endogenous variable.

(3) That even if the supply of something called "money" could be controlled, the availability of an endless array of substitutes would make such control useless.

(4) That the price level is a nonmonetary variable determined by the relationship of aggregate demand and supply. Therefore, production costs help to determine the price level.

In Chapter 12, the monetary controversy of recent times is summarized. There, it will be shown that the debate between the Currency and the Banking schools is both alive and well.

Selected References and Readings

BECKER, G. S., AND W. J. BAUMOL, "The Classical Monetary Theory: The Outcome of the Discussion," *Economica,* New Series, Vol. 19 (Nov. 1952).

BLAUG, MARK, *Economic Theory in Retrospect,* Rev. ed. (Homewood, Ill.: Irwin, 1968).

CRAMP, A. B., "Two Views on Money," *Lloyds Bank Review,* No. 65 (July 1962).

DAUGHERTY, M. R., "The Currency–Banking Controversy," *Southern Economic Journal* (Oct. 1942 and Jan. 1943).

DAVIS, J. RONNIE, "Chicago Economists, Deficit Budgets, and the Early 1930's," *The American Economic Review,* Vol. 58, No. 3 (June 1968).

————, *The New Economics and the Old Economists* (Ames, Iowa: Iowa State University Press, 1971).

FISHER, IRVING, *Appreciation and Interest* (New York: Macmillan, 1896).

————, *The Rate of Interest* (New York: Macmillan, 1907).

————, *The Purchasing Power of Money* (New York: Augustus Kelley, Reprints of Economics Classics, 1971).

————, *The Theory of Interest* (New York: Augustus Kelley, Reprints of Economic Classics, 1971).

HUME, DAVID, *Essay on Money* (1752).

HUMPHRIES, THOMAS, "The Quantity Theory of Money: Its Historical Evolution and Role in Policy Debates," *Economic Review*, Federal Reserve Bank of Richmond (May/June 1974).

KEYNES, J. M., *A Treatise on Money*, Vol. II, *The Applied Theory of Money* (London: Macmillan, 1930).

————, *A Tract on Monetary Reform* (New York: Harcourt, Brace & Co., 1924).

MARGET, ARTHUR W., *The Theory of Prices*, Vol. II (New York: Augustus Kelly, Reprints of Economic Classics 1966).

MARSHALL, ALFRED, *Principles of Economics*, 8th ed. (London: Macmillan, 1962).

————, *Money, Credit and Commerce* (London: Macmillan, 1923).

MUNDELL, ROBERT A., *Monetary Theory* (Pacific Palisades, Cal.: Goodyear, 1971).

PATINKIN, DON, *Money, Interest, and Prices*, 2nd ed. (New York: Harper & Row, 1965).

————, "On the Short-Run Non-Neutrality of Money in the Quantity Theory," *Banca Nazionale Del Lavoro Quarterly Review*, No. 100 (March 1972).

REEVE, JOSEPH E., *Monetary Reform Movements* (Washington, D.C.: American Council on Public Affairs, 1943).

SCHUMPETER, JOSEPH, *History of Economic Analysis* (New York: Oxford University Press, 1954).

THORNTON, HENRY, *The Paper Credit of Great Britain* (New York: Augustus Kelly, 1965). See especially the Introduction by F. A. Hayek.

TOOKE, THOMAS, *An Inquiry into the Currency Principle* (1844).

————, *History of Prices* (1928). See especially the review in the Introduction by T. E. Gregory.

VINER, JACOB, *Studies in the Theory of International Trade* (London: Allen & Unwin, 1935).

WICKSELL, KNUT, *Lectures on Political Economy*, Vol. II, *Money*, L. Robbins, ed. (London: Routledge and Kegan Paul, 1935).

chapter 4

Alternative Formulations
of the Quantity Theory

In Chapter 1, where the classical view of the forces determining the general level of prices was discussed, two approaches to the quantity theory were introduced. The formal classical model developed in that chapter made use of an explanation formulated by Professor Irving Fisher of Yale University, often called the income-velocity approach to the quantity theory. A graphical presentation of the Equation of Exchange, which he developed, was used to explain the general level of prices.

While the Fisherian approach became a part of the formal model, it was noted in Chapter 1 that the quantity theory could also be viewed in terms of a theory explaining the demand for money. This formulation, associated with Cambridge University, is frequently called the cash-balance approach to the quantity theory. The purpose of this chapter is to investigate these alternative approaches to the quantity theory and to note their relevance to contemporary monetary theory, even though on a purely mathematical level the two approaches are identical, that is, Fisher's *velocity* is merely the reciprocal of the Cambridge k.

THE FISHERIAN, OR INCOME VELOCITY, APPROACH

When the concept of velocity, or money's turnover rate against goods and services, was introduced in Chapter 1, careful attention was drawn to the fact that while its value can be determined mathematically once the values of the other variables in the equation of exchange are known, it must not be thought of as a constant. Far from being a constant, its value depends upon behavioral, technological, and institutional circumstances; as these change, the value of velocity ought also to change.

Fisher's most complete statement regarding velocity is found in *The Purchasing Power of Money.* Here the underlying factors are essentially divided between those which operate in the long run and those whose primary effect is during the period of transition, or the short run. His discussion of these long-run factors implies that velocity ought to have great stability, and while he suggests that these factors might change over time, they should do so very slowly. For this reason, subsequent textbook presentations have treated velocity as a constant, so it has been possible to treat the quantity theory as a very rigid theory of price-level determination, seriously distorting Fisher's presentation. Our discussion will show that Fisher never asserted the rigid quantity theory as did those who drew their intellectual inspiration from his work. Moreover, these scholars forgot almost totally the short-run factors which operate to alter velocity and which might have explained a good deal of its variability during the 1930's.

In order to appreciate the richness of Fisher's presentation of the quantity theory, those factors which operate essentially in the long run to affect velocity will be examined first; second, the short-run determinants of velocity will be reviewed; and third, the interdependence which exists among the variables in the Equation of Exchange will be investigated. An examination of point three will show that Fisher did not assert that the general level of commodity prices must vary in strict proportion to changes in the stock of money. However, while factors other than money in the Equation of Exchange might affect the price level, thus qualifying the proposition of rigid proportionality, Fisher's discussion implied that they were of secondary importance, for substantial changes in the price level, in his view, could only occur through a change in the money supply. Moreover, to the extent that interdependence exists between the variables in the equation of exchange, it will not be possible to assert that money is strictly neutral, and it may not be possible to assert the strict exogeneity of money. To the extent that interdependence is weak, money will be mostly neutral and mainly exogenous.

Long-Run Determinants of Velocity

Fisher conveniently subdivides the long-run determinants of velocity into three categories: habits of the individual, systems of payments in the community, and general causes. Changes in each of these categories will change the value of velocity. However, as these behavioral and institutional factors are discussed below, it will be obvious that they are not likely to change significantly in the short run, therefore they impart to velocity a high degree of constancy.

habits of the individual

Three habits of the individual were supposed to influence velocity: Those relating to thrift and hoarding, the use of book credit, and the use of checks (demand deposits).

Since velocity is calculated by dividing total money payments by the average stock of money, it follows that in a society where money hoards are large, average money holdings will be greater relative to money spending. Thus velocity must be less in societies where hoarding is practiced than in societies where it is not so common. As the analysis of Chapter 2 revealed, saving, or thrift, will not affect velocity so long as savings are held in a bond form. The only effect of a change in saving, in that analysis, was to change the natural rate of interest and the allocation of full employment output between investment and consumption.

A commercial system which permits individuals to use money substitutes (book credit or credit cards) will have a higher velocity than one which does not, for two reasons. First, when money must be accumulated in advance of purchase, there exists uncertainty as to when the money will be needed and how much will be needed. Such contingencies will lead to larger money holdings than when the time and amount of payments are known with certainty. A highly developed credit system will enable money payments to be made with certainty, thus lowering average money holdings and raising velocity. The second, related, factor is that money held in advance of payment must be held longer than money received after a use for it has been contracted. In the first instance, the individual must accumulate enough to pay cash bills, while in the latter, any difference between cash holdings and the bill can be covered by charging the remainder. Thus a developing credit system speeds up the velocity of circulation of money.

The existence of commercial banks issuing demand deposits ought also to speed up the velocity of money. It must be remembered that Fisher regarded demand deposits not as money proper but as a substitute which provided an outlet for surplus pocket or till money and so tended to prevent the existence of idle hoards; that is, individuals would place idle money balances in banks, which would lend them out, thereby reducing hoarding.

Concerning the habits of the individual, one can reasonably expect changes to occur over time in views relating to the desirability of hoarding, the spread and development of a commercial system using money substitutes, and the use of demand deposits. However, these changes are likely to be gradual rather than rapid so this determinant of velocity ought to impart a high degree of constancy to its magnitude of value.

systems of payments in the community

Fisher entitled the second broad classification of factors determining velocity "Systems of Payments in the Community." Three aspects of these systems could exert influence: The frequency of receipts and disbursements, the regularity of the receipts and disbursements, and the degree to which receipts and disbursements were synchronized.

In regard to the frequency of receipts and disbursements, Fisher believed that the more frequently receipts were received and disbursements made, the higher would be the value of velocity. For example, suppose that an individual who was paid once per week is now paid in equal sums twice per week. In both cases, he expends his income uniformly over the week.

Case I—Paid $6 once per week

$$\frac{\$6 + \$5 + \$4 + \$3 + \$2 + \$1 + \$0}{7 \text{ days}} = \frac{\$21}{7 \text{ days}} = \$3 \quad \text{Average money holdings per day}$$

$3 =$ Average money holdings per day
$3 \cdot V = \$6$ (money spending per week)
$V = 2$

Case II—Paid $3 twice per week

$$\frac{\$3 + \$2 + \$1 + \$3 + \$2 + \$1 + \$0}{7 \text{ days}} = \frac{\$12}{7 \text{ days}} = \$1\tfrac{5}{7} \quad \text{Average money holdings per day}$$

$\$1\tfrac{5}{7} \cdot V = \$6$
$V = 3\tfrac{1}{2}$

Thus, more frequent receipt of income will speed up the velocity of money. A similar example could be constructed for different distributions of payments.

By the regularity of receipts and payments, Fisher meant their degree of certainty as to time and amount. The greater this certainty, the smaller would be the average cash holding of the individual. On the other hand, when receipts and payments were irregular or uncertain, the prudent individual would hold larger sums to ensure against uncertainty or irregularity, thereby reducing velocity. Of course, in a system where book credit was allowed, this uncertainty or irregularity would exert a minimal influence on velocity.

The third characteristic of Fisher's systems of payments concerns the degree to which receipts of income and expenditure disbursements are synchronized. If they were perfectly synchronized, meaning that the individual receives in any day exactly the same amount that he spends, the individual would hold no cash balances. Thus, velocity would be infinite. When payments and receipts are not synchronized, they require the accumulation of cash balances, and this accumulation reduces the velocity of money. This situation is very common for labor. People's wages and salaries are usually paid in discrete intervals—weekly, fortnightly, or monthly; however, they make daily expenditures. Thus, a portion of wealth must be held in cash balances. The same is true for business units.

This determinant of velocity, like the previous one, imparts a high degree of constancy to its mathematical magnitude. While the systems of payments can change over time (and have done so), they should not change dramatically in the short run.

general causes

In this last category of long-run determinants of velocity, Fisher included density of population and rapidity of transportation. Both are linked to a common variable—the time which elapses between payments and receipts. Anything which reduces this time will increase velocity. Thus, the greater the density of the population in a given region, the less time that will elapse between receipts and payments. The greater the distance between people, the longer it will take to make payments and receive receipts. The same is true for systems of transportation; the development and spread of railroads and telegraphs in Fisher's time made money transactions much faster, thereby increasing velocity.

One might add, as a third general cause, the growing vertical integration of industry. Vertical integration permits transactions to be made between parts of a firm without the use of money. To this extent, it increases the velocity of money.

Each of these three broad determinants of velocity imparts to it a relatively high degree of constancy. It is little wonder that in subsequent textbook treatments, velocity came to be treated as a constant determined by commercial practices, the sophistication of the financial system, the behavior of the population regarding hoarding, the mobility of the population, and technological innovations primarily in transportation and communication.

The actual magnitude of velocity, especially during the decade of the 1930's, was anything but constant; this fact, coupled with the intellectual attack of the Keynesians, caused the quantity theory approach to fall into disfavor.

TABLE 4:1.   Index of the Income Velocity of Money

1929	1930	1931	1932	1933	1934	1935	1936	1937	1938	1939	1940	1941
100	91	83	71	72	78	74	73	76	71	68	65	70

Source: L. V. Chandler, *America's Greatest Depression, 1929–1941* (New York: Harper & Row, 1970), p. 185.

Short-run Determinants of Velocity

The almost 30 percent decline in velocity from 1929 to 1932 could hardly be explained by Fisher's long-run factors. However, besides these factors, Fisher included in his discussion of velocity three other variables whose effect on velocity ought to operate mainly in the short run: The rate of interest, expected changes in the general level of commodity prices, and the degree of "confidence" in the future course of events.

Thus, if interest rates rose, other things equal, individuals would seek to economize on the holding of cash balances, preferring instead to hold interest-bearing alternatives. Money would then be exchanged for bonds or capital goods, and the velocity of money would rise.

However, of concern is the extent to which Fisher integrated the interest rate as a basic determinant of velocity and, through it, as an influence on the business cycle. Patinkin[1] alleges that Fisher did not "fully recognize" the influence of the rate of interest on velocity, by which he means that Fisher did not consistently take account of this effect at appropriate points in his discussion. Paraphrasing Patinkin, he alleges that Fisher did not integrate the influence of the rate of interest into the general analysis of *The Purchasing Power of Money, The Rate of Interest,* or *The Theory of Interest.* It is but mentioned once in *The Purchasing Power*[2] and is not to be found in the analysis of the effects of higher interest rates which mark the "transition period" (Chapter 4), nor in the detailed description of the determinants of the velocity of circulation (Chapter 5), nor finally in the statistical investigation of the theory, with its description of how velocity varied during the time periods examined (Chapters 11 and 12). A possible reason for this omission may be that since market interest rates are influenced by expectations of price-level changes, inclusion of expectations as a variable explaining the observed movements in velocity will make it unnecessary to also include the interest rate, for both explanatory variables move in the same

[1] Don Patinkin, "The Chicago Tradition, the Quantity Theory, and Friedman," *Journal of Money, Credit and Banking,* Vol. 1, No. 1 (Feb. 1969), 58–59.

[2] The actual reference is to be found in Chapter 8, p. 152, and reads " . . . and on the other hand to avoid encumbrance, waste of interest, and risk of robbery, he will avoid carrying too much" [money].

direction (that is, if prices are expected to rise, the market interest rate ought also to rise).

Patinkin's analysis is of some importance, for if Fisher had in fact systematically included the rate of interest as a determinant of velocity, he would have successfully integrated the monetary and real sectors of the economy in one general equilibrium model, substantially diminishing Keynes' claim to having formulated a General Theory.

About Fisher's inclusion of the influence of expected price-level changes on velocity, there can be no doubt. As noted in Chapter 3, Fisher says that during an inflation or during periods when people expect commodity prices to rise, "We all hasten to get rid of any commodity which, like ripe fruit, is spoiling on our hands. Money is no exception; when it is depreciating, holders get rid of it as fast as possible." Conversely, during periods of deflation, people will hold on to cash balances, for their exchange value increases. Thus inflations will speed up velocity, while deflations will decrease it.[3]

Unfortunately Fisher, relying on an extensive elaboration of the long-run factors, never sufficiently emphasized these short-run determinants. Modern scholars in monetary economics, especially Friedman and his students, rely heavily on these short-run factors to explain the actual movement of velocity and pay little attention to the long-run determinants mentioned by Fisher. In Chapter 9, Friedman's concept of velocity and his reformulated quantity theory will be discussed in detail.

INTERDEPENDENCE AMONG THE VARIABLES IN THE EQUATION OF EXCHANGE

In order to rigidly assert that the general level of commodity prices varies in strict proportion with the stock of money, and therefore that money is neutral in the long run, it must be shown that the variables

[3] Later, in discussing Friedman's reformulated quantity theory, it will be shown that the concept of a stable velocity function is of great importance. Stability, as used by Friedman, means that movements in velocity can be accounted for by movements in its determinants, one of which is the expected rate of change of commodity prices. In a review article on the quantity theory, Friedman, taking note of Fisher's work, implies that Fisher had a similar view about the role of expected changes in prices as a determinant of observed variations in velocity (See M. Friedman, "Quantity Theory," *International Encyclopedia of the Social Sciences* (New York: MacMillan, 1968), pp. 433–46). However, Fisher's discussion of this point in *The Purchasing Power of Money* (pp. 63–64) reveals that he had another process in mind. For him, rising prices would set in motion expectations of a further rise, thereby increasing velocity and leading to a self-fulfilling rise in prices. The cycle repeats itself, producing a cumulative process of expansion which has no upper bound, save one institutionally imposed by bank reserves. This continual self-destructive flight from money, as viewed by Fisher, makes it unlikely that he was thinking of a stable velocity function in Friedman's terms. This observation is reinforced by reference to Fisher's assertion that velocity also depends upon public "confidence" in the future course of events.

in the Equation of Exchange, M, V, and Y, are independent of each other. That is, for example, that changes in money do not induce permanent changes in V or Y. If independence is not the case, one could not predict the consequences of, for example, money stock changes on the commodity price level.

Certainly, no reading of *The Purchasing Power of Money* would reveal that Fisher asserted the rigid quantity theory. Some of the ways in which Fisher believed the variables in the Equation of Exchange were interdependent, allowing changes in one to induce permanent changes in the others, can be briefly examined.

While the long-run growth of real output could not be changed by alterations in the stock of money, changes in it could affect both the stock of money and its velocity. As the discussion above has revealed, the level of real output depends upon the size of the labor force, the capital stock, and the productiveness of each. Since the labor force depends upon the size of the population, the capital stock upon the thriftiness of society, and productiveness partly upon the historic inventiveness of society, money has no role to play in increasing the long-run growth rate of real output.[4] Thus, except for transitory periods when sudden increases in the stock of money above its long-run average growth rate catch both labor and saver unaware of price changes, thereby inducing them to save more and offer more labor time at falling real wages, changes in the growth rate of the stock of money could not induce permanent changes in the long-run growth rate of real output.

However, changes in real output could affect both the money stock and velocity. Suppose that in an open economy, connected to others through a system of fixed exchange rates, a technological innovation raises the productivity of tradable goods and hence lowers their prices. Such an act will stimulate exports and retard imports, increasing the domestic stock of money (foreign monies will be attracted and domestic monies previously spent in foreign countries will now be spent at home) and the volume of money spending. This will raise domestic price levels back to equilibrium with those prevailing in the rest of the world. Additionally, innovations which decrease the cost of extracting gold from the ground ought also to raise the domestic money supply.

As to the effect of changes in real output on velocity, Fisher presented a number of arguments to show that this effect may be more pervasive than that on the money supply. First, changes in output could

---

[4] However, by making more efficient (saving time and effort) the process of exchange and production, money can enable labor and the existing capital stock to produce a larger volume of goods, services, and leisure. Hence, while the average level of output and its long-run change are largely independent of the quantity of money, they are not independent of the existence of a monetary economy. Any changes in the monetary system which make it more efficient can be expected to expand real output or leisure.

affect the efficiency of transportation and communication, thereby decreasing the time interval between the receipt of money and its subsequent expenditure and increasing velocity. Second, changes in real income might have distributional effects on income among people whose velocities are different, thereby changing aggregate velocity. Third and most important, a larger real income would permit certain economies in the management of money. Thus, as aggregate per-capita real income increases, velocity ought to increase.[5] This implies that money is a necessity, for as the real income of society rises, it demands relatively less money. This belief of Fisher, supported by primitive statistical evidence, is at variance with assertions and empirical testing by Friedman and his students, who work in the new quantity-theory tradition.[6]

While the preceding discussion is offered as evidence that Fisher did not assert the rigid quantity theory, it is equally true that, to the extent that these changes induce weak interdependent reactions, one could say with some confidence that changes in the stock of money adjust for changes in real output, and any secular trend in velocity would, in the long run, produce a proportional change in the level of commodity prices.

Our discussion of Fisher has shown that he was interested in the quantity theory and the Equation of Exchange as ways to explain the forces determining the general level of prices. We will now examine the alternative approach to the quantity theory, which, while it can also be used to determine the general level of prices, focuses attention on the factors which explain the demand for money.

THE CAMBRIDGE, OR CASH-BALANCE, APPROACH

The Cambridge approach to the quantity theory was primarily the work of five men: Alfred Marshall, A. C. Pigou, Frederick Lavington, Denis Robertson, and J. M. Keynes, even though it claims intellectual antecedents in the work of Petty (seventeenth century), Locke, Cantillon, and the venerable Adam Smith.[7]

The Cambridge approach is much more pleasing to the economist, for it involves the application of general demand analysis to the special

---

[5] Fisher, *The Purchasing Power of Money*, p. 167.

[6] *Studies in the Quantity Theory of Money*, M. Friedman, ed. (Chicago: University of Chicago Press, 1956), p. 18. Friedman's empirical work suggests an income elasticity of 1.8.

[7] We are warned by Patinkin that he regards the sharp distinction usually drawn between the "mechanical" Fisher and the "behavioristic" Cambridge economists to be largely a Cantabridgian tale. See Don Patinkin, "Keynesian Monetary Theory and the Cambridge School," in *Issues in Monetary Economics*, H. G. Johnson and A. R. Nobay, ed. (London: Oxford University Press, 1974), pp. 3–30. This section owes a heavy debt to Patinkin's excellent analysis.

case of money—inquiring into the utility of money, the nature of the budget constraint facing the individual, and the opportunity cost of holding money as opposed to other assets. These are all the considerations of the micro theorist when examining the demand for a commodity in general.

The Utility of Money

For Marshall, the utility of money derived from the fact that: "A large command of resources in the form of currency renders their business easy and smooth, and puts them at an advantage in bargaining. . . ."[8] Pigou provided a more general explanation:

> Hence, everybody is anxious to hold enough of his resources in the form of titles to legal tender [currency] both to enable him to effect the ordinary transactions of life without trouble, and to secure him against unexpected demands, due to a sudden need, or to a rise in the price of something that he cannot easily dispense with. For these two objects, the provision of convenience and the provision of security, people in general . . . elect to hold [money].[9]

Lavington's analysis parallels Pigou's:

> His stock [of money] yields him an income of convenience, for it reduces the cost and trouble of effecting his current payments; and it yields him an income of security, for it reduces his risk of not being able readily to make payments arising from contingencies which he cannot fully foresee.[10]

Thus the Cambridge scholars believed that money has utility for two reasons. First, because it is generally acceptable in exchange for goods and services, avoiding the inconveniences of barter transactions; second, because money holding provides a degree of security against future uncertainties. Since the Cambridge School excluded interest-bearing deposits from their definition of money, the yield on money is purely psychological, and its magnitude at the margin depends, as for all goods, upon its quantity in relation to the urgency with which these needs are held. The larger the supply of money, other things equal, the lower its marginal yield. In the Cambridge framework money was there-

---

[8] Alfred Marshall, *Money, Credit and Commerce* (London: MacMillan, 1923), p. 45.

[9] A. C. Pigou, "The Value of Money," *The Quarterly Journal of Economics*, Vol. 32 (1917–18), pp. 38–65. Reprinted in *Readings in Monetary Theory*, L. W. Mints and F. A. Lutz, ed. (Homewood, Ill.: Richard Irwin, 1951), p. 164. All subsequent citations are from the reprinted source.

[10] F. Lavington, *The English Capital Market* (London: Methuen, 1921), p. 29.

fore treated just like any other good, and its possession was subject to diminishing marginal utility.

The Budget Constraint

Given that money has utility, what did the Cambridge scholars believe determines the amount of money the average individual would be willing to hold? This depends first upon the nature of the budget constraint facing the individual and second upon the opportunity cost of holding money as opposed to other assets.

The nature of the budget constraint as viewed by the Cambridge School is somewhat confusing. The following statement, taken from Marshall, appears to spell it out quite clearly; however, subsequent discussion by Marshall and the work of his colleagues leaves the matter rather unclear.

Marshall, the leader of the Cambridge School, sets out the budget constraint as follows:

> . . . suppose that the inhabitants of a country . . . find it just worth their while to keep by them on the average ready purchasing power to the extent of a tenth part of their annual *income,* together with a fiftieth part of their *property;* then the aggregate value of the currency of the country will tend to be equal to the sum of these amounts.[11]

Thus, for Marshall, both income and wealth (or property) appear to be the relevant budget constraints.

However, in a later manuscript, Marshall does not sharply distinguish the stock from the flow and gives the impression that he considers them identical:

> Assuming the habits of business to remain unchanged, the amount of coin which a person finds it convenient to carry about, taking one with another, depends upon his general *wealth.* A shopkeeper with an *income* of £1000 a year would be likely to use a great deal more gold than an architect with the same income, but if prices rose generally so that the money income of each increased 10 percent, and the expenditures of each in every direction increased also 10 percent, then (their habits of business remaining unchanged) each of them would, I believe, keep 10 percent more money in his purse.[12]

His Cambridge colleagues are equally unclear. Keynes, in his *Tract on Monetary Reform,* tells us that the amount of purchasing power

[11] Marshall, *Money, Credit and Commerce,* p. 44.

[12] Alfred Marshall, *Official Papers* (London: MacMillan, 1926), quoted from Patinkin, "Keynesian Monetary Theory," pp. 23–24.

individuals desire to hold ". . . depends partly on their wealth, partly on their habits."[13] Several pages later, he repeats the quotation of Marshall in which both income and wealth appear as the constraints. Either Keynes did not distinguish wealth (a stock) from income (a flow), or he was unaware that his first statement in which only wealth appears as a constraint was incomplete.

For Pigou,[14] the constraint becomes the total resources of the community expressed in terms of wheat, which suggests that wealth is the relevant constraint. However, in his *Treatise on Money,* Keynes, in criticizing the Cambridge formulation of Pigou, interprets the term *resources* as being identical with *current income.*[15] Lavington links each motive for holding money to a relevant constraint. Since it is held to facilitate exchange, the amount held ought to vary with the volume of payments to be made. As it also serves as a reserve against an uncertain future, he believed that the amount held would depend upon the individual's estimate of his contingent payments.

As to the nature of the budget constraint, we might conclude that the Cambridge School recognized both total wealth and income as being the relevant variables, even though their statements and reasoning tend to be unclear. In addition, they failed to discuss the composition of wealth.

The Opportunity Cost of Money

Within the absolute constraint set by wealth and income, the actual proportion held in a money form depends, among other things, upon the yield of money in relation to the yield on the alternatives open to the individual.

For Marshall, the opportunity cost became ". . . an income of gratification if invested, say, in extra furniture; or a money income, if invested in extra machinery or cattle."[16] In addition, Marshall recognized that inflation would cause the demand for money to fall.[17] (These "incomes" can easily be converted to "own" rates of return by finding the discount rate which equates the money value or "gratification" with the present cost of furniture, machinery, cattle, and so forth, much as one would do in computing the marginal efficiency of investment or the own rate of return on capital goods.)

In his *Tract,* Keynes tells us that the money-holding habits of the

[13] J. M. Keynes, *A Tract on Monetary Reform* (New York: Harcourt, Brace and Co., 1924), pp. 83, 86.

[14] Pigou, "The Value of Money," p. 165.

[15] J. M. Keynes, *A Treatise on Money,* Vol. I (London: MacMillan, 1930), p. 232.

[16] Alfred Marshall, *Money, Credit and Commerce,* p. 45.

[17] *Ibid.,* pp. 47–48.

community ". . . are fixed by its estimation of the extra convenience of having more cash in hand as compared with the advantages to be got from spending the cash or investing it."[18] Thus for Keynes the yield from consumption and investment becomes the opportunity cost.[19] He also notes the effects of price-level changes on money demand.[20]

Lavington added little to Keynes and Marshall:

Resources devoted to consumption supply an income of immediate satisfaction; those held as a stock of currency yield a return of convenience and security; those devoted to investment in the narrower sense of the term yield a return in the form of interest . . . [thus] the quantity of resources which he holds in the form of money . . . yields him a return of convenience and security equal to the yield of satisfaction derived from the marginal unit spent on consumables, and equal also to the net rate of interest.[21]

For Pigou, the proportion of resources held as money will be larger

. . . the less attractive is the production use and the more attractive is the rival money use of resources. The chief factor upon which the attractiveness of the production use depends is the expected fruitfulness of industrial activity.[22]

In addition, movements in the general level of prices are expected to influence money demand, for according to Pigou:

Any holding of titles to legal tender is always capable of being exchanged against some quantity of commodities. Clearly, if it is expected that the quantity of commodities for which, say, a note for one pound can be exchanged will be greater a year hence than it is now, the inducement to hold

[18] J. M. Keynes, A Tract on Monetary Reform, pp. 85–86.

[19] By investing money, Keynes appears to have in mind, converting money balances into other financial assets. In the Treatise on Money (Vol. II, p. 45), we are told "When business is dull and investment unattractive, the cost of holding cash-deposits is merely the sacrifice of interest involved in holding them thus rather than as savings-deposits or bills or other liquid short-dated investments."

[20] In discussing the effects of price level changes on money demand, Keynes makes two very interesting observations. In The Treatise (Vol. II, p. 47), he tells us: "I am not clear that this cause (expectations of higher prices) is an important one in its direct influence on prices through increasing . . . velocity except in the extreme cases where the fear of depreciation of money is acute." In light of the fact that in The General Theory, real and nominal magnitudes are treated as equals, this statement is of interest.

In The Tract (pp. 89–90), Keynes notes that the effect may be to permanently alter the habits and practices of people which govern their money holdings. To the extent that price level changes, induced by prior changes in the money stock, permanently alter desired money holding, money is nonneutral in the long run.

[21] The English Capital Market, p. 30.

[22] "The Value of Money," p. 168.

pounds now is increased; and, conversely, if it is expected that a pound will buy fewer commodities a year hence; it is diminished.[23]

In summary, for the Cambridge School, the opportunity cost of holding money consists of the rate of interest, the yield on real capital, and the expected rate of inflation. These three yields also give a clue to the nature of the composition of individual wealth. It must have consisted of money, bonds, real capital goods including consumer durables, and inventories of commodities. Of course, no one Cambridge scholar brought together all the relevant assets and their respective yields in one coherent theory of portfolio choice. This task was left to others, especially Milton Friedman.

Other Factors Influencing Money Demand

The Cambridge School also mentioned as exerting an influence on money demand the list of variables given by Fisher—habits of the individual, the system of payments in the community, the availability of money substitutes, the density of the population, the system of communication, and so forth. They also mentioned the general level of confidence, or mood of the public and the business world, as an important factor determining the demand for money, especially that portion held to meet the uncertainties of the future.

THE CAMBRIDGE DEMAND-FOR-MONEY FUNCTION

By combining the analyses of the Cambridge School, it is possible to write a general demand function for money of the form:

$$M_D = \int(W, PY, i, r_K, r_C, U, X)$$

where: $W =$ wealth, $PY =$ money income, $i =$ the nominal interest rate, $r_K =$ the yield on real capital including consumer durables, $r_C =$ the yield on commodities, $U =$ the utility of money, and $X =$ all those factors of an institutional nature including the level of confidence mentioned by Fisher as influencing the demand for money. That demand was expected to be positively related to W and PY and negatively related to $i, r_K,$ and r_C.

Having formulated this generalized approach, let us discover to

[23] *Ibid.,* p. 169.

what use it was put and which of the variables in the function were regarded as most important in explaining the demand for money. Little evidence can be provided as to the relative importance of the variables, for the Cambridge School did not empirically test its formulation. On two occasions, however, limited empirical work was done,[24] and the principal factor explaining the change in the demand for money was changes in the price level, even though, in the case analyzed by Keynes, significant changes had occurred in both long-term and short-term interest rates. In fact, the first published empirical study linking the demand for money to the interest rate seems to have been done in 1939 by A. J. Brown.[25]

Other than the work of Keynes in *The General Theory,* it appears that the Cambridge scholars failed to integrate their demand-for-money function into the classical model and to explore its implications for the business cycle. As an example of possible integration, it might be remembered that a change in neither investment nor saving should, in the classical model presented in Chapter 2, have any effect on the level of money income, MV. It should only alter the composition of final output between investment and consumption goods. However, once the demand for money, or velocity, is made a function of the interest rate, a change in either saving or investment, which changes the interest rate, will also change velocity and money spending, MV. Thus, making the demand for money a function of the interest rate serves to integrate the real and monetary sectors. Unfortunately, such an integration and subsequent analysis was not performed.

Rather, Pigou made a number of simplifying assumptions to show that his version of the Cambridge approach and that formulated by Fisher achieve the same result. This reconciliation is important because Pigou was the first Cambridge scholar to put the cash-balance version of the quantity theory into an equation which could be compared with that formulated by Fisher. Reconciling the two tended to make many forget that the analysis of each sprang from fundamentally different approaches. The essence of Pigou's reconciliation was to show that the Cambridge k was the reciprocal of Fisher's V. In order to do this, Pigou first assumed that his budget constraint termed "resources" bore some constant relation to Fisher's "volume of transactions," or if one's concern is with income velocity, to the level of income.

Thus the Pigou demand function in which resources, R, the yield

[24] J. M. Keynes, *A Tract on Monetary Reform,* pp. 91–93; and A. C. Pigou, *Industrial Fluctuations,* 2nd ed. (London: MacMillan, 1929), pp. 163–72.

[25] A. J. Brown, "Interest, Prices, and the Demand for Idle Money," *Oxford Economic Papers,* No. 1 (1939), pp. 46–69.

on capital, r_K, and the yield on commodities (the expected rate of inflation), r_C, appear as arguments, could be transformed from:

$$M_D = \int(R, r_K, r_C)$$

to

$$M_D = \int(PY, r_K, r_C)$$

Then, Pigou assumed that expectations about r_K and r_C were constant, and that no economies were present in the holding of money balances which permitted him to specify the demand for money as a constant

$$M_D = k(PY)$$

portion of money income, PY, or where the value of k depends upon
those variables whose value is assumed constant, r_K and r_C. Any change
in these variables could cause changes in the magnitude of k and hence
in the proportion of money income the individual desires to hold in a
money form. These assumptions render the demand-for-money relationship a more or less short-run construct.

In order for equilibrium to prevail, the actual and desired money
stocks must be equal, or in other words the demand for money, M_D, must
be equal to the supply, MS. If MS should change, actual balances would
differ from those desired, which would require changes in either k or P
to restore equilibrium.

Once the Cambridge approach is formulated as $M_D = k(PY)$, it can
easily be shown (as in Chapter 1) that k is the mathematical reciprocal of
Fisher's V.

Pigou believed that his formulation of the quantity theory was no
"truer" than Fisher's; rather, it was a more "effective engine of analysis,"
for

it focuses attention on the proportion of their resources that people
choose to keep in the form of titles to legal tender, instead of focusing it on
"velocity of circulation." This fact gives it, as I think, a real advantage, because it brings us at once into relation with volition—an ultimate cause of
demand—instead of with something that seems, at first sight, accidental and
arbitrary.[26]

Unfortunately, it was this simplified version of the Cambridge cash
balance approach which ultimately came to be identified with that

---

[26] A. C. Pigou, "The Value of Money," p. 174.

school. As such, it abstracts from the richness of the true Cambridge tradition.

THE FISHERIAN AND CAMBRIDGE APPROACHES CONTRASTED

Contemporary scholars[27] have cataloged a number of differences between the Fisherian and Cambridge approaches to the quantity theory, which are summarized below.

First, they tend to lead to different definitions of money. The Fisherian approach makes it natural to define money in terms of whatever serves as a medium of exchange in effecting transactions, whereas the Cambridge approach, by stressing the store-of-value function of money, argues for a more comprehensive list of assets to be included in a definition of money.

Second, Fisher links money holding to the *flow of money expenditures*, while the Cambridge School links it to the *stock of wealth* held by the community. Thus Fisher's is a flow analysis, whereas the Cambridge scholars present a stock analysis.

Third, having emphasized wealth as the determinant of desired money holding, the Cambridge School is concerned about specifying the variables which determine what portion of their wealth the public desires to hold in a money form. Fisher, on the other hand, concentrating on the flow of money expenditures, is concerned about the factors governing how fast individuals can spend their money. Cambridge is therefore led to emphasize economic variables, whereas Fisher concentrates on institutional practices and technological changes which facilitate or impede exchange.

Fourth, Fisher believes that both velocity and real income are in the longer run independent of each other and of the supply of money. Under usual conditions, any change in the stock of money produces proportional changes in the general level of commodity prices. To the Cambridge School, the desired stock of money depends in part on the relative size of the stock of nonmonetary assets. Thus, if the supply of money changes, the price level may change by more or less than the change in the money supply. It depends upon what happens to the stock of nonmonetary assets and their expected yields.

Five, both Fisher and the Cambridge School provide the origins

[27] Dwayne Wrightsman, *An Introduction to Monetary Theory and Policy* (New York: The Free Press, 1971), pp. 105–8; David Laidler, *The Demand for Money: Theories and Evidence* (Scranton, Pa.: Intext, 1969), pp. 47–50; and Milton Friedman, *International Encyclopedia*, pp. 437–38.

for two quite different approaches to monetary theory which have been developed by contemporary scholars. Fisher's stress on the nonsynchronization of inpayments and outpayments has given rise to an inventory theory of money holding largely for transactions purposes. On the other hand, the approach pioneered at Cambridge has been developed into the portfolio, or capital theoretic, approach to money demand.

CONCLUSION

The concept of velocity, or the turnover rate of money, was first introduced in Chapter 1 as a mere number designed to balance two sides of an equation. At that time, it was specified that velocity was something more—it depended upon institutional and behavioral variables; in other words, velocity was a function of other variables, not a mathematical constant. One purpose of this chapter has been to detail the nature of these variables and their relationship to velocity.

A second purpose has been to provide a detailed analysis of the two contending approaches to the quantity theory, which center in the one case on velocity, and in the other on the demand for money. While by making appropriate assumptions both approaches can be made mathematically equivalent, from the analytical viewpoint they remain quite different. The prevailing tendency in modern analysis is to follow the Cambridge School and use what is now called the "capital theoretic approach" which it originated, emphasizing utility, budget constraints, opportunity costs, and stock adjustments as initiators of variations in flow variables and economic activity.

Selected References and Readings

BROWN, A. J., "Interest, Prices, and the Demand Schedule for Idle Money," *Oxford Economic Papers,* No. 2 (May 1939).

ESHAG, EPRIME, *From Marshall to Keynes* (Oxford: Blackwell, 1963).

FAY, C. R., "Obituary of Frederick Lavington," *Economic Journal,* Vol. 37, No. 147 (1927).

Fisher, Irving, *The Purchasing Power of Money* (New York: Augustus Kelley, Reprints of Economic Classics, 1971).

FRIEDMAN, MILTON, "Quantity Theory," *International Encyclopedia of the Social Sciences* (New York: Macmillan, 1968).

KEYNES, J. M., *Tract on Monetary Reform* (London: Macmillan, 1923).

———, *A Treatise on Money* (London: Macmillan, 1930).

LAIDLER, DAVID, *The Demand for Money: Theories and Evidence* (Scranton, Pa.: Intext, 1969).

LAVINGTON, FREDRICK, *The English Capital Market* (London: Methuen, 1921).

————, *The Trade Cycle* (London: King, 1922).

MARSHALL, ALFRED, *Money, Credit and Commerce* (London: Macmillan, 1923).

————, *Official Papers* (London: Macmillan, 1926).

PATINKIN, DON, *Money, Interest, and Prices,* 2nd ed. (New York: Harper & Row, 1965).

————, "The Chicago Tradition, The Quantity Theory, and Friedman," *Journal of Money, Credit and Banking,* Vol. 1, No. 1 (Feb. 1969).

————, "Friedman on the Quantity Theory and Keynesian Economics," *Journal of Political Economy,* Vol. 80, No. 5 (Sept./Oct. 1972).

————, "Keynesian Monetary Theory and the Cambridge School," in Johnson and Nobay, ed., *Issues in Monetary Economics* (London: Oxford University Press, 1974).

PIGOU, A. C., "The Value of Money," reprinted in Lutz and Mints, ed., *Readings in Monetary Theory* (Homewood, Ill.: Richard Irwin, 1951).

————, *Industrial Fluctuations,* 2nd ed. (London: Macmillan, 1929).

————, *The Theory of Unemployment* (London: Macmillan, 1933).

ROBERTSON, D. H., *Money,* 4th ed. (London: Pitman, 1948). (See also the 2nd and 3rd editions.)

SELDON, RICHARD, "Monetary Velocity in the United States," in *Studies in the Quantity Theory of Money,* M. Friedman, ed. (Chicago: University of Chicago Press, 1956).

SNYDER, CARL, "New Measures in the Equation of Exchange," *American Economic Review,* Vol. 14, No. 4 (Dec. 1924).

Classical Monetary Theory: Conclusion to Part I

In introducing this section, it was stated that the original and lasting contribution of the classical school to monetary theory was to be found in the hypothesis known as the *quantity theory of money*. This hypothesis was seen to rest on five essential propositions and one of the purposes of this section was to show how the classical economists arrived at these propositions and thus asserted the quantity theory. In the process of presenting the classical case, the long-run validity of these core propositions was distinguished from their inappropriateness to the short run, or period of transition. It was also noted that these propositions were not universally held among classical scholars and that counterpropositions were developed which in many instances have served as the basis for a continuing debate extending over several centuries.

The Proportionality of Money and Prices

For the price level to vary proportionately with changes in the stock of money, it is necessary that money have no effect on either output or velocity. In the classical concept of an economy, it was shown that so long as wages and prices had sufficient flexibility, a strong tendency toward full employment was the logical outcome. Several problems in

Chapter 2 demonstrated that money could not affect the level of real output.

Concerning velocity, in any society in which individuals hold money in more or less constant proportion to the volume of transactions to be made, that variable becomes relatively constant. In specifying the factors that could affect the turnover of money, the classical writers omitted money balances.

Thus in an analytical framework in which real output and velocity are determined by nonmonetary factors and can be regarded as relatively constant, changes in the money supply can only produce changes in the level of prices.

A counterview posited the existence of large idle balances in a society, and therefore changes in the money supply need only alter the volume of these stocks and not the price level. This argument attempts to break the convenient link between money and prices.

The Neutrality of Money

The neutrality of money appears at first glance to follow logically from the classical view on the forces determining the volume of employment, the level of real output, the composition of output, and the rate of interest. It was shown that these variables depended upon the capital stock, the state of technology determining the substitutability between factors, the preferences of individuals as to the desirability of work vs. leisure, the desire for present as opposed to future consumption, the resource endowment of the society, its method of economic organization, and so forth. However, it was shown that for strict neutrality to prevail, various conditions must be met: Prices and wages must be flexible, the participants in economic activity must be free from money illusion, the distribution of income must remain unaltered, and the productive factors must operate with perfect market information. Unless these conditions are met, money will not be neutral.

Reference to the works of many classical economists, especially the sophisticated analysis of Irving Fisher, showed that money is likely to be nonneutral in the short run.

While the counterargument was not well developed, it contains several lines of thought suggesting a general belief in nonneutrality. The supposed existence of money hoards implies that money can have some influence on real variables if the value of the hoarded stock is altered. Additionally, the belief that if the supply of money did not keep pace with the needs of business, real output would decline, suggests elements of nonneutrality.

Monetary Theory of the Price Level

In order to show that the price level was an exclusively monetary phenomenon, the orthodox theorists had to show that nonmonetary factors
such as taxes, prices of imported commodities, industrial structure, and
so forth, could have no lasting influence on the price level. To preclude
these factors from producing long-run effects on prices, it was shown
that their short-run effect was indeed to raise the price level. However,
this action reduced actual money balances below their desired level,
leading to a decrease in the rate of money spending and a consequent
fall in the general price level until actual and desired real money balances were again equal. When equilibrium was again restored, the price
level would be back to its original value.

This general conclusion regarding the inability of nonmonetary
forces to produce lasting effects on the price level was subject to the
qualification that taxes, the prices of imports, and the presence of
monopoly power could lead to less efficient production, reducing real
output and forcing up the price level.

However, in the analyses of the Tooke–Ricardo Conundrum and
Gibson's Paradox, an alternative nonmonetary theory of prices was advanced in which the price level is the joint outcome of the interaction of
forces of aggregate supply and demand. Since supply changes could influence the price level, this opened the possibility that changes in factor
costs as well as technological changes could alter the price level.

The Causality of Money

The discussion of Gibson's Paradox revealed a fundamental difference
among nineteenth-century economists on the causal role of money. By
use of the direct mechanism, the classical writers could show that whenever actual money balances exceeded those desired, both the rate of
money spending and the price level would increase, so that the level of
real money balances would remain unchanged. Using the indirect
mechanism, Thornton demonstrated that money creation, by lowering
the market interest rate, would create a gap between the actual and
desired capital stock, leading to a higher rate of investment, an increase
in money spending, and ultimately a rise in the price level. Both mechanisms were used to demonstrate the causal role of money in the business
cycle.

The nonmonetary theory of the cycle was advanced by Thomas
Tooke and his followers in the Banking School and consisted of their
endorsement and elaboration of the real bills doctrine, under which

commercial banks advance money in discount for short-term commercial paper needed by business. Thus the stock of money is demand-determined and since supply can never exceed demand, supply changes cannot induce the types of disparity envisioned by the direct and indirect mechanisms. If by some chance banks did independently expand their notes, the Law of Reflux was called into play, which specified that the redundant notes would promptly be returned to the banks as deposits, in repayment for loans, and for specie.

The Keynes–Wicksell resolution of Gibson's Paradox quite clearly sets out a nonmonetary theory of the cycle. However, if the banks would refuse to expand the money supply in response to the increase in demand, no series of events, such as reported by Gibson, would take place. Thus, while money does not cause the cycle, in their analysis its expansion is necessary for the cycle to take place.

The Exogeneity of Money

Related to the classical view on the monetary nature of the business cycle was the belief that the central bank could control the supply of money, by which they meant bank notes. Overissue of these notes or reckless contraction therefore must ultimately be due to ill-advised policies of the central bank. Thus *exogeneity* came to mean *ability to control,* and the basic policy prescription of the Currency School was a strict rule that the supply of bank notes be made to function exactly as would a pure specie system. This was achieved through the imposition of a 100 percent reserve requirement for the notes.

The counterargument was severalfold. First, it did not deal directly with the problem of whether the central bank could control the money supply if it desired. However, the argument that vast hoards of money existed appears to weaken substantially whatever power the central bank may have wielded. Second, it was argued that control of the money supply, even if it could be achieved, would not serve to minimize economic disturbances, for a number of money substitutes existed which could be used to make transactions, and the central bank could exercise no control over them. Third, since Currency School opponents were most vocal in arguing that the money supply expanded to meet the needs of trade, they insisted that the central bank had no power over the supply.

Of great interest, for a subsequent battle was raised over this same issue during the 1960's, is the question of characterizing a situation in which the central bank can control the money supply, but for some reason decides during some historical time periods not to do so. Should exogeneity still be used to describe the money supply during these periods? Such an issue is quite important when empirical tests are conducted to measure the causality of money.

KEYNESIAN
MONETARY THEORY

Part II

Introduction

In the introduction to the preceding section the essential propositions forming the quantity theory of money were stated in order to focus attention on the meaningful relationships embodied in the classical approach to monetary theory.

In introducing this section, we will show that much of the essence of the Keynesian Revolution lies in the denial of the validity of most of these five key propositions. Keynes' ability to deny them derives from his demonstration that an economy could achieve an equilibrium with substantial amounts of unemployment and that this unemployment could not be reduced by cutting money wages, as the classical economists had long supposed.

In terms of its theoretical formulations and policy prescriptions, the Keynesian approach has much in common with that of the discredited Banking School, even though Keynes believed he owed an intellectual debt to Parson Malthus and the mercantilists of the preclassical period.

Proportionality

At least three arguments from *The General Theory* can be used to deny the proportionality proposition. First, the existence of an unemployment equilibrium implies that expansion of the money supply can bring forth permanent increases in the level of real output rather than proportionate increases in the price level. Second, Keynes argued that velocity was an unstable and unpredictable variable; thus increases in the money supply could be partially or totally offset by velocity changes. Third, the possible existence of money hoards, whose total was sensitive to the money interest rate, served to break the close relationship between money and prices.

Money's ultimate influence on the price level came to depend upon its influence on aggregate demand and the elasticity of the supply schedule of aggregate output. While money was not precluded from exercising some influence on the price level, therefore, its effect was much less certain than in the classical model.

Neutrality

So long as an unemployment equilibrium was a possibility, changes in the money supply could permanently change real variables: The natural rate of interest, the level of real output, the volume of employment, and the mix of final output.

However, money could also be neutral in the Keynesian model if either or both of two conditions were present. First, if the demand for money were infinitely interest elastic, then changes in the money supply would merely be added to hoards and would change no variables at all in the Keynesian system. Second, money's influence on the real sector is transmitted through "the" market interest rate. If the spending categories comprising aggregate demand are totally inelastic to changes in the interest rate, money will be mostly neutral, that is, it will only change the rate of interest.

An interesting implication of nonneutrality is that the nominal interest rate can be used as a measure of monetary stringency, since it represents a proxy for the real rate. Those schooled in the Fisherian tradition would surely object to this use of market interest rates.

The existence of permanent nonneutrality implies a definite integration of the monetary and the real sectors of the economy.

Monetary Theory of Prices

The Keynesian approach to this proposition represents, in many respects, a return to the theory expounded by Thomas Tooke, for Keynes argued that prices are governed in large measure by costs of production. Since prime costs are determined by money wages, per-unit labor costs play an important role in formulating the general level of prices. Thus, while changes in the money stock can, by changing aggregate demand, change per-unit labor costs and the general level of prices, changes in factor remuneration can do the same thing. Hence, the money supply is not the sole determinant of the price level. Factor costs can play a significant role in determining prices, which opens the possibility for so-called "cost-push" theories of inflation.

Causal Role of Money

Nothing in the formal Keynesian framework excludes money from playing a significant causal role. The degree of money's importance depends upon its ability to alter money interest rates and upon the degree to which expenditure categories (consumption, investment, government outlays, and so forth) are sensitive to changes in the interest rate. To the extent that a given change in the money supply can induce large changes in the interest rate and that expenditures are highly sensitive to those changes, money matters very much in the Keynesian system.

However, Keynes' interpretation of historical events cast great doubt on the potency of money. He attributed The Great Depression of the 1930's to a collapse in the marginal efficiency of capital, and the great contraction in the money stock in the same era to a lack of demand for loanable funds.

The development of the Keynesian theory in terms of an income–expenditure model in which the multiplier, rather than velocity, plays a central role tended further to conceal the importance of money.

The strong emphasis on fiscal policy as the necessary means to restore and maintain full employment stands as additional testimony to Keynes' belief that if

. . . we are tempted to assert that money is the drink which stimulates the system to activity, we must remind ourselves that there may be several slips between the cup and the lip.[1]

Exogeneity of the Nominal Stock of Money

Little is said regarding the ability of the central bank to control the nominal money supply in *The General Theory*. However, the Keynesian interpretation of the great contraction of the early 1930's and the buildup of huge excess reserve balances by the American banking system during the later years of the 1930's and early 1940's, implies that the money supply is demand-determined and, hence, outside of central bank control.

However, the embodiment of the Keynesian model in the *IS–LM*

[1] J. M. Keynes, *The General Theory of Employment, Interest and Money* (New York: Harcourt, Brace and World, 1936), p. 173.

framework carries with it the implication that the money supply can be controlled by the central bank and hence is exogenous.

Little discussion is to be found in *The General Theory* on the role of money substitutes, the degree to which they can vary independently of the stock of money, and whether they are large or small relative to the group of assets defined to be money.

The purpose of the next four chapters will be to develop the Keynesian model to bring out these fundamental Keynesian views on the central propositions of the quantity theory and, hence, classical monetary theory.

chapter 5

The Keynesian Model

This introductory chapter in Keynesian monetary theory will parallel closely its classical counterpart. However, it will begin with a summary of Keynes' attack on classical theory, for only by seeing what basic tenets of that analysis he found objectionable can the truly innovative aspects of his own approach be appreciated and their merits evaluated.

After summarizing the objections to classical theory made by Keynes, a model derived from *The General Theory* will be constructed and, as far as possible, contrasted with corresponding components of its classical forebear. Lest the analysis get lost in the mechanics of the Keynesian approach, it should be remembered that Keynes told his readers that at full employment "the classical forces come into their own."

THE KEYNESIAN ATTACK

In Chapter 2, the functioning of the classical model was explored by positing a number of macro problems and examining the adjustment of the economic system to these problems. As long as money wages, commodity prices, and interest rates were flexible and moved relatively rapidly, the economy was self-adjusting and could maintain a tendency toward continuous full employment in the face of almost any type of macro disturbance. If unemployment did occur, the classical remedy was generally to call for a reduction in money wages, thereby reducing the real wage, increasing the quantity of labor demanded, and reducing the quantity supplied.[1] The reduction in money wages would ensure a reduction in real wages, because money wages and prices were not directly related except insofar as money wages affected the level of real output.

For the success of Keynes' argument, it was essential that he deny this postulate of classical theory—that wages and commodity prices are independent of each other. In Chapter 2 of *The General Theory,* he attacked the classical writers for an inconsistency between their micro and macro theory of prices. Claiming that they had ". . . taught us to believe that prices are governed by marginal prime costs in terms of money and that money-wages largely govern marginal prime costs,"[2] he formulated a new theory of price level determination for the macro model which was to emerge from *The General Theory*. Under it, the general level of commodity prices depends upon per unit labor costs plus a markup for the other factor payments which are conventionally called "profits." The only way changes in the stock of money can affect the price level is by changing per-unit labor costs; this is done by changing aggregate demand through prior changes in the rate of interest. In many respects, the price-level determination in the Keynesian model appears to be a reversion back to the ideas of Thomas Tooke and the Banking School. (See Chapter 3, pp. 64–65).

The direct linking of wages and prices has an important consequence. It means that reductions in money wages to solve an unemployment problem will no longer be effective, for they simultaneously reduce commodity prices in proportion, leaving the real wage unchanged.[3]

Additionally, Keynes denied one other postulate of the classical system—that the labor supply schedule was an upward sloping function of the *real* wage. He states that

. . . ordinary experience tells us, beyond doubt, that a situation where labor stipulates (within limits) for a money-wage rather than a real wage, so

[1] For historical accuracy, J. Ronnie Davis marshals considerable evidence that so-called American classical economists specifically rejected wage cuts as the means out of the great depression. The wage-cut thesis, Davis argues, if it can be called classical, is characteristic of European thought, not American. See his *The New Economics and The Old Economists* (Ames, Iowa: The Iowa State University Press, 1971), especially pp. 107–17.

[2] J. M. Keynes, *The General Theory of Employment, Interest and Money* (New York: Harcourt, Brace, World, 1936), p. 12.

[3] Keynes was aware that a reduction in money wages, by causing prices to fall, could, by changing relative prices in an international trade context, stimulate foreign demand for domestic products thereby raising employment. In addition, cuts in money wages might have consequences exactly as if the money supply had been increased. See *The General Theory,* Chapter 19, for a comprehensive discussion of Keynes' view of the effect of wage cuts on employment.

far from being a mere possibility, is the normal case. Whilst workers will normally resist a reduction of money-wages, it is not their practice to withdraw their labor whenever there is a rise in the price of wage-goods. It is sometimes said that it would be illogical for labor to resist a reduction of money-wages but not to resist a reduction of real wages . . . But, whether logical or illogical, experience shows that this is how labor in fact behaves.[4]

This Keynesian view has important implications for the shape of the labor supply schedule which will be explored in the section to follow.

Having linked wages and commodity prices directly, and denying that labor would withdraw its labor time for every small decrease in the real wage, Keynes posed a problem to the classical economists—the possibility of an unemployment equilibrium which could not be disturbed by reductions in money wages. That is, it was possible to have a situation in which people were willing to work for the going money wage but could not find employment, and that even if they were willing to take a cut in money wages, it would not bring them, in the aggregate, any more employment. This he called the paradox of poverty in the midst of plenty.

Such an unemployment equilibrium might emerge in a wealthy society where the level of saving, generated out of a full-employment income, would exceed the amount of resources desired for investment, since in such a society the production process may already be heavily capital intensive.

Figure 5:1 depicts such a situation, in which at a zero real interest rate desired saving out of a full-employment income exceeds desired investment. In the classical world, such a situation would lead to deflation, for more money is being withheld from the income stream via saving than is being returned via investment. Velocity would then fall, inducing subsequent reductions in commodity prices. If money wages were flexible, competition in the labor market would cause them to fall as well, preserving a constant real wage. So long as expectations did not change, a situation characterized by continual deflation would prevail. However, in the new Keynesian scheme of affairs this cycle of events would not occur, because prices are linked to money wages, not to the stock of money. Thus, whenever saving exceeds investment at a zero interest rate, aggregate demand, MV, falls, as in the classical system. But since the commodity price level depends upon per-unit labor costs, it is output rather than prices which must now give way to maintain equilibrium between aggregate demand, MV, and aggregate supply, or PY.[5]

---

[4] *The General Theory*, p. 9.

[5] This is not completely correct, for as will be shown subsequently, if the production process is subject to diminishing returns, decreases in output will raise the marginal product of labor, reduce per-unit labor costs, and cause the commodity price level to fall.

FIGURE 5:1.   Excess Supply of Saving

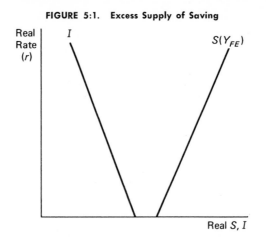

As the level of real income falls, the amount saved at each interest rate declines and the saving schedule shifts inward. Real income will continue to fall and the saving schedule to shift leftward until it intersects the investment schedule at a positive real rate of interest, as shown in Figure 5:2.

FIGURE 5:2.   Adjustment to a Fall in Real Income

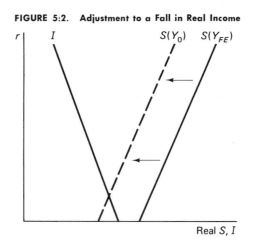

Once the schedules intersect, the economic system is again in equilibrium, but this time at an income level which is less than full employment.

In this unemployment equilibrium, money wage cuts were supposedly unable to move the system back toward a state of full employment because by reducing marginal prime costs, they reduced the price level proportionally. Rather than wage cuts to restore full employment, says Keynes, policy ought to be directed to the manipulation of aggregate demand along the lines suggested in *The General Theory*. However, what Keynes failed to perceive is that changes in the price level could alter the wealth position of society, and by so doing, alter society's consumption and saving patterns, thereby providing a mechanism for the restoration of full employment along classical lines. It was this failure of perception which opened the way for the classical theorists' counterattack on Keynesian theory; their case will be presented in Chapter 6.

THE LABOR AND OUTPUT MARKET

The preceding section has suggested that one Keynesian innovation is to be found in Keynes' view on the functioning of the labor market. The innovation is, however, confined exclusively to the labor supply schedule, for Keynes accepted the classical derivation of the demand schedule for labor which represents its marginal productivity.

As already indicated, Keynes denied the classical assumption, derived from a theoretical framework of utility maximization by labor, that the supply of labor time is a function of the real wage. By citing "ordinary experience," he concludes that within a certain range of price level changes, labor bargains for a money wage and not a real wage. Moreover, all declines in real wages produced by a rise in the price level were not expected to be matched by a withdrawal of labor time from the market. According to Keynes' critics, these conclusions mean that workers suffer from money illusion; that is, they do not distinguish between changes in money and real variables. Thus, they are willing to work for the same money wage even if it means a lower real wage. As the conclusions stated above note, however, Keynes conceived of this money illusion as operating only within a certain range of price level changes. Or, alternatively, labor may believe prices to be stable during the duration of the labor contract and may specify only a money wage, believing it to be an equivalent real wage.

For these reasons, Keynes thought that a more realistic analysis ought to draw the labor supply schedule horizontal at the prevailing *money* wage, sloping upward at the point where all labor time, offered at the going money wage, found employment. From that point on, the labor supply schedule could assume the classical form, that is, upward sloping in response to a rise in the real wage. This type of labor supply schedule is shown in Figure 5:3, where W_0 measures the prevailing *money* wage, and N_{FE} represents the total amount of labor time offered at the prevailing money wage, and, if achieved, measures full employment. Thus, *full employment* can be defined as a situation in which all labor time offered at the prevailing money wage finds employment. What unemployment is present can be called "involuntary," for people who offer their labor time at the going money wage cannot find employment. Moreover (subject to the qualifications of footnote 3) they cannot, in the aggregate, obtain jobs by standing willing to work for a lower money wage because this will not lower the real wage. The only way this type of unemployment could be corrected would be by expanding aggregate demand for output.

FIGURE 5:3.   The Supply of Labor

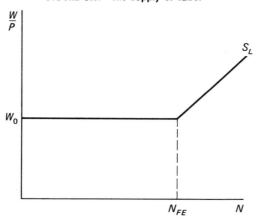

Before it is determined whether the real wage must fall to correct unemployment, two things should be noted about the supply schedule of labor. First, while the schedule is drawn with reference to a given money wage, W_0, that money wage divided by the prevailing index of commodity prices is a real wage as well, W_0/P_0, and can be drawn relative to a real wage axis. Every time commodity prices change with a constant money wage, the real wage, W_0/P_1, changes, and the labor supply schedule shifts. For example, if commodity prices should increase with a constant money wage, the real wage will fall and the supply schedule of labor will shift down, for the same amount of labor time is being offered at a reduced real wage ($W_0/P_1 < W_0/P_0$). This situation is exactly analogous to the Fisherian business cycle shown graphically in Chapter 3. There, the saving function shifted down when actual inflation exceeded that expected by savers.

Second, what forces determine the prevailing level of money wages, W_0? Historical and institutional circumstances, Keynes would reply. They might include minimum-wage legislation, the strength and militancy of trade unions, the effects of public opinion, the degree to which the recent past had been characterized by unemployment or conditions

FIGURE 5:4.   The Labor and Output Sector

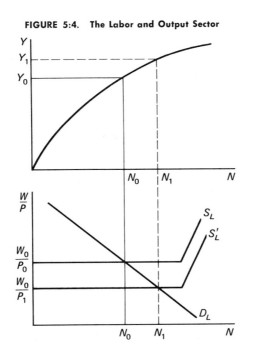

of excess demand, the amount of past price changes, and so forth. For these reasons, in the Keynesian model the level of money wages is usually said to be given or exogenously determined.

In Figure 5:4, the complete labor and output sectors are shown together to determine whether real wages must fall to increase the volume of employment. In order to answer the question, it must be remembered that for Keynes the commodity price level depends upon per-unit labor cost plus a markup for the other factors.

Now let it be assumed that, through ways yet unspecified, an increase in the supply of money has led to an increase in aggregate demand. This increase in demand will cause output to rise, and since labor suffers from diminishing marginal returns, the marginal product of labor will fall. Given the money wage, W_0, a diminished marginal product will increase per-unit labor cost. This must be translated into rising commodity prices. The increase in commodity prices—given the money wage, W_0—means a lower real wage, W_0/P_1. In terms of Figure 5:4, the supply schedule of labor shifts downward from S_L to S'_L. Output expands to Y_1, and the volume of employment increases to N_1. In the end, labor has accepted a lower real wage.[6]

---

[6] James Tobin, among other neo-Keynesians, argues that Keynes was not guilty of such an elementary mistake as attributing to labor money illusion in the sense in which the term is usually used in a strict and static equilibrium analysis. That is, Keynes would never have argued

So far the analysis indicates that to increase employment the real wage must fall. A case exists where this decline need not occur, but it seems relevant only to periods of high unemployment. Let it be supposed that a portion of the total output schedule yields constant output for given uniform increments of labor input. The total output schedule then appears as a straight line in the relevant range. This is shown in Figure 5:5; the relevant range lies between N_a and N_b. Corresponding to this section is a portion of the demand curve for labor which yields a constant marginal product and is therefore horizontal. If the expansion in output, in response to a change in aggregate demand, occurs in this region, employment will increase without any need for the real wage to decline. This example does not seem relevant as full employment is approached; in fact, returns are likely to diminish rather sharply, so that substantial decreases in the real wage are necessary to increase employment. If this is the case, the assumption of money illusion on the part of labor is questionable, and the ability to increase employment in the long run via demand manipulation is doubtful.

THE SAVING/INVESTMENT SECTOR, OR THE COMMODITY MARKET

The classical model predicted that with flexible wages, prices, and interest rates, full employment would always result. The basic function of the interest rate was to allocate the resulting full-employment output be-

---

that if prices and nominal wages were decreased tenfold, leaving real wages unchanged, that labor would voluntarily withdraw its time from the market.

Rather, the early chapters in *The General Theory* must be viewed in a different context. First, the use of the word *equilibrium* to describe a labor market in which unemployment is present is most unfortunate and such a market should be viewed as one of persistent disequilibrium. Second, the comparative static analysis used by Keynes should, in Tobin's view, be interpreted as a shrewd and incisive, if somewhat awkward, attempt at dynamic analysis. In this new interpretation of Keynes, involuntary unemployment is taken to imply that labor markets are not in equilibrium and the resistance of money wages to decline in the face of an excess supply of labor becomes a feature of the adjustment process rather than an indication that the unemployment present is really voluntary.

The downward rigidities in the time path of money wages in the face of an excess supply of labor is due, as Tobin reads Keynes, to the view that workers are more concerned with relative than absolute real wages. However, in a market-oriented economy there is an absence of any central economy-wide mechanism for altering all money wages together which preserves the relative wage structure. It is because relative real wages are important in the supply of labor time to any one market that workers will resist cuts in money wages which serve to alter what they regard as a normal wage relationship to other labor markets.

Thus, expansions in demand which reduce real wages by causing rising prices will not be resisted by labor so long as the relative wage structure is left intact. Therefore, expansions in demand will lead to a larger volume of employment even though it reduces real wages. See James Tobin, "Inflation and Unemployment," *American Economic Review,* Vol. 62, No. 1 (March 1972), 1–18.

tween consumption and investment goods. If the society's propensity to save changed or its incentive to invest altered, nothing would happen to the level of income, only to its composition, that is, the mix of investment and consumption goods.

FIGURE 5:5. Constant Marginal Productivity of Labor

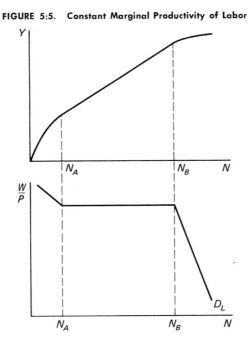

A second aspect of the saving/investment process was that monetary manipulations were incapable of changing the natural rate of interest. In the short run, such manipulations changed money interest rates and in the longer run, the general level of commodity prices.

In the Keynesian model, saving and investment perform other functions. First, their equality basically determines the level of aggregate output and may influence its composition. Once full employment is achieved, changes in the schedules only change output composition; that is, in order to have more goods for investment or public uses, it will be necessary to save more. Second, as long as unemployed resources exist, it will be possible through monetary manipulation to change the natural rate of interest. When full employment is reached, this will no longer be possible, and one is once again in the classical economy. Third, contrary to many statements made by Keynes in *The General Theory*, changes in either the saving or the investment schedule will, by themselves, change the natural rate of interest, except in the special case of the liquidity trap. Once the entire model has been developed, it will be possible to show how changes in saving or investment are able to change the interest rate.

investment

Derivation of the investment demand schedule is exactly the same as in the classical model presented in Chapter 1. In Figure 5:6, the investment demand schedule is reproduced.

As for the saving schedule, Keynes specified that its principal determinant was the level of real income, although he accorded the rate of interest some influence. In order to avoid a third dimension in the diagrams, we will assume that saving depends only on the level of real income. Later, when the *IS–LM* apparatus is used, this restriction can be removed and the saving schedule made a function of both real income and real interest rates, as in its derivation in Chapter 2. The saving schedule is shown in Figure 5:7.

Whether the origin of the saving schedule is the origin of the

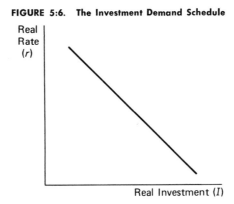

FIGURE 5:6.   The Investment Demand Schedule

Real Rate (r)

Real Investment (I)

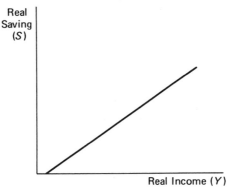

FIGURE 5:7.   The Saving Demand Schedule

Real Saving (S)

Real Income (Y)

FIGURE 5:8.   Equilibrium in the Commodity Market

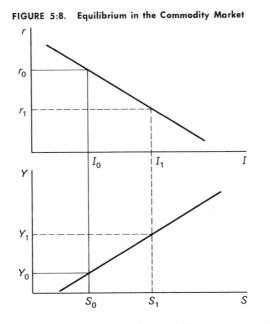

diagram or some intermediate position (indicating negative saving at low levels of real income)[7] is immaterial for the purposes at hand. It is the slope of the schedule which is important, for it determines the value of the Keynesian multiplier. Since the simple multiplier is $1/MPS$ and the MPS is the value of the slope of the saving schedule, the reciprocal of the slope is the simple multiplier; it shows by how much real income will change for a given change in any expenditure category, such as investment or government outlays. It is the multiplier which is the focus in the Keynesian analysis, for it links changes in expenditures to the resulting change in real income or output. By concentrating on the multiplier, attention is shifted away from the classical emphasis on velocity as the link between the money supply and the level of real income.

In order that equilibrium can prevail in the nonmonetary sector, saving and investment must be equal to each other. This means that the goods available for investment (saving) must be equal to the demand for goods for investment. In Figure 5:8, it can be seen that r_0 and Y_0 are a combination of the real interest rate and real income that will make saving and investment equal. Any other real rate combined with Y_0 or any other level of real income combined with r_0 will not yield equilibrium, for these combinations will yield either excess supply (saving will exceed investment) or excess demand (investment will exceed saving).

[7] For purposes of our analysis, the terms *real income* and *real output* will be used interchangeably.

However, r_0 and Y_0 are only one combination giving equilibrium in the nonmonetary sector. Another such combination would be r_1 and Y_1. It is possible to put together, in a single schedule, all such combinations of real interest rates and real income levels which yield $I = S$. Such a schedule is the familiar IS curve graphed in a set of axes whose vertical dimension is the real rate of interest and whose horizontal dimension is the level of real income. Figure 5:9 shows a hypothetical IS curve.

A similar IS schedule can be derived if saving and investment are a function of both the real interest rate and the level of real income.[8]

FIGURE 5:9.   The IS Schedule

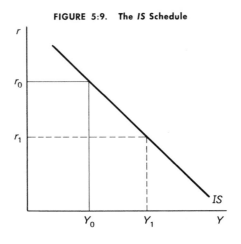

THE MONETARY SECTOR

The monetary sector has rightly been recognized as an original contribution by Keynes, one which has been the subject of a great deal of controversy—attacked especially by those whose allegiance is to the quantity theory approach.

Unfortunately for subsequent analysis and for a rigorous comparison with earlier thoughts, Keynes presented his analysis of the demand for money in a way somewhat different from that of his Cambridge colleagues, and he made claims for his analysis—especially for the theory of interest rates—which were basically incorrect.

To make the analysis more orderly, this chapter will examine Keynes' presentation and his claims for it. Chapter 8 will concentrate

[8] As is well known, if the investment function has greater elasticity with respect to the level of real income than does saving, the IS schedule will have a positive slope, and, given a positively sloped LM curve, the macro economy may have stability problems. However, an upward-sloping IS schedule yields the interesting conclusion that an increase in the money supply will result in a rising level of real income and a rising real rate of interest!

on some extensions made by Keynesians to the basic **Keynesian model,** recast Keynes' demand-for-money function into a mold more consistent with his Cambridge colleagues', note the originality of his contribution, and examine the objections raised by the quantity theorists to Keynes' claims. That chapter will conclude by examining recent work which reinterprets what Keynes was trying to impart.[9]

the keynesian thesis

According to Keynes, the function of the monetary sector is to determine the rate of interest, which results from a balancing of the demand for money with the available supply. In this early expression of his general theory, the rate of interest becomes a purely monetary phenomenon. Its function is to induce people to give up the liquidity of money for the illiquidity of the other available asset for wealth holding—long-term bonds.[10] For this reason, it is often called the *liquidity preference theory* of interest rates. In sharp contrast to this monetary theory of interest rates stands the classical nonmonetary theory in which the function of the interest rate is to induce people to give up present consumption (that is, save) for future consumption. Sir John Hicks[11] first suggested that a complete theory of the interest rate must include both Keynesian and classical causes. Later it will be shown that, except in the special cases of full employment and the liquidity trap, both the Keynesian and the classical theories are needed to yield a determinate theory of the rate of interest.

Sources of Liquidity Preference

Liquidity preference, or the demand for money, is said to arise from three sources. The first is the long-familiar desire for money to make transactions, because in daily life individual or business income and ex-

[9] Anyone who attempts to evaluate Keynes' contribution to monetary economics will bear a heavy debt to the masterful surveys of the subjects made by Harry G. Johnson. See his "Monetary Theory and Policy," *The American Economic Review,* Vol. 52, No. 3 (June 1962); "Recent Developments in Monetary Theory," in *Money in Britain,* D. R. Croome and Harry G. Johnson, ed. (London: Oxford University Press, 1970), pp. 83–121; "The General Theory after Twenty-five Years," *The American Economic Review,* Vol. 51, No. 2 (May 1961), 1–17; "Recent Developments in Monetary Theory," *Indian Economic Review,* Vol. 6, No. 3 (Feb. 1963), 29–69 and Vol. 6, No. 4 (Aug. 1963), 1–28. Much of the analysis in this section is shamelessly taken from these sources.

[10] By this standard, money consists of demand deposits and the noninterest-bearing debt of the government. Keynes says (*The General Theory,* p. 167) that the definition ought to be determined by the particular problem one seeks to analyze. In *The General Theory,* he assumes that money is coextensive with bank deposits. This does not preclude time deposits from his definition of money; however, the basic implication of his theory of interest rates is that money does not have an explicit yield, thus ruling out time deposits.

[11] Hicks, J. R., "Mr. Keynes and the Classics: A Suggested Interpretation," *Econometrica,* Vol. V (1937), pp. 147–159.

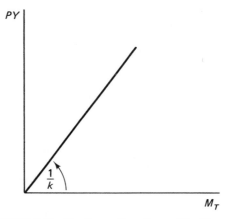

FIGURE 5:10.   The Transactions Demand for Money

penditures are never perfectly synchronized. Money will therefore be desired to perform the basic function of a medium of exchange. Given society's basic institutional and technical arrangements (as discussed by Fisher in his analysis of velocity), the higher the level of money income, the greater the demand for money to make transactions. This *trans-actions demand* can be functionally expressed in the familiar Cambridge equation:

$$M_T = k(PY)$$

where M_T represents the transactions demand for money, k expresses the fraction of money income society desires to hold as money because its income and expenditures are not perfectly synchronized, and PY represents money income. The value of k is determined by the institutional and technological relationships determining the payment and receipt of money; its value is assumed to be constant during the short run. Figure 5:10 graphs this relationship—it is the familiar Cambridge treatment of the quantity theory and was acknowledged by Keynes to be equivalent to the classical treatment of velocity.

The second general reason for preferring the liquidity of money, Keynes labels the *precautionary motive,* which arises

to provide for contingencies requiring sudden expenditures and for un-foreseen opportunities of advantageous purchases, and to hold an asset of which the value is fixed in terms of money to meet a subsequent liability fixed in terms of money. . . .[12]

[12] *The General Theory,* p. 196.

This desire to hold money will be substantially weakened if a highly organized financial exchange exists, for in that case bonds can be quickly converted into money to meet unforeseen contingencies. Since the precautionary demand for money is unrelated to any economic variables in the system, it will be subsumed under the transactions demand.[13]

The third source of liquidity preference represents the unique Keynesian contribution, for he, at last, provides a reason why the rational man will prefer to hold money rather than bonds, even though in doing so he gives up the interest yield of bonds for the zero return of money.

On a more theoretical level, Keynes' *speculative demand for money* finally enables the economist to integrate the monetary sector of the economic model with the real sector in a general equilibrium model which simultaneously explains interest rates, velocity, money income, and the general level of prices. It permits changes in the stock of money to change the equilibrium value of real variables. Money is then no longer just a more efficient substitute for a highly developed barter system. Indeed, Harry Johnson once proclaimed that this was what the Keynesian Revolution was all about. Once one accepted the speculative demand for money, one accepted the Keynesian Revolution and Keynes' attack on the quantity theory.[14] In addition, the speculative demand for money has important implications for the effectiveness of monetary policy.

It is of some importance, therefore, that the nature of the speculative demand for money and its implications for the macro model be fully understood. This is the substance of monetary theory!

In deciding whether to hold wealth in a money or a bond form (for purposes of this analysis, the bond is assumed to be a perpetuity, or consol), the individual compares the current rate of interest, i_c, with the rate of interest expected to prevail in the near future, i_e, called by Keynes the individual's "normal" interest rate. If the current rate is expected to

[13] Harry Johnson maintains that *The General Theory's* treatment of the relative importance of the precautionary demand is rather confusing. When it is introduced in Chapter 13, it is the senior partner in determining liquidity preference, "intrusted with the important business of avoiding uncertainty about the future rate of interest." Indeed, Keynes goes so far as to state, "There is, however, a necessary condition failing which the existence of a liquidity preference for money as a means of holding wealth could not exist. This necessary condition is the existence of *uncertainty* as to the future rate of interest . . . " (*The General Theory*, p. 168). James Tobin interprets this to mean disagreement among investors concerning the future rate rather than subjective doubt in the mind of an individual investor. See his "Liquidity Preference as Behavior Towards Risk," *Review of Economic Studies*, Vol. 25 (Feb. 1958), p. 72.

However, in Chapter 15: " . . . the precautionary motive has been reduced to a poor relation eking out his existence in the household of transactions demand." This remarkable switch in importance Johnson calls a *transmogrification*—unexplained by Keynes. See Johnson, "The General Theory after Twenty-Five Years," p. 8.

[14] H. G. Johnson, "A Quantity Theorist's Monetary History of the United States," *Economic Journal*, Vol. 75 (June 1965), p. 396.

rise in the near future (that is, if the individual's normal rate is above the current rate), a capital loss will result if the consol is held. For example, if $i_c = .02$ and $i_e = .04$, the market value of one dollar invested today in a consol paying 2 percent per year would be expected to decline to 50 cents and the bond holder to suffer a potential capital loss equal to one-half the value of the holding of consols. The expected capital gain or loss can be computed easily by subtracting the current investment of one dollar from the market value of the consol or $g = \dfrac{i_c}{i_e} - \$1$. For the case in point, $g = \dfrac{.02}{.04} - \$1 = \$.50 - \$1$, or $\$-.50$.

Thus, in deciding whether to hold bonds or money, the wealth owner must not only be concerned with the present interest rate, but with the rate expected to prevail in the near future, for that rate will govern whether a capital gain or loss will accrue as a result of holding bonds. So long as the net yield, which consists of the interest paid on the bond plus or minus the capital gain or loss, is greater than zero, the individual will hold only bonds. If the net yield is less than zero, only money will be held; whereas, if it is exactly zero, the individual will be indifferent between bonds and money. (The preceding discussion ignores transactions costs.)

Given the formula for computing the capital gain or loss, one can compute a critical value for the current interest rate, i_c, which will leave the individual indifferent between money and bond holding. Then, at any current rate above this critical value only bonds will be held because their net yield will be positive; at any rate below this critical value only money will be held, for the net yield on bonds will be negative. To solve for the critical value of the current rate, i_c,

$$g + i_c = 0 \; ; g = \frac{i_c}{i_e} - 1 \tag{5:1}$$

thus,
$$\frac{i_c}{i_e} - 1 + i_c = 0 \tag{5:2}$$

and
$$\frac{i_c}{i_e} + i_c = 1 \tag{5:3}$$

then,
$$i_c \left(\frac{1}{i_e} + 1 \right) = 1 \; ; i_c \left(\frac{1 + i_e}{i_e} \right) = 1 \tag{5:4}$$

$$i_c = \frac{1}{\frac{1 + i_e}{i_e}} \tag{5:5}$$

and
$$i_c = \frac{i_e}{1 + i_e} \tag{5:6}$$

In the example above, for an $i_e = .04$, the critical value of the current rate becomes .0385. Whenever the current market rate is above this value, the wealth owner, whose $i_e = .04$ will hold only bonds and, when the current rate is below .0385, he will hold only money.[15] This produces for the individual a discontinuous demand function as shown in **Figure 5:11**. At a current market rate above critical rate $\bar{i}_c$, only bonds are held; below $\bar{i}_c$, the entire portfolio measured as W_0 nominal dollars will be held as money balances.

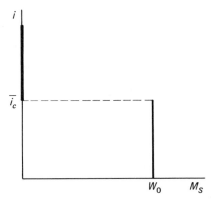

FIGURE 5:11. Keynesian Demand Function for Speculative Balances by the Individual

From the analysis above, for an individual, a demand schedule for speculative balances can be derived for all individuals which will relate money holdings to the current rate of interest. This can be done in several steps. First, a maximum critical value of the current rate is selected which will produce only bond holders for the society. That is, at that value of the current rate and above, everyone in the society will hold only bonds. In Figure 5:12, let this rate be designated as i_A.

Let the current rate then be reduced to one lower than i_A. When the current rate is lowered, some individuals will be encountered who have critical current rates above the new rate, but below rate i_A. These individuals will then become money holders, because their critical current rate lies above the current rate and to hold bonds will impose on them a net loss. Thus, at a rate such as i_B, some small demand for money to hold as an asset will start to emerge, say, M_0 amount.

Let the present rate be lowered below i_B to a point such as i_C. A still larger group will now be encountered whose critical current rate lies above i_C. These individuals will hold money rather than bonds to avoid a net loss. Let them hold M_1 amount of speculative balances. If points

---

[15] For example, suppose $i_e = .04$ and $i_c = .039$. Then by holding bonds, the wealth owner will realize a net gain of 1.4¢ per \$1 invested.

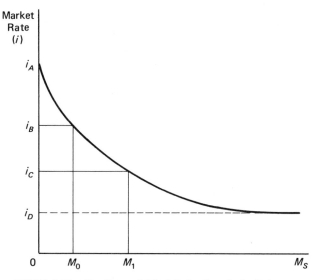

FIGURE 5:12.   The Demand Schedule for Speculative Balances

i_A–0, i_B–M_0, and i_C–M_1 are connected, a demand schedule for speculative balances will result.

As a part of the derivation of the speculative demand schedule, Keynes supposed some minimum value of the critical interest rate to exist above which everyone's critical rate would lie. Let this minimum rate be designated as i_D. At that rate, everyone becomes a money holder, for holding bonds means a net loss. At designated rate i_D, the demand for speculative balances becomes absolute—infinitely elastic. This portion of the demand schedule is the familiar liquidity trap and has played a rather prominent role in the early monetary policy implications drawn from *The General Theory*, although Keynes stated that he never knew of any instance in the world when absolute liquidity preference prevailed.[16]

To round out this discussion, two additional aspects of the speculative demand schedule should be considered. First, what determines its overall elasticity, and second, is the function a stable one?

Elasticity depends upon the divergence of opinion among wealth holders as to their critical current rate. If many critical rates are present which differ by very slight amounts, the demand schedule ought to be relatively inelastic. If only a narrow difference separates all critical rates, the demand schedule will be relatively elastic and similar to that for an individual. In the limiting case, where everyone has the same critical rate, the demand schedule is infinitely elastic and identical to that shown in Figure 5:11. If the present rate is above the critical rate, everyone holds bonds. If it is below that rate, everyone holds money.

The ultimate resolution of the elasticity question must rest upon empirical studies. Available information suggests an elasticity range of -0.12 to -0.17, when short-term interest rates are used, and a range of -0.12 to -0.8, when long-term rates are used.[17] The results of empirical work therefore suggest that the interest elasticity of money demand is low. There is no evidence which suggests that a liquidity trap has ever existed in the United States.[18] However, the nature of the empirical analysis, resting on time series regressions, may preclude determining its existence on a short-run basis.

The stability of the schedule is seldom discussed and its importance is not fully recognized by many Keynesians. When the speculative demand schedule was derived, it was assumed that each wealth holder had in mind an expected future rate toward which the present rate would move in the near future. Expectations about future rates are far from static. Depending upon how they are formed, they may be in a constant state of revision upward or downward. *The General Theory* implies that they are in a state of change and can even be influenced by announced policies of the central bank. If such an institution announced that it was committed to a policy of lower interest rates, it might be able to achieve the objective without the necessity of monetary expansion, for every wealth holder might revise downward his expected rate, causing a downward shift in the speculative demand schedule and lower interest rates.

If instability exists, it can have a profound influence on monetary policy by rendering its effects uncertain. The monetary authorities will no longer be able to gauge accurately the impact of a change in the money supply unless they can depend on the stability or predictability of the demand function. If this function is subject to random shifts, monetary policy may be either ineffective or supereffective. The wealth of empirical studies generated by Friedman and his supporters suggests that the demand function is remarkably stable in the functional sense; that is, while it does shift, its shift depends on movements in a few economic variables, and the magnitude of the shift can be predicted by changes in the value of those variables.

[17] The range depends, in part, on the definition of money and the length of the sample period.

[18] See, however, a very early paper by Tobin which suggests that a liquidity trap may have been present in the pre–World War II period. See his "Liquidity Preference and Monetary Policy," *Review of Economics and Statistics*, Vol. 29 (May 1947), pp. 124–31.

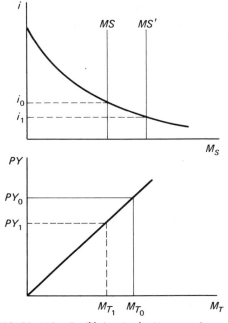

FIGURE 5:13.   Equilibrium in the Monetary Sector

The Combined Monetary Sector

Now that the three reasons for liquidity preference have been discussed, the Keynesian monetary sector can be presented graphically and the conditions for monetary equilibrium can be specified. This is shown in Figure 5:13.

In order to determine the market rate of interest, the level of money income must first be specified. This determines the quantity of money demanded for transactions, which when subtracted from the available supply of money (assumed to be given by the central bank) yields the residual supply of money available for speculation. If money income is assumed to be equal to PY_0, the corresponding quantity of money demanded for transactions will be M_{T_0}. If M_{T_0} is subtracted from the available supply, the residual, MS, is plotted in the speculative portion of the diagram, yielding a money interest rate equal to i_0.

Given PY_0 and i_0, the necessary conditions for monetary equilibrium in the Keynesian model are present, for at that combination of money income and money interest rate, the demand for money, $M_T + M_S$, is equal to the supply of money, $M\overline{S}$. In a more formalized fashion, the functional relationships and equilibrium can be stated as:

$$M_T = k(PY)$$

$$M_S = \int(i)$$

$$M_T + M_S = M\overline{S}$$

However, PY_0 and i_0 indicate only one of an infinite number of possible combinations of money income and money interest rates which yield monetary equilibrium. PY_1 and i_1 is another possible combination. The schedule relating all possible combinations of PY and i which yield monetary equilibrium $(M_T + M_S = M\overline{S})$ is the familiar LM curve shown as Figure 5:14.

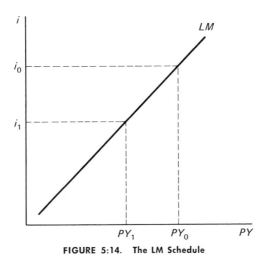

FIGURE 5:14.   The LM Schedule

In order to make the horizontal axis of Figure 5:14 correspond with that of Figure 5:9, that is, so both are expressed in real terms, it will be necessary to make the transactions demand—a demand for real balances. This is done by dividing both sides of the equation $M_T = k(PY)$ by the index of the general level of commodity prices, P. However, this formula still leaves a potential problem, because the money rate of interest, not the real rate, measures the opportunity cost of holding wealth in a money form (in a world of commodity price stability and in which bonds are the only alternative asset to money). The vertical axis remains the money rate, or i, and not the real rate, or r. Hence, changes in the money rate are equal to changes in the real rate. To the economist schooled in the Fisherian tradition, this is apt to be a very misleading simplification with potential for grave policy error if the money rate is used to judge the impact of monetary policy. In more sophisticated models of the

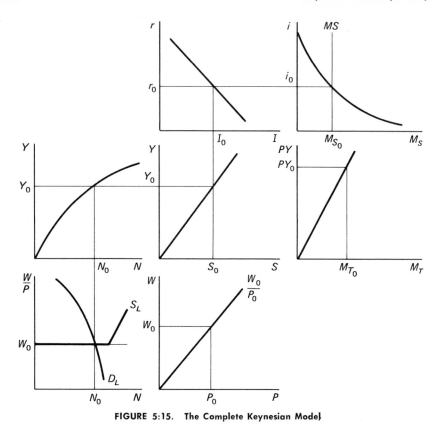

FIGURE 5:15.   The Complete Keynesian Model

type developed by Martin Bailey,[19] for example, it is possible to incorporate the Fisherian distinction between real and nominal interest
rates into the *IS–LM* framework.

THE COMPLETE KEYNESIAN MODEL

Before presenting a critique of the liquidity preference theory of interest
rates, the complete Keynesian model which emerges from the preceding
discussion will be examined. This is shown as Figure 5:15.

    In order to generate a unique equilibrium, the stock of money, the
level of money wages, and the general level of commodity prices must be
given. The first is assumed to be determined by the central bank and the
second by historical and institutional circumstances, while the third
depends upon per unit labor costs plus a profit markup. Note that the

[19] M. J. Bailey, *National Income and the Price Level* (New York: McGraw-Hill, 1962), pp.
49–54. In Chapter 12 of this text, such a distinction is made.

transactions diagram stands by itself—its vertical axis measures money income, not real income. If the price level is assumed to be unity and unchanging, then changes in PY are equal to changes in Y. However, in the problems analyzed in Chapter 7, this will not be a reasonable assumption.

Since each diagram represents an equation in a general-equilibrium framework, the complete model in function form can be expressed as:

$$I = f(r) \tag{5:7}$$

$$S = f(Y) \tag{5:8}$$

$$I = S \tag{5:9}$$

$$M_T = k(PY) \tag{5:10}$$

$$M_S = f(i) \tag{5:11}$$

$$M_T + M_S = \overline{MS} \tag{5:12}$$

$$Y = f(N) \tag{5:13}$$

$$D_L = f\left(\frac{W}{P}\right) \tag{5:14}$$

$$W = W_0 \tag{5:15}$$

$$D_L = N \tag{5:16}$$

where equations (5:9), (5:12), and (5:16) express the necessary conditions for equilibrium in the model, that is, that saving equal investment, a condition for equilibrium in the commodity market; that money demand equal money supply, a condition for equilibrium in the money market;

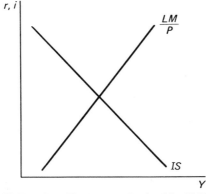

FIGURE 5:16.   The Economy Depicted by *IS–LM*

and that the demand for labor equal the number of workers employed, a condition for equilibrium in the labor market.

The Keynesian system can also be shown in terms of the *IS–LM* apparatus; however, this system does not permit the labor market to be examined. It is, nevertheless, shown as Figure 5:16.

A SUMMARY AND CRITIQUE OF LIQUIDITY PREFERENCE AS A THEORY OF INTEREST RATES

We will conclude the formal presentation of the Keynesian model with an examination of the liquidity preference theory of interest rates and its implications. (It will, of necessity, involve some repetition.) Since the unique aspect of the Keynesian monetary sector centers on the speculative demand for money, most of the discussion will concern this innovative concept.

In *The General Theory,* asset aggregation was carried to a relative extreme and only two types of assets were admitted—money, which has no explicit yield, and the long-term bond, which pays an explicit rate of interest. All nonmonetary assets were incorporated into the bond alternative. Thus, physical capital and its proxy, the equity, and physical commodities were assumed to be perfect substitutes with bonds. Keynes tried to remedy this shortcoming in an article published shortly after the appearance of *The General Theory.*[20] Here the equity is added as an explicit option, but it was not integrated into subsequent Keynesian monetary analyses until the post–World War II period.

While this assumption of a two-asset world vastly simplifies monetary analysis, it presents two basic problems. First, it implies that the wealth owner holds either all bonds or all money depending upon the critical value of the current interest rate. Thus, a diversified portfolio of bonds and money will never be held—a kind of portfolio behavior seldom, if ever, observed. Second, the two-asset model consists of two instruments whose nominal value is fixed. Commodity price inflation will thus have no effect on asset selection, for the real value of each alternative changes in exactly the same way. This phenomenon hampers analysis of the effects of inflation on portfolio decisions.

Related to the point above is the assumption of actual or expected price stability. Since this assumption permits money to have the absolutely certain yield of zero percent, its opportunity cost can be measured by the money interest rate, and changes in the money rate can be taken

---

[20] Keynes, J. M., "The General Theory: A Reply," *The New Economics,* S. E. Harris, ed. (London: Dobson, 1947), pp. 181–93. See also Hansen's attempt to integrate Keynes' analysis into the cycle, in *A Guide to Keynes* (New York: McGraw-Hill, 1953), pp. 134–39.

as an indication of monetary ease or tightness. It also means that one need not distinguish between money and real rates, for every change in the former is regarded as an equivalent change in the latter. Such neglect may have disastrous policy consequences, for in an inflation, high money interest rates may be taken as an indication of monetary stringency, when they may, in fact, indicate low real rates.

As Keynes presented liquidity preference, it is obvious that he regarded the interest rate as a purely monetary phenomenon. However, the analysis leading to the derivation of the *LM* curve shows that money demand and supply cannot explain the equilibrium, or natural, rate; this rate will depend on the real sector as well. Only in the case of the liquidity trap does Keynes' monetary theory of interest rates provide the correct explanation.

The complete model of the Keynesian economy, shown in Figure 5:14, reveals that the only way monetary impulses can be transmitted to the nonmonetary sector is through changes in the money rate of interest. If the money rate cannot be altered, changes in the money supply will have no effect on the economy. This model has limited scope for a direct mechanism, however that mechanism operates. Moreover, it fails to explain how the net increase in financial assets accompanying the financing of a government budget can have an effect on the economy. Such an increase may directly influence consumption and investment without the necessity of any change in the interest rate. Moreover, it may influence the demand for money as well. Thus, monetary impulses are forced to react through one narrow channel—the interest rate—whereas they may operate through a wealth channel as well.

It has already been noted that the liquidity preference theory really implies that monetary policy will have an uncertain effect on the economy because of the instability of the money demand function. Empirical work has cast doubt on the validity of the assumption that the demand function is unstable.

What happens to this theory of liquidity preference if a single market interest rate prevails in the long run? First, much uncertainty about future rates will vanish and with it the speculative demand for money. Second, this long-run actual rate ultimately ought to become the normal rate for everyone. If it does, it will produce a positive net yield on bonds and everyone will hold bonds. Thus, liquidity preference will vanish—it cannot prevail in a long-run equilibrium!

The last point to note in this critique of liquidity preference (one which will be further analyzed in a later chapter) is that if an autonomous change in the money supply is posited in the Keynesian model shown in Figure 5:15, it can yield results between interest rates and commodity price inflation which are absolutely inconsistent with the findings of Tooke and Gibson. In fact, liquidity preference can be made to produce results exactly like those predicted from the work of Thornton—and this from a man who named—and provided a resolution to—Gibson's Paradox!

CONCLUSION

The purpose of this chapter has been to construct the basic Keynesian model and to contrast and compare it in limited ways with the classical model presented in Chapter 1. A principal difference is that the commodity, monetary, and employment sectors form an integrated whole in the Keynesian model, whereas they did not in the classical model.

Our presentation has shown that Keynes borrowed heavily from his classical forebears. He assimilated their labor and investment demand schedules and the equation of exchange into his model. He made the labor supply and saving schedules respond to different motivation than the classics did. In addition, his price-level determination was differently specified, and he added more motives for holding cash balances. Within the mechanism of the model emerging from *The General Theory*, it is possible to change real variables by changing monetary ones, an integration that may well be the essence of the Keynesian Revolution—it no longer relegates money to the role of a mere veil thrown over an essentially barter economy. Money now matters a great deal, subject to Keynes' caveat that there may be several slips between the cup and the lip.

Selected References and Readings

ACKLEY, GARDNER, *Macroeconomic Theory* (New York: Macmillan, 1961).

BAILEY, MARTIN, *National Income and the Price Level* (New York: McGraw-Hill, 1962).

CLOWER, ROBERT, "Keynes and the Classics: A Dynamical Perspective," *Quarterly Journal of Economics,* Vol. 74, No. 2 (May 1960).

FELLNER, WILLIAM, "What is Surviving?" *American Economic Review,* Vol. 47, No. 3 (May 1957).

HANSEN, ALVIN, *A Guide to Keynes* (New York: McGraw-Hill, 1953).

HARRIS, SEYMOUR, *The New Economics* (London: Dobson, 1960). An exceptional collection of early views on Keynes' *General Theory.*

HARROD, ROY, *The Life of John Maynard Keynes* (London: Macmillan, 1951).

HICKS, JOHN, "Mr. Keynes and the 'Classics': A Suggested Interpretation," reprinted in *Critical Essays in Monetary Theory* (London: Oxford University Press, 1967).

JOHNSON, HARRY, "Monetary Theory and Policy," *American Economic Review*, Vol. 52, No. 3 (June 1962).

————, "The General Theory After Twenty-Five Years," *American Economic Review*, Vol. 51, No. 2 (May 1961).

————, "A Quantity Theorist's Monetary History of the United States," *Economic Journal* (June 1965).

KEYNES, J. M., *The General Theory of Employment, Interest and Money* (London: Macmillan, 1936).

KLEIN, LAWRENCE, *The Keynesian Revolution*, 2nd ed. (New York: Macmillan, 1966).

LEKACHMAN, ROBERT, ed., *Keynes' General Theory: Reports of Three Decades* (London: Macmillan, 1964).

PATINKIN, DON, *Money, Interest, and Prices*, 2nd ed. (New York: Harper & Row, 1965).

SCHLESINGER, JAMES, "After Twenty Years: The General Theory," *Quarterly Journal of Economics*, Vol. 70, No. 4 (Nov. 1956).

SMITH, WARREN, "A Graphical Exposition of the Complete Keynesian System," *Southern Economic Journal*, Vol. 23, No. 4 (Oct. 1956).

WRIGHT, A. L., "The Genesis of the Multiplier Theory," *Oxford Economic Papers*, Vol. 8, No. 2 (June 1956).

chapter 6

The Classical Reply

Revolutions against long-entrenched regimes, political or intellectual, seldom meet with unequivocal success. After an initial advance, they generally must face a reaction or counterattack. So it was with the Keynesian Revolution. Under the aegis of Professor A. C. Pigou, the counterrevolution was mounted. The mantle of leadership passed successively to Don Patinkin, Milton Friedman, and most recently to Karl Brunner and Allan Meltzer.

This chapter will discuss the initial reaction presented by Pigou and its extensive development during the late 1960's by Boris Pesek and Thomas Saving. In Chapter 12, the more general criticism of the Keynesian approach, called Monetarism, will be examined.

THE KEYNESIAN INNOVATION

One of the central themes of *The General Theory* was the possibility of the existence of an unemployment equilibrium impervious to correction by the use of money wage reductions. Having linked wages and prices directly in his theoretical apparatus, Keynes noted that reductions in wages would in the aggregate reduce prices in proportion, leaving unchanged the real wage, the determinant of the quantity of labor demanded. Thus the economic system was not self-adjusting along the lines suggested by classical analysis. Keynes speculated that rather than a continuous tendency to full employment, there existed in developed, capital-rich economies a chronic tendency toward unemployment for which the decade of the 1930's stood as evidence.

THE CLASSICAL REACTION

The classical reaction against *The General Theory* was almost instantaneous and was frequently confined to unfavorable book reviews which attacked various theoretical formulations, especially the liquidity preference theory of interest rates.

It was not until 1943, some seven years after *The General Theory* appeared, that Professor Pigou—now a harsh critic of his former colleague—was able to mount an effective intellectual counterattack designed to show that so long as wages and prices were flexible, an unemployment equilibrium was impossible.[1]

The initial reaction of many economists, including Pigou himself, was that sane public policy could not be based upon his intellectual formulation. Subsequent opinion, discussed below, has not always been so certain.

A simple statement of what is now immortalized as the *Pigou Effect* would omit much of its content. Therefore, to fully understand Pigou's contribution it will be necessary both to state his argument and explore its implications in greater depth.

The "Pigou Effect"

Suppose that over time in a capital-rich society, the incentive to invest declines relative to the volume of saving, so that at a zero real interest rate, saving from a full-employment income now exceeds investment—a situation similar to that shown in Figure 5:1. In such a situation, Pigou was willing to concede, the level of real income will fall and unemployment will emerge much as Keynes supposed and as was shown in Figure 5:2. In this world, an unemployment equilibrium becomes a distinct possibility. However, suppose the unemployed offer their labor services at a lower money wage or the government cuts money wages by decree (either action being in accord with classical policy prescriptions); either way, in the Keynesian model, the commodity price level will fall. In the classical model, the excess of saving over investment will cause MV to decline, reducing both wages and prices. In the Keynesian model, the reduction in wages will not directly reduce unemployment, for since commodity prices will have fallen in proportion, the real wage will remain unchanged. However, with the fall in commodity prices, the real value of the community's wealth (measured in terms of its command over goods and services) will rise. Feeling wealthier, the community will lose incentive to save for future consumption at each interest rate, because

[1] A. C. Pigou, "The Classical Stationary State," *Economic Journal*, Vol. 53 (1943), pp. 343–51.

the marginal utility from each additional increment to wealth will have fallen. Thus, as the commodity price level declines, the saving schedule will shift to the left, as in Figure 5:1, and continue to shift until it intersects with investment at a positive interest rate. Once intersection occurs at a positive rate, full-employment equilibrium is again ensured.

In a Keynesian framework, such as shown in Figure 6:1, the reduction in the price level following a wage cut will shift the saving schedule downward from $S(P_0)$ to $S(P_1)$, expanding both the level of income, from Y_0 to Y_1, and the volume of employment. If one wage cut is insufficient to restore full employment, others must be implemented.

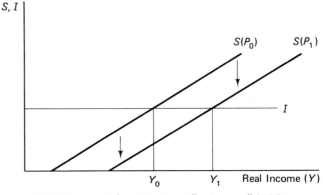

FIGURE 6:1.   A Decline in Saving Following a Fall in Prices

Therefore, if a tendency exists for full-employment saving to exceed investment, resulting in unemployment, the remedy of money wage reductions is still an effective cure and the self-adjusting nature of the classical system is preserved, at least in theory.

To fully understand the Pigou Effect and its ramifications, the range of assets it depends upon must be examined, its operational content for public policy investigated, and its implications for the classical theory of interest rates explored.

Pigou-type Assets[2]

The Pigou Effect specifies that whenever commodity price levels change, thereby causing the real wealth of a society to change, they induce a permanent change in the division of income between consumption and saving (that is, the average propensity to save will change). Thus, crucial to the operation of the Pigou Effect is a type of wealth whose real value

[2] The discussion in this section depends heavily on Don Patinkin, "Money and Wealth: A Review Article," The Journal of Economic Literature, Vol. 8, No. 4 (Dec. 1969), pp. 1140–60.

or purchasing power is affected by changes in the price level. This type of wealth can be singled out if all assets can be grouped into two categories. The first category will consist of those assets whose nominal value changes in proportion to changes in the general level of prices and whose real values are therefore constant. Real property (including inventories and equities in general) might be an example of the kind of assets included in the first category. Quite clearly, the Pigou Effect is not related to this group of assets, for movements in the price level do not affect their purchasing power.

The second category of assets includes all those whose nominal value is fixed and whose real value therefore varies inversely with changes in the general level of prices. Assets in this classification are obviously money, bonds, and a host of near-monies (saving-and-loan shares, saving and time deposits, cash surrender values of insurance policies, and so forth). It is upon this type of asset that the operation of the Pigou Effect must hinge. In the year following the publication of Pigou's original article in 1943, Michael Kalecki[3] pointed out that a further division of the second category's assets appeared desirable because, for the Pigou Effect to operate, changes in the price level must make the community as a whole feel better or worse off. In the creation of bank money, money substitutes, and bonds, whether issued by private enterprise or the government, a clear debtor–creditor relationship arises. For example, for the creditor, the bond represents an income stream consisting of annual interest payments, while for the debtor, it represents a claim on a certain portion of the goods and services produced by his enterprise. Therefore, while a fall in commodity prices makes the creditor feel better off, or wealthier, it impoverishes the debtor by increasing the real burden of debt, for more goods and services must be sold at a lower price to service the obligations of the bond. If the same rate of discount is used by both creditors and debtors to value their respective streams of income and obligations, a change in the price level will leave the real value of this type of social wealth unchanged, for the increase in the real value of assets is exactly offset by the increase in the real value of liabilities. Thus the net wealth position of society is left unchanged. However, if unequal discount rates are used by creditors and debtors, net wealth might be changed. In addition, the position of government debt obligations is somewhat ambiguous, for some economists believe that taxpayers consistently undervalue or neglect altogether the tax liabilities attached to the outstanding issue of government bonds. Hence, government bonds are regarded by their owners as an asset, but appear on no one's balance sheet as a liability, or if they do, at a substantial discount relative to their asset value. According to Kalecki and, subsequently, the conven-

[3] Michael Kalecki, "Professor Pigou on the 'Classical Stationary State'—A Comment," *Economic Journal*, Vol. 54 (1944), pp. 131–32.

tional wisdom of economics, the Pigou Effect is made to hinge on that portion of the money stock and the stock of bonds in which no actual or perceived debtor–creditor relationship exists. Hence, the kind of wealth crucial to the Pigou Effect consists of the amount of government paper money and coin in existence, as well as the amount of government bonds outstanding. The latter will qualify only to the extent that the taxpayers do not regard themselves as the debtors of the bondholders. In 1960, this division of Category-Two wealth was formalized in the work of John Gurley and Edward Shaw.[4] That range of assets on which the Pigou Effect depends they called *outside money or wealth,* while bank money and private bonds were called *inside money* and were excluded from Pigou-type wealth.

The validity of this distinction between inside and outside money has been successfully challenged by a work of Boris Pesek and Thomas Saving.[5] They argue convincingly that under certain conditions bank money ought to be included in the group of Pigou-type assets. Note carefully, however, that the inclusion of bank money is due solely to its being used as a surrogate for the net worth of the banking system. Whether it is included, in part or in total, will depend upon how commodity price changes affect the net worth position of commercial banks. The examples below are constructed so that the conditions under which bank money is or is not included in the range of Pigou Effect assets might be clearly observed. The development of Pesek and Saving's argument will follow closely the excellent presentation by Patinkin,[6] for his work avoids two shortcomings in the original book. First, it avoids some confusion in Pesek and Saving's work, especially their exclusion of time and savings deposits from bank money. Second, Patinkin casts their argument into the mold of conventional accounting analysis similar to that in any text which explains the fundamentals of money creation.

To see the essence of Pesek and Saving's contribution, we will proceed from a simple case to one which, being closer to the world about us, is more complicated.

Our analysis starts by assuming that Table 6:1 states the balance sheet of individuals who comprise the economy and that, until now, the right to print money has resided exclusively with the government. However, the government now extends to private citizens the monopoly right to produce $5,000 of "bank money," which is equally as acceptable as that issued by the government. The individuals who possess this monopoly right now exercise it by selling bank money for the private debts of

[4] J. G. Gurley and E. S. Shaw, *Money in a Theory of Finance* (Washington, D.C.: Brookings Institution, 1960).

[5] B. P. Pesek and T. R. Saving, *Money, Wealth and Economic Theory* (New York: MacMillan, 1967).

[6] "Money and Wealth."

individuals. In conventional texts on money, this would be described as the creation of $5,000 of demand deposits. A typical bank balance sheet would show an asset, "debts of the private sector," and an equivalent liability, "bank money." This is shown in Table 6:2; in Table 6:1, the

TABLE 6:1. Balance Sheet of the Private Sector

Assets		Liabilities	
Gov't. fiat money	$ 20,000		0
Other real assets	100,000	Net worth	$120,000
	$120,000		$120,000

TABLE 6:2. Balance Sheet of the Bank

Assets		Liabilities	
Debts of the private sector	$5,000	Bank money	$5,000

two entries must be reversed, showing "bank money" as an asset and "debts of the private sector" as a liability. Since both assets and liabilities increase by the same amount, the net worth of the private sector remains unchanged.

Quite clearly, a decrease in commodity prices would impoverish the debtor while increasing the wealth of the creditor; as Gurley and Shaw explain, no Pigou Effect is obtained from this type of bank money. However, the source of error in the conventional analysis becomes readily apparent when a simple question is asked. How much would an individual be willing to pay to purchase this banking business? Since its assets are exactly equal to its liabilities, it has zero net worth, as shown by its balance sheet. Does this mean that its price on the market would be zero? "No" would be the answer from Pesek and Saving's work. The grant of the monopoly right to create $5,000 of bank money means that, when the right is exercised, the bank will acquire an equal value of assets which yield the going rate of interest. It is, then, the capitalized value of these interest receipts which represents the net worth of the bank and its maximum market value to the potential buyer. If one assumes that bank money can be produced at no cost, the bank's net worth is then equal to the capitalized or present value of its interest receipts, or income. This can be easily calculated by the formula for a perpetuity:

$$\text{PRESENT VALUE} = \frac{\text{INTEREST RECEIPTS PER PERIOD}}{\text{MARKET RATE OF INTEREST PER PERIOD}}$$

It makes no difference whether the market rate of interest is assumed to be either 3 percent or 8 percent; the present value of each interest income stream which results when $5,000 of earning assets are acquired becomes $\frac{\$150}{.03} = \frac{\$400}{.08} = \$5,000$. Thus the net worth of the bank is equal to the value of the money it is empowered to create, $5,000 (if bank money is costless to produce).

Should commodity prices fall, this monopoly grant to print money would command the same nominal value (which would, of course, represent a larger real value for those individuals who possess it). Thus, in deciding which assets are Pigou Effect assets, government paper money could be added to the monopoly right to print bank money or, alternatively, government money plus bank money (true only if it is costless to produce bank money), or the total money supply would be the appropriate sum.

It is important to see that in this simple example the Pigou Effect would occur even if no bank money were created. The mere possession of the monopoly right increases the net worth of society, for it represents an asset for its owners for which there is no offsetting liability on any balance sheet in the society. The value of the monopoly right can be recognized when the bank is established by listing it as an asset equal to the net worth of the bank. Tables 6:3 and 6:4 record the bank's net worth when it is formed and the increase in the net worth of the private sector which owns the bank.

TABLE 6:3.   Balance Sheet of the Bank

Assets		Liabilities	
Debts of the private sector	$5,000	Bank money	$5,000
Monopoly right to produce bank money	$5,000	Net worth	
		Common stock	$5,000

When these two balance sheets are consolidated, bank money will be canceled against the debts of the private sector to the bank ($5,000) leaving a grand total for assets of $125,000 and a total for net worth of $125,000. When these totals are compared to comparable totals in Table 6:1, it will be seen that both net assets and net worth are increased by $5,000, representing the nominal value of the monopoly grant. A decrease in commodity prices will increase the real value of this component of net worth and will be one source of the Pigou Effect.

TABLE 6:4. Balance Sheet of the Private Sector

Assets		Liabilities	
Gov't. fiat money	$ 20,000	Debts to the bank	$ 5,000
Common stock	5,000		
Other real assets	100,000		
Bank money	5,000	Net worth	125,000
	$130,000		$130,000

Before this presentation is complicated, two things should be noted. First, the banking system is not in equilibrium, as that term is usually understood, for its marginal revenue or interest income is positive, while its marginal costs to produce bank money are assumed to be zero. Its "equilibrium" is forced upon the banking system by its charter, which limits its money-creating capability. Second, in constructing the preceding example, we assumed that the government grants banks the right to create a certain sum of money. While the example may seem unrealistic, it is actually a good deal closer to reality than one might at first imagine. So long as the ability of commercial banks to create money is limited by the availability of high-powered money, or reserve requirements, an approximation to the monopoly case exists, as a simple example will show. Assume that only $1,000 of high-powered money is available and that banks operate under a 20 percent reserve requirement imposed either by the government or by experience. Entry A in Table 6:5 records the receipt of the high-powered money. Of the $1,000 of reserves, $800 is excess and usable to create additional bank money in exchange for the debts of the private sector. A maximum of $4,000 of these debts can be purchased in return for the creation or sale of bank money. This is shown by entries labeled B. In this situation, the net worth of the banking system is only $4,000, or the capitalized value of the interest income from its assets (only if this bank money is produced at zero cost). In this case, the Pigou Effect will operate on the amount of government money in the hands of the public plus the total amount of bank money, or equivalently, the total amount of government money (held by the public and the banks) and the net worth of the banking system.

TABLE 6:5. Balance Sheet of the Bank

A.	Govt. fiat money (Reserves)	$1,000	Bank money	$1,000 A.
B.	Debts of the public	$4,000	Bank money	$4,000 B.

Now let a final complication be introduced by assuming that the maintenance of the stock of bank money involves costs, including possible interest payments on bank deposits. To the extent that interest payments are involved, time and savings deposits fall within the definition of bank money. The effect of these production costs is to reduce the income earned from the assets purchased. Continuing the example introduced at the beginning of this section, assume that on the $5,000 of assets acquired, the banks earn 5 percent, or $250 of gross income, per year. Associated with the maintenance of $5,000 of bank money, we will further assume are costs of $100. Thus net income is $150 per year, and its capitalized value is $\frac{\$150}{.05}$, or $3,000. Therefore, the monopoly right to produce $5,000 of bank money is worth only $3,000, and this sum becomes part of the net wealth of society. So in calculating the range of assets on which the Pigou Effect depends, only three-fifths of the value of bank money ought to be included. If declines in commodity prices leave unchanged the expected net income from the assets, the Pigou Effect will depend on only $3,000 of bank money. However, if banks expect costs to fall relative to interest income, the nominal net worth of banks will increase and a larger nominal value of assets will be available for the operation of the Pigou Effect.

The contribution of Pesek and Saving is important because it shows that traditional analysis, by neglecting the net worth which accrues to the owners of commercial banks when they create money, fails to include in the range of assets on which the Pigou Effect depends for its operation a potentially significant nominal sum, which can be approximated by a portion of the nominal value of bank money.[7] Henceforth, the distinction in the literature between inside and outside money should be forgotten, for the really crucial distinction, insofar as the Pigou Effect is concerned, is between money whose marginal cost of production is less than its marginal value and money whose marginal cost of production equals its marginal value.[8] The former is a Pigou-type asset, for it will represent positive net wealth; the latter will not.

A TERMINOLOGICAL CONFUSION

Frequently in the literature of economics the terms *real-balance effect* or *wealth effect* are used synonymously with the Pigou Effect, when in fact they are not properly the same things.

[7] It should be noted that in defining social wealth, Pesek and Saving double-count bank money, for it is included as a part of the money supply, and the net worth of the banking system is included in another entity. Clearly, one or the other should be counted, but not both. See *Money, Wealth, and Economic Theory*, p. 289.

[8] This implies that, if banking had free entry and its output of money were pressed to the point of competitive profit maximization, bank money would not be counted as a Pigou-type asset. The conclusion requires further that average variable cost be constant so that at the intersection of the marginal cost and value schedules, no clear profit emerges.

The Pigou Effect refers to a permanent change in the consumption/ saving distribution of a given income or change in the average propensity to save, which occurs when the general level of commodity prices changes. It could be called a price-induced wealth effect. However, a change in the general level of commodity prices also affects the level of real cash balances, creating (other things being equal) a divergence between actual real cash balances and those desired relative to a given nominal interest rate. Thus if commodity prices fall, society's actual real cash balances will exceed its desired real balances, and in a Keynesian model these excess real balances will lead to the purchase of bonds, forcing up their price and reducing the nominal rate of interest (except in the special case of the liquidity trap). The decrease in interest rates may lead to a higher level of investment and an increase in real income. This change in interest rates caused by changes in the real money supply is called the *Keynes Effect,* because Keynes admitted it as a qualification to his unemployment equilibrium and its inability to be disturbed by cuts in money wages. The Keynes Effect may properly be viewed as the substitution effect resulting from a decrease in the level of commodity prices. The excess real cash balances are used to buy bonds or bonds are substituted for the excess real balances.

This impact of excess real cash balances on the bond market and on interest rates occurs in the Keynesian model because bonds and real assets are assumed to be perfect substitutes and their joint yield given by the market interest rate. To the extent that these two assets are imperfect substitutes, there is no reason why these excess real balances should not lead to the direct purchase of real assets—both producer and consumer durables—for then the holding of real money balances must be related to both the market interest rate and the yield on real capital. Excess real balances are then spent in both markets until the respective yields on money, bonds, and real capital are restored to equilibrium.

It is a combination of the Pigou and Keynes effects which should properly be called the *real balances effect*—one which embodies both the wealth (Pigou) and the substitution (Keynes) effects. Using the Hicks–Hansen *IS–LM* framework, the Pigou Effect proper operates only on the *IS* schedule, while the Keynes Effect, within the confines of the narrow Keynesian model, operates only on the *LM* schedule. In a more general model in which real assets and bonds are not perfect substitutes and in which they can be substituted for money, the Keynes Effect then has shift implications for both schedules. Thus if commodity prices fall the Pigou Effect will shift the *IS* curve to the right and the Keynes Effect will shift at least the *LM* curve (and possibly the *IS* curve as well) in the same direction. In the narrow Keynesian model, the liquidity trap renders the Keynesian substitution effect inoperative. However, in a more general model, the Keynesian substitution effect may contribute to a rightward shift in the *IS* schedule.

Our discussion thus far has assumed that a decrease in commodity prices is necessary to produce a "real balance effect." This need not be the case—any increase in the nominal supply of money in an environment of stable prices could set in motion a real balance effect. The increase in nominal balances would increase real balances, creating a divergence between actual and desired magnitudes leading to a substitution of financial and real assets for money. Whether a wealth effect also occurs may depend upon how the nominal money supply is increased. Increases in money from past gold-mining or greenback-financed wars must be distinguished from similar increases resulting from open market purchases. The former add to net wealth, for they represent assets to their owners and occur as liabilities to no one, while the latter do only to the extent that government bonds are inside wealth (that is, both the interest and tax liability streams, represented by the bonds, are fully and equally discounted).

Before we examine the policy implications of the Pigou Effect, an additional complication must be introduced—the real balance effect may cause nominal interest rates to decline. To the extent that it does, the capitalized value of the interest income stream (represented by bonds) will increase, thereby increasing the nominal wealth of bond owners. This phenomenon is often called the *Keynesian windfall effect,* or an interest-rate–induced wealth effect, to distinguish it from the wealth effect of the real balance variety. A crucial question concerns the extent to which the windfall effect influences the consumption/saving behavior of the community. The answer to the question depends upon the extent to which the community views government bonds as outside wealth. To the extent that the tax liability for servicing these evidences of social indebtedness is fully realized, interest rate changes will induce no consumption effect. For while a change in market rates will alter the asset position of those who own the bonds, it will also change the indebtedness position of those who owe the bonds (that is, the taxpayers) by an exactly offsetting amount. If such is not the case, the windfall effect will be either positive or negative depending upon the movement of the interest rate. Private debt obligations are of course excluded from the windfall effect.

THE PIGOU EFFECT AS A POLICY TOOL

In discussing the policy implications of the Pigou Effect, initial reactions must be distinguished from subsequent reactions; they are remarkably dissimilar.

Initially, professional opinion held that for the Pigou Effect to be considered a serious policy tool, saving and consumption would have to be highly sensitive to changes in the real value of a rather narrow range of assets, whose nominal value is a small fraction of total wealth. In addition, the effects on expectations of commodity price changes, generated by actual changes in commodity prices, would also have to be minimum. If every time a deflation were contrived to restore full employment, people expected prices to fall more in the future than they actually did in the present, rather than saving less and consuming more, they would do just the opposite. The same pattern holds true for inflations. Finally, severe deflations of the type which early empirical research indicates was necessary to produce a significant Pigou Effect may rob money of a property essential to its functioning as a medium of exchange —relative stability of purchasing power. It was pointed out, for example, that in severe inflations the monetary system often breaks down and people resort to barter. The same thing was thought to be possible during a severe deflation.

Early reaction to the Pigou Effect, then, was to regard it as an intellectual curiosity unworthy of serious consideration as a policy tool, especially since there were more certain ways to eliminate unemployment than to cut money wages and reduce prices. Nevertheless, the existence of the Pigou Effect permitted the classics to assert that the economic system is self-adjusting and will always tend to produce full employment as long as wages and prices are flexible. Thus, the only way Keynes was able to show the existence of an unemployment equilibrium was to assume implicitly that wages and prices were rigid in the downward direction, despite his disclaimer to the contrary. Because of this, the classics asserted that Keynes' book ought not be called *The General Theory,* for it really represented only a special case of the classical model—that specific case in which wages and prices were inflexible in the downward direction.[9]

Subsequent discussion of the Pigou Effect and, more generally, the real balance effect, has centered around its implications for the potency of monetary policy as a stabilization tool. According to Friedman:

The intellectual importance of the forces brought to the fore by Haberler and Pigou was the emphasis they placed on the possibility of substitution

---

[9] It was shown in the problems outlined in Chapter 2 that when wages and prices are inflexible in the downward direction, a deflation will result in unemployment. Modern Keynesians would agree that his unemployment equilibrium does depend on institutionally induced wage rigidities. However, they would argue that this is not an unrealistic assumption, but may be due to a very slow wage-adjustment process which for short-run periods enables wages to be treated as though they were inflexible. Leijonhufvud's analysis, to follow in Chapter 8, can also explain the inflexibility in the short run without the necessity of saying that it is due to trade union practices or other institutional rigidities.

between cash, on the one hand, and real flows of expenditures on the other. This contributed to a reemphasis on the role of money.[10]

Thus, changes in the real quantity of money can directly affect real aggregate demand, even if such changes in real balances do not alter the rate of interest. This gives monetary policy a second channel through which it can affect real aggregate demand. This means that if the central bank can increase the supply of real balances through open market operations, and if aggregate expenditures (investment and consumption) are insensitive to any resulting interest rate changes, or if the interest rate will not change, the real sector may nevertheless feel stimulation from a spillover from the monetary sector. The degree of the spillover and the expansion of real expenditures will depend on the degree to which real assets are regarded as substitutes for money.

It was because of the recent emphasis on the real balance effect that the work of Pesek and Saving was so carefully scrutinized and the subject of much controversy when it appeared. To the extent that their thesis—that the distinction between inside and outside money is false— has validity, the potency of monetary policy is greatly enhanced, for by increasing the reserves of the banking system, the monetary authorities increase the banks' lending power, the discounted value of potential interest income, the net worth of the banking system, and the net wealth of the community. Monetary policy thus is able to alter directly the net wealth of the community. Whether this alteration in wealth level is permanent or transitory depends on the price level ramifications of any change in the money stock. Rising prices following an expansionary monetary policy would reduce the real value of wealth and in the long run no net real wealth would result from the increase in the money stock.

To strengthen the case that monetary policy can create wealth, the proponents of this view argue that interest-bearing government debt should be included in the inside wealth category, for taxpayers, being rational individuals, should include the tax liability attached to government securities as an asset offset on their individual balance sheets. Therefore open market operations, which replace government interest-bearing debt with noninterest-bearing debt, should create net private wealth for the community. On the other hand, if the tax liability goes unrecognized, such direct swaps of interest-bearing for noninterest-bearing debt will have no effect on net private wealth. This will minimize substantially the real balance effect and confine its influence to a

[10] M. Friedman, "Postwar Trends in Monetary Theory and Policy," *The National Banking Review*, Vol. 1, No. 1 (Sept. 1964), p. 1.

substitution of other assets for money. The wealth portion of its total influence will be absent.

Thus, from the viewpoint of subsequent analysis, the real balance effect is seen as having important implications for the potency of monetary policy, for it broadens substantially the potential effect of money on economic activity. A direct channel is now open by which money can change aggregate expenditures without first having to alter the rate of interest.

However, lest anyone believe that the level of real balances is the fulcrum on which the entire economy turns, we are told by such erstwhile supporters of the money-only view as Brunner and Meltzer:

> Like Friedman . . . we believe that the real-balance effect is one of several explanations of long-run changes in the IS curve. We agree, also, that the short-run importance of the real-balance effect is small enough to neglect in most developed economies where real balances are a small part of wealth. In our analysis, the size of the traditional real-balance effect depends on the proportion of money to total nonhuman wealth, a factor that is less than .05 for the United States.[11]

THE PIGOU EFFECT AND THE
CLASSICAL THEORY OF INTEREST RATES

When the classical theory of interest rates was examined in Chapter 1, we noted that while monetary expansion and contraction could alter the money rate of interest, neither could have any effect on the natural rate of interest; that was determined exclusively by saving and investment. Thus the natural rate was a completely nonmonetary phenomenon. However, once the level of saving is made to depend upon both the rate of interest and the value of wealth, variations in the supply of nominal money balances, to the extent that they can change the real value of wealth, can, by causing the saving schedule to shift, change the natural rate of interest. This ability of the money stock to change the natural rate and the mix of final output between consumption and investment goods implies that money is nonneutral and that the natural rate is no longer determined exclusively by the real factors of thrift and the productivity of capital.

By making the Pigou Effect an integral part of the classical model, integration is achieved between the real and monetary sectors and money becomes more than a mere veil thrown over what is essentially a barter system.

[11] Karl Brunner and Allan Meltzer, "Friedman's Monetary Theory," *Journal of Political Economy*, Vol. 80, No. 5 (Sept./Oct. 1972), p. 847, footnote 8.

CONCLUSION

The purpose of this chapter has been to present the substance of the early classical reply to the Keynesian propositions, which rested on the assumption that an unemployment equilibrium was a possibility.

A. C. Pigou, supported subsequently by many others, was the first to show that insofar as theory was concerned, an unemployment equilibrium could not exist in a world with flexible wages and prices. If in the face of unemployment money wages were reduced, the price level would decline, thereby increasing the real value of money. The increase would, in turn, decrease the desire to save, shifting the saving schedule until full-employment saving was equal to investment. The process by which cuts in money wages, by decreasing the desire to save, restore full employment has come to be called the Pigou Effect.

In the investigation of the operation of Pigou's creation, we noted the range of assets critical to its success (those denominated in fixed nominal terms and which constitute part of the net wealth of society), the use made of the effect in the development of monetary theory (it opens additional avenues for money to affect the real sector), its limited operational content from a policy viewpoint, and the way in which it contributes to the integration of the monetary and real sectors of the classical model by making the natural rate partially a monetary phenomenon.

Selected References and Readings

FRIEDMAN, MILTON, "Postwar Trends in Monetary Theory and Policy," in *Money and Finance: Readings in Theory, Policy, and Institutions,* Deane Carson, ed. (New York: John Wiley, 1966).

GURLEY, JOHN, AND SHAW, EDWARD, *Money in a Theory of Finance* (Washington, D.C.: Brookings Institution, 1960).

HABERLER, GOTTFRIED, *Prosperity and Depression* (Geneva: League of Nations, 1941).

JOHNSON, HARRY, "Inside Money, Outside Money, Income, Wealth, and Welfare in Monetary Theory," *Journal of Money, Credit and Banking,* Vol. 1, No. 1 (Feb. 1969), and "Comment" (same journal), Vol. 1, No. 3 (August 1969).

KALECKI, MICHAEL, "Professor Pigou on the 'Classical Stationary State': A Comment," *Economic Journal,* Vol. 54 (1944).

LLOYD, CLIFF, "The Real Balance Effect, *Sine Qua* What?" *Oxford Economic Papers,* Vol. 14 (Oct. 1962).

MARTY, ALVIN, "The Real Balance Effect: An Exercise in Capital Theory," *Canadian Journal of Economics and Political Science*, Vol. 30 (Aug. 1964).

NEWLYN, W. T., "Definitions and Classifications," *Theory of Money* (Oxford: The Clarendon Press, 1962). See Chapter 1, pp. 1–11.

PATINKIN, DON, "Price Flexibility and Full Employment," *American Economic Review*, Vol. 38 (Sept. 1948).

————, *Money, Interest, and Prices*, 2nd ed. (New York: Harper & Row, 1965).

————, "Money and Wealth: A Review Article," *The Journal of Economic Literature*, Vol. 8, No. 4 (Dec. 1969).

PESEK, BORIS, AND SAVING, THOMAS, *Money, Wealth and Economic Theory* (New York: Macmillan, 1967).

PIGOU, A. C., "The Classical Stationary State," *Economic Journal*, Vol. 53 (1943).

SCITOVSKY, TIBOR, "Capital Accumulation, Employment and Price Rigidity," *Review of Economic Studies*, Vol. 8 (1940–41).

TOBIN, JAMES, "Asset Holdings and Spending Decisions," *American Economic Review*, Vol. 42 (May 1952).

YEAGER, LELAND B., "Essential Properties of the Medium of Exchange," *Kyklos*, Vol. 21, Fasc I (1968).

chapter 7

An Analysis
of Problems in
a Keynesian Framework

In order to explain the operation of the classical model, Chapter 2 was devoted to an analysis of problems within that model's framework. This chapter is designed as a parallel exposition of similar problems within the Keynesian frame of reference. As such, it will enable a direct comparison to be made between the two models as well as afford a deeper understanding of the Keynesian approach. However, the analysis contained in this chapter will be more complex than that in Chapter 2, for two reasons.

First, there appears to be some confusion among economists as to exactly how the Keynesian model functions. Professor Friedman, in his 1968 presidential address before the American Economic Association, discussed the influence of money on economic activity.[1] He described its influence as distributed among three different effects, whose impact is felt sequentially. The first and most immediate consequence of an expansion in the money stock is designated by Friedman as the *liquidity effect* and represents, in terms of the model developed in Chapter 5, a movement of the money supply schedule down the speculative demand-for-money schedule. As such, the liquidity effect is felt only on interest

---

[1] M. Friedman, "The Role of Monetary Policy," *The American Economic Review*, Vol. 58, No. 1 (March 1968), pp. 1–17.

rates because the level of income is held constant.

In response to the lower interest rate, various categories of expenditures expand, driving up aggregate demand and increasing income. The increase in income requires a larger quantity of money, thereby feeding back on the interest rates and causing them to rise somewhat. This feedback Friedman calls the *income effect*. A third consequence, operating in the longer run, completely reverses the initial liquidity influence and actually serves to increase interest rates above those prevailing before the expansion of the money stock. This longer-run rise in interest rates is due to expectations of continuing inflation set in motion by some price increases associated with the income effect. In the tradition of Irving Fisher, Friedman calls this last influence the *price expectation effect*. While Friedman's theoretical framework will be examined in greater depth in Chapters 9, 11, and 12, his claim that the Keynesians only recognize the liquidity effect is manifestly incorrect and is one reason why the analysis in this chapter must be more detailed.

A second reason for a more extensive analysis is that the responses occurring in the Keynesian model to a change in some variable depend critically on the state of unemployment in the economy when the variable changes. Therefore the state of unemployment must be specified before a change in any variable can be analyzed. In this regard, it is important to note again Keynes' statement that when full employment is achieved, the classical forces come in to their own. The analysis to follow ought to indicate exactly what Keynes meant by that expression.

As in Chapter 2, an Appendix to this chapter analyzes each problem in the *IS–LM* framework.

AN INCREASE IN THE SUPPLY OF MONEY

When this problem was analyzed according to the classical model, utilizing Thornton's indirect mechanism, it resulted in lower money interest rates in the short run and produced proportionate changes in the general level of commodity prices in the longer run.

To analyze the impact of an increase in the money supply in the Keynesian model, three employment situations will be specified: (A) deep unemployment, (B) full employment, and (C) moderate unemployment.

The Keynesian World with Deep Unemployment

initial effect

The expansion of the residual money supply in Figure 7:1 from *MS* to *MS'* will have no effect whatever on the rate of interest, for individuals will stand ready to surrender unlimited quantities of bonds for money at the price indicated by market interest rate i_0.

As the interest rate remains unchanged, the increase in the money supply will have no effect on the nonmonetary, or real, sector, for it is the market rate of interest which transmits the influence of changes in the money supply to the real sector.

In this case, the minimum money rate of interest, i_0, is above the full-employment real rate (which lies below r_0), or that real rate at which full-employment saving, S, is equal to investment, I. This is merely a special case of the possibility of full-employment saving being greater than investment at a zero real interest rate. Here the floor on the money rate prevents that real rate from prevailing which would ensure full-employment saving being equal to investment (if such a real rate is a possibility).

Since Keynes neglected the Pigou Effect, the unemployment equi-

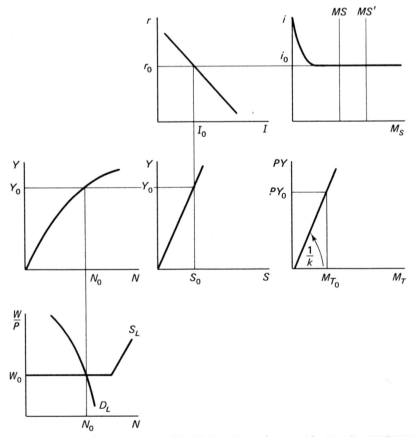

FIGURE 7:1. The Keynesian World with Deep Unemployment (the Liquidity Trap)

librium shown is made implicitly to depend upon downward rigidities in wages and prices.

The Keynesian World with Full Employment

In this situation the classical forces come in to their own; that is, changes in the stock of money will produce only proportionate changes in the general level of commodity prices, and the equilibrium level of interest rates will depend on saving and investment. In more general terms, money will be neutral.

In Chapter 5 we noted that by *full employment* the Keynesians mean that everyone seeking a job at the going money wage finds one. From historical analysis of the post–World War II period, the Keynesians generally conclude that when the unemployment rate is between 3 percent and 4 percent, full employment prevails.

initial effects

The expansion in the residual supply of money (in Figure 7:2) from MS to MS' will lower the money rate of interest below the full-employment real rate r_{FE}. This is what Friedman calls the *liquidity effect*. In response to this reduction in the real rate, marginal increments of investment unprofitable at r_{FE} now become profitable, causing businessmen to attempt to expand the rate of investment.

Aggregate money demand will rise, stimulating the desire of entrepreneurs to expand production in response to the increase in demand. To do this they must attract additional labor, so money wages in the aggregate will rise.

secondary effects

The increase in money wages will increase per-unit labor costs, and since prices depend on labor costs, they will rise in proportion to the increase in wages, for the productivity of labor at full employment is unchanged. Since prices have risen in proportion to wages, the real wage is constant as is the volume of employment.

The rise in the general level of prices will increase the value of nominal income, PY, which will increase the quantity of money required for transactions. This is the feedback of income on money, called by Friedman, the *income effect*. Since more money is required for transactions, a smaller quantity is available for speculation, putting upward pressure on interest rates and tending thereby to reverse the initial effect; in other words, the rise in the price level reduces the real value of cash balances.

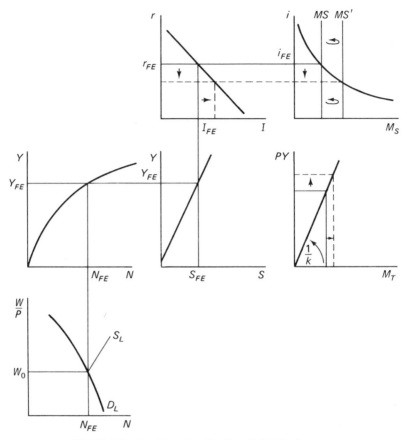

FIGURE 7:2. The Keynesian World with Full Employment

How long must commodity prices and the money rate of interest rise? Until the rate of interest returns to i_{FE}, where full-employment investment is again equal to full-employment saving. In this equilibrium situation, the real money supply will again be equal to what it was before nominal balances were increased, an indication that money is neutral.

ultimate effects

Given the position of the savings function, real output cannot expand. Thus, the general level of commodity prices will have increased in proportion to the increase in the supply of money, and since the real wage remains unchanged, money wages will have increased in proportion to the change in the nominal stock of money. Unlike in the classical model, however, the chain of events went from money to money wages to commodity prices rather than from money to commodity prices to money wages. In the end, the changes in $M\overline{S}$, P and W are the same regardless of what model is used. The classical forces explaining the price level are valid. In addition, monetary expansion was unable to change the equilibrium rate of interest, r_{FE}. That could be changed only by altering either the position of the savings or investment schedules. Hence, the equilibrium rate of interest is determined by nonmonetary forces at full employment.

Several other aspects of this problem should be noted. First, the Keynesian model embodies both a liquidity and an income effect, contrary to Friedman's assertion. But it says nothing about the effect (if any) of the change in commodity prices on expectations of future price changes. Thus it avoids the supposed divergence between money and real rates caused by expectations of inflation which were at the center of Fisher's discussion of the short run.

Second, in a problem in which an autonomous increase in the stock of money is posited, the result is identical to the discredited analysis of Henry Thornton; that is, low interest rates and rising or high commodity prices go together, contrary to the results of Tooke and Gibson. The Keynesian response to this allegation is that this is not how the money stock is increased. It rises to accommodate the "needs of business," so one must first assume a rise in investor expectations and an accommodating increase in the supply of money to finance their projects.

The Keynesian World with Moderate Unemployment

This problem might be called a typical Keynesian situation, in which the unemployment rate is above 4 percent but below a depression rate and in which discretionary monetary policy is called upon to increase the volume of employment.

initial effects

The initial increase in the residual stock of money (in Figure 7:3) from MS to MS' will lower the money rate of interest, constituting the liquidity effect. As the quantity of investment expands, it will, via the multiplier (the reciprocal of the slope of the saving schedule), expand real output. Real output will continue to increase until it generates a volume of additional saving equal to the new investment. At that point, saving is again equal to investment, and equilibrium will prevail in the commodity market.

This discussion of the effect of money on the level of real output quite clearly shows the crucial role of the multiplier in Keynesian analysis. This is now the variable which ultimately links money to economic activity.

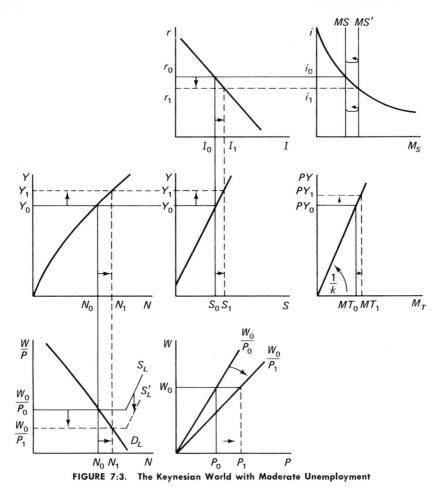

FIGURE 7:3.   The Keynesian World with Moderate Unemployment

secondary effects

The rise in real output will bring diminishing returns to labor, raising per-unit labor costs and the price level. The degree to which this occurs will depend on how rapidly returns to labor diminish. To the extent that prices rise, the real wage will fall, and the supply schedule of labor, drawn for a given money wage, W_0, will shift downward from S_L to S'_L, for the same labor time is now being provided at the lower real wage.

The rise in both real output, Y, and the price level, P, will increase nominal income, PY, causing money balances to be diverted to transactions needs. This will raise interest rates, thereby setting in motion a partial reversal of the initial expansion; this, of course, is the essence of Friedman's income effect.

ultimate effects

The ultimate effects will be lower money and real rates of interest, a lower real wage, a higher price level, and a larger volume of real output and employment. Here monetary expansion causes permanent changes in real variables, demonstrating that so long as unemployment equilibrium prevails, money can be nonneutral.

The expansion of the money supply causes some rise in the price level, but the rise in prices depends on the diminishing returns to labor, which govern the rise in per-unit labor costs and are not proportional to changes in the money stock. If labor time did not suffer from diminishing returns, per-unit labor costs would remain constant and the price level would not change.

This problem permits the basic determinants of the effectiveness of monetary policy in the Keynesian framework to be highlighted.

First, such effectiveness depends upon the inelasticity of the speculative demand schedule. The more inelastic the schedule, the greater the decline in the money rate of interest for a given expansion of the money supply. Second, the more elastic the investment demand schedule, the larger the response of investment for a given change in the interest rate. Third, the less elastic the saving schedule, the larger the value of the multiplier, hence the greater the increase in real output for a given change in investment. Fourth, the more elastic the demand for labor, the larger the increase in employment for a given change in the real wage. Lastly, the smaller the value of k, the smaller the reversal effect for a given change in money income. It is upon the value of these variables that any discussion of the importance of money in the Keynesian system must center.

WAGE AND PRICE RIGIDITIES

In a Keynesian model with full employment, the imposition of wage and price controls to halt an inflation caused by the overissue of money will yield a result identical to that of the classical model. It will artificially raise the value of k, leading to the holding of larger transactions balances for each level of nominal income. As soon as the controls are removed, k will return to its normal magnitude and the price level will rise; therefore the imposition of controls will not be examined in depth.

However, in this section we will examine whether a cut in money wages to reduce unemployment will be effective, as the classical writers had long supposed.

A Cut in Money Wages to Reduce Unemployment

In the classical world, a cut in money wages was regarded as an effective policy tool for reducing unemployment, considered to be symptomatic of too high a money wage. An analysis of this problem will also allow us to measure the potency of the Keynes Effect discussed in Chapter 6.

In analyzing the effects of this policy tool, Keynes assumed that a cut in money wages would not alter business expectations, would not cause labor unrest, would not alter the distribution of income, and would not alter the relative prices of exports and imports.

initial effects

Since commodity prices are linked to per-unit labor costs, a cut in money wages will reduce commodity prices proportionately leaving the real wage unchanged. Hence, the supply schedule of labor remains in its initial position, even though money wages are now lower than before the cut.

However, the reduction in prices, which follows from the reduction in money wages, will reduce the value of nominal income (in Figure 7:4) from PY_0 to PY_1, reducing the quantity of money required to make transactions from M_{T_0} to M_{T_1}. A larger quantity of money is now available for use as speculative balances shifting out the residual supply from MS to MS' (the total money supply $\overline{MS}$ has not changed), and reducing the rate of interest from i_0 to i_1, unless the economy is in the liquidity trap.

Alternatively, the above analysis could have been so framed that the reduction in the price level left the level of real income and money demand constant, but increased the real supply of money. Since the real supply has increased, the population would not be content to hold the increased balances at the prevailing interest rate. Thus, since actual balances exceed desired balances at the prevailing interest rate and level of real income, spending is stimulated, which expands the level of real income. The expansion of real income will continue until actual real balances are again equal to their desired level. In addition, if market interest rates change, they can serve as an alternative force restoring equilibrium.

secondary effects

If the economy is not in the liquidity trap and if the investment demand schedule has some elasticity, the economy will expand in response to this stimulus, just as though the money supply had been increased.

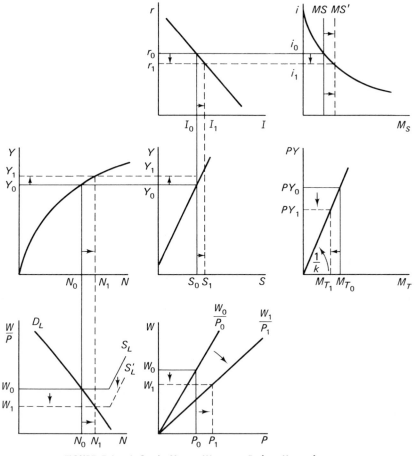

FIGURE 7:4. A Cut in Money Wages to Reduce Unemployment

Whether or not labor suffers from diminishing returns, real output and employment will expand. If labor does suffer from diminishing returns, the expansion in real output will cause per-unit labor costs to rise, pushing up the price level. This will drive down the real wage and shift S_L downward to S'_L in Figure 7:4.

This process, whereby a cut in money wages leads to a reduction in the rate of interest, is the Keynes Effect, and was admitted by Keynes as a qualification to his conclusion that a cut in money wages would not disturb his unemployment equilibrium. Moreover, since the cut in money wages has the same impact on the interest rate and on the economy as an expansion in the supply of money, Keynes argued for the latter, for surely a flexible monetary policy would be regarded by all as superior to a flexible wage policy.

ultimate effects

If the reduction in money wage were successful, money wages, commodity prices, and interest rates would all be lower; the real wage might be lower, while the volume of real output and employment would be higher. If a liquidity trap situation prevailed, the wage cuts would be useless, neglecting, of course, the Pigou Effect.

AN INCREASE IN THE SUPPLY OF LABOR

An increase in the supply of labor will have no discernible effect on the Keynesian model to the extent that it has no effect on the going money wage. As seen in the labor market, an increase in the supply of labor merely extends the supply schedule rightward, as in Figure 7:5, increasing the amount of labor time now offered at the prevailing money wage.

If, however, the increased supply of labor goes unemployed, it might have an effect on the historically and institutionally determined money wage, W_0.

AN INCREASE IN THE DEMAND FOR LABOR

As with the classical model, the demand schedule for labor can increase only if capital stock accumulates relative to labor time or if technological innovations raise the marginal productivity of labor.

In this problem, both the volume of employment and the real wage are likely to rise, demonstrating the frequently observed phenomenon of a rising standard of living over time, which most developed economies have experienced. It also shows that all increases in employ-

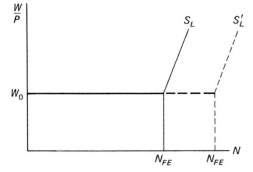

FIGURE 7:5. An Increase in the Supply of Labor

ment need not be associated with a decline in the real wage. The situation analyzed in this example can also affect the investment demand schedule, but any shift induced by capital accumulation or technology will be neglected.

initial effects

The change in technology or the increase in capital per unit of labor time will shift up the total product schedule from Y to Y' and shift out the marginal product or demand schedule for labor from D_L to D'_L. This, in itself, will not change the real wage unless it cuts the supply-of-labor schedule in its rising portion.

However, the increase in the marginal product of labor will, given a constant money wage, reduce per-unit labor costs and the price level. The decline in the price level, given the money wage, will cause real wages to rise from W_0/P_0 to W_0/P_1, shifting up the supply schedule of labor from S_L to S'_L.

secondary effects

The decline in the price level must exceed the rise in real income for, in terms of Figure 7:6, the interest rate must decline to r_1 to make the level of investment again equal to the higher level of saving generated by the rise in real income, Y. The necessary decline in the interest rate will occur because the decline in the value of nominal income, PY, will enable money balances used previously for transactions to be made available for holding for speculative purposes. This will drive down market interest rates from i_0 to i_1.

ultimate effects

When equilibrium is again restored, real output, employment, and the real wage will have risen; money wages will be unchanged; and commodity prices and interest rates ought to be lower.

As did its classical counterpart, this problem raises the possibility of alternative monetary policies. As the problem was originally presented, the nominal money supply was held constant and real balances were expanded by having the price level decline.

A possible alternative is to allow money wages to rise by as much as labor productivity increases. This would serve to maintain a constant price level and nominal income would then rise by the amount of the expansion in real income. The money supply would then have to be increased by some fraction of the rise in nominal income to accommodate the larger balances required for transactions plus a sum sufficient to drive down market interest rates to i_1. Perhaps an increase in the nominal

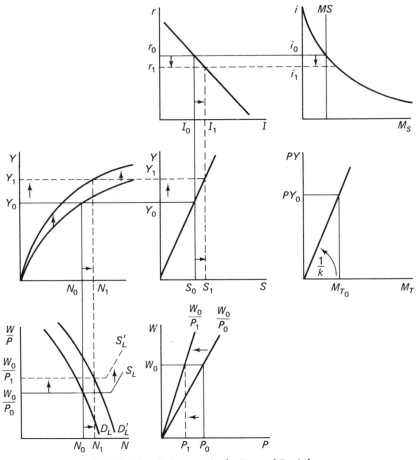

FIGURE 7:6.   An Increase in the Demand For Labor

money supply paralleling the rise in labor productivity or the rise in real output would be sufficient.

A RISE IN THE LEVEL OF THRIFT

Nothing prevents the Keynesian man from suddenly placing a higher value on future consumption and a correspondingly lower value on current consumption, thus raising the level of thrift.

initial effects

The rise in the level of thrift is shown in Figure 7:7 as an outward shift in the saving schedule, for at each level of real income a larger volume

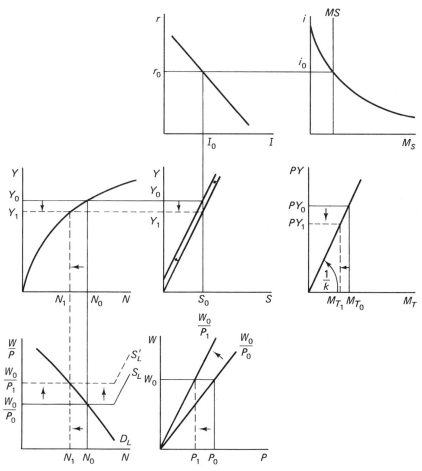

FIGURE 7:7. A Rise in the Level of Thrift

of resources is now available for nonconsumption uses (whether both the *MPS* and *APS* change will not be of concern).

The increase in thrift reveals that a new lower real income level is consistent with the interest rate, r_0, in preserving equilibrium between saving and investment. As such, the economy starts to deflate, with real income declining from Y_0 toward Y_1.

secondary effects

The contraction of real income has the effect of raising the marginal product of labor, and given the money wage, of raising the real wage of labor by reducing per-unit labor costs and the price level. Thus, the labor supply schedule starts shifting upward from S_L toward S'_L, producing unemployment as it moves upward.

The decline in the price level, P, and the level of real output, Y, reduces nominal income from PY_0 to PY_1, and the amount of money balances necessary to carry on transactions from M_{T_0} to M_{T_1}. Thus, balances are set free for speculative holding, forcing down nominal interest rates. This sets in motion a partial reversal effect, for it stimulates the economy. The degree of stimulation will depend upon the elasticity of both the speculative demand schedule and that for investment demand.

If the liquidity trap prevails, no reversal effect is forthcoming, and the full effects of deflation will be felt.

ultimate effects

In the final equilibrium, the level of real output, employment, and nominal income will be lower, the real wage will be higher, and if no liquidity trap is present, both nominal and real interest rates will be lower. This example serves to demonstrate that in the Keynesian model the interest rate is not a purely monetary affair, for a rise in thrift can succeed in lowering the rate. However, contrary to the classical model, the level of output and of employment declined.

A RISE IN MONEY HOARDING

In the Keynesian model, a rise in hoarding is merely another name for a rise in the desire to hold speculative balances; that is, at every current market interest rate the society desires to hold larger balances for speculative purposes.

initial effects

The speculative demand schedule will shift to the right (in Figure 7:8), raising the money rate of interest unless the economy is in the liquidity trap. If it is, nothing will happen.

The rise in the money rate will also raise the real rate by an equal amount, decreasing the quantity of investment and setting in motion a negative multiplier effect upon real income and the volume of employment.

secondary effects

The decline in income will reduce the quantity of labor demanded and raise the marginal product of labor, which (given money wages) will reduce per-unit labor costs and the price level. The real wage will rise and the labor supply schedule shift upward. The combined fall in output and

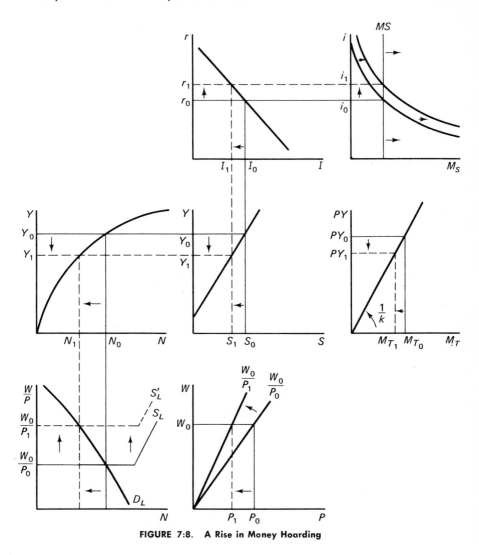

FIGURE 7:8.   A Rise in Money Hoarding

prices will reduce nominal income, PY, reducing the quantity of balances required for transactions and increasing those available for speculation. The subsequent fall in the interest rate will set in motion a reversal process to counter the initial decline.

ultimate effects

In the new equilibrium, the level of real income and volume of employment will be lower, the real wage will be higher, and since both the price level and real income are lower, nominal income, PY, will be lower.

Lastly, both the nominal interest rate and the real interest rate will be higher.

So long as the economy is not in a liquidity trap situation, correct central bank policy would be to permit a sufficient increase in the supply of money so that interest rates do not rise—a policy prescription identical to that given for the classical model.

FISCAL POLICY IN A KEYNESIAN WORLD

An analysis of fiscal policy in a Keynesian framework has two objectives. First, it will permit the Keynes–Wicksell explanation for Gibson's Paradox to be presented within a Keynesian model, and second the "crowding-out" effect of government expenditures can be examined. Except in the case of full employment, and provided that either money demand or supply is at all responsive to the interest rate, the crowd-out will not be complete, thereby providing a rationalization for compensatory or stabilizing fiscal policy.

Before analyzing its effects, *fiscal policy* must be defined, for as Chapter 12 will reveal, a common definition is not to be found among economists. For purposes of our discussion, fiscal policy is any action which alters the rate of government expenditures or taxation while the money supply remains unchanged.

To explain the crowding-out effect, only two states of employment will be used: (A) some unemployment and (B) full employment.

A. Some Unemployment

initial effects

A rise in government expenditures is shown in Figure 7:9 by an outward shift of the investment demand schedule from I to I', where the difference between the two schedules represents government expenditures not covered by tax receipts.

The rise in government outlays will set in motion the familiar multiplier process, stimulating a rise in real output and (to the extent that labor suffers diminishing returns) a rise in the level of commodity prices. The degree to which prices rise is usually believed related to the extent of the unemployment prevailing when the stimulus occurs. The closer the economy is to full employment, the greater should be the degree of price-level change for any given increase in government expenditures.

Any rise in the price level will reduce the real wage, shifting downward the supply schedule of labor.

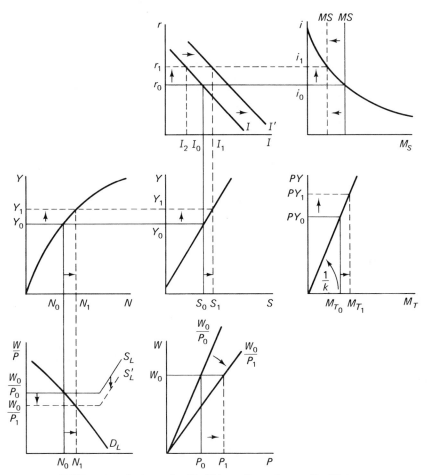

FIGURE 7:9. The Keynesian World in an Unemployment Equilibrium

secondary effects

Since output and perhaps commodity prices will have risen, the value of nominal income, PY, will also have risen, thereby increasing the quantity of money required for transactions. A rising transactions demand will decrease the quantity of money available for speculation, putting upward pressure on the interest rate unless: (a) the rise in government expenditures is financed in a money-creating way, (b) compensatory increases in the supply of money can be induced, or (c) the economy is in a liquidity trap when the rise in expenditures takes place—in that case, money doesn't matter. However, if the money supply increases via routes (a) or (b), the pure effect of fiscal policy may be difficult to measure, for now both government expenditures and increases in the money supply are working to expand income and only the first act comes within the definition of fiscal policy given above.

ultimate effects

Given that the money supply was held constant, the ultimate effect would be for the interest rate to be higher (above i_0), the level of output and employment larger, the real wage lower (although depending on the initial state of unemployment it may be unchanged), and the level of nominal income, PY, higher.

It is the rise in the nominal interest rate which causes the fiscal crowd-out, or the displacement of private investment outlays by government expenditures. This phenomenon is shown in Figure 7:10. Let MS, I, i_0, and r_0 represent initial positions. After I shifts to I', the multiplier effect will raise nominal income, requiring larger transactions balances and forcing the residual money supply to contract from MS to MS' and the interest rate to rise from i_0 to i_1. As the money rate rises, some investment projects previously profitable at real rate r_0, OI_2, are no longer worth undertaking. To measure the crowd-out, the original equilibrium position on I, OI_0, must be compared with the point on the same schedule given by the change in the interest rate from r_0 to r_1, or OI_3. Thus, the rise in government spending has displaced some previously profitable projects. In terms of Figure 7:10, the fiscal crowd-out is equal to I_0I_3. The closer to full employment, the more complete will be the crowd-out. Obviously, if a liquidity trap situation prevails, there will be no crowd-out.

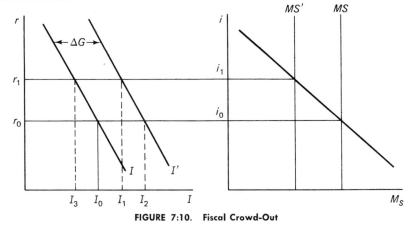

FIGURE 7:10. Fiscal Crowd-Out

This analysis of crowd-out suffers from one serious flaw. Some of the rise in nominal income which caused the nominal interest rate to rise was due to an increase in the price level; however, this rise in the price level is disregarded in the analysis. All changes in nominal variables are taken to be equivalent changes in real variables.

Full Employment

In a full-employment setting, the fiscal crowd-out will be complete. In addition, in this problem, as in the previous example, the Keynes–Wicksell explanation for the findings of Gibson can be developed.

initial effects

As in the preceding example, the rise in government expenditures shifts the investment schedule from I to I' in Figure 7:11. In response to the rise in investment, businessmen try to hire more labor; however, as full employment prevails, they must raise the money wage to attract additional employees. The rise in money wages produces a proportional rise in the price level. Thus, the position of the labor supply schedule remains unchanged.

secondary effects

The rise in the price level will cause nominal income, PY, to rise, diverting money balances to transactions needs, thereby forcing up the nominal rate of interest. If the money supply is increased for any reason, the degree of inflation will be intensified, for it will take a large rise in prices to force up the money rate from i_0 to i_1. Once the money rate has increased to i_1, the necessary expansion of the price level should cease unless government expenditures continue to rise, for at money rate i_1, the corresponding real rate, r_1, ensures that investment and saving are equal, and the economy is back in equilibrium.

As shown in this analysis, the crowd-out is complete, for each dollar of government expenditures has displaced an equal dollar of private expenditures.

ultimate effects

Ultimately, when the new equilibrium prevails, money wages and commodity prices will have risen in proportion, leaving the real wage, the level of employment, and the volume of output unchanged. Nominal income will be higher, and real money balances will be smaller.

A Keynesian Resolution of Gibson's Paradox

If the data generated by the movement from the initial to the ultimate equilibrium were plotted, they would show that as the price level rose so did the interest rate, and that high prices were therefore positively correlated with high interest rates. Consistent with the analysis above, there are several ways in which this Gibson's Paradox might have come

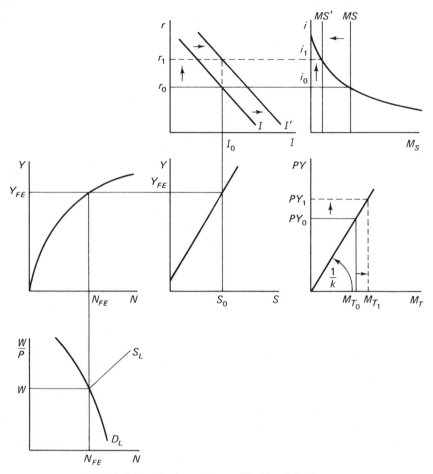

FIGURE 7:11. The Keynesian World with Full Employment

about. First, either the social rate of return rose (causing government expenditures to rise) or the natural rate rose (a shift of I to I' could be accounted for on those grounds). Either act, by expanding aggregate demand, would put pressure on market interest rates, causing the velocity of money to rise. Second, if the rise in government or private investment expenditures is financed in money-creating ways, a greater force is brought to bear forcing up the price level and (more slowly than in the first case) the nominal rate of interest.

It should be noted that Keynes rejected the Fisherian explanation that inflation would cause nominal interest rates to rise.[2] Recent work

---

[2] See *The General Theory*, pp. 141–44. Keynes argues that to the extent that inflationary expectations exert an expansionary influence on economic activity, they cannot raise the rate of interest as Fisher supposes. (Keynes says that this would be a paradoxical way of stimulating

by Shiller and Siegel[3] using spectral analysis also rejects the Fisherian explanation for the paradox. They argue that a variation of the above two considerations can explain, in part, the Gibson relationship. They theorize that during wartimes, the increased volume of government expenditures puts upward pressure on interest rates. The central bank or the government, reluctant to see these rates rise, attempts with less than complete success to prevent their rise by increasing the supply of money, thus producing both rising prices and interest rates. For the interwar years, they rely on an argument put forth by an early investigator of Gibson's paradox, Frederick Macaulay.[4] Macaulay assumed that unanticipated inflation caused wealth redistributions from lenders to borrowers as the burden of debt declined. Such transfers increased the desire of debtors to borrow and decreased the ability of lenders to lend, thereby putting upward pressure on interest rates and producing Gibson's Paradox for peacetime years.

COST-OF-LIVING INDICES IN LABOR CONTRACTS

In the initial discussion of the Keynesian labor market made in Chapter 5, it was noted that since the supply schedule of labor was made a function of money wages and not of real wages, workers appear to suffer from money illusion, or to take a considerable period of time to adjust to changes in the price level. In the analysis to follow, the assumption of money illusion will be dropped and we will assume that all labor contracts contain a cost-of-living clause giving to the money wage, W_0, a constant purchasing power.

It will be assumed that unemployment is present and that to reduce its magnitude the government undertakes an expansionary monetary policy. However, labor identifies the prevailing money wage, W_0, as equivalent to a particular real wage, W_0/P_0, which it desires to maintain.

output.) Rather, anticipations of inflation will shift outward the investment demand schedule. Since investment is now more profitable, it will lead to a bidding-up of the prices of the currently existing capital stock (or its equity equivalent) relative to the price of new production, encouraging thereby production of the latter which expands economic activity. It is not clear from Keynes' presentation if he and Fisher are using the same model or if they have the same time span in mind. In addition, in terms of the Keynesian model, for inflationary expectations to exert no influence on interest rates but at the same time expand real output, the money demand schedule must be in a liquidity trap. In the graphical presentation of Fisher's cycle in Chapter 3, it was shown that inflation can exert an expansionary influence on economic activity to the extent that lenders and borrowers do not equally anticipate inflation.

[3] Robert J. Shiller and Jeremy J. Siegel, "The Gibson Paradox and Historical Movements in Real Long-Term Interest Rates," Unpublished.

[4] Frederick R. Macaulay, *The Movement of Interest Rates, Bond Yields, and Stock Prices in the United States Since 1856* (National Bureau of Economic Research, 1938), Ch. VI, "Interest Rates and Commodity Prices."

initial effects

The expansion in the supply of money (in Figure 7:12) shifts the residual money supply from *MS* to *MS'*, driving down the money interest rate, increasing the quantity of investment, and (via the multiplier) expanding aggregate demand. If deep unemployment is present, it is likely that the additional employment of labor will not be subject to diminishing productivity. However, the closer the economy is to full employment, the more likely it is that labor productivity will diminish, raising per-unit labor costs and commodity prices. The initial decline in the real wage will lead to an increase in employment. However, as labor sees its real wage fall, it demands increases in the money wage to compensate for the rise in prices. When such increases are granted, the supply schedule of labor shifts back to its original position. But since money wages have risen, per-unit labor costs rise and the price level is pushed up again, depressing the real wage. Again labor demands compensatory money adjustment. This process can go on and on; however, it cannot continue indefinitely unless the money supply is continually increased.

secondary effects

Every rise in the price level increases the value of nominal income and the quantity of money required for transactions. This increase in transactions demand forces up the money rate of interest, decreasing investment and thereby depressing the original stimulus given the economy by the expansion in the supply of money.

ultimate effects

As this analysis shows, the widespread insertion of cost-of-living clauses in labor contracts will render monetary and fiscal policy fairly impotent as a stabilization device, except in those circumstances where changes in output do not bring diminishing returns to labor.

This analysis has additional relevance, however. It implies that whenever labor does not suffer from money illusion, monetary and fiscal policy can have only a relatively short-run effect on output and employment, thus robbing them of their effectiveness as stabilization tools. This point will be further discussed in Chapter 11, when various theories of inflation are investigated. It has additional relevance to the controversy between the Monetarists and the Keynesians investigated in Chapter 12.

CONCLUSION

The purposes of this chapter have been to pose and solve various problems within the Keynesian framework and to contrast the solution of

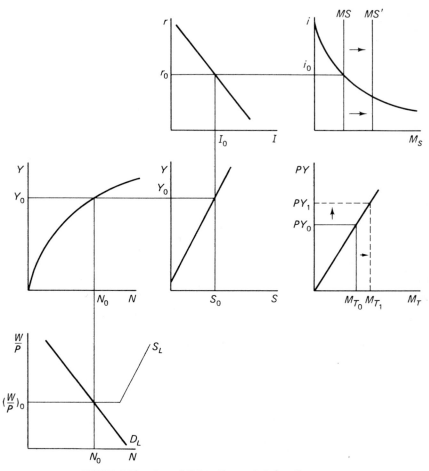

FIGURE 7:12.   Cost-of-Living Clauses in Labor Contracts

each of these problems with that given by the classical model. Both sets of analyses have had two problems associated with them. First, these problems were developed in a comparatively static framework; that is, two different equilibria are compared, one characterizing the initial state and the other the state after the postulated change has taken place. The shortcoming of that method is that the dynamic adjustment path is not developed nor is the length of time it takes to move from the initial to the ultimate state specified. Time can be of great importance, especially if some policy changes to counteract undesirable changes in other variables are contemplated.

Second, of potentially great importance, changes in critical nominal variables (for example, the interest rate) are treated as equivalent changes in real variables. Such an assumption has obvious limitations in societies where inflation is more or less endemic, and some economists believe that such an assumption for the United States has led to grave policy errors.

While a more extensive discussion of the relation between nominal and real variables will be given in Chapter 12, models which embody such a distinction are outside the scope of this introductory analysis.

APPENDIX 7:1

This Appendix is designed to supplement the preceding discussion by presenting the same problems within the *IS–LM* framework. As such, it parallels its counterpart in Chapter 2.[5]

An Increase in the Supply of Money

In Figure 7:13, graph *A* corresponds to the liquidity trap of deep depression, while graphs *B* and *C* refer to moderate unemployment and full employment respectively; full-employment income is defined as that level of real income where everyone willing to work at the going money wage finds employment.

In the liquidity trap case, an increase in the money supply does no good. It will not increase real income, for the position of the *LM* schedule remains unchanged.

In the moderate-employment case, graph *B*, an increase in the money supply will shift the *LM* schedule to the right, from LM_0/P to LM_1/P, raising the level of real income and lowering the interest rate. The degree of change in either variable depends on the slope of the *IS* schedule. The movement from *A* to *B* will correspond to the liquidity effect, that from *B* to *C*, the income effect. Any rise in the price level, by reducing the real value of money balances, will shift the *LM* schedule leftward, moving the ultimate equilibrium value of real income, *Y*, and the interest rate to a point left of *C*.

If the initial position is one of full employment, any change in nominal money supply will push the *LM* schedule temporarily to the right. The induced rise in the price level will then reduce the real value of money balances back to the level given by LM/P. In this case, a price expectation effect along the lines suggested by Friedman is a greater possibility than in the case in which unemployment exists. If such an

---

[5] The reader should beware of a slight difference between the analysis of the Appendix and that of the main body of Chapter 7. In the six-section diagram, the demand for and supply of money is measured in nominal terms and related to nominal income, *PY*. In the analysis of the Appendix, demand and supply are measured in real terms and related to real income.

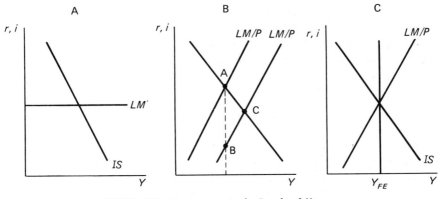

FIGURE 7:13. An Increase in the Supply of Money

effect is present, the analysis given in the preceding sentences is inadequate. In Chapter 12, Friedman's full presentation of the price expectation effect is given in terms of the *IS–LM* schedules.

A Cut in Money Wages

The reduction in money wages will, by reducing per-unit labor costs, reduce the price level in proportion. The fall in the price level will increase the real stock of money, shifting the *LM* schedule (in Figure 7:14)

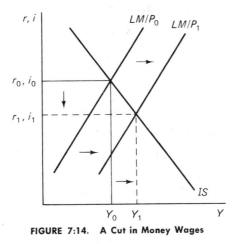

FIGURE 7:14. A Cut in Money Wages

from LM/P_0 to LM/P_1, causing the rate of interest to fall and the level of real income and employment to rise. This Keynes Effect could also have been produced by increasing the nominal supply of money with a given price level.

If we drop the assumption that bonds and real capital are perfect substitutes, the rise in real cash balances could cause the *IS* schedule to shift rightward as well, as new physical capital is purchased with the rise in real balances. In addition, a Pigou-type effect on consumption could also shift out the *IS* schedule.

A Rise in the Level of Thrift

Since at each real-income level individuals desire to save more and consume less, the saving schedule shifts upward, and (in Figure 7:15) the *IS* schedule moves downward from IS_0 to IS_1. The effect on the level of real income and on the rate of interest will depend on the slope of the *LM* schedule. If the liquidity trap prevails (LM_2), only the level of real income and employment will decline. If the classical *LM* schedule prevails (LM_0), the entire effect of a rise in thrift will be to reduce the interest rate. If a more normal *LM* schedule prevails (LM_1), both the interest rate and the level of real income will be affected.

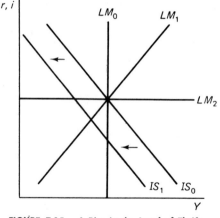

FIGURE 7:15.   A Rise in the Level of Thrift

This exposition permits us to make a generalized statement on the degree to which the interest rate is a monetary or a real phenomenon in the Keynesian model. So long as the liquidity trap prevails, the interest rate is a purely monetary affair. If the *LM* schedule is a perfectly vertical line and full employment prevails, the interest rate can only be influenced by changes in the real sector (variations in the productivity of capital and the level of thrift). If the *LM* schedule is upward-sloping and an unemployment equilibrium prevails, changes in either the monetary or the real sector will be capable of changing the equilibrium rate of interest. If full employment prevails, even though the *LM* schedule slopes upward only the real-sector variables of saving and investment can change the interest rate.

An Increase in the Supply of Labor

An increase in the supply of labor by itself has no effect on either the IS or LM schedule. Its only direct effect is to shift rightward the level of real income designated as full employment.

If it happens to result in a fall in the money wage level, the resulting analysis will parallel that presented above for a cut in money wages, as both are the same in the end.

An Increase in the Demand for Labor

As with the case in which the supply of labor changes, an increase in the demand for labor has no direct effect on either the LM or IS schedule. It serves to shift to the right the full-employment level of output or of income. As the rise in labor's marginal product serves to reduce per-unit labor costs and the price level, the value of the real money supply will rise, shifting the LM schedule to the right (in Figure 7:16) from LM/P_0 to LM/P_1, thereby reducing the level of interest rates and raising the level of real income and employment. Since money wages were held constant, the fall in the price level indicates that the real wage and the standard of living rose.

If it is desired to keep the price level constant and allow money wages to rise as productivity rises, the supply of money will have to be

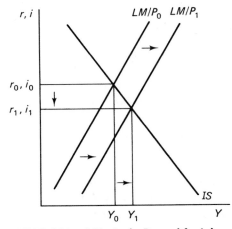

FIGURE 7:16.   A Rise in the Demand for Labor

increased. In that case, the *LM* schedule will still shift out, for the value of real balances will have risen.

A Rise in Hoarding

By desiring to hold larger money balances at each interest rate, the total demand for money rises, shifting the *LM* schedule (in Figure 7:17) to the left from LM_0/P to LM_1/P, raising the interest rate, and decreasing the level of real income and employment.

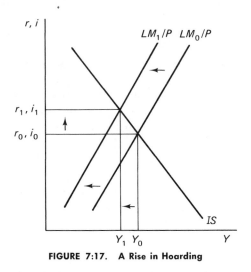

FIGURE 7:17.   A Rise in Hoarding

If the central bank expands the supply of money to accommodate the increased demand for hoarded balances, the *LM* schedule need not shift inward.

Fiscal Policy

The examination of fiscal policy in the *IS–LM* context is designed to show the degree to which government expenditures displace, or crowd out, private expenditures.

The rise in government outlays will shift the *IS* schedule from IS_0 to IS_1 in Figure 7:18. To measure the crowd-out, the original equilibrium position on IS_0 must be compared with the point on that same schedule given by the change in the interest rate, if one occurs.

If the LM schedule is perfectly horizontal (LM_2), no crowd-out occurs. However, the more vertical the *LM* schedule becomes, the larger

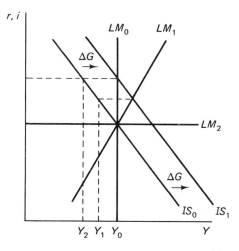

FIGURE 7:18.   A Rise in Government Expenditures

the degree of displacement from a purely fiscal act. With LM_1, the displacement is $Y_0 - Y_1$, whereas with LM_0, the displacement is complete, that is, government expenditures crowd out private expenditures dollar for dollar and are measured by the distance $Y_0 - Y_2$, equal to ΔG.

Cost-of-Living Index

The purpose of cost-of-living clauses in labor contracts is to maintain the purchasing power of money wages. Their effect may be to weaken substantially the ability of compensatory monetary and fiscal policy to reduce unemployment. To see this, we assume that unemployment exists and that the money supply is expanded to increase real output and employment. In Figure 7:19, the LM schedule shifts rightward from LM_0/P to LM_1/P.

To the extent that it is necessary to reduce the real wage through price increases to achieve the expansion of income and employment, the objective is self-defeating. For the rise in prices will cause a rise in money wages, necessitating a rise in prices, begetting another rise in wages, and so on. Each rise in the price level will reduce the real value of the money supply, shifting the LM schedule leftward. As unemployment grows, the ability of labor to demand compensatory salary increases may be diminished. Moreover, every wage increase need not raise prices in proportion, as labor productivity does not remain constant and the demand schedule for each product is not vertical.

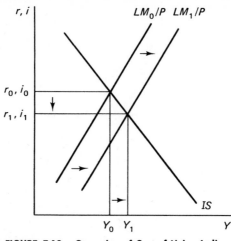

FIGURE 7:19.   Operation of Cost-of-Living Indices

Nevertheless, the universal inclusion of cost-of-living clauses in labor contracts does weaken the potency of discretionary fiscal and monetary policy.

chapter 8

Keynesian Monetary Theory: Extensions, Criticisms, and Reinterpretations

In developing the monetary sector of the Keynesian model, several questions have arisen either implicitly or explicitly but have been left largely unanswered. Before concluding the presentation of Keynesian monetary theory, these loose ends ought to be dealt with in a satisfactory manner.

At various points in the preceding pages, it was suggested that money balances held to make transactions may not be linearly related to the level of income, but that certain scale economies might be present in the holding of those balances. Nevertheless, in the formal presentation of both the classical and Keynesian models, linearity was assumed. During the 1950's, two Keynesian-oriented economists applied optimum inventory analysis to cash-balance holding, yielding the result that strict linearity need not characterize the transactions demand for money. This analysis also had the additional desirable consequence of making consistent the theoretical treatment of the transactions and speculative demands for money.

In the critique of the liquidity preference theory of interest rates at the end of Chapter 5, the unrealistic composition of the portfolio of assets held by the individual was discussed: It would consist either of all bonds or all money, but not a combination of both. A successful attempt has been made to construct a model of portfolio behavior in which a rational individual will hold both assets and in which the shape of the speculative demand schedule is retained.

Among the several implicit questions raised, two are especially noteworthy and are analyzed in the pages to follow. First, what difference, if any, exists between the monetary theory of Keynes and that of his Cambridge associates? That is, does *The General Theory* represent merely a restatement of the Cambridge approach to which Keynes' earlier work was a contribution, or does it embody something fundamentally different? Second, what are the implications, if any, of the Keynesian innovation of the speculative demand for money for the quantity theory and the quantity theorist?

Finally, the presentation of Keynesian monetary theory found in this text, as well as in others, is influenced strongly by the interpretation of *The General Theory* made by Sir John Hicks and Alvin Hansen, often called the Hicks–Hansen *IS–LM* approach. Recently, this interpretation has been questioned by several economists, notably Axel Leijonhufvud.[1] This chapter will conclude with a summary of his work.

EXTENSIONS OF KEYNESIAN MONETARY THEORY

Capital Theory Applied to the Transactions Demand

As presented by Keynes, the aggregate demand for money rested upon two primary determinants: A transactions motive and a speculative, or asset, motive. This combination of motives represented an unfortunate and inconsistent union of two quite different approaches to monetary theory.

The transactions demand was made to depend upon the technical and institutional customs and practices in a community which governs its receipt of income and subsequent flow of expenditures. For convenience, it was assumed that these customs and practices would change gradually over time so that the relationship of money holding to income could be assumed to be constant and linear. Thus, Keynes assimilated into his monetary theory the classical tradition normally associated with the work of Irving Fisher.

On the other hand, in developing the speculative, or asset, demand for money, Keynes used the portfolio, or capital theoretic, approach, which is built upon an analysis of utility, budget constraints, and opportunity costs. Combining as he did these two quite different approaches

[1] Axel Leijonhufvud, *On Keynesian Economics and the Economics of Keynes* (New York: Oxford University Press, 1968).

to monetary theory under the general label of liquidity preference created an unsettled state of affairs for many monetary economists who preferred a more uniform application of methodology to the demand for money. In the post–*General Theory* period, several attempts have been made to correct this inconsistency. First, there has been a tendency to blur the sharp distinction between motives for holding money balances, emphasizing instead that money is held for many purposes and that the amount held in this common fund is sensitive to various economic variables—income, interest rates, expectations of commodity price changes, and so forth. Second, two well-known economists, William Baumol and James Tobin,[2] in separate papers, applied the capital theoretic, or portfolio, analysis to the transactions demand, thereby making consistent the methodology applied to the total demand for money.

Drawing their inspiration from a problem common to the asset management of business—that of determining the optimum inventory of raw materials—they were able to draw some interesting conclusions, one of which was that monetary policy had the potential to be much more powerful than many Keynesians at that time were willing to concede.

Following the general outlines of the Baumol–Tobin approach, in applying capital theory to the transactions demand for money, money balances held to make expenditures are considered a sort of inventory and the goal of the individual is to minimize the costs associated with that inventory. When money is held to make expenditures, two costs are associated with its holding. The first involves the expenses necessary to convert other assets (in this case, bonds) to money. These expenses are both monetary—the fee necessary to sell bonds on an organized financial market—and nonmonetary—the physical exertion and inconvenience involved in making the conversion. Both expenses are called the *brokerage fee*. Second, each dollar held as money involves the loss of interest which the individual could have earned by holding his wealth in a bond form. In deciding how much money to hold over any given period, the goal is to minimize the sum of these costs. It is assumed that in order to compute his optimum inventory of money the individual has given uniform expenditures to make over a given time period, symbolized by Y.

At the beginning of the period over which the expenditures are to be made, the individual can make one conversion of bonds for money equal to the total of his planned expenditures, or he may make as many uniform conversions as he wishes over the expenditure period. Each conversion will involve a brokerage fee, as defined above, and the total brokerage fee will be equal to the number of conversions into money

[2] W. J. Baumol, "The Transactions Demand for Cash: An Inventory Theoretic Approach," *Quarterly Journal of Economics,* Vol. 66, No. 4 (Nov. 1952), pp. 545–56. James Tobin, "The Interest-Elasticity of Transactions Demand for Cash," *Review of Economics and Statistics,* Vol. 38, No. 3 (Aug. 1956), pp. 241–47.

times the brokerage fee, or $(Y/M)(b)$, where M denotes the amount of bonds converted to money and b is the brokerage fee per conversion.

Also, every time bonds are converted into money, the individual foregoes interest income and the total interest income foregone over the expenditure period is equal to the average money holding per *conversion* period or, $M/2$, multiplied by the interest rate applicable to the *expenditure* period, or i.[3]

The problem then posed to the individual is to minimize the sum of these two costs, symbolized by C, associated with his money holding over the expenditure period, or:

$$\text{Minimize } C = \frac{Y(b)}{M} + \frac{M(i)}{2} \qquad (8:1)$$

This can be done by differentiating C with respect to M, setting the result equal to zero and solving the equation, or:

$$\frac{dC}{dM} = \frac{-Y(b)}{M^2} + \frac{i}{2} = 0 \qquad (8:2)$$

$$\frac{Y(b)}{M^2} = \frac{i}{2} \qquad (8:3)$$

$$\frac{1}{M^2} = \frac{i}{2Y(b)} \qquad (8:4)$$

$$M^2 = \frac{2Y(b)}{i} \qquad (8:5)$$

$$M = \sqrt{\frac{2Y(b)}{i}} \qquad (8:6)$$

Since the average money holding of the individual per period is $\frac{2}{M}$, $(8:6)$ becomes

$$\frac{M}{2} = \frac{1}{2}\sqrt{\frac{2Y(b)}{i}} \qquad (8:7)$$

Therefore, the nominal money holdings for the cost-minimizing individual will vary directly with the square root of planned nominal ex-

---

[3] For example, if the expenditure period is one year and bonds are converted into money at the beginning of the year, average money holding is $(M/2)$ and the interest foregone is $(M/2)(i)$, where i is the annual rate of interest. If bonds are converted into money twice per year, the semiannual cost consists of the average money balances held per half-year, $(M/2)$, multiplied by the semiannual interest rate $(i/2)$ or $(M/2)(i/2)$. The annual cost is, therefore, $(M/2)(i/2) + (M/2)(i/2)$, or $(M/2)(i)$, or the average money holding per *conversion* period (half-year) multiplied by the annual rate of interest, or the rate prevailing over the *expenditure* period.

penditures and inversely with the square root of the market interest rate. The function can be made into one for real money balances, M/P, by making expenditures and the brokerage fee real magnitudes, that is, by dividing each nominal magnitude by a suitable price index, P.

Before the implications of the Baumol–Tobin construct are explored, several factors qualifying the analysis ought to be understood.

First, the brokerage fee has obvious importance. If its value were zero, no money would be held to make transactions and the wealth owner would merely synchronize bond sales with planned purchases. Second, the brokerage fee has been assumed to be constant regardless of the size of the conversion of bonds for money. This may be unrealistic to a degree, but the principal cost involved in the brokerage fee is supposedly the time and inconvenience involved in converting bonds into money. It is not the commission charged by the intermediary to dispose of the issue on the financial market. When viewed in this way, any lack of realism seems minimal.

Finally, omitted from the discussion has been any cost associated with the acquisition of the bonds. That is, at the beginning of the planned expenditure period, an individual could have received some portion of his income which was then used to add to his stock of bond holdings. The acquisition of these bonds obviously involves costs, both monetary and nonmonetary. The occurrence of such costs is usually handled by saying that their explicit consideration does not alter the ultimate conclusions of the analysis, so long as they do not vary directly with the amount of bonds purchased and are relatively small. Thus, they enter the analysis much as do the disposition or conversion costs.

The implications of the Baumol–Tobin model are several. First, the demand for real cash balances, M/P, will rise by less than the rise in real income (or real expenditures), implying both that substantial scale economies exist in holding money balances, and that in the terminology of micro theory, money is a necessity. One therefore ought to observe a secular rise in the velocity of money over time. Data produced by Friedman would tend to contradict this implication.[4] Second, in this model, the demand for real balances is invariant with respect to changes in the price level and therefore inflation can only affect the demand for money by altering the rate of interest. Third, the power of monetary policy is greatly enhanced. Suppose, for example, that the supply of money is increased, creating a disparity between actual and desired balances. This model implies that for a given interest rate nominal income must rise by the square of any increase in nominal balances before equilibrium can be restored. Fourth, no doubt should exist that the transactions demand has been formally recognized on a methodological level with the

---

[4] M. Friedman and A. J. Schwartz, *A Monetary History of the United States* (Princeton, N.J.: Princeton University Press, 1963), pp. 678–79.

speculative demand, for now the individual, in deciding whether to hold wealth in a money or a bond form for transactions purposes, must consider (among other variables) the market rate of interest. This permits the total demand for real money balances to be written in one general functional form as:

$$\frac{M}{P} = f\left(\frac{Y}{P}, i\right)$$ (8:8)

Extensions to the Money–Bond Model

In addition to a combination of two quite different approaches to monetary theory, liquidity preference was subject to two further limitations. First, the asset selection open to the wealth owner was limited to bonds and money. Physical capital, equities, commodities held as inventories, and so forth, were all made perfect substitutes for bonds. Thus the model had to explain only one yield—that on bonds. Second, the theory of liquidity preference imposed unrealistic behavior on the wealth holder. His portfolio consisted of either all bonds or all money, but not both assets. Experience shows that such behavior, if it exists at all, is clearly the exception. It also shows us that when wealth holders expect interest rates to rise, they generally shift from long-maturity securities to those with short maturities rather than to money. This type of behavior is also precluded in a model in which all securities except money are grouped together as though they were perfect substitutes.

Work by both Friedman[5] and Tobin[6] was designed to overcome the first objection by specifying the financial sector of a model which included a more extensive asset menu and which was part of a generalized portfolio, or capital theoretic, approach to money holding. While Friedman's work is taken up later in Chapter 9, the asset structure in Tobin's model includes government long, short, and demand debt, bank deposits, private debts, and capital stock. The yield on each would depend upon their relative supplies and would be linked, depending on their respective cross-elasticities of substitution, in portfolios. Monetary policy in Tobin's model would function by altering the relative supplies of government debt, thereby changing their yields. Portfolio shifts, set in motion by these initial yield changes, would generalize them to other assets.

[5] Milton Friedman, "The Quantity Theory of Money—A Restatement," in M. Friedman, ed., *Studies in the Quantity Theory of Money* (Chicago: University of Chicago Press, 1956), pp. 3–21.

[6] James Tobin, "Monetary Theory: New and Old Looks, Money, Capital, and Other Stores of Value," *American Economic Review*, Vol. 51, No. 2 (May 1961), pp. 26–37; and "An Essay on the Principles of Debt Management," *Fiscal and Debt Management Policies* (Englewood Cliffs, N.J.: Prentice-Hall, 1963), pp. 143–218.

Ultimately, real capital output would be stimulated and income would expand.

These expanded asset models of the type formulated by Tobin carry with them an interesting implication for the speculative demand for money. They transform the speculative motive for holding money as opposed to long-term bonds into a speculative motive for holding short-maturity securities rather than those of a longer maturity. In such a situation, the only reason for holding money comes principally to depend on the lack of synchronization between income and expenditures and to be explainable in terms of the Baumol–Tobin inventory model.

In the late 1950's, the fertile mind of James Tobin formulated a model in which the simultaneous desire to avert risk and to maximize the utility from wealth would lead an individual to choose a diversified portfolio consisting of both money and bonds.[7] The presentation of the Tobin model, given below, is based on simplifications introduced by David Laidler.[8]

As stated above, Tobin's demonstration of a diversified portfolio is based on the premise that an individual desires to maximize the utility from his wealth and seeks to avoid the risk associated with holding his wealth in various forms. Since the portfolio will consist only of bonds and money, the type of risk associated with bond holding involves alteration in their market value (capital gains or losses) due to uncertainty over the future rate of interest.[9] If the portfolio consists only of money, this risk is zero, for risk arises only if bonds are held. On the other hand, if the portfolio consists only of bonds, the risk is maximized. Portfolios consisting of both bonds and money involve intermediate levels of risk depending on the extent to which they approach either extreme.

However, despite the risk attached to bond holdings, such a portfolio has an advantage over a portfolio consisting of money—it yields an explicit income. This income is composed of two parts, an interest income known with certainty and capital gains or losses depending upon the movement in the interest rate. After Tobin, the expected value of the capital gain or loss will be assumed to be zero, which means that for

---

[7] James Tobin, "Liquidity Preference as Behavior Towards Risk," *Review of Economic Studies*, Vol. 25 (Feb. 1958), pp. 65–86. The principles stated in this analysis can also be applied to an expanded portfolio. However, in a world that includes equities and commodity inventories, movements in commodity prices may be important because they affect the yield on money. In the two-asset world of money and bonds, changes in the price level can be neglected for they affect money and bonds in the same way. Thus, money can be assumed to have a zero explicit yield.

[8] David E. W. Laidler, *The Demand for Money* (Scranton, Pa.: Intext, 1969), pp. 67–76.

[9] Uncertainty over the future rate of interest is one feature distinguishing this model from Keynes'. In the derivation of the speculative demand schedule, the assumption was made that each individual had a "normal" rate in mind to which the current rate was expected to move in the near future. In this model, the individual is uncertain about the future rate and views it in terms of a probability distribution of possible rates.

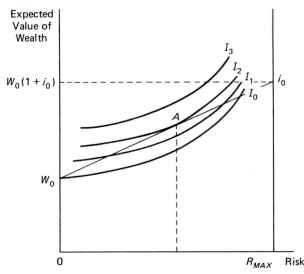

FIGURE 8:1. Portfolio Choice Under Uncertainty

the individual wealth owner there is equal probability that the present interest rate will double or fall by one-half, regardless of its present level. If this assumption is made, the expected yield from holding bonds will be equal to the market rate of interest.[10]

In order to determine the optimum combination of money and bonds for the individual, it will be necessary for him to express his subjective preferences between the utility from his expected wealth and his aversion to risk. In addition, it will be necessary to determine the tradeoff which exists in the market place between wealth and risk. Thus, the problem which must be solved is very similar to the constrained welfare maximization problem of consumer choice presented in micro textbooks.

Figure 8:1 represents the graphical construct in which the Tobin approach can be developed. Its horizontal axis measures the risk of capital gain or loss associated with uncertainty about the future rate of interest. As the portfolio becomes more heavily concentrated in bonds, the degree of risk increases, reaching a maximum when all assets have been converted to bonds. That maximum is denoted as R_{MAX}. The vertical axis measures the expected value of the portfolio. For the end of any given period, it may not be the actual value, but the value the individual

---

[10] The assumption of a zero expected capital gain or loss is not critical. It could be positive or negative. However, if an alternative value is used, the growth path or budget constraint which transforms present wealth into future wealth would depend not only on the present rate of interest, but on the adjustment for the expected rate of capital gain or loss. Such an adjustment complicates the analysis, for it makes it difficult to relate the speculative demand for money to the rate of interest unless it can be shown that the expected rate of capital gain or loss is related systematically to the rate of interest.

believes will prevail, given his expectations of future interest rates. If actual events correspond with those expected, the actual and expected values of the portfolio will then be equal.

If the initial position of the portfolio is given by W_0, the expected value of it at the end of the period under consideration, if the entire portfolio were invested in bonds, would be $W_0(1 + i_0)$. Thus, the growth of the value of assets would depend on the market interest rate, i_0, for it has been assumed that the expected value of capital gains or losses is zero. The growth path by which W_0 approaches $W_0(1 + i_0)$ is shown by the solid line designated (i_0). This growth path can be conceived of as the analog of the budget constraint in the theory of consumer behavior, for it gives all combinations of risk and expected wealth objectively open to the individual in the market place.

The subjective trade-off of the individual is given by indifference curves, each of which measures alternative levels of expected wealth and risk which leave the individual equally well off. To induce the individual to bear more risk, the expected value of his wealth must be increased, and because the individual avers risk and increases in wealth yield diminishing utility, ever-larger increases in expected wealth are necessary to induce him to bear uniform additional increments of risk. Thus, the indifference curves slope downward and to the left. Additionally, higher-level indifference curves are preferred to those lying at lower levels, for they yield higher expected wealth for the same level of risk, or for a given level of expected wealth, they represent lower levels of risk.

These indifference curves are shown, in Figure 8:1, as I_0, I_1, I_2 and I_3.

The optimum, or utility-maximizing, portfolio for the individual will result when his subjective trade-off is equal to the objective or market trade-off. Such a situation is shown in Figure 8:1, by a point such as A, which indicates a portfolio weighted more heavily toward bonds than toward money. Given this portfolio, its expected value at the end of the period can be obtained by moving directly over to the vertical axis.

In order to derive a demand schedule for idle or speculative balances, Figure 8:1 must be amended to show alternative rates of interest. If the rate is not i_0, but a higher rate such as i_1, the growth path of expected wealth must be above that for i_0 so long as the evaluation of risk remains constant, for the slope of the path is given by:

$$\frac{W_0 (1 + i) - W_0}{R_{MAX}} \tag{8:9}$$

or

$$\frac{iW_0}{R_{MAX}} \tag{8:10}$$

So long as W and R_{MAX} remain constant, the value of the slope of the expansion path will depend on i. Figure 8:2 gives several points of equilibria for various values of the market rate of interest. These are designated as A, B, and C, and they indicate that as the market interest rate rises, the individual is willing to bear more risk by holding more bonds and less money.[11] When this inverse relationship is graphed, it will yield the usual continuous speculative demand schedule, shown as Figure 8:3. It is important to note that this demand schedule is for the

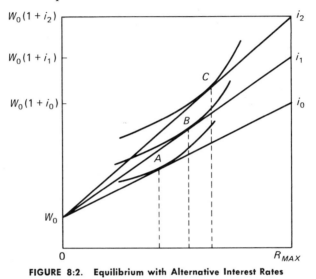

FIGURE 8:2.   Equilibrium with Alternative Interest Rates

individual wealth owner. In the formal Keynesian model developed in Chapter 5, such a continuous schedule did not emerge, for the individual had an either/or choice and acted as if he knew with certainty the future rate of interest. This knowledge permitted the computation of the critical current rate (i_c), and whenever the actual current rate was above its critical value, the individual held only bonds, and when below, he held only money. Such reasoning would produce for the individual a discontinuous demand function such as shown in Figure 8:4. The smooth, continuous downward-sloping function was produced by summing these individual demand functions and assuming that the individuals had diverse normal rates and therefore diverse critical values of the current market rate.

Tobin's model can also be altered by allowing for changes in the

[11] It should be obvious that this conclusion results from the position of the indifference curves. Had the indifference map been centered more to the left, it would have produced the opposite conclusion. Whether rising interest rates increase or decrease, the demand for money can only be resolved empirically. The available evidence using both short and long interest rates, is that an inverse relationship is present.

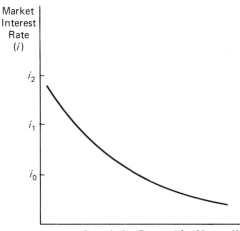

FIGURE 8:3.   Demand for Money by a Utility-Maximizing Individual

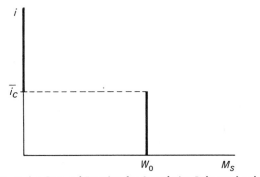

FIGURE 8:4.   Keynesian Demand Function for Speculative Balances by the Individual

level of risk attached to portfolios containing various combinations of bonds. While this refinement will not be presented here, its general conclusion should come as no surprise: If the level of risk rises, for the same interest rate, i_0, fewer bonds and more money will be held in the individual's portfolio.

In summary, the work of Tobin permits the derivation of a demand schedule for speculative balances and explains a diversified portfolio which corresponds to those observed in the real world. His theorizing is based upon the wealth level of the individual, the current rate of interest (which actually serves as a proxy for the expected yield on bonds), and the risk of changes in the capital value of bonds. In many respects, Tobin's formulation of the problem is markedly similar to the constrainted welfare-maximization problems of micro theory.

LIQUIDITY PREFERENCE AND THE CAMBRIDGE TRADITION

In Chapter 4, the Cambridge approach to monetary theory was shown to consist of what is now called the portfolio, or capital theoretic, approach to money. The writings of this school made it clear that in their discussion of the utility of money they recognized what Keynes was to call the *transactions* and *precautionary* motives for holding cash balances. They also recognized as budget constraints both income and wealth, although the evidence is unclear whether they really understood the difference between the two. They also recognized several forms, in addition to money and bonds, which could serve as the means for holding wealth, although they appear to have made limited use of this insight, preferring instead to reconcile their version of the quantity theory with that given by Fisher.

What then (if any) is the unique contribution by Keynes to monetary theory that is not to be found in the Cambridge tradition, and might not his work, by making all other assets perfect substitutes for money, represent a step backwards?

In his several pieces on the history of doctrine in monetary economics, Patinkin has concluded that Keynes in *The General Theory* did, in fact, make a significant departure from his previous work and that of his Cambridge associates.[12] So significant was the Keynesian formulation that Patinkin believes liquidity preference worthy of being called a new theory of money.

Keynes' first point of departure was to see clearly that the budget constraint must consist both of income and wealth. The former was relevant to the transactions demand for money, whereas the latter was pertinent to the speculative, or asset, demand for money. Thus, any increase in wealth could lead directly to an increase in the demand for money. Such a clear distinction embodied in an analytical framework is not to be found in his earlier writings or those of his Cambridge associates.

Second, and most important, while both the Cambridge School and Keynes approached monetary theory from the viewpoint of an optimum portfolio, Patinkin concludes that:

. . . the Cambridge School did not realize the full implications of the

---

[12] See Don Patinkin, "The Chicago Tradition, the Quantity Theory, and Friedman," *Journal of Money, Credit and Banking*, Vol. 1, No. 1 (Feb. 1969), pp. 46–70; "Friedman on the Quantity Theory," *Journal of Political Economy*, Vol. 80, No. 5 (Sept./Oct. 1972), pp. 883–905; and "Keynesian Monetary Theory and the Cambridge School," in Johnson and Nobay, ed., *Issues in Monetary Economics* (London: Oxford University Press, 1974), pp. 3–30.

portfolio approach to monetary theory. Conversely, it is the systematic application of this approach that is the hallmark of Keynesian monetary theory.[13]

The systematic application of this approach, which is supposedly the hallmark of Keynesian monetary theory, is most clearly seen in the way each side analyzed an increase in the money supply.

According to *The General Theory,* an increase in the money supply should lead directly to lower money rates of interest. The increase in money balances will throw the portfolios of individuals into disequilibrium and they will seek to get rid of the now excess money balances by *substituting* them for bonds and real capital goods. Only when the rates of return on all assets alternative to money have fallen will the public be content with holding the now larger supply of money.

However, in the process of getting rid of the redundant cash balances, the public is led to purchase new capital goods and perhaps consumer durables as well. This disturbs the equilibrium in the goods market, leading to an increase in output and/or prices, depending upon the state of unemployment present when the money stock is increased. In addition, nothing would exclude the wealth-owning individuals from issuing more liabilities to borrow the now more-plentiful funds available from the banks.

Thus, the Keynesian description of the adjustment process recognizes clearly the distinction between the stock adjustment of portfolios and the subsequent change in the rate of flow of income, and that as a minimum, a general lowering of the yield on all assets alternative to money is necessary to induce the public to hold the now larger money balances.

Patinkin shows that the Cambridge School's concept of the adjustment process was different in the sense that it never recognized that a change in the interest rate would have any effect on the desired money holding of the population. Rather, the analysis is essentially similar to that given in Chapter 3 by Henry Thornton. An increase in the lending capability of commercial banks is reflected in a lowering of the money rate of interest relative to the natural rate, creating a stock or portfolio disequilibrium, for the actual capital stock is less than that desired at the now lower interest rate. This leads wealth owners to issue liabilities (bonds) in an effort to raise funds from the banks, hence to an increase in the demand for capital goods, and ultimately to a rise in the general level of prices and nominal income. Nowhere in this discussion is it recognized that the lowering of the rate of interest will have an effect upon the amount of money the public desires to hold or upon velocity.

Patinkin shows, in addition, that this absence of a discussion of the

---

13 Don Patinkin, "Keynesian Monetary Theory," p. 15, by permission of Oxford University Press.

influence of the interest rate on velocity is also characteristic of the empirical work of the Cambridge School. This was noted in Chapter 4.

Last of all, Patinkin cites as further evidence that the Cambridge School did not approach monetary theory from the viewpoint of an optimum portfolio, the absence of any analysis about the effects on the rates of return of assets alternative to money resulting from a change in tastes as to the form in which wealth is to be held. Liquidity preference, with its emphasis on a normal or expected rate of interest, does provide such an analysis.

Thus from the viewpoint of Patinkin the speculative demand for money and the portfolio-type analysis to which it gives rise represent the unique Keynesian contribution which differentiates him from the Cambridge School.

THE QUANTITY THEORISTS' CONCERN WITH LIQUIDITY PREFERENCE

The Keynesian monetary theory of interest rates was challenged very soon after the publication of *The General Theory,* especially by those scholars whose allegiance was to the classical tradition. At least three aspects of liquidity preference caused them concern. One, however, can be dismissed with brief discussion—the precautionary demand for money. The fact that wealth owners will hold money as a safeguard against an uncertain future will (in the period when it occurs) increase the demand for loanable funds, causing the money rate to rise above the natural rate, thereby setting in motion deflationary forces. The only solution to this problem is for the central bank to engineer an appropriate expansion in the supply of loanable funds. As seen from this viewpoint, the problem posed by a precautionary demand for money is identical to the problem posed by hoarding. In Chapter 2, the solution for this problem also lay in a suitable expansion in the supply of loanable funds, which would serve to keep the money rate of interest from rising.

It is the existence of the speculative demand for money which poses the real difficulties for the quantity theorist. These difficulties are two in number and relate to the supposed instability of the function caused by changes in expectations about the future or normal rate of interest and the existence of a liquidity trap. Both problems have the potential for robbing monetary policy of its effectiveness and certainty. With this potential destroyed, the quantity theorist's principal tool for stabilization disappears.

This becomes obvious when the method used by the quantity theorists to expand aggregate demand is reviewed. In pre-Friedman days, they would have relied upon a fairly constant value for velocity. Then, in order to obtain an increase in the money value of aggregate output, or *PY*, they would have brought about an increase in the supply of money. Given any increase in the supply of money, the quantity theorist could have predicted the increase in money income. In this world, where velocity was essentially determined by the institutional arrangements governing the payment and receipt of money, monetary policy was all powerful. In terms of the *IS–LM* apparatus, a velocity of money unrelated to the rate of interest would produce a vertical *LM* schedule. As shown in Figure 8:5, the only way real income can be increased is by shifting the *LM* schedule. Any shifts in the *IS* schedule by themselves will only change the rate of interest and will not produce any change in the level of real income.

If it is true, as Keynes conjectured, that the demand for money, or velocity, is highly unstable because the individual's concept of a normal interest rate changes over time as his expectations are either over- or underfulfilled, the policymaker cannot predict the consequences of a change in the supply of money. It may be overeffective if the demand for money happens to fall when the supply is increased, it may be ineffective if demand changes in a way to exactly offset the planned change in supply, or it may have some intermediate influence. Because the central bank cannot predict the value of velocity, monetary policy is rendered ineffective as a stabilization tool.

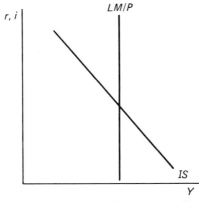

FIGURE 8:5. All-Powerful Monetary Policy

Because of a belief in functional instability, economists in the Keynesian tradition do not use the money supply and velocity for predictive purposes in their economic models. Instead, they believe the saving/ consumption relationship to be fundamentally stable, that is, their values depend on economic variables and changes in these variables lead to predictable changes in these two aggregates. For forecasting purposes, they use autonomous expenditures and the multiplier derived from the saving function to predict changes in income. In elementary textbooks, students are often asked to forecast or predict the change in income for a given change in investment. They duly multiply the change in investment by a multiplier to derive the change in income. There is no reason why such forecasting could not be done by taking a change in the money supply and multiplying it by velocity to derive the change in income. The Keynesian preference most likely arises from a belief that the velocity function is unstable.

Whether velocity is stable or not cannot be resolved in theory, for it is an empirical question to which Friedman and his followers have devoted considerable research effort. In a controversial piece published with David Meiselman,[14] they sought to show that velocity was more stable then the Keynesian multiplier and that better predictive results would emerge if the money supply and velocity were used rather than autonomous expenditures and the multiplier.

However, lest too much be made of what Friedman has tried to do, it should be remembered that a stable demand-for-money function is implicit in the *LM* schedule used in the standard Keynesian general-equilibrium model. Thus, while Keynes may have believed the function to be unstable, those who have propagated his theories do not. This, of course, raises the question of why they continue to forecast in the Keynesian way.

As far as the liquidity trap is concerned, in the traditional *IS–LM* framework, it makes the *LM* schedule horizontal so that all changes in real income must come about through shifts in the *IS* schedule. In terms of the quantity theory approach, the existence of a liquidity trap, or highly interest-elastic demand for money, is to reduce velocity at the margin to zero or a value close to zero. In such a situation, changes in the money supply will have no effect on money income and employment.

Because the perfectly elastic *LM* schedule renders monetary policy ineffective, whereas a perfectly vertical schedule makes it the only effective tool for stabilization, professional interest was soon aroused among economists in estimating the interest elasticity of the demand for money.[15] Among those contributing a relatively early work was Friedman, who

[14] M. Friedman and D. Meiselman, "The Relative Stability of Monetary Velocity and the Investment Multiplier in the United States, 1898–1958," Commission on Money and Credit, *Stabilization Policies* (Englewood Cliffs, N.J.: Prentice-Hall, 1963), pp. 165–268. See also, A. Ando and F. Modigliani, "Velocity and the Investment Multiplier," M. DePrano and T. Mayer, "Autonomous Expenditures and Money," and Friedman and Meiselman, "Reply" and "Rejoinders," *The American Economic Review*, Vol. 60, No. 4 (Sept. 1965), pp. 693–728, 729–52, 753–85, 786–90, 791–92.

[15] Later, when more fully developed theories of the supply of money were articulated, it was realized that the *LM* schedule could slope upward and to the right because the supply of money was sensitive to the interest rate as well as the demand.

reported that he was unable to find any close connection between changes in velocity and any of a number of interest rates.[16] This statement was widely interpreted as a finding of zero elasticity of velocity, or money demand, with respect to the interest rate, that is, a vertical *LM* schedule. Friedman subsequently disclaimed any such notion and in his work with Anna Schwartz, *A Monetary History of the United States,* they assigned a value of $-.15$ to the elasticity. This figure is noticeably smaller than any that 30 or 40 other studies have been able to find. No study, however, has been able to substantiate the existence of a liquidity trap.

However, this concession by Friedman did not end the controversy about the elasticity of the *LM* schedule, for many Keynesian economists thought that the slope of the *LM* schedule distinguished them from the Friedman-type quantity theorists. To them, a vertical or near-vertical *LM* schedule implied at least three things contrary to either Keynesian theory or the Keynesian interpretation of history. First, to them a vertical *LM* schedule implies that only money matters, that is, is capable of changing income and employment. Second, fiscal policy for stabilization purposes was seen to be useless for it would only change the interest rate (because it acts only on the *IS* schedule); and third, all cyclical instability observed in the economy could be attributed to changes in the money supply and not to the erratic behavior of the capitalist. As late as 1972, James Tobin could say about the controversy with Friedman:

> First, let me explain what I thought the main issue was. In terms of the Hicksian language of Friedman's two articles, I thought (and I still think) it was the shape of the LM locus.[17]

Not so, says Friedman:

> . . . the main issue between us clearly is not and never has been whether the *LM* curve is vertical or has a positive slope [but] . . . while the *LM* curve slopes positively, it is very far from being horizontal . . . [and] In my opinion, no fundamental issues in either monetary theory or monetary policy hinge on whether the estimated elasticity . . . can for most purposes be approximated by zero or is better approximated by $-.1$ or $-.5$ or -2.0, provided it is seldom capable of being approximated by $-\infty$.[18]

Thus, while admitting that the *LM* schedule sloped upward, Friedman nevertheless maintained that the core propositions constituting the

[16] M. Friedman, "The Demand for Money: Some Theoretical and Empirical Results," *Journal of Political Economy*, Vol. 67 (Aug. 1959), pp. 327–51.

[17] "Friedman's Theoretical Framework," *Journal of Political Economy*, Vol. 80, No. 5 (Sept./Oct. 1972), p. 853.

[18] "Comments on the Critics," *Journal of Political Economy*, Vol. 80, No. 5 (Sept./Oct. 1972), pp. 913, 916, 917.

quantity theory of money were valid, that is, in reference to the above controversy, the cycle is monetary in nature, money is all-powerful for stabilization purposes, and fiscal policy is useless to smooth out the cycle. At this time, the reasons for Friedman's rejection of the Keynesian contentions will not be discussed. In Chapters 9, 11, and 12, the core of Friedman's theory will be presented and the reasons for his views analyzed in great detail. But the conclusion remains: One can still believe in an upward-sloping *LM* schedule and be a quantity theorist.

KEYNES REINTERPRETED

This final section of Chapter 8 will summarize the recent scholarly contribution of Axel Leijonhufvud,[19] which is devoted to a reinterpretation of the message Keynes intended to impart to posterity. In the process of summary, great injustice may be done this work, for it presents the distinct impression that it and the work upon which it builds represent the future direction for monetary economics. This future direction will be concerned with a microdynamics analysis of labor and goods markets, based on the concept of information as an economic good and the fact that transactions and searches for jobs involve costs. However, much of this work is still in an embryonic state. In Chapter 11, it will be used to explain the neo-Fisherian, or Monetarist, theory of inflation and in Chapter 12 it will be shown to form the theoretical core of the anti-Keynesian position.

According to Leijonhufvud, one must sharply distinguish Keynesian economics from the economics of Keynes. The former is to be found in the general-equilibrium model summarized by the *IS–LM* schedules propagated by Sir John Hicks and Professor Alvin Hansen. This, according to Leijonhufvud, is *not* the economics of Keynes.

Paralleling, in some of his arguments, recent work by his mentor Robert Clower,[20] Arman Alchian,[21] and others, Leijonhufvud believes that *The General Theory* represents a continuation of Keynes' reasoning in *The Treatise on Money* and that the essence of his message is to be found by comparing how he and the classics analyzed the reaction of an economy to a decrease in effective demand.

In the classical model of the type developed in Chapter 1, if *MV*

---

[19] A. Leijonhufvud, *On Keynesian Economics and the Economics of Keynes* (New York: Oxford University Press, 1968). For a more concise presentation of the material in this section, see Leijonhufvud, "Keynes and the Effectiveness of Monetary Policy," *Western Economic Journal,* Vol. 6, No. 1 (1967), pp. 97–111.

[20] R. W. Clower, "A Reconsideration of the Microfoundations of Monetary Theory," *Western Economic Journal,* Vol. 6, No. 1 (Dec. 1967), pp. 1–8.

[21] A. A. Alchian, "Information Costs, Pricing, and Resource Employment," *Western Economic Journal,* Vol. 7, No. 2 (June 1969), pp. 109–28.

declines for any reason, wages and commodity prices are assumed to move instantaneously, thereby ensuring the continuation of full employment. All adjustments in the classical system are to be made by prices and wages. In the Keynesian model, however, if aggregate demand declines, the adjustment is confined basically to output and employment, not to prices and wages, which conventionally are treated as inflexible in the downward direction. When the reason for the reversal of the adjustment parameters is understood, Leijonhufvud believes that part of the essential Keynesian contribution will be realized and appreciated.

The reason for the pure price–wage adjustment in the classical model follows from an assumption seldom explicitly stated, but an essential part of the model—the assumption of the *Walrasian auctioneer*. Whenever aggregate demand declines, this imaginary auctioneer (who is, really, the source of perfect market information) calls off a price in the commodity market and another in the labor market, soliciting offers to supply and demand quantities of commodities or labor services. If the markets fail to clear at the prices called, that is, if supply and demand are unequal, all contracts to sell or buy are negated and he calls off another set of prices. He continues to do this until all commodity and labor markets are cleared. The only thing the auctioneer must do is see that no false trades take place, that is, trades at other than equilibrium prices. It is this highly specialized assumption of the auctioneer, or the provision of perfect market information, which permits the classical model to posit complete price adjustments to maintain equilibrium in all relevant markets.

According to Leijonhufvud, it was this theory of adjustment with its imaginary auctioneer providing costless information to the markets from which Keynes was trying to break away. When aggregate demand declines, sellers in the commodity market have no information on whether the initial decline is temporary or of a longer-run nature. Since it would be unwise to adjust prices to clear a market or maintain sales if the decline in demand were only temporary, sellers will probably wait to form opinions concerning the permanency of the decline before they adjust prices to maintain sales. While they wait, inventories are likely to accumulate, providing, in part, the information as to the extent of the decline in demand. To the extent that this type of information convinces sellers that the decline in demand is more than merely transitory, they will cut back production in order to adjust the inventories downward. The cutback in production leads to unemployment and (via the destructive workings of the multiplier) to further unemployment.

Once sellers are convinced that the decline in demand is permanent, they will begin to adjust prices. This price-adjustment process is also likely to be time-consuming, as sellers explore market conditions trying to discover the best bargains they can strike with buyers. However, this analysis indicates that a rational seller, in the absence of perfect market information, will first adjust output in response to a decline in demand, then price. Moreover, the period of disequilibrium may be rather long, depending on the time which must lapse before sellers are convinced that the decline in demand is permanent and determine what the new market price must be.

Now, what about the adjustment made by the worker rendered unemployed by the sellers' decision to cut production? Does he immediately enter the marketplace and accept the best available job at whatever wage is being paid? Most likely not, for he does not know if the decline in demand for his services is temporary or permanent—he also suffers from a lack of relevant market information.

In time, the unemployed worker will come to a conclusion regarding the status of the decline in demand. He will then try to find a job at a wage reasonably close to what he was previously paid. If one is unavailable, he then lowers the wage at which he would be willing to accept employment. Suppose he lowered it to the level at which he would immediately find a job. Would it be to his advantage to accept employment? Not if he thought he could get a better position by searching the job market for a longer time period. However, the time taken in the search has a cost—the income foregone from the best alternative available. It also has a benefit—the present discounted value of the extra income from the job he expects to get over his best available option today. By balancing marginal costs against marginal benefits he decides when the search ought to end. Nevertheless, during the time he gathers market information and makes his job search, he remains unemployed, and for the rational worker, unemployment is a viable alternative until he is convinced that he cannot improve his income prospects by continuing the job search.

Thus, for both the seller of commodities and the seller of labor services, the initial decline in demand will be met by quantity adjustments rather than price adjustments. It is the quantity adjustment which is the prominent feature of the Keynesian model.

As Leijonhufvud reads Keynes, this deflationary process with falling output and employment need not occur if only the money rate of interest would fall sufficiently, for by so doing it would simulate both investment and consumption, restoring full employment. The rise in consumption would be stimulated by what was earlier called the *Keynesian windfall effect,* which results from an increase in the bond holder's perceived wealth due to a fall in the money interest rate.[22] Moreover, a lowering

---

[22] In *The General Theory,* Keynes attempted to capture this windfall effect by formulating what he called the second law of consumption. The law postulated that unforeseen changes in nominal wealth due to interest rate movements may be among the major factors causing short-run changes in the propensity to consume. See pp. 92–93.

of the interest rate, by increasing the capitalized value of investment projects, stimulates the quantity of investment. If the money rate of interest would only fall sufficiently, the stimulus of increased consumption and investment ought to push the economy back toward full employment and prevent the multiplier from working its destruction. But something stands in the way of the necessary fall in the interest rate—inelastic expectations about the future rate of interest on the part of wealth owners. In order to see exactly what this means, recall the Keynesian formulation of the speculative demand for money. According to that approach, in deciding whether to hold money or bonds, each individual compared the current rate with the expected, or normal, rate. Given any individual's normal rate, a critical value of the current rate could be computed which, when compared to the actual current rate, could be used to predict his behavior. However, what happens if, over time, the individual's initial expectations about the future interest rate are not borne out? According to Keynes, they will be revised in light of experience.

Thus, a deflation set in motion by, perhaps, a decline in investor optimism about the future, will produce downward pressure on interest rates as smaller cash balances will be needed for transactions as nominal income declines. Wealth owners, basing their expectations of the future rate of interest on the current rate, will be led to revise downward their expected normal rate. This will cause their critical value of the current rate to fall and their individual demand function for speculative balances to shift downward. However, because their expectations are inelastic, their normal rate of interest will not fall sufficiently to permit the aggregate demand for speculative balances to shift downward by an appropriate amount. Thus, the money rate of interest is kept above the rate necessary to maintain a full-employment equilibrium, that is, the money rate is kept above the natural rate.

Inelastic expectations need not have harmful effects on the economy if the central bank acts with sufficient force to increase the money supply, thereby forcing downward the rate of interest to a level consistent with full employment. In his day, Keynes believed that such institutions were guided by timid souls who would fail to seize the appropriate opportunity and thereby allow the economy to drift about in an unemployment equilibrium.

The attractiveness of the Leijonhufvud analysis to the quantity theorist is that in order to maintain the economy close to a full-employment equilibrium, stabilization efforts should rely primarily on monetary policy to keep the money rate of interest in line with the natural rate, regardless of the initiating cause of cyclical disturbances.

In the Leijonhufvud interpretation of the economics of Keynes, money matters a great deal and monetary policy becomes an effective tool for keeping an economy close to a full-employment path. All of this is supposed to stand contrary to the general assessment of Keynesian economics.

Of doctrinal interest is the fact that by not making the assumption of the auctioneer, Keynes can lay claim to having produced a general theory in which the classical model embodying this highly restrictive assumption emerges as a special case. Thus *The General Theory* does merit its name, contrary to the classical claim.

In Figure 8:6, Leijonhufvud's analysis is applied to a Keynesian model. The only alteration of this model, one that is consistent with an approach in which market information is important, is to make the supply-of-labor schedule conform to its classical specification. This change does not alter the conclusions emerging from the analysis.

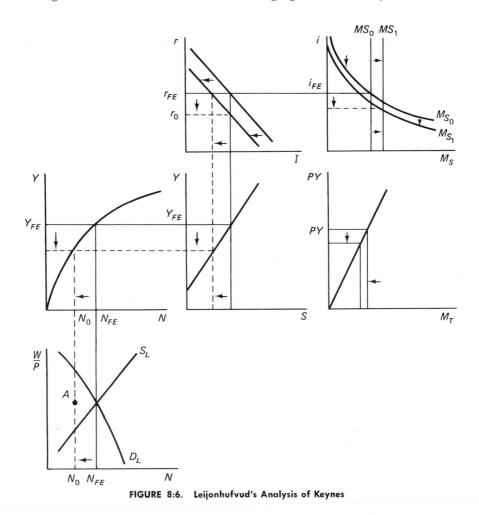

FIGURE 8:6. Leijonhufvud's Analysis of Keynes

Initially, it is assumed that a full-employment equilibrium prevails, and for some reason investor expectations about the future become less optimistic, causing the investment demand schedule to shift inward and the natural rate of interest (that consistent with full employment) to decline to r_0. This action sets in motion a deflation, but neither wages nor prices decline initially because of a lack of market information about the degree of permanency of the decline in demand. As output declines with a constant real wage, the economy operates off the demand-for-labor and supply-of-labor schedules at a point such as A.

As nominal income declines, money balances are set free for speculative purposes, shifting MS_0 toward MS_1 and driving down the interest rate. The fall in the interest rate accomplishes two things. First, by lowering the money rate it serves to increase the quantity of investment and (because of the windfall effect) to shift inward the saving function. Both actions serve to partly offset the initial downswing. Second, the fall in interest rates causes wealth owners to revise downward their normal rates, thereby shifting downward the speculative demand schedule from Ms_0 to Ms_1. However, the combination of the downward shift in the speculative demand schedule and the rise in money balances available for speculation is insufficient to drive the money rate to equality with the now lower natural rate, r_0, which would be consistent with full employment. A sort of equilibrium then emerges with unemployed resources, but the unemployment does not depend upon wage rigidities due to trade unions or to the pricing policies of oligopolistic industries. It depends on the time it takes to acquire and adjust to market information.

In the face of this failure of the market interest rate to decline sufficiently, the obvious policy is for the central bank to expand the money stock to drive down the money rate to the level consistent with the now lower natural rate.

CONCLUSION

The purpose of this chapter has been to deal with several topics related either to the incompleteness or the methodological problems of the Keynesian model and to several implicit questions raised during the discussion of the contribution of Keynes to monetary theory.

The application by Baumol and Tobin of optimum inventory analysis to the transactions demand unified Keynesian monetary theory methodologically and made it possible to express the total demand for money in one functional form, in which real income and the interest rate appear as arguments. Tobin's work on portfolio behavior made it possible to explain diversified asset holding while retaining the slope of the speculative demand schedule.

Several implicit questions were also discussed, especially concerning the problems posed for the quantity theory by the speculative demand for money and the aspects of the Keynesian monetary theory which distinguish it from the general Cambridge approach. As to the first question, the mere linking of the demand for money to the interest rate was seen not to differentiate the Keynesian from the quantity theorist and, in this regard, it must be the belief in a liquidity trap and the absence of functional stability which serves, in part, to distinguish the two.

The work of Patinkin showed the uniqueness of *The General Theory* approach to monetary theory to be the speculative demand for money and the recognition that changes in the interest rate affect the desired money holding of society and velocity, these having not been recognized by the Cambridge School.

Last of all, the reassessment of Keynes' message to posterity was viewed through the work of Axel Leijonhufvud and a group of able scholars at the University of California at Los Angeles. In commenting on works such as Leijonhufvud's involving discussion of "what Keynes really meant," Harry Johnson observes that they represent:

. . . a tendency which usually indicates that a field of study has lost its way and is searching for clues as to how to proceed by re-examining the works of the master for hitherto neglected ideas and insights.[23]

In the chapters to follow on inflation and the great debate, the degree to which monetary economics has lost its way will become evident.

Selected References and Readings

ALCHIAN, ARMAN, "Information Costs, Pricing, and Resource Employment," *Western Economic Journal*, Vol. 8, No. 2 (June 1969).

BAUMOL, WILLIAM, "The Transactions Demand for Cash: An Inventory Theoretic Approach," *Quarterly Journal of Economics*, Vol. 66, No. 4 (Nov. 1952).

BRONFENBRENNER, MARTIN, AND MAYER, THOMAS, "Liquidity Functions in the American Economy," *Econometrica*, Vol. 28, No. 3 (Oct. 1960).

CLOWER, ROBERT, "A Reconsideration of the Microfoundations of Monetary Theory," *Western Economic Journal*, Vol. 6, No. 1 (Dec. 1967).

FRIEDMAN, MILTON, "The Quantity Theory of Money—A Restatement," in M.

[23] Harry G. Johnson, "Major Issues in Monetary Economics," *Oxford Economic Papers* (New Series), Vol. 26, No. 2 (July 1974), p. 213, by permission of the Oxford University Press.

Friedman, ed., *Studies in the Quantity Theory of Money* (Chicago: University of Chicago Press, 1956).

————, "The Demand for Money: Some Theoretical and Empirical Results," *Journal of Political Economy*, Vol. 67, No. 4 (Aug. 1959).

————, "Interest Rates and the Demand for Money," *The Journal of Law and Economics*, Vol. 9, No. 3 (October 1966).

————, "Comments on the Critics," *Journal of Political Economy*, Vol. 80, No. 5 (Sept./Oct. 1972).

————, AND MEISELMAN, DAVID, "The Relative Stability of Monetary Velocity and the Investment Multiplier in the United States, 1898–1958," Commission on Money and Credit, *Stabilization Policies* (Englewood Cliffs, N.J.: Prentice-Hall, 1963).

————, AND SCHWARTZ, ANNA, *A Monetary History of the United States* (Princeton, N.J.: Princeton University Press, 1963).

LAIDLER, DAVID E. W., *The Demand for Money* (Scranton, Pa.: Intext, 1969).

LEIJONHUFVUD, AXEL, "Keynes and the Keynesians: A Suggested Interpretation," *American Economic Review, Papers and Proceedings*, Vol. 57, No. 2 (May 1967).

————, *On Keynesian Economics and the Economics of Keynes* (New York: Oxford University Press, 1968).

————, *Keynes and the Classics* (London: The Institute of Economic Affairs, Occasional Paper 30, 1969).

PATINKIN, DON, "The Chicago Tradition, The Quantity Theory, and Friedman," *Journal of Money, Credit and Banking*, Vol. 1, No. 1 (Feb. 1969).

————, "Friedman on the Quantity Theory of Money," *Journal of Political Economy*, Vol. 80, No. 5 (Sept./Oct. 1972).

————, "Keynesian Monetary Theory and the Cambridge School," in Johnson and Nobay eds., *Issues in Monetary Economics* (London: Oxford University Press, 1974).

TOBIN, JAMES, "Liquidity Preference and Monetary Policy," *Review of Economics and Statistics*, Vol. 29, No. 2 (May 1947).

————, "The Interest-Elasticity of Transactions Demand for Cash," *Review of Economics and Statistics*, Vol. 38, No. 3 (Aug. 1956).

————, "Liquidity Preference as Behavior Towards Risk," *Review of Economic Studies*, Vol. 25, No. 1 (Feb. 1958).

————, "Money, Capital and Other Stores of Value," *American Economic Review, Papers and Proceedings*, Vol. 51, No. 2 (May 1961).

————, "An Essay on the Principles of Debt Management," *Fiscal and Debt Management Policies* (Englewood Cliffs, N.J.: Prentice-Hall, 1963).

————, "Friedman's Theoretical Framework," *Journal of Political Economy*, Vol. 80, No. 5 (Sept./Oct. 1972).

Keynesian Monetary Theory: Conclusion To Part II

In the preface introducing this section on the monetary theory of Keynes, it was noted that the essence of what has come to be called the Keynesian Revolution is to be found in his denial of the basic propositions constituting the quantity theory of money. This denial of long-held beliefs is based either on his alternative theoretical formulation or on his interpretation of economic history. Whichever was responsible, the economics profession came to view the functioning of a market economy in very different ways after 1936 than before. Both policy prescriptions and theoretical formulations emanating from Keynesian economists were different from those of individuals clinging to more traditional beliefs.

The Proportionality of Money and Prices

Crucial to the denial of the proportionality proposition was to show that a long-run unemployment equilibrium could exist in the face of flexible wages and prices. This Keynes was able to accomplish by showing that at a hypothetical full-employment level, saving would exceed investment. This would occur because the real rate of interest could not be pushed low enough to bring forth sufficient investment to utilize the full-employment volume of saving. Either a zero real rate stood as a barrier or the money rate could not be pushed below some downward floor (that is, the so-called *liquidity trap*). Thus the economy came to rest at some level less than full employment at which saving and investment were equal.

Given such an unemployment equilibrium, increases in aggregate demand, stimulated perhaps by changes in the money stock, might bring forth output changes with no changes in the level of prices. The exact distribution of any change in aggregate demand between an output and a price level component was left unspecified theoretically and came to depend upon the degree to which the prevailing equilibrium, prior to the expansion in demand, approximated the Keynesian definition of full employment.

Of additional importance in denying the proportionality postulate, although it hinges on the existence of an unemployment equilibrium, was the speculative demand for money. By linking the demand for money to the interest rate, changes in the money supply, to the extent they changed the interest rate, would be added in part to idle balances and have no proportional effect on money spending and the price level. Of course, in the liquidity trap all changes in the money supply are merely added to money hoards.

The last Keynesian proposition used to deny proportionality arises from his view that the demand-for-money function is highly unstable, or subject to erratic and unpredictable fluctuations, as wealth-owning individuals changed their views periodically as to their normal rate of interest. Each change affected the individual demand schedule for speculative balances and hence shifted the aggregate function as well. Therefore in Keynes' view velocity was not as stable as Fisher and the early quantity theorists supposed. With velocity shifting erratically, one could not predict what effect money-supply changes would have on the price level.

The Neutrality of Money

That Keynes was able to demonstrate the long-run permanent non-neutrality of money was a consequence of his demonstration of an unemployment equilibrium. In such a situation, an expansion of the money supply could permanently change real variables, such as interest rates, output, employment, the rate of capital formation, and so forth.

In certain situations, the ability to lower real interest rates, increase the rate of capital formation, and lower the unemployment rate rests clearly on the presence of money illusion. That is, the expansion in the money stock which accomplishes nonneutrality does so in an environment in which inflation takes place while the participants in the economy are oblivious to it. Such behavior was seen to produce temporary nonneutrality in the Fisherian model, but not permanent nonneutrality as the Keynesian model implies.

Two interesting situations exist in the Keynesian model which render money largely neutral. The first is the liquidity trap. In such a state of affairs, all changes in the money supply are simply added to idle balances and have no affect on any real variable; money is thus neutral. Second, in the Keynesian model the only channel by which money can affect the real sector is through the interest rate. If expenditures are insensitive to changes in the interest rate, money is mostly neutral, meaning that it can change the interest rate but will have a minimal impact on all other real variables.

In those situations in which money is nonneutral, the magnitude of nonneutrality depends upon the interest and income elasticities of money demand, the interest elasticity of expenditures, the income elasticity of the saving schedule (which governs the value of the multiplier), the degree to which the marginal productivity of labor diminishes, and the extent to which the productive factors suffer from money illusion.

The fact that money is seen to have permanent nonneutral effects in the Keynesian model has led to the treatment of changes in nominal variables as though they were equivalent changes in their real counterparts. Such treatment of nominal magnitudes may lead to very serious policy errors, especially since the nominal interest rate has frequently been used by Keynesians as a measure of monetary tightness or ease.

Monetary Theory of the Price Level

A necessary condition for showing that an unemployment equilibrium could exist even if wages and prices were flexible was to link wages and prices, thereby precluding a cut in the former from inducing a rise in employment via a reduction in the real wage.

Thus, the price level was made to depend upon per-unit labor costs, which was represented as the true classical view. Labor costs were then made to depend upon forces lying outside the formal structure of the model, that is, on historical and institutional circumstances. This rendered the initial price level exogenous. It may be a fatal weakness of the Keynesian system that it fails to specify the long-run determinant of wages, and thus of prices. In such a theory of price-level determination, the only way that money is able to change the level of prices is through its effects on per-unit labor costs. Once full employment is achieved, it is shown that prices do move in proportion to changes in the money stock even though the mechanism is slightly different than in the classical model.

However, nonmonetary theories of the price level lead naturally to nonmonetary theories of inflation; and latter-day Keynesians have been in the forefront of those expounding cost-push theories of inflation and demanding the implementation of incomes policies to curb inflation.

The Causality of Money

Utilizing only the indirect money mechanism of Thornton, the Keynesian approach, while narrowly circumscribing the money transmission mechanism to the interest rate channel, does not preclude it from having a significant causal role. The importance of money can be inferred exclusively from the elasticities of the *IS–LM* schedules and knowledge about the marginal productivity of labor and the degree of money illusion on the part of workers. The more elastic the *IS* schedule and inelastic the *LM* schedule, the greater the likelihood that money really matters.

Even if changes in the money stock do not precede changes in real income, with a relatively inelastic *LM* schedule changes in the IS schedule induced, for example, by fiscal policy measures, will have little effect on real income and employment.

However, the Keynesian interpretation of the business cycle as being caused by waves of investor optimism and pessimism, its emphasis on the liquidity trap, the possibility that expenditures may not be responsive to interest rate changes, and the general emphasis on compensatory fiscal policy, lead to the conclusion that Keynes had great reservations about the causal role of money.

In addition, Keynes' revival of the income–expenditure approach, whose central feature is the multiplier linking autonomous expenditures to income, further obscures the role of money in the model, for money enters indirectly as a determinant of autonomous expenditures.

It should be remembered that the theory of liquidity preference permits a more complete statement of the portfolio approach to monetary theory and the effect of money upon economic activity.

Last of all, by neglecting the real-balance effect, Keynes and the Keynesians have neglected a potentially disturbing consequence for their conclusions. First, it showed that the unemployment equilibrium depended upon wage-and-price rigidities. Second, the existence of such an effect broadened substantially the channels through which money could exert its influence on the real sector, thereby weakening the Keynesian reliance on the liquidity trap and elasticity pessimism to conclude that money doesn't matter much. Thus, the influence of money can no longer be measured by the slope properties of the *IS–LM* schedules. Rather, the degree to which they shift in response to changes in real balances may be very important.

The Exogeneity of Money

From the viewpoint of theory, nothing prevents the central bank from exercising control over the money supply in the Keynesian model. Indeed, it is implicit in almost all money and banking textbooks, which explain money creation and the tools of monetary management available to the central bank. It is also a part of the *IS–LM* apparatus that the central bank can control the *LM* schedule within some reasonable range of time.

However, many Keynesians would deny that historically the money supply has, in fact, been exogenous, holding instead that the central bank has either willingly supplied money on request from the Treasury or simply allowed the commercial banks and the public to determine the supply regardless of the consequences. During some historical periods, especially the great contraction of 1929–33, some Keynesians (including Keynes himself) argued that the central bank was powerless to halt the deflation and that the contraction was due to an absence of borrowers, thus reverting back to the idea that the supply of money is demand-determined (a sort of real bills doctrine). In addition, the resolution of Gibson's Paradox, in terms of the Keynesian model, clearly implies that the banking system passively supplies money on request. Thus if the central bank could control the money supply, it must decide not to exercise its power.

The ultimate importance of the exogeneity issue is to be discovered when individuals conduct empirical tests on the causality of money. Thus, for the validity of their conclusions that money causes the cycle, the money supply must be exogenous in the statistical sense, that is, it must be a truly independent variable whose magnitude does not depend upon prior changes in the dependent variable (for example, income) which it seeks to explain. In the empirical sense, mere ability to control by the central bank is not enough to prove the case if it can be shown that in the past the central bank did not exercise control.

The exogeneity issue will be discussed extensively in Chapter 12, for it forms an issue of central contention between the Keynesians and their antagonists, the Monetarists.

CONTEMPORARY MONETARY THEORY

Part III

Introduction

Unlike the Prefaces to parts I and II, a summary of the views of contemporary monetary theorists on the five key propositions of the quantity theory will not be given here, nor will a separate summary under these five points conclude this section. However, Chapter 12, the final one in this text, will summarize the modern views on the validity of these key propositions, for they form the crucial elements in the controversy over the effect and duration of changes in the supply of money on the level of economic activity.

In several ways, the first three chapters in this section lay the groundwork for the summary of the great debate. First, developments in the theory of money demand (specifically the portfolio, or capital theoretic, approach) are presented which, from the diversity of views of their respective contributors, provide a common ground for unifying the profession. That is, contributions developing the portfolio approach to money demand will be shown to originate from both Keynesian economists and those whose intellectual inspiration is said to come from the quantity theory. The fact that both traditions are evolving a common approach to the demand for money serves to draw together members of the economics profession.

Second, the quantity theory, which has been associated with the analysis of the long run to the neglect of periods of transition, has been amended. Much theoretical work on the subject of inflation, discussed in Chapter 11, has been formulated by quantity theorists which permits them to discuss the short run in terms of theoretical framework evolved from the work of Irving Fisher. It is this framework and the interpretation of historical events which flows from it which permits a sharp contrast to be drawn between it and the alternative Keynesian formulation.

Third, a survey of the literature on the supply of money is undertaken. The principal conclusion to emerge from this review is that theorists are developing a supply function for money on grounds paralleling that of demand. That is, the portfolio, or capital theoretic, approach is being applied to the money supply and it is shown that the supply depends upon the portfolio behavior of the public, commercial banks, and the central bank. An important part of this discussion concerns the extent to which the money supply is an exogeneous variable, a topic which assumes great importance in the current great debate. Finally, an alternative to the quantity theory view that the economy must adjust to an excess supply of money is examined and its merits evaluated.

Of somewhat lesser interest are other subjects to be found in these three chapters which were of interest during the late 1950's and early 1960's. A subject first examined by the participants in the Banking–Currency School controversy—the proper definition of money—is raised again. The modern replay of this discussion concerns, in addition, the special place accorded commercial banks in monetary theory, the role of nonbank financial intermediaries, and a new mechanism by which the supply of money is to affect the pace of economic activity.

Thus, the purpose of these three chapters is both to lay the groundwork for the summary of the great debate presented in Chapter 12 and to present an analysis of several other topics concerned only indirectly with that debate.

chapter 9

The Monetary Theory of Milton Friedman

That a chapter in a textbook is devoted exclusively to an examination and explanation of the monetary theory identified with a single individual stands as a measure of his influence and importance.

Some might find surprising this chapter's conclusion that Friedman's monetary theory is very Keynesian in spirit and owes a great debt to the Cambridge cash-balance approach to the quantity theory. In fact, when the empirical Friedman is separated from the theoretical Friedman, the debt owed Keynes is glaringly apparent. Before this striking similarity is examined, however, Friedman's theoretical approach will be developed at great length. In the final pages of the chapter, the theoretical Friedman will be distinguished from his empirical counterpart.

THE ORIGIN OF FRIEDMAN'S MONETARY THEORY

Beginning in the immediate post–World War II period, Milton Friedman, then a recent Columbia Ph.D., began the publication of a continuing series of empirical studies designed to distinguish him from, and question the assumptions, relevance, and predictive capability of, the ruling Keynesian model. It was not until 1956 that he formalized, to a limited degree, the model which formed the theoretical underpinnings for his empirical work. In his now classic and widely reprinted, "The

Quantity Theory of Money—A Restatement," he informs us that the model set forth represents an attempt "to convey the flavor of the oral tradition" of the University of Chicago, to which he was privy first as a graduate student and later as a colleague of its formulators. This quantity theory tradition was supposedly shaped during the 1930's and 1940's by such formidable intellects as Henry Simons, Lloyd Mints, Jacob Viner, and Frank Knight. Unlike the earlier Fisherian approach to the quantity theory, this Chicago tradition was not a "theory of output, or of money income, or of the price level." Rather, it was "in the first instance a theory of the demand for money" which, for "ultimate wealth-owning units in the society, can be made formally identical with that of the demand for a consumption service."

Given much of the earlier discussion of the origin of the quantity theory, especially that in Chapter 4, it would appear that at Chicago tion" at Chicago in what seems to me the much more important sense in which the liquidity preference theory of Keynes was seen to be a distinct advancement over the atrophied simplification of A. C. Pigou.

As early as 1963[1] and again in 1964,[2] Friedman, in discussing the revived quantity theory, no longer linked it to a Chicago tradition developed during the 1930's and 1940's. Referring to developments in monetary theory, he states:

A second and more basic effect of the post-war reaction [to policy dictated by Keynesian analysis] has been a reformulation of the quantity theory. This reformulation has . . . been much affected by the Keynesian formulation. The Keynesian approach, as embodied in liquidity preference analysis, emphasizes the role of money as an asset to be compared with other assets such as bonds. Recent quantity theory thinking has tended to adopt the same emphasis and to look at the problem of monetary theory as a part of capital theory.[3]

With this admission of indebtedness to Keynes, one is left with the uneasy feeling that Friedman's 1956 statement about the intellectual origin of his quantity theory restatement is slightly exaggerated. Indeed, in 1968 Don Patinkin showed conclusively that no such oral or written tradition, supposedly summarized in 1956 by Friedman, ever existed. He concludes that: ". . . Milton Friedman provided us in 1956 with a most elegant and sophisticated statement of modern Keynesian monetary theory—misleadingly entitled, 'The Quantity Theory of Money—A Re-

---

[1] Milton Friedman, "The Present State of Monetary Theory," *The Economic Studies Quarterly*, Vol. XIV, No. 1 (Sept. 1963), pp. 1–15.

[2] Milton Friedman, "Postwar Trends in Monetary Theory and Policy," *The National Banking Review*, Vol. 1, No. 1 (Sept. 1964), pp. 1–10. See especially p. 5.

[3] "The Present State of Monetary Theory," p. 9.

statement.' "[4] Some four years later, Friedman vigorously answered Patinkin's allegation that he had manufactured a Chicago tradition. He
summarized his defense with:

> I shall not defend my "Restatement" as giving the "flavor of the oral
> tradition" at Chicago in the sense that the details of my formal structure have
> precise counterparts in the teachings of Simons and Mints. . . . But I cer-
> tainly do defend my "Restatement" as giving the "flavor of the oral tradi-
> tion" at Chicago in what seems to me the much more important sense in which
> . . . the oral tradition "nurtured the remaining essays in" *Studies in the
> Quantity Theory of Money,* and my own subsequent work.[5]

By Friedman's own admission, the Chicago School did not formulate a precise theoretical structure such as is to be found in his famous
"Restatement," and if Patinkin is to be believed, the structure is
markedly different. Thus, the importance of the tradition arises because
it served as the inspiration for his own research effort. Friedman tells us
that the true Chicago tradition consists of some three elements: Its interpretation of short-run movements, the reasons for the Great Depression,
and the role of monetary and fiscal policies. While Friedman offers
various quotations to support this contention, he fails to give any indication of the theoretical framework from which the interpretations, conclusions, and policy recommendations of the Chicago School flow. All he
says is that the teaching of Chicago economists was markedly different
from their quantity theory counterparts in at least the London School
of Economics, and because their policy prescriptions were so similar to
those coming from Keynes, the latter: ". . . had nothing to offer those
of us who had sat at the feet of Simons, Mints, Knight, and Viner."[6]

---

[4] Don Patinkin, "The Chicago Tradition, the Quantity Theory and Friedman," *Journal of
Money, Credit and Banking,* Vol. 1, No. 1 (Feb. 1969), p. 61. This article provides, in addition to a
critique of Friedman, an excellent insight into the Chicago view of the quantity theory and the
state of monetary theory developed by quantity theorists at the time of the Keynesian Revolution.
Thomas Humphrey offers some compelling evidence why Friedman's intellectual debt ought to be
owed to non-Chicago quantity theorists. In particular, he argues that positions currently advanced by Friedman can only be found in the works of four non-Chicago quantity theorists who
during the 1930's and 40's were making substantial contributions to that approach. From the
collective works of Carl Snyder, Lionel Edie, Lauchlin Currie, and Clark Warburton, Humphrey
cites three important propositions long associated with Friedman. First is the famous money-
supply growth rule necessary to stabilize the price level; second, that deviations in the growth
of the money supply from its trend are the cause of business cycles, and, third, that the
Federal Reserve System was responsible for both initiating and aggravating the great depression. In addition, these four were among the first to offer detailed empirical verification of
their views. See Thomas M. Humphrey, "Role of Non-Chicago Economists in the Evolution of
the Quantity Theory in America," *Southern Economic Journal,* Vol. 38, No. 1 (July 1971), pp.
12–18.

[5] Milton Friedman, "Comments on the Critics," *Journal of Political Economy,* Vol. 80, No.
5 (Sept./Oct. 1972), p. 941.

[6] *Ibid.,* p. 937. In particular the Chicago School was calling for deficit spending by the

Whatever the true source of Friedman's ideas on monetary theory and policy, he has made a substantial contribution to our understanding of how a monetary economy operates. However, the analyses to follow will show that Friedman's work can be made to look substantially like that deriving from the Cambridge approach to the quantity theory. As such, a brief review of the Cambridge cash-balance formulization follows.

A REVIEW OF THE CAMBRIDGE APPROACH
TO THE QUANTITY THEORY

Using the work of A. C. Pigou as typical of a pre–*General Theory* Cambridge economist, it was shown that the Cambridge cash-balance approach represented the application of demand analysis to money as a special case. Pigou specified that the utility of money lay in its ability to eliminate the inconvenience of barter and to serve as a convenient safeguard against an uncertain future. Next, he spelled out the nature of the budget constraint determining maximum money holdings. This turned out to be resources, with the precise definition of the term left unsettled—it presumably could be either the income or the wealth of the individual. Lastly, he specified the nature of the opportunity costs of holding money as opposed to other assets, these being the yield on real capital and the expected rate of change of commodity prices. Rather than draw out the implications of his analysis, Pigou instead rigidified it by making assumptions about the relationship of current income to resources and the constancy of expectations about price changes and capital yields. These assumptions allowed him to express the demand for money as a constant proportion of money income—the derivation of the Cambridge k, the reciprocal of Fisher's velocity.

An essential contribution of *The General Theory* was the explicit introduction of the money interest rate as an argument in the demand function for money along with the current level of nominal income. However, commodity price stability was assumed, and capital assets and commodity inventories were made perfect substitutes for bonds. In a 1937 article,[7] though, Keynes was willing to concede and introduce the

---

Federal government. Whether this policy prescription arose from an analytical framework in which compensatory deficit finance was viewed as an offset to variations in private expenditures in order to iron out the business cycle is doubtful. It is more likely that the Chicago School called for deficits because they felt this to be the best way to achieve sufficient expansions in the supply of money to compensate for the great contraction of 1929–1933.

[7] J. M. Keynes, "The General Theory," *Quarterly Journal of Economics*, Vol. 51 (Feb. 1937), pp. 209–23. The analysis contained in this article is very brief, and how the bond and real capital or equity differ is not discussed. Supposedly, it is self-evident.

yield on real assets as an independent variable in the demand function for money balances. Except for limited discussion by Hansen,[8] this concession never entered the mainstream of Keynesian-inspired analysis.

It should also be remembered that the notion of the liquidity trap and the instability of the money demand function generally serve to foreclose the use of the quantity theory approach by Keynesians for forecasting or research purposes.

If the liquidity trap and functional instability are ignored, the following three equations may be used to summarize the theoretical development of the Cambridge approach to the quantity theory through *The General Theory:*

Pigou	$M_D = k(PY)$	(9:1)
Keynes I	$M_D = \int(r_B, PY)$	(9:2)
Keynes II	$M_D = \int(r_B, r_E, PY)$	(9:3)

where PY is current money income; r_B, the current yield on bonds relative to the expected future or normal yield; and r_E, the yield on real capital or its equity equivalent.[9]

It is at this point in the development of a generalized demand function for money that Friedman enters with his 1956 restatement of the quantity theory.

THE FRIEDMAN DEMAND-FOR-MONEY FUNCTION

General Concepts

At the outset, Friedman states that he will apply general demand analysis to the case of money. This application of demand analysis can be made only to ultimate wealth-owning units. Following Friedman, the explanation below will indicate what modifications must be made when the demand for money by "productive enterprise" or business units is discussed.

As noted in the discussion of the Cambridge School, money is held

---

[8] Alvin Hansen, *A Guide to Keynes* (New York: McGraw Hill, 1953), pp. 135–39.

[9] The question arises whether wealth ought to be included in addition to income as an explicit argument in the function, since it obviously serves as a constraint on the speculative and precautionary demand for money. From a theoretical viewpoint, nothing would preclude its insertion as an additional argument. From an empirical viewpoint, however, its effect can be captured by PY and r_B or, if r_B and r_E are both included, by their average, because the present value of wealth can be viewed as roughly approximated as PY/r, depending on how wealth is defined. In addition, if the analysis is confined to the short run, wealth can be ignored as a determinant of money demand and treated as a constant.

as an asset because it yields utility, or a flow of services, to its owner (the avoidance of the inconveniences of barter and the provision of security against an uncertain future), or in some cases because it has an explicit return—money interest.[10] The exact nature of these service flows, or utility, is vaguely defined by Friedman and actually confined to two words, "convenience and security." Perhaps the purpose of this vagueness is to draw attention from the motivational trichotomy put forth by Keynes. In fact, Friedman emphasizes that he does not distinguish between active and idle balances or the closely related concepts of transactions and speculative balances. Rather, money is regarded as rendering a variety of services deriving from the fact that it serves as a temporary abode for generalized purchasing power, which permits the individual to separate the act of sale from the act of purchase.[11]

As with the general theory of demand, it is further stipulated that the tastes and preferences of money holders must be constant over significant stretches of time and space and subject to diminishing utility at the margin.

The Budget Constraint

For the ultimate wealth owner, the analogue of the budget constraint in consumer demand theory is of course total wealth. It may be natural to think of wealth as consisting of the tangible and intangible assets owned by individuals, for they set the upper limit on the ability of society to hold money balances. However, Friedman has a broader concept in mind. For him, wealth consists of anything which is capable of generating an explicit income stream or one measured in kind (for example, that from the services of money), and as such includes all the conventional assets. In addition, this definition of wealth implies that human assets which are capable of generating income ought also to be included as a part of wealth. So wealth should, by Friedman's definition, include the present value of the individual's future expected labor income. For many individuals the greater part of their wealth may well take the human form.

However, human wealth differs from the nonhuman variety in one fundamental respect: While the nonhuman forms may be freely substi-

---

[10] As discussed in the pages to follow, Friedman's definition of money includes an interest-bearing form—time deposits. That it includes this form has influenced his empirical findings and affects the explicit nature of the arguments to be included in the demand function itself. Until Friedman's definition of money is discussed, it can be assumed to consist only of demand deposits and currency.

[11] A fundamental question arises as to whether these services cannot be rendered by other short-term assets, for example, treasury bills. If so, this becomes a theory of the demand for short-term assets and not for money. Alternatively, it may become a theory to explain the term structure of interest rates.

tuted one for the other without limit, one cannot freely substitute non-human for human capital. That is, in the absence of slavery, a person cannot sell his human capital for equities, money, bonds, and so forth. He may, to a degree, borrow against his future labor income or sell claims to future services (for example, a lawyer's retainer) and may invest in himself through education or training in an attempt to improve his future labor income. All these forms of substitution are limited when compared to the substitutions which are possible among the nonhuman forms of wealth. This lack of general substitutability of human for non-human wealth influences the money demand function in a way discussed more extensively below.

Since Friedman's initial interest is in emphasizing the major outlines of his approach, he distinguishes five highly aggregated forms in which wealth can be held: (1) money, defined as claims or commodity units that are generally accepted in payments of debts at a fixed nominal value; (2) bonds, defined as a claim to a time stream of payments that are fixed in nominal units; (3) equities, defined as a claim to a time stream of payments that are fixed in real units; (4) physical goods, such as inventories of producer and consumer durables; and (5) human capital.

Each of these five forms of wealth yields an income stream either explicitly, for example, interest, dividends, labor income, and so forth, or implicitly, for example, the services (convenience and security) of money and inventories. The present discounted value of these expected income flows constitutes the current value of wealth, which serves as the budget constraint in the demand function for money.

Symbolically, if r is selected to represent the "rate of interest" (a concept discussed below) and Y the expected income flow from the five forms in which wealth can be held, the present value of the stock of wealth, W, can be calculated as if it were a perpetual security, or

$$W = \frac{Y}{r}$$

Thus, in place of wealth, "income," as defined above, can serve as the budget constraint.[12]

Since the Friedman approach has ultimate empirical implications, the method used by Friedman to reduce this very broad definition of wealth and its related concept of income to a variable which can be

---

[12] In Friedman's view, "This emphasis on income as a surrogate for wealth, rather than as a measure of the 'work' to be done by money, is conceptually, perhaps, the basic difference between the reformulation and the earlier versions of the quantity theory." See Friedman, "Quantity Theory," *International Encyclopedia of the Social Sciences*, Vol. 10 (New York: Macmillan and the Free Press, 1968), p. 440.

measured will be discussed below. For the time being, concern is with the theoretical rather than the empirical Friedman.

The legal and institutional constraints imposed on the conversion of human wealth to nonhuman wealth discussed above has implications for the variables that ought to be included in the demand function for money. In particular, this imperfection in the market can affect the quantity of money demanded in two different and opposite ways. First, if most of an individual's wealth is concentrated in the form of his future earning capacity, that is, the human form, the lack of substitutability may encourage him to remain more liquid than otherwise; other things equal, he will hold larger money balances. Second, rather rough empirical studies have shown that the yield on human capital generally exceeds the yield on nonhuman capital. If they are correct, they imply that the rate of return sacrificed by holding cash is greater when the alternative is human wealth rather than nonhuman wealth. Thus, when the individual's wealth is concentrated in the human form, it ought to reduce the quantity of money demanded.

For these reasons, Friedman introduces the ratio of nonhuman to human wealth as a variable in the demand function. Generally denoted by the symbol w, it is approximated by the ratio of income from nonhuman wealth to income from human wealth. In studies conducted, it has no empirical significance, indicating perhaps that its two opposite effects on the quantity of money demanded exactly counteract each other.

Given that each form of wealth has either an explicit or implicit flow associated with it, what determines the exact combination of assets which maximizes the utility of an ultimate wealth owner? As with the Cambridge School, this depends upon the opportunity cost, or yield on money relative to other nonmonetary assets.

The Yield on Wealth

money

In conventional demand analysis, the answer to the utility-maximizing combination would lead to an investigation of the price of the commodity in question and its substitutes and complements. Inquiry, then, should be directed to an investigation into the prices or yields associated with each of the five forms of wealth.

Since the definition of money thus far used includes only those assets utilized as media of exchange, that is, demand deposits and paper currency, money's *nominal* yield must necessarily be zero (if service charges are assessed against demand deposits, their yield will be negative). As explained by Friedman, individuals hold money for the services it yields them, and these services arise because of money's command over goods and services. It is the real value or physical amount of these goods and services which must be of concern; therefore, the *real* yield on money will depend upon the price index, denoted as P, for the level of prices governs the ability of money to command resources. The price index, Friedman believes, is broadly based and corresponds to the one implicit in estimating national income at constant prices. Whether the actual or expected value of that price index should be used is discussed below, but for the time being the analysis remains ambivalent on this point.

If time and savings deposits are added to the definition of money, an explicit argument must be added to the demand function denoting the interest payable on these deposits, or r_M.

bonds

For Friedman, in this highly aggregated asset structure, the bond is thought to be a perpetual security, or consol, which represents a claim to an income stream whose value is fixed in nominal terms. Thus, the yield on the consol, designated as r_B, consists of the sum of its coupon plus any anticipated capital gain due to an expected fall in the market rate of interest or less any anticipated capital loss arising from an ex-pected rise in the market rate.

For example, if a \$1,000 bond bore a coupon of 10 percent, or \$100, and it was expected that one year hence the market interest rate would be 8 percent, the expected price of the bond would be \$1,250 with a capital gain of \$250, or 25 percent. The total nominal yield on the bond, r_B, would then be \$350, or 35 percent. The real yield would, as with money, depend upon the value of P.

equity

The equity option is virtually identical to the bond except that it con-tains a cost-of-living escalator clause, thus ensuring that its income stream always maintains constant purchasing power. Therefore, its nominal yield can be thought of as being composed of three elements: its coupon yield, any expected capital gains or losses due to changes in interest rates, and expected changes in the general price level. The sum of these three elements, together with P, specify the real yield on equities.

That the equity contains the cost-of-living escalator ensures that, in Friedman's analysis, a Fisherian relationship between the price level and money interest rates will prevail. If it is assumed that everyone expects no change in future interest rates and that everyone has an opinion about future price level movements, then the money rate of interest, or yield on bonds, r_B, ought to be equal to the yield on equities plus the weighted average of the public's expected rate of change of commodity prices. Thus, market interest rates ought to rise during periods when the public has positive expectations about the future course of prices. In

Friedman's model, a force bringing about a rising interest rate would involve shifts from bonds to equities as inflationary expectations gripped the society.

commodities

The third form in which wealth can be held consists, for Friedman, of physical goods, that is, stocks of producer and consumer durables. These are similar to equities except that the income stream which they yield is in kind rather than in money and might be conceived to be the convenience and avoidance of risk and loss to which the holding of inventory gives rise. Thus, the basic yield on commodities is an implicit one. However, commodities also have an explicit yield consisting, in the first instance, of expected movements in their price. Thus, if their price is expected to appreciate their expected yield is positive, and conversely if their price is expected to decline.

In addition, offsetting the gross yield on commodities may be a negative return approximated by their storage costs and rate of depreciation or deterioration. For convenience, Friedman generally considers the nominal yield on commodities, r_C, to consist of their expected rate of price change per unit of time. Their real yield is of course calculated with reference to P.

human capital

In the absence of slavery, no market price for human capital exists and thus a rate of return or yield on this form of wealth cannot be computed directly. Some indirect methods have been used to approximate it. Nevertheless, following Friedman, any explicit rate of return on this asset will be excluded from the demand function for money.

other variables

Lastly, Friedman introduces a variable designated by u to stand for any influence other than income that can be expected to affect tastes and preferences for money, or "in Keynesian terminology, to determine the value attached to liquidity proper," for example, the degree of uncertainty attached to the future course of events.[13]

---

[13] "The Present State of Monetary Theory," p. 11. It is of interest that a Chairman of the Federal Reserve Board of Governors, Arthur Burns, places great emphasis on confidence as a determinant of velocity. We are told that "The high dynamic variable in the business cycle is not the stock of money but the rate of turnover of money, the willingness to use the existing stock, and this depends basically on the state of confidence . . . " See Hearings Before the Committee on Banking, Housing and Urban Affairs, U.S. Senate, 94th Congress, 1st Session, April 29 and 30; and May 1, Washington, D.C.: U.S. Government Printing Office (1975): pp. 176–77. According to Burn's statement, uncertainty of the future may be a principal factor precipitating the business cycle.

Combining all the above factors permits the theoretical Friedman to derive the following demand function for nominal money balances[14]:

$$M = \int\left(\frac{Y}{r}, w, P, r_B, r_E, r_C, u\right) \qquad (9{:}4)$$

If this Friedmanian demand for money function is compared to that distilled from the writings of the pre–*General Theory* Cambridge School, it might be concluded that Friedman's contribution is other than substantial. Such a conclusion would be a gross error, however, for while the functions look much alike on a purely mathematical level, Friedman's was developed from one lucid and concise statement. As such, it set forth very clearly the utility of money, the composition of wealth, and the yield on assets alternative to money. The Cambridge distillation, on the other hand, was never set forth in total by one person and was never developed to the degree of Friedman's "Restatement."

Simplifications

In order to simplify this demand function and measure the empirical relevance of each of its arguments, Friedman notes that the function in Equation (9:4) contains three interest rates: r_B, r_E, and one intended to apply to all types of assets, r, where r can be interpreted as a weighted average of r_B and r_E plus the unobservable rate applicable to human capital and physical goods (r_C in Equation (9:4) is actually the expected rate of change of prices). If the latter two rates are assumed to vary in a systematic way with the observable approximations for r_B and r_E, the generalized rate, r, can be dropped from the function, treating its influence as fully accounted for by the formal inclusion of r_B and r_E. If this is done, Y/r is reduced to Y.

Next, the price level variable, P, can be removed by making the function a demand for real balances, M/P, rather than for nominal balances.[15] When P is removed by dividing the function by its value, Y then becomes real income, or Y/P. As noted above, when the discussion returns to the empirical Friedman, close attention must be paid to the relevant concept of the price level which should be used to deflate the nominal money and income series.

What relationship should be expected to prevail between the quan-

---

[14] If money is defined broadly to include time deposits, r_M must be introduced as an explicit argument in the function.

[15] When P is removed by division, making the function a demand for real balances, this assumes that that demand is homogeneous of degree one, or a doubling of the price level will double the demand for nominal money. It should be noted that the homogeneity assumption is inconsistent with the Tobin–Baumol inventory model developed as Equation (8:6).

tity of money demanded and each of the arguments in the demand function? Theory tells us that a negative relationship ought to prevail between the quantity of money demanded and the yield on each money alternative; that is, as r_B, r_E, and r_C increase, the quantity of money demanded ought to decrease, other things equal. However, a positive relationship should exist with respect to wealth; as wealth increases over time, it should lead to larger money holdings. Exactly how much is the subject of both theoretical and empirical dispute. When certain extensions to the Keynesian model were discussed, the application of inventory analysis to money demand yielded the square root rule of Baumol, which suggests less-than-proportional growth. Similarly, when discussing Fisher, note was made of his belief that money holding ought to be subject to certain scale economies, so that as real income grew, the income elasticity of money demand would be less than unity. The ultimate resolution of these theoretical considerations is an empirical problem. Last of all, discussed above were the two opposing ways in which human capital ought to influence the quantity of money demanded. Whichever effect is the stronger will determine whether money demand, with reference to this variable, is positive or negative.

Only empirical investigations can determine how important any of these arguments are for a given time period and place as an explanation for the quantity of money demanded. However, almost every empirical study done for any time period for any country reveals that real income explains the vast majority of money demand.

The Demand for Money by Productive Enterprise

At the beginning of this chapter, when developing Friedman's generalized demand function for money, it was noted that the discussion would apply only to ultimate wealth owners and, with modification, to productive enterprise. We will now examine the modifications which must be introduced when the focus is on business units; they appear to be three in number.

First, for business, real money balances must be treated as a factor of production, just as they were treated as a source of utility for ultimate wealth owners. For business enterprise, the possession of money avoids the hazards and inconveniences of barter and provides a safe reserve for future contingencies. As a productive factor, real money balances are combined with capital and labor to maximize profits. Unlike the ultimate wealth owner, however, business enterprise can increase its money balances by borrowing in the capital market, and hence faces no budget constraint analogous to wealth or real income. When marginal profitability conditions dictate, the enterprise will borrow to augment its capital. Since these real balances are regarded as a productive factor, Friedman argues that a variable ought to be included in the demand function for money to indicate the scale of the enterprise and hence its importance as a source of money demand. He is not certain what it should be, but suggests that perhaps some measure such as total transactions, net value added, net income, net worth, or total capital in a nonmoney form might suffice. But until relevant empirical research can give an acceptable answer, it will do no harm to the conclusion of his work to use wealth or real income as a surrogate.

Second, unlike the case of ultimate wealth owners, no distinction need be made between human and nonhuman capital, for both are available to the productive enterprise in the market place with no difference in substitution possibilities as far as business is concerned.

Third, certain refinements may be called for with regard to the variables expressing the opportunity cost of holding money, that is, r_B, r_E, and r_c. This is not to suggest that the concept of opportunity cost is irrelevant for business. Quite the contrary, rates of return on money and on alternative assets are highly relevant. However, the particular rates that are relevant may differ from those of concern to ultimate wealth owners. The rates charged by banks, for example, on loans which are of minor importance for wealth owners, are likely to be extremely important for business, since such loans may be the source of business assets embodied in cash balances. In the absence of relevant information on the set of rates applicable to business, Friedman assumes that they are the same as those to which wealth owners respond.

The factors included in the generalized variable denoted by u may be similar to those for ultimate wealth owners, for example, uncertainty about the future course of events. It will also include all other factors affecting the productivity of money balances in business except those related to the size of the enterprise.

With the exception of w, it appears that the generalized demand function given as Equation (9:4) can be made applicable to business enterprise as well. Various problems of aggregation should be noted if the function is to be tested empirically; for example, one may be concerned with the distribution of real income and the distribution of wealth between its human and nonhuman components.

PERMANENT INCOME AS A SUBSTITUTE FOR WEALTH

One of the ultimate purposes of deriving the theoretical demand for money is to test it empirically to see if the quantity of money demanded, or velocity, depends on a few variables, and to determine the relative importance of these variables in explaining the observed variations in money demand, or velocity. If variations in these variables can explain a high proportion of the variation in the demand for money, it can be asserted that the demand function is stable in terms of these variables. Stability, in this sense, is an important part of Friedman's restatement of what it means to be a quantity theorist.

In order to accomplish his empirical tests, Friedman must transform his broad measure of income, Y, used in place of wealth, into a variable for which data exist. It will be remembered that included in Y are both the expected values of all items that appear in the national income accounts, that is, wages, salaries, interest, rents, profits, and various imputations (owner-occupied housing, food consumed on farms); and the imputed value of services for which no sum appears in the national income statistics, for example, the services from money balances and inventories of goods.

It might be tempting to simplify things by just including the value of national income for a given year as an approximation for Y. However, Friedman objects to this simplification because his concept of Y is that of *expected* income, whereas the national income statistics record measured, or actual, income for a given year. Expected and actual magnitudes may differ because of unexpected or transitory events, and these transitory phenomena ought not to affect the demand for money. In order to approximate his ideal of expected income, Friedman introduces what has come to be called *permanent income*. This measure of income can be generated from actual national income statistics if it is assumed that expectations about future income are based on some weighted average of past actual income. In developing this concept of income for his theory of the consumption function, the more recent the income, the greater the weight applied to it in computing the expected, or permanent, income of the consumer. In all, a 17-year time horizon was used for calculating the permanent income related to consumption; it need not, however, be the optimal time horizon for money demand.

It is this definition of income which Friedman substitutes for his broad unmeasurable concept of income, the theoretical proxy for wealth in the demand function. It should be noted that permanent income includes only those imputed services which are to be found in the national income accounts. Therefore, it is best regarded as a proxy for a somewhat narrower concept of wealth than he has in mind—one which excludes money balances.

THE REAL YIELD ON ASSETS

When the yield on money and other assets comprising wealth was discussed, a distinction was made between their nominal yield and their real yield. The latter depended upon the value of a broad-based price index denoted in Equation (9:4) as P. As viewed by Friedman, the index consists of measured prices, not the prices expected to prevail.[16] However, in some of his empirical work testing this demand function, he introduces the concept of expected, or permanent, prices, a concept analogous to permanent income and computed in the same fashion.[17]

The inclusion of expected prices as an argument is more consistent than the insertion of measured prices, for the idea lying behind a demand function for money balances is that it expresses a desired demand for money as a function of the expected value of a limited number of variables. If r_M, r_B, r_E, and r_C are expressed as expected yields, consistency and theory would call for the inclusion of the expected price level as a variable, not its measured or actual value. However, Friedman is not consistent in his explanation and use of this variable. It is best to think of it as the expected level of prices.

FRIEDMAN'S DEFINITION OF MONEY

Before Friedman's theoretical work on the demand for money can be summarized and compared with that emerging from the Cambridge School, his definition of money should be explained, as it is the only remaining variable in Equation (9:4) left undiscussed.

In a companion volume to their *Monetary History of the United States* entitled *Monetary Statistics of the United States,* Friedman and his collaborator, Anna Schwartz, devote more than 110 pages to a discussion of the appropriate definition of money. They conclude:

> . . . that the definition of money is to be sought for not on grounds of principle but on grounds of usefulness in organizing our knowledge of economic relationships. "Money" is that to which we choose to assign a number by specified operations; it is not something in existence to be discovered like the American continent; it is a tentative scientific construct to be invented like "length" or "temperature" or "force" in physics.[18]

On the basis that the empirical content of money ought to be determined "on grounds of usefulness in organizing our knowledge of economic relationships," Friedman and Schwartz reject both the tradi-

---

[16] See Friedman, "The Quantity Theory of Money—A Restatement" and *International Encyclopedia of the Social Sciences,* Vol. 10, p. 440.

[17] See Milton Friedman, "The Demand for Money: Some Theoretical and Empirical Results," *Journal of Political Economy,* Vol. 67, No. 4 (Aug. 1959), pp. 327–52.

[18] Milton Friedman and Anna Schwartz, *Monetary Statistics of the United States* (New York: National Bureau of Economic Research, 1970), p. 137.

tional definition (that which specifies money's function) and the more modern liquidity definition associated with the Radcliffe Report[19] and the work of Tobin[20] and Gurley and Shaw.[21]

As far as a specific definition of money is concerned, Friedman and Schwartz explain:

> . . . the desideratum is a monetary total whose real value (measured as the ratio of the total to a price index or as a ratio to a measure of total income or transactions, i.e., as the inverse of a velocity) bears a relatively stable relation (as between the different time periods or geographical areas under study) to a small number of variables that theoretical considerations lead us to believe affect the real quantity of money demanded—in particular, real wealth or income and the cost of holding money as measured by interest rates and the rate of change in prices.[22]

After considering the monetary history of the U.S. from at least the Civil War through the mid-1960's and correlating various asset collections with per-capita personal income on a cross-section basis for six selected years (1929, 1935, 1940, 1950, 1955, 1960), Friedman and Schwartz conclude that the proper definition of money for their purposes consists of the sum of currency held by the public plus adjusted deposits of commercial banks, both demand and time. However, the correlation evidence for 1950, 1955, and 1960 would suggest a broader definition of money, including mutual savings bank deposits and savings-and-loan shares.

One cannot help but be left with an uneasy feeling when a definition of money is determined by empirical methods and rests on no sound theoretical basis. The post–World War II empirical evidence suggests that Friedman may have to face problems in the future as his definition of money changes. It goes without saying that his definition of money has been the subject of a great deal of controversy. It will serve no purpose to review that literature, but the crux of the issue is that an obvious conflict emerges between his empirically derived definition and that emerging from his specification of money's economic function—to serve

[19] *Report of the Committee on the Working of the Monetary System*, Command 827 (London: Her Majesty's Stationary Office, 1959).

[20] James Tobin, "Commercial Banks as Creators of Money" in *Banking and Monetary Studies*, D. Carson, ed. (Homewood, Ill.: Richard D. Irwin, 1963), pp. 408–19.

[21] John G. Gurley and Edward S. Shaw, "Financial Aspects of Economic Development," *American Economic Review* (Sept. 1955), pp. 515–38; "Financial intermediaries in the Saving–Investment Process," *Journal of Finance* (May 1956), pp. 257–76; "The Growth of Debt and Money in the United States, 1890–1950: A Suggested Interpretation," *Review of Economics and Statistics* (Aug. 1957), pp. 250–62; *Money in a Theory of Finance* (Washington, D.C.: Brookings Institution), 1960.

[22] *Monetary Statistics*, pp. 139–40.

as a temporary abode for generalized purchasing power. Obviously, if time deposits can perform this function, a whole host of other assets exist which can serve the same purpose, and to exclude them from a definition of money on the basis of correlation evidence and a visual inspection of historical time series is to raise serious questions about the theoretical underpinnings of Friedman's definition. However, the whole controversy is similar in structure to that between the Banking and Currency schools over the same issue. Matters of little substance are involved. The crucial issue from Friedman's viewpoint is the degree to which the inclusion of time deposits in a definition of money increases the control which the monetary authority exercises over the course of national income, prices, and employment.

THE INFLUENCE OF TIME DEPOSITS ON FRIEDMAN'S EMPIRICAL FINDINGS

The inclusion of time deposits in the definition of money may contribute to the extremely small elasticity of money demand with respect to the interest rate which Friedman, alone among all other scholars, has discovered.

As observed in discussing the quantity theorists' uneasiness with various aspects of the Keynesian model, if the demand for money were sensitive to the money interest rate, the monetary and real sectors were integrated. In fact, Harry Johnson proclaimed this the essence of the Keynesian Revolution. So the interest sensitivity of money demand is important. As will be recalled, Friedman produced an extremely low elasticity, −.15, a number so low as to be almost equal to zero as far as practical policy is concerned. Part of the reason for this low elasticity may be that as the rate of interest changes, individuals merely shift the composition of their money balances from demand to time deposits without affecting the total amount held. If this is the case, interest rate changes will be weakly related to changes in total money balances and hence will produce a low elasticity. Thus, Friedman's definition of money may have influenced his empirical findings, which served either to confirm or to reformulate his theoretical propositions.

THE COST OF MONEY

Previously, the nominal yield on each form in which wealth can be held was distinguished from its real yield. Regardless of whether the variable to be explained in Equation (9:4) is nominal balances, M, or real balances, M/P, the opportunity cost of holding money as opposed to these other assets is measured by what is foregone, and this is the nominal yield on the nonmonetary alternative.

However, if time deposits are included as a part of the money stock, then a specific variable denoting their nominal yield must be included in the demand function for money. Then, when reference is made to the cost of holding money, it must be to the net cost, which is equal to the nominal yield on the alternatives to money, namely, r_B, r_E, and r_C, less the explicit yield on money, r_M. The difference measures the opportunity cost of money and should be the variable considered in empirical work.

FRIEDMAN SUMMARIZED

The time is now at hand to summarize the theoretical Friedman in order to compare him with the demand-for-money function set forth in *The General Theory:*

$$M_D = f(Y^e, w, r_M, r_B, r_E, r_C, P, u) \qquad (9:5)$$

Friedman's theoretical demand function for money states that the demand for nominal balances, M_D, defined as currency plus adjusted demand and time deposits, depends upon expected income, Y^e, which serves as a proxy for wealth and the magnitude of business enterprise; the distribution of wealth between human and nonhuman capital, w; the expected yield on time deposits, r_M; the total yield on bonds, r_B, envisioned as the sum of their coupon plus or minus capital gains or losses due to expected changes in the market rate; the yield on equities, r_E, which is the same as r_B, adjusted for any expected changes in commodity prices; the yield on durable commodities, r_C, which for simplicity is set equal to the rate at which prices are expected to change; the anticipated level of prices, P, which serves to define the real yield of the services of money and its alternatives; and u, symbolizing all other factors affecting the utility or productivity of money to economic units which are not explicitly accounted for in the function.

FRIEDMAN AND KEYNES COMPARED AT THE THEORETICAL LEVEL

Friedman's theoretical demand function differs from that developed by Keynes and reproduced at the beginning of this chapter in several ways.

First, it employs a definition of money which is broader than that associated with the Keynesian definition, which is usually taken to consist of demand deposits and the noninterest-bearing debt of the government.

Second, Friedman both includes additional variables to express the opportunity cost of money and specifies their value differently from Keynes. Thus, a yield on money, r_M, is introduced to account for time deposits. The yield on bonds, r_B, is the sum of the coupon and capital gain or loss arising from expected movements in the market rate of interest. In the Keynesian formulation, the interest rate is the current rate relative to some normal, or expected, rate. Moreover, in Friedman's work an explicit rate is introduced for the equity and commodity option, both generally excluded by the Keynesian assumption that they are perfect substitutes for bonds.

Third, Friedman introduces permanent income and prices as arguments, whereas in the Keynesian formulation they generally are taken to be the current measured magnitudes of these variables. However, what emerges as permanent income in Friedman's specification entered his theoretical discussion as wealth. In the Keynesian specification no such distinction is made.

Fourth, Friedman makes no distinctions between the motives for holding money balances; rather, money is held because it is a temporary abode for generalized purchasing power which provides various services to its possessor, including services as a productive factor. If for no other reason than the very elaborate way in which he has described the nature and composition of wealth, the specification of the opportunity costs of holding money, and the distinction between the motives of business and ultimate wealth owners as money demanders, the contribution of Friedman to monetary theory would be substantial.

THE EMPIRICAL FRIEDMAN

With regard to the empirical testing of his demand function, Friedman acknowledges that:

> the major problems that arise in practice . . . are the precise definitions of Y [his inclusive measure of income] and w, the estimation of expected rates of return as contrasted with actual rates of return, and the quantitative specification of the variables designated by u.[23]

It is when the empirical Friedman (who has emerged in attempting to deal with the above problems) is compared to Keynes that much of the difference in their theoretical constructs disappears.

[23] *International Encyclopedia of the Social Sciences*, Vol. 10, p. 441.

For the United States, up until 1973, Friedman and others have found only permanent income, Y^e, and actual market rates of interest, both long and short, as explaining most of the movements in the quantity of money demanded. No one has been able to show that the rate of change in the price level has any effect, no doubt because the rate of inflation in the United States has been mild and has seldom followed a single direction for a sustained period.[24] Moreover, Friedman himself tells us that w is insignificant as an explanatory variable.

Note that Friedman uses the actual rate of interest in his empirical work rather than the expected rate. The difficulties in computing the latter have generally led to a compromise in which the actual rate is used as a substitute.

Using only the significant variables, the demand function of the empirical Friedman emerges as Equation (9:6), which differs from its Keynesian counterpart in using a broader definition of money and in substituting permanent income for current measured income.

$$M_D = \int(Y^e, i) \tag{9:6}$$

THE THEORETICAL USE OF FRIEDMAN'S DEMAND FUNCTION

The discussion presented thus far has served merely to derive a formal demand function for money. It is not the derivation of a complete model of an economy; for example, the commodity, output, and labor markets remain unspecified. For many years following the 1956 "Restatement," little supplementary analysis was forthcoming to fill the void. In Friedman's 1968 presidential address before the American Economic Association[25] and in several articles in 1971,[26] the void was partially filled by a more complete statement of his model. In the interim, this demand function was used as a framework for the articulation of a generalized portfolio, or capital theoretic, approach to explain how money exerts its effects on the real sector of the economy. The general contours of Friedman's approach can be gleaned from the quotation to follow. It should be noted carefully that this statement by Friedman contains the essence of what Patinkin claims represents the fundamental advancement

[24] For a summary of the empirical evidence, see Laidler, David, *The Demand for Money: Theories and Evidence* (Scranton, Pennsylvania: International Textbook Company, 1969), pp. 89–119.

[25] M. Friedman, "The Role of Monetary Policy," *The American Economic Review*, Vol. 58, No. 1 (March 1968), pp. 1–17.

[26] M. Friedman, "A Theoretical Framework for Monetary Analysis," *Journal of Political Economy*, Vol. 78, No. 2 (March/April 1970), pp. 193–238; and "A Monetary Theory of National Income," *Journal of Political Economy*, Vol. 79, No. 2 (March/April 1971), pp. 323–37. Both papers are combined and slightly extended in *National Bureau of Economic Research Occasional Paper 112*, 1971.

of Keynes over his Cambridge associates. That is, that the increase in the stock of money can only be absorbed by a general decrease in the yields of all other assets and that this occurs via the attempt to substitute those assets for the larger money balances. In addition, the stock adjustment generating the flow adjustment is clearly distinguished. This should come as no surprise, for Friedman includes the interest rate as a variable explaining the holding of money.

Let us now suppose that an unexpected rise to a new level occurs in the rate of change in the money stock, and it remains there indefinitely . . . [and] let us suppose it comes from an increased rate of open-market purchases by a central bank.

Although the initial sellers of the securities purchased by the central bank were willing sellers, this does not mean that they want to hold the proceeds in money indefinitely. The bank offered them a good price, so they sold; they added to their money balances as a temporary step in rearranging their portfolios. If the seller was a commercial bank, it now has larger reserves than it has regarded before as sufficient and will seek to expand its investments and its loans at a greater rate than before. If the seller was not a commercial bank, he is not likely even temporarily to want to hold the proceeds in currency but will deposit them in a commercial bank, thereby, in our fractional reserve system, adding to the bank's reserves relative to its deposits. In either case, therefore, in our system, commercial banks become more liquid. In the second case, in addition, the nonbank seller has a higher ratio of money in his portfolio than he has had hitherto.

Both the nonbank seller and commercial banks will therefore seek to readjust their portfolios, the only difference being that the commercial banks will in the process create more money, thereby transmitting the increase in high-powered money to the total money stock. . . .

It seems plausible that both nonbank and bank holders of redundant balances will turn first to securities comparable to those they have sold, say fixed-interest coupon, low-risk obligations. But as they seek to purchase these they will tend to bid up the prices of those issues. Hence they, and also other holders not involved in the initial central bank open-market transactions, will look farther afield: the banks, to their loans; the nonbank holders, to other categories of securities—higher-risk fixed-coupon obligations, equities, real property, and so forth.

As the process continues, the initial impacts are diffused in several respects: first, the range of assets affected widens; second, potential creators of assets now more in demand are induced to react to the better terms on which they can be sold, including business enterprises wishing to engage in capital expansion, house builders or prospective homeowners, consumers who are potential purchasers of durable consumer goods—and so on and on; third, the initially redundant money balances concentrated in the hands of those first affected by the open-market purchases become spread throughout the economy.

As the prices of financial assets are bid up, they become expensive relative to nonfinancial assets, so there is an incentive for individuals and enterprises to seek to bring their actual portfolios into accord with desired portfolios by acquiring nonfinancial assets. This, in turn, tends to make existing nonfinancial assets expensive relative to newly constructed nonfinancial assets. At the same time, the general rise in the price level of nonfinancial assets tends to raise wealth relative to income, and to make the direct acquisition of current services cheaper relative to the purchase of sources of services. These effects raise demand curves for current productive services, both for producing new capital goods and for purchasing current services. The monetary stimulus is, in this way, spread from the financial markets to the markets for goods and services. . . .

On the basis of the sketch so far, we should expect it to have its first impact on the financial markets, and there, first on bonds, and only later on equities, and only still later on actual flows of payments for real resources. . . .

To return to our sketch, we had reached the stage at which the demand for the services of factors of production was rising, which means, of course, a rise in money incomes. This will tend to be partly reflected in a rise of the prices of resources and of final goods; at the same time, the prices of nonfinancial assets will already have been rising as demand shifted to them from financial assets. These price rises themselves tend to correct portfolios by making the real value of monetary assets less than they otherwise would be. The result is to reduce the relative redundancy of monetary assets, which sets the stage for a rise in the structure of interest rates in place of the prior decline. The exact sequence of rises in prices, whether it affects first prices of final products, and only later prices of factors and so shifts profit margins— and so on—depends on the structure of the product and factor markets . . . .

The central element in the transmission mechanism, as we have outlined it, is the concept of cyclical fluctuations as the outcome of balance sheet adjustments, as the effects on flows of adjustments between desired and actual stocks.[27]

WHAT IT MEANS TO BE A QUANTITY THEORIST[28]

Notwithstanding this close similarity between Keynes' and Friedman's empirical forms, Friedman, at the conclusion of his 1956 Restatement, spells out what it means to be a quantity theorist.

---

[27] Milton Friedman and Anna Schwartz, "Money and Business Cycles," *The Review of Economics and Statistics,* Vol. 45, No. 1, Part 2 (Feb. 1963), pp. 32–79. Quoted with permission of the authors and the North-Holland Publishing Company.

[28] Much of this section is taken verbatim from Friedman's "Restatement."

First, the quantity theorist accepts the empirical hypothesis that the demand for money is highly stable—more stable than functions like the consumption function that are offered as alternative key relations. A stable function, Friedman emphasizes, does not mean a constant velocity, but that the function is stable in terms of the variables which determine its value. Thus, an increase in velocity during a period of inflation or a rise in the interest rate is consistent with functional stability. In addition, this functional stability must depend upon only a few variables because, as Friedman rightly believes, little difference exists between asserting that the demand for money is highly unstable and asserting that it is a perfectly stable function of an indefinitely large number of variables.

From the assertion that the velocity function is more stable than the consumption function comes the belief that it plays a vital role in determining variables the quantity theorist regards as highly important for the analysis of the economy, for example, money income and the level of prices. He therefore prefers to perform analysis in terms of changes in the money supply and a money multiplier derived from the velocity relationship rather than use autonomous expenditures and the multiplier which emerges from the consumption function (the latter emphasized by Keynesians).

Second, the quantity theorist holds that there are important factors affecting the supply of money that do not affect the demand for money. The notion of a stable demand function is useful in order to trace out the effect of changes in supply, but it is useful only if supply is influenced by at least some factors other than those regarded as affecting demand. Thus, the quantity theorist would reject the notion that the supply of money expands or contracts according to the "needs of trade" —an idea traceable to the Banking School and Adam Smith, but also used by Keynes–Wicksell in their explanation for Gibson's Paradox.

Third, the quantity theorist rejects the concept of a Keynesian liquidity trap, or infinite elasticity of demand for money. While Friedman does not tell us what the elasticity ought to be, he obviously makes a stronger case for the quantity theory if the value approximates zero.

Other unspecified differences of the kind developed throughout this text as the fundamental propositions of the quantity theory must also exist between the two approaches, for if none other exists than the three given above, empirical testing would determine to what extent "we are all Keynesians now."

CONCLUSION

The purpose of this chapter has been to develop the theoretical underpinnings of Professor Friedman's basic monetary theory. This has led to an investigation in great detail of his now classic article restating the quantity theory. A central purpose has been to show how it can be viewed as a logical progression of a theme initiated by the Cambridge cash-balance approach to the quantity theory of which the liquidity preference theory of Keynes is a direct descendant. Therefore, Friedman can indeed be viewed as being in the Cambridge tradition and one of the central formulators of the capital theoretical approach to monetary theory.

Any differences between Friedman and the Keynesians shrink considerably when we view their respective empirical work.

However, basic differences still remain, and in the chapters to follow these differences will be spelled out, centering in part on the short-run nonneutrality of money and the channels through which money affects the real variables of the economy.

Selected References and Readings

FRIEDMAN, MILTON, "The Quantity Theory of Money: A Restatement," in M. Friedman, ed., *Studies in the Quantity Theory of Money* (Chicago: University of Chicago Press, 1956).

————, "The Supply of Money and Changes in Prices and Output," in *The Relationship of Prices to Economic Stability and Growth*, 85th Congress, 2nd Session, Joint Economic Committee (Washington, D.C.: U.S. Government Printing Office, 1958).

————, "The Demand for Money: Some Theoretical and Empirical Results," *The Journal of Political Economy*, Vol. 67, No. 4 (July/Aug. 1959).

————, "The Present State of Monetary Theory," *Economic Studies Quarterly*, Vol. 14, No. 1 (Sept. 1963).

————, "Postwar Trends in Monetary Theory and Policy," *The National Banking Review*, Vol. 1, No. 1 (Sept. 1964).

————, "Interest Rates and the Demand for Money," *The Journal of Law and Economics*, Vol. 9 (Oct. 1966).

————, "Quantity Theory," *International Encyclopedia of the Social Sciences*, Vol. 10 (New York: Macmillan, 1968).

————, "Comments on the Critics," *Journal of Political Economy*, Vol. 80, No. 5 (Sept./Oct. 1972).

————, AND SCHWARTZ, ANNA, "Money and Business Cycles," *Review of Economics and Statistics*, Vol. 45, No. 1, Part 2: Supplement (Feb. 1963).

————, *A Monetary History of the United States, 1870–1960* (Princeton, N.J.: Princeton University Press, 1963).

————, *Monetary Statistics of the United States* (New York: National Bureau of Economic Research, 1970).

HANSEN, ALVIN, *A Guide to Keynes* (New York: McGraw-Hill, 1953).

JOHNSON, HARRY, "The Keynesian Revolution and the Monetarist Counter-Revolution," *American Economic Review*, Vol. 61, No. 2 (May 1971).

KEYNES, J. M., "The General Theory," *Quarterly Journal of Economics*, Vol. 51, No. 1 (Feb. 1937).

PATINKIN, DON, "The Chicago Tradition, The Quantity Theory and Friedman," *Journal of Money, Credit and Banking*, Vol. 1, No. 1 (Feb. 1969).

————, "Friedman on the Quantity Theory and Keynesian Economics," *Journal of Political Economy*, Vol. 80, No. 5 (Sept./Oct. 1972).

chapter 10

Modern Monetary Theory

The purpose of this chapter is to discuss several specific topics in monetary economics which are either refinements of a theoretical approach or revivals of an old controversy. When the discussion to follow is combined with the analysis in the two subsequent chapters, the dimensions of modern monetary theory and its controversies can be fully appreciated.

The specific topics addressed in this chapter include the portfolio approach to money demand, various questions related to the uniqueness of money and commercial banks (including a review of the work of the Radcliffe Committee in England and that of Gurley, Shaw, and Roosa in the United States), and a survey of the literature developing the theory of the supply of money.

THE PORTFOLIO APPROACH TO MONEY DEMAND

The portfolio approach to money demand was introduced in Chapter 4 as the Cambridge, or cash-balance, formulation of the quantity theory of money and consisted of the application of micro-demand analysis to the specific commodity called money. As developed by the Cambridge scholars, the cash-balance approach explains the factors determining the optimum portfolio of assets.

In Chapter 8, the work of James Tobin was introduced as a major contribution to portfolio analysis to correct the unsatisfactory state of affairs found in *The General Theory:* The highly aggregated state of assets (only money and bonds), the result that individuals hold either all money or all bonds in their portfolios, and the combination of two quite different approaches to monetary theory.

Last, work by Milton Friedman was introduced in the preceding chapter as an elegant elaboration of the portfolio approach which, like the work of Tobin, intended to amend the shortcomings found in the monetary theory of Keynes.

There were, however, others outside of the Cambridge tradition and antecedent to Tobin and Friedman who made valuable contributions to the analytical structure of the portfolio approach as it now stands.

Foremost among these is Sir John Hicks, who in 1935, one year before the appearance of *The General Theory,* published "A Suggestion for Simplifying the Theory of Money."[1] Called by G.L.S. Shackle, ". . . one of the most remarkable papers contributed to the journals of theory in our period,"[2] it represented a specific application of general demand analysis, or value theory, to money. As such, it sets forth the marginal productivity of money, the nature of the opportunity cost, the budget constraint, and how changes in each ought to affect the demand for money. All this is spelled out quite clearly, without the obscurity which often mars the work of the Cambridge scholars. Because of the clarity, and thus seeming originality, of Hicks' exposition, some have argued that the cash-balance formulation of the quantity theory ought to be viewed as the Oxford approach even though Hicks acknowledges that the works of Lavington ". . . come very close to what I am driving at."

An extensive list of assets is set forth by Hicks, which includes consumption goods, both durable and nondurable; money; bank deposits; short-term and long-term debts; stocks and shares; and productive capital. Unfortunately, in the tidal wave caused by *The General Theory,* Hicks' paper was not immediately followed up, as it should have been, by a more extensive analysis integrated into a theoretical framework which would permit contrasts and comparisons to be made between it and the traditional theory extant at the time.

Two other contributions to the portfolio approach are also noteworthy. The first, published in 1938, was by Helen Makower and Jacob Marschak[3] and applies such concepts as time, imperfect competition, and uncertainty to explain the holding of the stock of money in a general equilibrium framework which includes other assets. The second

[1] John R. Hicks, "A Suggestion for Simplifying the Theory of Money," *Economica,* New Series, Vol. 2 (1935), pp. 1–19.

[2] G.L.S. Shackle, *The Years of High Theory* (London: Cambridge University Press 1967), p. 222.

[3] Helen Makower and Jacob Marschak, "Assets, Prices and Monetary Theory," *Economica,* New Series, Vol. 5 (1938), pp. 261–88.

paper, by Harry Markowitz,[4] was a first attempt to apply the concept of risk, as represented by the variance in the expected rate of return from an asset, to explain the holding of a diversified portfolio. The idea that the wealth holder must consider both the expected rate of return from an asset and the variance in that rate of return, if diversified portfolios are to be explained, represents a major theoretical contribution which was later considered by Tobin using indifference curves and budget lines (See Chapter 8, pp. 204–09).

MONETARY AND FISCAL POLICY IN A PORTFOLIO FRAMEWORK

Given this brief survey of the literature, our next step is actually to work out two problems within the confines of the portfolio approach. This may not be as easy as it seems, for the ultimate answers derived from the analysis can depend critically on the asset mix selected and the assumptions made concerning the degree to which one asset is a substitute for another. For example, it has already been shown that in the highly aggregated two-asset Keynesian world inflation will have no direct effect on asset selection, for the purchasing power of both assets is eroded equally by rising commodity prices. Conversely, in the more extensive asset menu emerging from the work of Friedman, the inclusion of the equity option makes a distinction between real and nominal interest rates imperative.

With this general caveat in mind, the portfolio selected for the problems presented below will include the following assets:

Money

    Governments Noninterest-Bearing Debt

    Bank Deposits

Government Interest-Bearing Debt

    Short-Term

    Long-Term (Bonds)

Private Debt

    Short-Term

    Long-Term (Bonds)

Equities

[4] Harry Markowitz, "Portfolio Selection," *Journal of Finance*, Vol. 7, No. 1 (March 1952), pp. 77–91. See also his *Portfolio Selection: Efficient Diversification of Investments* (New York: John Wiley, 1959).

> Real Capital
>> Producers' Durables
>> Consumers' Durables

As such, this portfolio should be about as acceptable to the Friedmanians as it would be to the followers of Keynes.[5]

We begin the analysis of each problem by assuming that a state of equilibrium prevails, which means that the price of each asset, or its yield, is such that the society is just willing to hold the existing stock, that is, that it desires neither to add to nor decrease its existing holdings of each asset. The prevailing prices, or yields, of assets need not be equal at the margin, but ought to differ depending upon such characteristics as default risk, variance of expected earnings, time to maturity, expected yields, and so forth.

Monetary Policy

initial influences

In the first problem, the central bank will engage in an expansionary monetary policy in which it purchases government interest-bearing debt from the public and the banking system, giving in return noninterest-bearing debt, or money. In order to induce individuals, both bank and nonbank, to reduce their stock of government noninterest-bearing debt, the prices of those assets must be increased, which as a consequence reduces their yield.

This open-market operation by the central bank will set in motion substitution and wealth effects which will serve ultimately to expand aggregate money demand and (depending on the state of the economy) to expand real output, employment, and the level of prices. Whether the impact of the increase in the supply of money is permanent or transitory is still a matter of controversy.

substitution effects

Nonbank Public. In the portfolios of those individuals who sold their bonds for money to the central bank, the yield on those two assets has fallen relative to the yield on all other assets, thereby setting in motion an adjustment process wherein higher-yielding assets are substituted

<hr>

[5] See, for example, Tobin's portfolio in "Money, Capital and Other Stores of Value," *American Economic Review*, Vol. 51, No. 2 (May 1961), pp. 26–37 and "An Essay on the Principles of Debt Management" in Commission on Money and Credit, *Fiscal and Debt Management Policies* (Englewood Cliffs, N.J.: Prentice-Hall 1963), pp. 143–218.

For an alternative portfolio which includes the claims of nonbank intermediaries as well as other differentiating criteria, see John Gurley, and Edward Shaw, *Money in a Theory of Finance* (Washington, D.C.: Brookings Institution, 1960), pp. 159–77.

for lower-yielding ones, that is, money is exchanged for private debt securities, equities, and real capital. The exact chain of events by which these securities are purchased depends upon the degree to which each is more or less substitutable for the government securities given up. Most likely if a short-term government security were sold, a private short-term security would be purchased as a replacement, for the marginal yield differential between them would have been altered. Since the yield on private short-term debt would then be altered relative to private long-term debt, wealth owners might then be induced to purchase the longer-term security. In doing so, the yield on that class of security might then be altered relative to the equity inducing its purchase, and so on to the purchase of the existing stock of real producer and consumer durables.

As the operation of the substitution effect serves to alter the yield on all other assets, it throws into disequilibrium the portfolios of those individuals who did not initially sell their government securities in response to the central bank purchase. They also are then induced to sell some assets and purchase others in an attempt to restore equilibrium to their asset structure.

Commercial Banks. The purchase of government interest-bearing securities from the banking system serves to augment the monetary base, or bank reserves, and, by reducing the implicit yield on those reserve assets relative to others, induces the commercial banks to increase their rate of lending. The rise in lending serves to monetize part of the existing stock of privately owned assets. In addition, the easier terms on which loans are made may persuade the nonbank public to issue more liabilities in order to raise loanable funds for expanded asset purchases.

The substitution effect thus far appears to constitute only a rearrangement of the ownership of the existing stock of assets. This need not be so. To the extent that the price of equity shares and the existing stock of producer and consumer durable goods increases relative to the price of newly produced durables, a gap is opened between the actual and the desired stock of those capital goods, leading to an increase in the rate of flow of production of new durables.

The purpose of the substitution effect is therefore to generalize the initial change in the interest yield on government securities to all of the other assets owned by the public. How successful this will be depends on the magnitude of the change in the yield on government securities and the degree to which the other real assets are substitutes for government securities, that is, the degree to which high cross-elasticities of demand prevail. If the interest rate is low to begin with, or if low cross-elasticities of other financial assets for government bonds and a high cross-elasticity of these assets for money prevails, the substitution effect is likely to be relatively weak.

wealth effects

Regarding the wealth effect, a good deal of controversy is to be found between the Friedmanians and the Keynesians. The problem centers around the extent to which government interest-bearing debt should be counted as a part of net wealth. Clearly, to the individuals who own the government securities, such debt is an asset and is included on their balance sheets. But each bond has attached to it a tax liability to service it for future interest payments and its ultimate redemption. Thus, according to Friedman, each taxpayer ought to include a proportionate share of the national debt as a liability on his personal balance sheet. To the extent that the same discount rate is used to discount the future interest income from the bond and the future tax liability for debt service, government bonds cannot constitute a part of net wealth. To argue that they are part of net wealth is to argue that the future tax liability for debt service is discounted at an infinite rate of interest or that for some reason the public does not perceive its future tax liability for debt service.

Nevertheless, various economists generally identified as Keynesians regard government interest-bearing debt as a part of net wealth. For them, open-market operations which substitute noninterest-bearing debt (money) for interest-bearing debt do not create a direct wealth effect because the net wealth of society is not altered; only its composition is changed.[6] However, for the followers of Friedman, open-market operations such as discussed above can directly create wealth, for the bond, which is not wealth, is replaced by money, which is a part of net wealth, for it has no tax liability attached to it for debt service. It is further alleged by these Friedmanians that the power of monetary policy lies in the wealth effect, for it leads to the purchase of all types of assets by directly expanding the budget constraint.[7]

It is the use made of the wealth effect which serves to differentiate the use of the portfolio approach by Keynesians and Friedmanians. In the Keynesian approach, the substitution effect will directly expand income, setting in motion the well-known Keynesian multiplier and leading to an expansion in the demand for consumer nondurable goods. In the Friedmanian framework, the wealth effect can directly expand

[6] In some Keynesian models, open-market operations can directly affect consumption when that variable is made to depend upon the liquidity, or "moniness," of assets. Thus, if long-term bonds are replaced by money, the liquidity of the economy will be increased and the consumption function will shift upward. This effect is unlikely if Treasury bills are purchased.

[7] The wealth effect is analogous to the income effect of conventional demand analysis. Whether it will lead to an increase in the holding of all assets depends upon their respective wealth elasticities of demand, although they ought all to be normal goods, that is, have a wealth elasticity greater than zero.

the demand for nondurable goods, thereby circumventing the necessity for the multiplier to operate.

Also generally acknowledged is a second type of wealth effect, which arises because the open-market operation leads to a general decrease in the yields of all assets. The decrease in yields raises the capitalized values of the income streams associated with each asset, making the owners of these assets better off. Again, however, as with government interest-bearing securities, private debt securities are not a part of net wealth and hence should be excluded when calculating this second wealth effect. In principle its magnitude appears confined to durable goods or their equity equivalent.

To the extent that the combined wealth effects bring up the price of the existing stock of assets relative to the price of new production, they also serve to increase the rate of flow of output of new producer and consumer durables. In addition, the wealth effects may serve directly to stimulate the purchase of consumer nondurable goods.

ultimate influences

Both the substitution and the wealth effects set in motion stock adjustments in which individuals seek to restore equilibrium between their actual holdings of each asset and their desired holdings. These stock adjustments are not the end of the process, however, for they in turn alter the rate of flow of durable and nondurable goods production. Changes in these flows can also give rise to changes in the supply of assets, which in turn, by altering relative supplies and stocks, can initiate further substitution and wealth effects in a complex pattern which defies verbal description. Interwoven in this description of an expanding economy ought to be a discussion of the effect of a rising demand for paper currency (government noninterest-bearing debt) relative to bank money, and the effects on asset selection which any inflation might generate. However, the discussion soon becomes unmanageable.

Fiscal Policy

While some controversy surrounds the definition of fiscal policy (the topic is discussed in Chapter 12), for purposes of this analysis, it will be defined as any acts of government expenditure or taxation undertaken while holding the stock of money constant.

Initial Influences. Starting from a balanced budget, the initial rise in expenditures or reduction in taxes is intended to directly enlarge the flow of real income, for it represents the direct alteration of the purchase of goods and services. Supplemented by the operation of the

Keynesian multiplier, the fiscal act leads to a rise in the demand for money, which puts upward pressure on interest rates. In addition, the sale of government interest-bearing debt to finance the budget deficit puts additional upward pressure on interest rates in order that these bonds might be sold.

The rise in the stock of government interest-bearing debt and the upward pressure on interest rates sets in motion substitution and wealth effects such as those discussed above.

substitution effect

The operation of the substitution effect is the reverse of that described above. The rise in the yield on government interest-bearing securities induces their holders to substitute them for the now lower-yielding private debts, equities, and durable goods. The sale of these latter assets causes their prices to fall and their yields to rise, which generalizes the effects of the rise in the yield of government securities.

If the prices of equities and the existing stock of durable goods fall below their current reproduction costs, the actual stock of capital (producers and consumers) then exceeds the desired stock, leading to net disinvestment and a decrease in the rate of flow of new producer and consumer durable goods.

The behavior of the banking system may be in the direction of expanding the supply of bank money. The general rise in yields will lead banks to use more intensively any holdings of excess reserves, perhaps even inducing an attempt to borrow reserves from the central bank. Any increase in the supply of money will mean a monetization of some of the stock of existing assets, thereby moderating the rise in yields.

Quite clearly, if the behavior of the banking system is disregarded, the substitution effect of a fiscal policy act works to offset the expansionary influence of any direct increase in the purchase of goods and services induced by a cut in taxes or an increase in government expenditures. This offset produces what in Chapter 8 was called the crowding-out effect.

wealth effects

The net impact of the wealth effects is difficult to describe, for it works both to expand and to contract the economy.

From the Keynesian viewpoint, the additional bonds required to finance the deficit constitute an addition to net wealth, which increases period after period as long as the deficit continues. Because these bonds serve to shift out the budget constraint on portfolios, they serve to expand the demand for all assets including consumer nondurable goods. From the viewpoint of expanding demand for durables and nondurables, this Keynesian wealth effect is expansionary. This wealth-induced expansion in income serves also to increase the demand for money, and an increasing demand for money serves to raise interest rates and in general to exercise a contractionary influence on economic activity.[8]

In addition, the generalized rise in asset yields following from the fiscal action tends to decrease the capitalized values of each asset, thereby impoverishing the owners and contracting their demand for all assets (this does not apply to private debt securities unless the wealth elasticity of bond owners and issuers is different). To the extent that this wealth effect is strong, as some econometric models indicate it is for monetary policy, it should exercise a powerful contractionary influence tending to offset the direct expansionary force of the deficit.

On balance, and in the long run, it would appear that a strong argument could be made that the negative wealth and substitution effects ought ultimately to offset the expansionary influence of the initial deficit in the government budget caused by higher expenditure levels or lower taxes. To the extent that this occurs, fiscal crowd-out is complete and government fiscal policy has no net expansionary influence. This topic is treated more extensively in Chapter 12.

The ultimate impact of this fiscal act will necessitate a discussion paralleling that given above for monetary policy and including consideration of movements in the public's holding of paper currency.

Of great importance is the fact that to draw a complete set of conclusions regarding the effectiveness of monetary and fiscal acts a consistent methodology ought to be applied to each. It is gratifying, then, that a common approach embodied in portfolio analysis is available as well as an appropriate methodology to assess the relative importance of each act at the theoretical level.

THE PORTFOLIO APPROACH—
SOME ADDITIONAL CONSIDERATIONS

A basic conclusion to emerge from an examination of problems of monetary and fiscal actions is that the portfolio approach may not be conveniently summarized in terms of the conventional *IS–LM* framework. The wealth effects cause one or both schedules to shift, and such shifts may be more important quantitatively than an analysis confined to the substitution effect alone would indicate. In most problems using

---

[8] The Friedmanians would deny this Keynesian wealth effect. However, in their view, the increase in the stock of government bonds continues and bonds accumulate in portfolios relative to other assets. This continued accumulation of bonds ought to give rise to a diversification demand for money which should then serve to exercise a deflationary influence on the economy.

the *IS–LM* framework, usually only the substitution effect is discussed, as the discussion is generally confined to the short run. Whether the magnitude of the wealth effects dominates that of the substitution effect is purely an empirical issue.

Thus, while a discussion of the portfolio adjustment process is certainly more intricate than that given by a more traditional *IS–LM* analysis, it provides a more rigorous treatment of the subject and gives richer insights into the actual means by which economic activity responds to either a monetary or a fiscal stimulus.

THE RADCLIFFE REPORT, GURLEY–SHAW, AND ROOSA

In the 1950's, by a remarkable coincidence, in both Great Britain and the United States various individuals in both academic and public policy circles questioned the adequacy or sophistication of conventional monetary theory to serve as the underpinning for monetary policy. In retrospect, the issues which they raised and the alternative theoretical propositions which they advanced can largely be seen as signs of an extreme movement away from the quantity theory with its emphasis on the supply of money as the all-important economic variable.

The British and American inquirers into the role of money in an economy came from different backgrounds, but all addressed similar issues and arrived at somewhat similar conclusions on theory and policy. Common to both discussions was a subject debated a century or more before, during the famous Currency–Banking School controversy. This concerned the unique attributes of a small group of assets which alone among all others were to be called money. The issues raised during the 1950's go far beyond a mere sterile discussion of what is and is not money, and concern questions fundamental to both monetary policy and theory. At the center of the discussion is the question of the stability of the velocity function and the uniqueness of commercial banks among financial intermediaries, such that monetary policy ought to concentrate exclusively on regulating their ability to create demand deposits. Obviously, if money is undefinable or includes a broad category of assets, it may either be impossible to discuss the policy actions of central banks, or monetary policy tools for accomplishing stabilization objectives which center on commercial banks may be inadequate and require supplementation. Moreover, if money cannot be defined, a monetary theory is impossible, or depending on how money is defined, radically different theories may be advanced concerning the way in which money influences economic activity.

It is for these reasons that a review of the discussions which took place on both sides of the Atlantic during the 1950's should be of interest. Before considering the arguments, it should be noted that these discussions came to very little. They altered neither monetary theory nor policy in any fundamental respect. Several of the issues raised in these discussions were subjected to empirical investigations which in the main did not lend support to the position of those who questioned the orthodoxy of the day. Ironically, monetary theory is once again moving in the direction of one of the approaches specifically rejected by those who questioned the conventional analysis.

THE RADCLIFFE REPORT

The Committee on the Working of the Monetary System, known as the Radcliffe Committee, was appointed by Britain's Chancellor of the Exchequer in May 1957 "to inquire into the working of the monetary and credit system and to make recommendations." The Committee was composed of the Chairman, Lord Radcliffe, two businessmen, two bankers, two trade union leaders, and two academic economists (Professors A. K. Cairncross and R. S. Sayers). During the 59 days of hearings, scattered from July 1957 to April 1959, evidence was obtained from the Treasury, the Bank of England, clearing banks and other financial institutions, dozens of trade associations, business leaders, and many economists. In addition, the Committee received memoranda from many of these witnesses and from others, including the National Institute of Economic and Social Research, the Central Statistical Office, and, inevitably, a few monetary cranks.[9]

The unanimous *Report* of the Committee was published in August 1959. This was followed in March 1960 by four volumes of evidence: ". . . as a rough guess, the Report and the four volumes of evidence are packed with upwards of $3\frac{1}{2}$ million words. . . ."

Because of the dearth of relevant statistical information, the principal hypotheses of the Committee were not subject to any but the most primitive empirical verifications. Rather, the methodology of the *Report* is that of "informed opinion," "insider information," and "personal conjecture" on the cause of economic events and the effectiveness of public policy. Nowhere in the *Report* is a formal Radcliffe economic model set forth. This must be constructed from the written *Report,* which consists of 986 numbered paragraphs interspersing theory, conjecture, and historical analysis of past events.

---

[9] This paragraph and the succeeding one are taken from John G. Gurley, "The Radcliffe Report and Evidence: A Review Article," *American Economic Review*, Vol. 50, No. 4 (Sept. 1960), pp. 672–700.

Assessment of Prevailing Monetary Theory

Starting from the premise that the important variable for determining the level of employment and the rate of change of the price level is the state of aggregate demand, the Committee investigated the way in which money was supposed (according to prevailing monetary theory) to influence that variable. This led inevitably to a consideration of the direct and indirect linkage of money to economic activity.

The direct linkage was identified with the classical quantity theory, whereas the second, or indirect, mechanism, emphasizing interest rates, was thought to best characterize the Keynesian approach.

The direct mechanism embodied in the Equation of Exchange, $M \cdot V = P \cdot Y$, was denied emphatically as an explanation of the linkage of money and economic activity on several grounds. First, the Committee could discover no tight relationship between the supply of money as defined, and the level of economic activity (national income), although only several years were compared. Second, it was argued that in a highly developed financial system with many financial intermediaries, grave theoretical difficulties were posed in identifying or labeling some quantity as "the supply of money."[10] Third, the Committee viewed the veloc-

---

[10] The inference is frequently made that the Committee itself did not or could not define the supply of money for Great Britain. This is totally incorrect. Early in the *Report*, in commenting on demand deposits, the statement is made: "Their value being absolutely fixed in terms of the unit of account, these balances are 'money' to a degree shared by no other asset except, for smaller transactions, notes and coin." (¶129, p. 43. Hereafter this notation will be used to indicate the relevant paragraph and page of the *Report* from which the quotation is taken.) Later, the *Report* states: " . . . and the quantity of 'money,' meaning by 'money' [in the British context] notes plus bank deposits" (¶388, p. 132). Nevertheless, at various places in the *Report* the words—supply of money—are put in quotation marks followed by such phrases as "however that is defined" (¶125, p. 42) or "whatever that may be made to mean" (¶504, p. 179), giving rise to the inference that the relevant quantity could not be defined.

It is a subsequent article by R.S. Sayers, widely regarded as providing the theoretical substructure for Radcliffe monetary theory, that raises the issue whether money can, in fact, be defined. We are told, "The difficulty of identification has derived from the two-fold nature of money . . . as a medium of exchange and as a store of value . . . There are articles which are stores of value but are clearly not money because they are *never* used as media of exchange. But are we to label as money all other stores of value, that is to say, all those which are ever brought into use, whether commonly or occasionally or only rarely, as media of exchange? The usual answer is that we should include as money only those assets which are commonly used as media of exchange. Resort to the adverb 'commonly' at once emphasizes the absence of any sharp line of distinction.

"A similar attempt to escape from the difficulties of identification of money is to be found in the distinction sometimes drawn between 'active money' and 'idle money' . . . But the distinction is at best misleading. No asset is in action as a medium of exchange except in the moment of being transferred from one ownership to another, in settlement of some transaction, and no class of assets used in this way can logically be excluded from the class of active money. Between transactions all money is idle. Yet if activity is held to cover the state of being held in readiness against possible use in exchange, then all monetary assets

ity of money as it was usually viewed in pre-Friedman days: As a numerical constant devoid of any behavioral content and as a variable whose value changed as the definition of money was altered. The Committee went so far as to say that they had not made use of the concept of velocity

> . . . because we cannot find any reason for supposing, or any experience in monetary history indicating, that there is any limit to the velocity of circulation; it is a statistical concept that tells us nothing directly of the motivation that influences the level of total demand.[11]

Even if all the theoretical difficulties surrounding the definition could be resolved, the Committee would still reject the direct mechanism as an explanation of the link between the money supply and economic activity, because in a system of highly developed financial intermediaries providing substitutes for narrowly defined money, the velocity of circulation was thought to be indeterminate. In the words of the Committee ". . . all the haziness of the connection between the supply of money and the level of total demand remains: the haziness that lies in the impossibility of limiting the velocity of circulation."[12]

Thus, if the central bank sought to restrain the growth of aggregate demand (MV) by restraining the growth of the money supply (M), financial intermediaries other than banks were supposed able to activate idle demand deposits and currency, raising velocity (V) sufficiently to offset the restriction on the money supply and leave aggregate demand (MV) largely unaltered. This power of nonbank intermediaries was thought to be unlimited![13] In addition, the volume of trade credit, many

---

are active all the time. It is not merely that we cannot easily earmark for statistical assessment the quantity that is active: there is no such quantity . . . ." See R.S. Sayers, "Monetary Thought and Monetary Policy in England," *Economic Journal*, Vol. 70, No. 4 (Dec. 1960), pp. 710–24.

[11] ¶391, p. 133.

[12] ¶523, p. 187.

[13] There is remarkably little analysis in the *Report* of how velocity can be raised by nonbank intermediaries. Supposedly, a slight increase in the amount paid on their deposits or the sale of assets, for example, government securities, should attract previously idle demand deposits which can then be re-lent to those who have been refused bank loans. Other actions are available to the potential borrower, including running down his own idle balances, obtaining longer credit from suppliers, using hire purchase (buying on time), mortgaging his properties, raising money on insurance policies or against marketable securities, and so forth. (See ¶316, pp. 107–108). The view is also expressed that the availability of funds for borrowers in some unspecified way depends on the number of intermediaries.

The Radcliffe view on the velocity of money parallels remarkably that of the Banking School. It will be recalled from Chapter 3 that the Banking School ridiculed the Currency School policy prescription centering on control over the supply of Bank of England notes in the presence of various other means which could serve as media of exchange. On the other hand, the Radcliffe Committee argued the futility of control of money (defined as notes and

times the size of the British money supply, was thought capable of being lengthened, providing an effective offset to monetary stringency.[14]

In this fashion, the Committee dispensed with the direct mechanism and the quantity theory approach to monetary theory and policy.

By appeal to crude empirical tests, the indirect mechanism was also found to be inapplicable as an explanation of the link between money and economic activity. According to the Committee, it found no evidence that higher interest rates, in and of themselves, reduced consumption; there was practically no indication that interest rates were important to large firms with respect to investment in either inventories or fixed capital; expenditures of the nationalized industries were also largely impervious to changes in interest rates; the same was true for local authorities' expenditures; and spokesmen for the smaller firms treated the interest rate effect with general skepticism.[15] Thus, "It has become clear that, as the system works at present, changes in rates of interest only very exceptionally have direct effects on the level of demand. . . ."[16]

The Radcliffe View on the Effectiveness of Money

Since neither the direct nor the indirect mechanism was thought able to explain the influence of the money supply on the pace of economic activity, it would seem valid to conclude that the Radcliffe Committee held that money does not matter and that monetary policy has no role to play in economic stabilization. However, this is not the case, for the *Report* set forth the outlines of a new transmission mechanism explaining the role of the money supply, commercial banks, and monetary policy.

The new transmission mechanism centered on what the *Report* called *liquidity*.

---

bank deposits) in the presence of a financial system which provides a large number of substitutes for conventional money as a store of value. On this comparison, see A.B. Cramp, "Two Views on Money," *Lloyds Bank Review*, No. 65 (July 1962), pp. 1–15.

[14] On the issue of trade credit, the *Report* states: "Trade credit thus introduces considerable elasticity into the response of business to efforts by the monetary authorities to compress liquidity. In conditions of boom it can be used to finance a continuing expansion, even when bank credit is being contracted, so long as business expectations remain sanguine. . . . Moreover, trade credit is so large in relation to bank credit that a comparatively small lengthening of trade credit would normally offset quite a large proportionate reduction in bank credit." (¶300, p. 103).

[15] This summary is taken from Gurley, "The Radcliffe Report," p. 681. As Gurley notes, the evidence on the effects of interest rate changes was gathered largely by surveys and, if read carefully, may not in fact support the conclusions deduced by the Committee. In addition, the Committee tended to badger and hound witnesses reporting on these surveys in an effort to elicit from them the view that interest rates were unimportant in investment decisions of the type summarized above.

[16] ¶487, p. 174.

It is this wide concept of liquid assets that we must put in the place conventionally occupied by "the supply of money," as the monetary quantity influencing total effective demand for goods and services. And we must interpret it widely enough to include credit that can be brought into existence concurrently with a decision to exercise demand.[17]

Surprisingly, nowhere in the *Report* is there a definition of liquidity or liquid asset. The most nearly precise definition is contained in an opinion of the Committee that

. . . spending is not limited by the amount of money in existence; but it is related to the amount of money people think they can get hold of, whether by receipts of income (for instance, from sales), by disposal of capital assets or by borrowing.[18]

Thus, liquidity consists of the amount of money people think they can get hold of from their own resources, which might be called "old" liquidity, and from unused borrowing power, or "new" liquidity. Supposedly, if liquidity were reduced, expenditures, to the extent they exceeded current income, ought to decline and vice versa. This is the first element in the Radcliffe view of the transmission mechanism.[19]

The second element of the transmission mechanism concerns the way in which the monetary authority can influence the overall level of liquidity and hence the level of aggregate expenditures. Varying the amount of liquidity is to be accomplished by manipulating the structure of interest rates, which can directly change the "old" liquidity of spenders and make it more difficult for them to acquire "new" liquidity. Clearly, according to the Radcliffe Committee, it was the increasing difficulty of acquiring "new" liquidity that was to be the major effect of monetary policy and this difficulty was to act upon the ability of lenders to lend, not upon the ability of borrowers to borrow. Thus, rising interest rates brought about by conventional monetary contraction [20] were to reduce the ability of lenders to lend, since they were not supposed to have much effect upon the borrower's desire to borrow. Rising interest rates reduce liquidity because they serve to reduce the capital value of assets held by individuals and financial institutions. Thus, the "old"

---

[17] Sayers, "Monetary Thought," p. 1.

[18] ¶390, p. 133.

[19] It should be noted that this quantity called liquidity cannot be measured, which makes it impossible to test directly the hypothesis that aggregate spending depends upon the liquidity of the economy. Thus, the central proposition of the Radcliffe *Report* is untestable!

[20] The same effect could be produced by changing the composition of the national debt, for example, selling long-term bonds and buying short-dated securities. The Committee envisioned just such a role for debt management policies.

liquidity of individual spenders is reduced directly, and because financial institutions especially were thought reluctant to accept capital losses, they were locked into their portfolios and thus sources of "new" liquidity were also reduced. It was this so-called "locking-in" effect that was to operate in the face of rising interest rates to reduce "new" liquidity and the supply of loanable funds from the financial intermediaries. Thus, while rising interest rates have little effect upon the demand for loanable funds, they supposedly reduce the available supply, and since the public cannot get hold of funds, they must reduce their planned level of expenditures.[21]

The Importance of Banks and the Money Supply

Following this line of reasoning, it is the entire structure of interest rates which becomes "the centerpiece of monetary action," and the money supply becomes a very important means for influencing the structure of rates, as does the management of the national debt by the Treasury. Moreover, in this view commercial banks are important, for

> In the liquidity structure . . . the banks hold a special position, in that they are, for most borrowers and for most short-term purposes, much the most convenient institutional source of funds and often the only source.[22]

However, this new transmission mechanism did not, in the Committee's view, enhance the potency of monetary policy, for it concluded:

> But, when all has been said on the possibility of monetary action and of its likely efficacy, our conclusion is that monetary measures cannot alone be relied upon to keep in nice balance an economy subject to major strains from both without and within. Monetary measures can help but that is all. . . . We envisage the use of monetary measures as not in ordinary times playing other than a subordinate part in guiding the development of the economy. . . .[23]

[21] In a contrary situation, "A fall in rates, on the other hand, strengthens balance sheets and encourages lenders to seek new business" (¶393, p. 134). However, monetary policy was viewed as asymmetrical and not working as well to encourage an upswing for "In general, the potentialities of monetary policy alone in the face of a severe slump are well represented by the proverb that you can take a horse to water but you cannot make him drink" (¶521, p. 186).

[22] ¶395, p. 134.

[23] ¶514, p. 183 and ¶511, p. 182. The prejudice against reliance on monetary policy as a stabilization tool appears based on the opinion that for it to be effective, interest rates would have to fluctuate markedly, which could disrupt London's function as an international capital market, call into frequent doubt the solvency of financial institutions which hold large quantities of government securities, and compound the problems of financing the budget deficits of the British government.

Insofar as stabilization policy was concerned, the Committee recommended greater reliance on fiscal policy and, in extraordinary times, measures to strike directly and rapidly at the liquidity of spenders: Control of capital issues, bank advances or loans (not their deposits),[24] and consumer credit. In addition, the Committee rejected controls over the lending capability of nonbank financial intermediaries because of additional administrative burdens and because the further development of new financial institutions would allow the situation continually to slip from the grip of the authorities.[25]

For purposes of further analysis, the Radcliffe *Report* raises several interesting issues. First, is it important to be able to define money? Second, are commercial banks in some fundamental and important respects different from other intermediaries? Third, does the existence of a highly developed system of financial intermediaries render the velocity function unstable? Fourth, is the transmission mechanism formulated by the Committee a valid explanation of the way in which monetary policy operates? Before considering these questions, our discussion turns briefly to an account of the controversy raised in the United States by the publication of papers by Gurley–Shaw and Roosa.

THE GURLEY–SHAW THESIS

Unlike the Radcliffe *Report,* which sets forth the findings of a Parliamentary Committee of inquiry, the work of John Gurley and Edward Shaw[26] was inspired by the publication in the early 1950's of a monumental piece of work by Raymond Goldsmith on saving and its institutionalization through financial intermediaries.[27] Goldsmith's work showed that while all financial intermediaries grew rapidly during the first half of the twentieth century, the claims of nonbank intermediaries

---

[24] This emphasis on controlling bank loans but not deposits will be shown below to be a view long popular with banks and to involve a confusion between money and credit.

[25] ¶394, p. 134.

[26] See J. G. Gurley and E. S. Shaw, "Financial Aspects of Economic Development," *American Economic Review,* Vol. 45, No. 4 (Sept. 1955), pp. 515–38; "Financial intermediaries and the Saving–Investment Process," *Journal of Finance,* Vol. 11, No. 2 (May 1956), pp. 257–76; "The Growth of Debt and Money in the United States, 1800–1950: A Suggested Interpretation," *Review of Economics and Statistics,* Vol. 39, No. 3 (Aug. 1957), pp. 250–62; and *Money in a Theory of Finance* (Washington, D.C.: Brookings Institution, 1960). See also J. G. Gurley, *Liquidity and Financial Institutions in the Postwar Economy,* Study Paper 14, Joint Economic Committee, 86th Congress, 2nd session (Washington, D.C.: U.S. Government Printing Office, 1960).

[27] Raymond W. Goldsmith, *The Share of Financial Intermediaries in National Wealth and National Assets, 1900–1949* (New York: National Bureau of Economic Research, Occasional Paper 42, 1954); *A Study of Saving in the United States* (Princeton, N.J.: Princeton University Press, 1955); and *Financial Intermediaries in the American Economy Since 1900* (Princeton, N.J.: Princeton University Press, 1958).

increased relative to the demand deposit claims of commercial banks, causing commercial banks to diminish in importance among all intermediaries.

The conclusions drawn from Goldsmith's work by Gurley–Shaw and others were that the relative decline of commercial banks weakened the ability of the central bank to control economic activity, that direct control of nonbank intermediaries is called for, and that the distinction drawn in the literature between commercial banks and other financial institutions is invalid.

Before the analysis of Gurley–Shaw is discussed, it should be noted that the assertion that commercial banks have diminished in relative importance has not gone unchallenged. For example, Joseph Aschheim was among the first to question the validity of this conclusion.[28] While it is true that the ratio of commercial bank assets to total assets of all financial institutions decreased from 52.8 percent in 1900 to 33.9 percent in 1952, the ratio stood at 33.5 percent in 1933. Thus, the decline was completed by 1933, some 25 years before Gurley–Shaw sounded the alarm. However, Aschheim attributed this decline to the growth of government financial institutions: The Federal Reserve, government lending agencies, Social Security pension fund, government pension funds, and so forth. If bank assets are compared to the assets of private financial institutions, the decline is much less marked, from 52.8 percent in 1900 to 44.5 percent in 1952. Aschheim shows that the decline can be accounted for not by the relative diminution of demand deposits, but by the failure of time deposits to grow at their trend rate (time deposits being that line of commerce in which commercial banks are most like other financial institutions).

Be that as it may, Gurley–Shaw draw conclusions from Goldsmith's data concerning the implications of the rapid growth of nonbank intermediaries for both the secular and cyclical conduct of monetary policy.

Secular Monetary Policy

As to the conduct of monetary policy in the long run, if it is desired to maintain some optimum rate of interest over time which is to be consistent, say, with full employment, Gurley–Shaw contend that no simple rule can be adopted for the increase in the conventionally defined money supply. This conclusion follows from their analysis of the process of financial growth which parallels real economic growth. The process of economic growth inevitably involves external finance in which surplus spending units (those whose income exceeds expenditures) transfer their

---

[28] Joseph Aschheim, "Commercial Banks and Financial Intermediaries: Fallacies and Policy Implications," *Journal of Political Economy*, Vol. 67, No. 5 (Sept./Oct. 1960), pp. 59–71."

saving to deficit units with the bond serving as the means of transfer. In a simple world with only commercial banks, as this transfer process continues, the portfolios of surplus spending units become increasingly encumbered with bonds, creating a "diversification demand for money" based on the fact that money has superior liquidity relative to bonds. Unless the supply of money is expanded, the surplus spending units will only be willing to absorb the bonds at rising rates of interest. Similarly, the deficit units, not wishing to accumulate endless debts, are not willing to spend unless interest rates are eased.

Since, other things being equal, the diversification demand would impart a downward secular trend to velocity depending on the degree and extent of external finance, Gurley–Shaw believe that an appropriate adjustment in the supply of money is required if a rise in interest rates, with its deflationary impact on national income, is to be avoided. However, the actual process of financial development is more complicated than an analysis confined to a simple money/bond world would suggest. In addition to direct lending, a good deal of indirect lending is to be found, involving nonbank financial intermediaries who stand between the surplus and deficit spending units.

The relative growth of these nonbank intermediaries is interpreted by Gurley–Shaw to mean that the liabilities of these institutions, called *indirect financial assets*, are better substitutes for meeting the diversification demand than is money. While it is true that these indirect financial assets offer less liquidity than money in many instances, they can offer the same degree of security and, perhaps insurance, interest yield, and other services as well. Thus, the magnitude and direction of the diversification demand for financial assets is more complicated than when money is the only alternative to bonds. Moreover, as the quotation to follow indicates, it becomes difficult to specify the exact nature of the secular trend in demand for money, and hence the best monetary policy.

Gurley–Shaw believe that in a model with a variety of money substitutes, the appropriate monetary policy to keep interest rates on an optimal, or full-employment, trend is not a simple function of trends in income or even of income and debt. In their words:

> The necessary growth in the money supply may be high or low, positive or negative, depending on the growth of income, the share of spending that is externally financed (especially by long-term securities), the growth in demand by spending units for direct relative to indirect financial assets, and on the development of financial intermediaries whose indirect debt issues are competitive with money.[29]

[29] J. G. Gurley and E. S. Shaw, "Financial Aspects of Development," p. 531.

Cyclical Monetary Policy

It was not the Gurley–Shaw discussion of the long-run implication of nonbank intermediaries which received the most attention, but their conclusion that short-run, or countercyclical, monetary policy can be effectively sabotaged by nonbank intermediaries. Their argument is similar to that given by the Radcliffe Committee. If commercial banks are restricted by Federal Reserve policy, nonbank intermediaries have ways to offset the decline in the rate of growth of the money supply, by increasing the velocity, or turnover rate, of the existing money stock. First, by a small increase in the rate they pay on deposits they can attract hitherto idle bank deposits, and by re-lending them raise the velocity of the money stock.[30] Second, Gurley–Shaw allege that the existence of a large and widely held public debt enhances the ability of nonbank intermediaries to raise velocity, for they possess an instrument easily disposable on a highly organized financial market. By selling government securities to holders of idle bank deposits, the nonbank intermediaries can activate the deposits and raise velocity.

Policy Implications

Because of the potential for both long-run and short-run problems for monetary policy when that policy operates only through commercial banks, Gurley–Shaw and a host of others call for direct control of velocity through the regulation of the lending policies of nonbank intermediaries. In the words of Gurley–Shaw:

> The lag of regulatory techniques behind the institutional development of intermediaries can be overcome when it is appreciated that "financial control" should supplant "monetary control." Monetary control limits the supply of one financial asset, money. With a sophisticated financial structure providing financial assets, other than money and bonds, in increasing proportion to both, control over money alone is a decreasingly efficient means of regulating flows of loanable funds and spending on goods and services. Financial control, as the successor to monetary control, would regulate creation of financial assets in all forms that are competitive with direct securities in spend-

---

[30] It should be noted that this implies that discriminatory control of commercial banks permits the relative expansion of nonbank financial intermediaries. This discrimination is alleged to account for part of their growth and, consequently, the weakening of the power of the central bank to stabilize the economy. Note also that the emphasis in the Gurley–Shaw work is on the fact that intermediaries provide substitutes for money as a store of value.

ing units' portfolios. "Tight finance" and "cheap finance" are the sequels to "tight money" and "cheap money."[31]

One financial control suggested by Gurley–Shaw was similar to a proposal of the Radcliffe Committee. If the central bank could influence the structure of interest rates, it might affect the availability of loanable funds from financial intermediaries. But, since Gurley–Shaw could not be certain that the portfolio practices of these institutions would lead to this result, they suggested this control as only one of several possible measures.[32]

THE UNIQUENESS OF MONEY

Unlike the Radcliffe Committee, Gurley–Shaw do not discuss the supply of money as though the variable is undefinable nor do they add any derogations after a specific definition. Rather, they emphasize that commercial banks and demand deposits are very important: The latter because they are the principal medium of exchange and the former because they administer the payments system and are one of the largest single financial intermediaries. But they are careful to draw attention to the fact that commercial banks are similar in many respects to other financial intermediaries, each of which produces a differentiated product substitutable for the others in the portfolios of spending units.

Thus, the purpose of their work is not to formulate a new definition of money based upon liquidity, but to contribute to an understanding of the relationship of money to other financial assets regardless of what definition is given for money.[33]

ROOSA'S AVAILABILITY DOCTRINE

In the discussion of the new transmission mechanism formulated by the Radcliffe Committee as well as in a suggestion made by Gurley–Shaw on

[31] "Financial Aspects of Development," p. 537.

[32] *Ibid.*, p. 538.

[33] However, Gurley himself has experimented with a definition of money in which weights are assigned to financial assets based upon their "liquidity," or degree of substitutability for demand-deposit money. For example, if demand deposits were reduced by 10 percent and it required a 30 percent expansion in financial asset A to keep interest rates constant, financial asset A is 1/3 as liquid as demand deposits and, in calculating a monetary total based upon liquidity, asset A would receive a weight of 1/3. Similar considerations would guide the weights applied to other assets. See "Liquidity and Financial Institutions," pp. 7–8. In a discussion primarily of monetary policy, Shaw defined money as equal to currency plus demand deposits adjusted. See "Money Supply and Stable Economic Growth," *United States Monetary Policy* (New York: American Assembly, 1958), pp. 49–71.

a possible method for central bank control of nonbank financial intermediaries, the availability of loanable funds assumed primary importance. While this doctrine of the availability of loanable funds has an
ancient and venerable ancestry,[34] its most recent formulation was the
work of Robert V. Roosa (sometimes spelled Rosa), a former official of
both the Federal Reserve System and the U.S. Treasury.[35]

To appreciate fully the wide popular acceptance of the Roosa doctrine, the historic circumstances immediately antecedent to its restatement must be appreciated.

In the period immediately preceding World War II, many economists in the Keynesian mold were extremely skeptical of the ability of
monetary policy to combat economic downturns, because the available
evidence suggested that investment and consumption expenditures were
highly insensitive to changes in market interest rates.[36] To stimulate
these two categories of outlay would require very large changes in interest rates. During World War II, the public debt increased manyfold and
in the postwar period, the Federal Reserve was committed to a price-
support program which had been commenced during the war partly out
of fear that to abandon such a program would destroy public confidence
in government debt. Thus, monetary policy was caught in a terrible
bind, for in order for it to be effective, large interest rate changes were
thought necessary. On the other hand, changes of that magnitude would
weaken public confidence, leading to a refusal to hold and buy government securities, and thus complicate subsequent Treasury efforts to
underwrite government borrowing requirements.

In this environment the Roosa doctrine would have great appeal,
for he was to argue that the support program could be dropped without

[34] W. Randolph Burgess, long associated with the Federal Reserve System, wrote in 1927:
"Interest rates in themselves have, of course, some importance for business. When money can
be borrowed at 3 per cent, the costs of doing business are less than when rates are 6 per cent.
But the difference . . . is usually a small item in the businessman's total costs. The real question
for him (as far as money is concerned) is whether he can get money when he needs it, and
whether his banker will give him assurance of future accommodation. When interest rates are
high and rising, it is usually a little less easy for the businessman to be sure of borrowing
money. It is from this point of view that interest rates are chiefly important, as an outward
evidence of changes in underlying credit conditions." See The Reserve Banks and the Money
Market (New York: Harper and Bros., 1927). Quotation taken from p. 195, 1946 edition.

[35] Robert V. Roosa, "Interest Rates and the Central Bank" in Money, Trade, and Economic Growth: Essays in Honor of John H. Williams (New York: MacMillan, 1951), pp. 270–95.

[36] The empirical evidence available in 1950, the year Roosa wrote his paper, consisted
largely of two surveys made by Oxford University (See J. E. Meade and P. W. S. Andrews,
"Summary of Replies to Questions on Effects of Interest Rates," Oxford Economic Papers, No. 1
(Oct. 1938). pp. 14–31; and P. W. S. Andrews, "A Further Inquiry into the Effects of Rates of
Interest," Oxford Economic Papers, No. 3 (Feb. 1940), pp. 32–73; a case study by Professor
John Ebersole of the Harvard Business School, "The Influence of Interest Rates upon Entrepreneurial Decisions in Business: A Case Study," Harvard Business Review, Vol. 17 (1938), pp. 35–39;
and the interpretation of the Great Depression made by Keynes and reported in Chapter 12 of
this text.

causing large changes in interest rates and at the same time the presence of a widely held public debt would vastly strengthen the leverage of monetary policy to control the course of economic activity.

Basically, the Roosa hypothesis contains two essential elements. First, a large government debt, widely held by financial institutions, would increase the scope and power of open-market operations, enabling them to exercise an influence on economic activity far beyond that originating from the banking system. Second, and serving as an explanation for the first, was Roosa's conjecture that a small change (either a rise or fall) in the interest rate would greatly affect the supply of loanable funds and have a significant impact on aggregate demand, even if the credit demand by borrowers were highly interest inelastic, as the Oxford surveys purported to show.[37] Slight interest rate changes were supposed to have a pronounced effect on the supply of loanable funds for two reasons. First, they were supposed either to decrease or increase the capital value of government securities held by financial institutions. If interest rates rose, the assumed desire to avoid capital losses by selling securities in an effort to activate idle balances would lock lenders into their existing portfolios, thus reducing the supply of new loanable funds. Second, the effect of interest rate changes was expected to create or dispel uncertainty about the future course of interest rate movements, hence further retarding or encouraging lending. Given a rise in rates,

. . . the uncertainty over further rises will cause hesitation, an unwillingness to go all the way in a new commitment if rates may be generally higher a few weeks later on, a shortening in commitment terms, and a general desire "to wait and see."[38]

The implication of the above is that open-market operations have a pervasive influence far beyond their power to regulate the lending of commercial banks and that monetary policy exercises its impact by influencing the availability of credit to borrowers. This is why the name *availability doctrine* came to be applied to Roosa's thesis.

As to the stabilization power of credit availability, Roosa's conclusion was about as pessimistic as that contained in the Radcliffe *Report:*

No doubt the restraint or the stimulus provided to credit expansion through changes in long-term rates will never turn the course of economic

[37] Roosa notes that roughly a quarter of the replies to the 1940 Oxford Survey ". . . indicated that the *availability* of bank credit, or of funds obtained through the securities markets, affected businessmen's decision to make (or the *timing* of their decisions to make) expenditures upon new plants, or upon repairs and maintenance, or upon inventories." "Interest Rates and the Central Bank," p. 275.

[38] *Ibid.*, p. 287.

activity alone. But rate changes can certainly exert some influence upon the flow of funds and the timing of new undertakings . . . Properly guided . . . the long-term market can, by spacing the flow of funds into longer-term investment opportunities, make a positive contribution toward lessening the amplitude of booms and depressions.[39]

The work of Gurley–Shaw supplemented by the availability doctrine of Roosa raises several important issues requiring further analysis. These are quite similar to those raised by the Radcliffe *Report* and concern the importance of the definition of money, the unique attributes of commercial banks, the ability of nonbank intermediaries to render the velocity function unstable, and the validity of the availability doctrine.

THE DEFINITION OF MONEY

Thus far, the question of what group of assets should be designated as money has not received wide attention in this text. It has, nevertheless, been touched upon in several places, when it was usually presented as a matter of controversy.

The importance of the definition has most often been related to its implications for monetary policy and, often, for monetary theory. Thus in Chapter 3 it was noted that for the Currency School, the medium of exchange role served as the defining characteristic of money. On that basis, the Currency School concluded that the supply of money consisted only of Bank of England notes and sought by Act of Parliament to regulate the issue of such notes. Pointing to the fact that other assets were also used as media of exchange, the Banking School called their definition arbitrary and their policy conclusions ineffective.

The definition of money put forth by the Currency School, which considers money as a medium of exchange, is only one of several possible definitions. Harry Johnson[40] has provided a fourfold classification; the Currency School choice can be designated the *traditional* definition, for it is to be found in the great majority of economic textbooks dealing with money. Close to the traditional definition is one formulated by Milton Friedman and often called the Chicago definition. From the discussion in Chapter 9, according to this definition, money is any asset capable of serving as a temporary abode of purchasing power, which would suggest, for most societies, a broader range of assets than those used commonly as means of exchange. In his empirical work, Friedman

[39] *Ibid.,* p. 291.

[40] Harry G. Johnson, "Monetary Theory and Policy," *The American Economic Review,* Vol. 52, No. 3 (June 1962), pp. 351–54.

derives as the counterpart of this definition the sum of currency plus adjusted bank deposits or a range of assets very close to those meeting the medium-of-exchange test.[41] In more recent work, Friedman now distinguishes between a narrow definition of money, designated M_1, in which money consists of currency and adjusted demand deposits and M_2, in which money consists of the empirical counterpart of temporary abodes of purchasing power.

Both the traditional and Chicago definitions of money are quite compatible with either a quantity theory or Keynesian approach to economic stabilization, for each regards the velocity of the money or demand function as stable in terms of a limited number of variables.[42] Monetary policy can thus continue to be centered on its present instruments for control, emphasizing reserve requirement changes and open-market operations.

A third definition of money, very different from the two above, says that money consists of a broad group of assets which can be converted or used to finance purchases. According to Johnson, this definition is most often used by those interested in policy. This group of assets may be subject to measurement; often it is not. A measure of this definition of money emphasized by central banks, including our Federal Reserve, is the volume of bank credit outstanding taken as the sum of commercial bank loans and investments.[43]

---

[41] Various studies have attempted to measure the degree to which time and savings deposits ought to be included in a definition of money. See G. S. Laumas, "The Degree of Moneyness of Savings Deposits," *American Economic Review*, Vol. 58, No. 3 (June 1968), pp. 501–503; and his "Savings Deposits in the Definition of Money," *Journal of Political Economy*, Vol. 77, No. 6 (Nov./Dec. 1969), pp. 892–96; T. H. Lee, "Substitutability of Non-Bank Intermediary Liabilities for Money: The Empirical Evidence," *Journal of Finance*, Vol. 21, No. 4 (Sept. 1966), pp. 441–57; and R. H. Timberlake, Jr., and James Fortson, "Time Deposits in the Definition of Money," *American Economic Review*, Vol. 57, No. 1 (March 1967), pp. 190–94.

[42] Brunner and Meltzer, while generally in accord with the Chicago approach to money, find Friedman's definition of money as a temporary abode of purchasing power unacceptable. They prefer a definition which groups as money all assets used in "dominant transaction chains" or dominant media of exchange. The emergence of currency and demand deposits as dominant transaction assets is explained by the fact that these instruments reduce the time and cost, including the cost of market information on asset quality and availability, required to convert an initial endowment of resources possessed by an individual, including his own labor time, into a preferred bundle of goods and services. Therein lies the marginal utility of money. Thus for Brunner and Meltzer the medium-of-exchange role is the distinguishing characteristic of money. They seek to provide a rationale why some small group of assets among numerous possible ones emerges in this role. See Karl Brunner and Allan Meltzer, "The Use of Money: Money in the Theory of an Exchange Economy," *American Economic Review*, Vol. 61, No. 5 (Dec. 1971), pp. 784–805 and Karl Brunner, "A Survey of Selected Issues in Monetary Theory," *Schweizerische Zeitschrift Für Volkswirtschaft und Statistic*, Vol. 107 (Winter 1971), pp. 1–17.

[43] Robert V. Roosa, "The Change in Money and Credit, 1957–59" and Woodlief Thomas, "How Much Can Be Expected of Monetary Policy," in "Controversial Issues in Recent Monetary Policy: A Symposium," *Review of Economics and Statistics*, Vol. 42, No. 3 (Aug. 1960), pp. 261–63 and 272–76. For earlier Federal Reserve views, see W. R. Burgess, *The Reserve Banks and The Money Market*.

There can be little doubt that the Federal Reserve has often been more concerned with regulating such a volume of assets than the money supply.

The liquidity of the economy emphasized by the Radcliffe Committee, including the potential elasticity of commercial credit, is a prime example of an unmeasurable magnitude. In its extreme form, the Radcliffe definition suggests that velocity is a completely meaningless statistic, devoid of behavioral significance (it is no more than a number derived by dividing national income by a given collection of assets). Thus the Radcliffe Committee stands quite apart from the stable velocity views emerging from the first two definitions. Depending on the collection of assets used to calculate velocity, its numerical value will differ. The more extensive the collection, the smaller becomes the value of velocity and the less will it fluctuate over time. As noted, consistent with its view of money the Committee recommended that in extraordinary times, the central bank should have direct control over commercial bank advances or loans in order to control spending, or MV.

A fourth definition, somewhat similar to that of the Radcliffe Committee, is suggested by the work of Gurley–Shaw. Since they hold that nonbank intermediaries have the ability to frustrate conventional monetary policy by altering the velocity of money on a secular and cyclical basis, their work leads naturally to the conclusion that an appropriate definition of money ought to include the liabilities of nonbank intermediaries. While the two authors have never jointly advocated such a definition, Gurley's work, formulating a liquidity definition of money, might be taken as the logical extension of their analysis.

Which of the four definitions is in some sense "best" cannot be decided as a matter of principle, but must be resolved on the basis of its usefulness in either theory or policy, for depending on criteria, each definition is in some sense arbitrary.

For a critique of each definition, showing the problems involved, or the inconsistencies likely to arise, the interested student is referred to Friedman and Schwartz.[44] Often, in empirical work, several definitions are used to show that the hypothesis tested does not depend on which measure of money is used.

THE UNIQUENESS OF COMMERCIAL BANKS

The alternative definitions of money given above suggest different answers to the question of whether commercial banks are in some sense

[44] Milton Friedman and Anna Schwartz, Monetary Statistics of the United States (New York: Columbia University Press, 1970), pp. 89–198.

different from other financial intermediaries. Basically, two different views concerning the uniqueness of commercial banks can be distinguished, depending on whether one accepts the Traditional–Chicago or the Radcliffe–Gurley–Shaw approach.

We remark first that there are many obvious similarities between commercial banks and other financial intermediaries. First and most obviously, both are intermediaries which serve the function of transmitting the saving of surplus economic units to deficit units, permitting lending to assume an indirect dimension. To the extent that all intermediaries serve to diffuse the risks inherent in lending and borrowing, and serve as the means for securing scale economies in the lending process, they tend to lower the structure of interest rates.

Second, both types of financial intermediaries have the ability to create loanable funds over and above the amount made available through saving. For each, this ability depends upon their reserve base; their own portfolio behavior determining the ratio of reserves to liabilities; and the portfolio behavior of the public expressed in its holdings of bank deposits, paper currency, and the liabilities of nonbank intermediaries. There are, however, some differences.

The Traditional–Chicago view would hold that commercial banks as a group can expand their liabilities as a multiple of their reserves to a degree not even remotely approximated by the other financial intermediaries. This is due largely to the fact that the demand deposits of banks serve as the principal medium of exchange. As a consequence, the banks administer the payments system of the country. Disregarding Federal Reserve and Treasury acts, the commercial banks lose reserves principally when paper currency in circulation rises. Transfers of demand deposits from banks to nonbank intermediaries do not cause losses of bank reserves, but only a transfer of deposit ownership, because nonbank intermediaries hold their reserves principally as deposits in commercial banks. Thus, when the commercial banks expand deposits on the basis of an increase in their reserves, they can expect to retain a substantial portion of those reserves even if some of the funds lent are ultimately deposited in nonbank intermediaries. On the other hand, if a credit union or savings-and-loan institution lends funds entrusted to it, the likelihood that the group of credit unions or savings-and-loan institutions will be the recipient of the redeposit is small, because the marginal propensity of the public to hold additions to its wealth in the form of claims on nonbank intermediaries is small. Thus, nonbank intermediaries can be expected to lose a substantial amount of reserves per dollar lent. Only if nonbank intermediaries hold their reserves, as do commercial banks, as deposits at the central bank, would their credit-creation potential be as great as that of commercial banks when the two sectors are the same size (as measured by their liabilities). So long as nonbank intermediaries hold all their reserves as deposits at commercial banks, Guttentag and Lindsay have estimated that the credit-creation potential of banks will be about 17 times that of nonbank intermediaries when their deposit liabilities are equal, given the reserve ratios prevailing in 1968. They imply that the uniqueness of banks is to be found in their ability to create credit in excess of nonbank intermediaries, thereby justifying the special apparatus of central bank controls applied to commercial banks. However, Joseph Aschheim asserts strongly that this is not the essential attribute of uniqueness. He elaborates on an oblique reference made by Guttentag and Lindsay that central to the true uniqueness of banks is their ability to create the means of payment used in the economy. Because they provide these means, banks among all intermediaries are forced to provide an absolute promise to convert their demand deposits into currency on demand. As a consequence of this promise, they are used as depositories by nonbank intermediaries. Hence, the greater credit-creating ability of banks is a consequence of uniqueness not its source. Aschheim asserts, correctly, that even if the nonbank intermediaries hold all their reserves as deposits at the central bank (or as currency) and hence possess the same credit-creating potential as banks, banks would still be different, for their absolute rather than conditional promise of convertibility would justify the imposition of controls on their reserve base and the implementation of deposit insurance to prevent bank runs.[45] The argument on the uniqueness of banks has thus come full circle and finds their uniqueness to reside in their ability to create the means of payment.

The ability of the commercial banking system to retain the reserves lent to a far greater degree than is possible for nonbank intermediaries has been likened to the widow's cruse.[46]

[45] Guttentag and Lindsay have estimated that nonbanks and banks could expand credit by the same amount for an equal change in their reserve ratios only if the public was content to hold 16 dollars of claims against nonbank intermediaries for every dollar held by them as bank deposits. Since the actual amount was in the range of two dollars for every one dollar held as demand deposits, they concluded that the credit-creating potential of nonbanks was severely limited. See Jack Guttentag and Robert Lindsay, "The Uniqueness of Commercial Banks," *Journal of Political Economy*, Vol. 76, No. 5 (Sept./Oct. 1968), pp. 991–1014. The subject of the uniqueness of commercial banks is further explored in John H. Wood, "Two Notes on the Uniqueness of Commercial Banks," *Journal of Finance*, Vol. 25, No. 1 (March 1970), pp. 99–108. Here the arguments of Guttentag and Lindsay are shown to parallel an argument made a century earlier by Walter Bagehot on the uniqueness of the Bank of England. For Joseph Aschheim's analysis, see "Commercial Bank Uniqueness," *Journal of Political Economy*, Vol. 78, No. 2 (May/June 1970), pp. 353–56.

[46] The cruse was a vessel containing an oil used for cooking. When the prophet Elijah was sent to Zarephath, the widow of that city gave him lodging and provided him with water and a morsel of bread, even though severe drought had exhausted her cooking oil and meal for bread. For her kindness and faith, she was told by Elijah that the pot of meal shall not waste, nor the cruse of oil be diminished, until the day wherein the Lord will give rain upon the face of the earth (See I Kings, 17: 10–16). The ability of the cruse to yield an unfailing supply of oil has been likened by Tobin to the theoretical ability of the banking system to re-

For the most part, those adhering to the so-called "New View," who hold that commercial banks are not unique but produce only one of a spectrum of differentiated products which are substitutes for each other in the portfolios of wealth owners, appear rather long on rhetoric and short on substantive analysis. For example, Gurley–Shaw tell us that while banks alone have the capacity to create demand deposits, only savings-and-loan associations can create savings-and-loan shares.[47] Tobin tells us that while the means-of-payment characteristic of demand deposits is a feature differentiating these bank liabilities from those of other intermediaries, insurance against death is equally a feature differentiating life insurance policies from the obligations of other intermediaries including banks.[48] Finally, Sayers, noting that the policy of the Currency School which centered on control of Bank of England notes became increasingly inadequate as demand deposits became the principal means of payment, questions whether control of money alone among all liquid assets is adequate. Might we not, he asks, be in a situation in which bank deposits have become the small change of the financial system just as Bank of England notes were some 100 years earlier?[49]

Karl Brunner, a foremost critic of the New View, is especially hostile to such statements, for he claims that they contribute little to our systematic knowledge and yield no informative hypotheses. After all, just because banks and other intermediaries supply liabilities to satisfy the preferences of ultimate lenders, this doesn't mean that they are identical; even differences in degree may be systematically significant.[50] The trouble with the New View is that the public has not decided to hold the liabilities of nonbank intermediaries to the extent needed to make their credit-creating ability as significant as that of banks, and those who advance the New View have failed to show why it would matter if the public should exhibit that type of behavior.

NONBANK FINANCIAL INTERMEDIARIES AND MONETARY POLICY

Both the Radcliffe Committee and Gurley–Shaw were of the opinion that the rapid growth of nonbank intermediaries posed special problems

---

tain its reserves after it expands deposits. See James Tobin, "Commercial Banks as Creators of Money," in Deane Carson, ed., Banking and Monetary Studies (Homewood, Ill.: Richard D. Irwin, 1963), pp. 408–19.

[47] "Financial Aspects of Development," p. 521.

[48] "Commercial Banks as Creators of Money," p. 412. The name "New View" was given to the group by Tobin.

[49] "Monetary Thought," p. 724.

[50] "A Survey of Selected Issues," p. 104.

for the secular and cyclical conduct of monetary policy. Given the traditional definition of money, the activities of nonbank intermediaries must
show up mainly in the velocity, or turnover rate, of conventional money.

On a secular basis, since nonbank intermediaries have been growing faster than banks, their liabilities are supposedly better substitutes
for bonds than is conventional money in the portfolio of wealth owners.
If this is true, one ought to observe a secular rise in velocity. On a purely
theoretical basis, a secular trend in velocity should pose no difficulty for
monetary policy. It merely requires that the supply of money be adjusted for this trend in order to ensure that the growth of money spending should expand at some desired rate. Whether a secular trend in
velocity has in fact been observed is an empirical issue. For the entire
period from the Civil War to the present, the secular trend appears
downward, not upward, although the period subsequent to World War
II conforms more nearly to that predicted by Radcliffe–Gurley–Shaw.[51]
Most empirical work on the long-run demand for money has been able
to adequately explain movements in the function without including the
yield on the liabilities of nonbank intermediaries as one of its arguments.[52]

It is, however, on the cyclical level that the weight of the argument
against traditional monetary policy has been placed. The argument
holds that the activities of nonbank intermediaries can partially or
totally offset cyclical variations in the supply of conventional money. In
other words, procyclical variations in velocity ought to be observed.
From the Radcliffe view, the ability of nonbank intermediaries to thwart
the monetary authorities was complete, while Gurley–Shaw did not advance such an extreme position. However, both argued that monetary
policy ought to be replaced by a more comprehensive financial policy
which included the power to control velocity directly. Whether the nonbank intermediaries have such power is essentially an empirical issue,
although a review of how they are able to accomplish this can lend insights into the validity of the proposition. Supposedly, by extending the
maturity of book credit and activating idle demand-deposit balances,
nonbank intermediaries can raise velocity. Activating idle balances is to
be accomplished either by inducing wealth owners to swap demand
deposits for intermediary claims or by selling securities from their portfolios. The incentive to activate the idle balances and increase the degree

---

[51] See the work of V. K. Chetty, "On Measuring the Nearness of Near-Money," *American Economic Review*, Vol. 59, No. 3 (June 1969), pp. 270–81. If a more comprehensive definition of money were used, Chetty's results would indicate that velocity would have been a constant since 1950.

[52] See Allan Meltzer, "The Demand for Money: The Evidence from the Time Series," *Journal of Political Economy*, Vol. 71, No. 3 (May/June 1963), pp. 219–46; and Allan Meltzer and Karl Brunner, "Predicting Velocity: Implications for Theory and Policy," *Journal of Finance*, Vol. 18, No. 2 (May 1963), pp. 319–54.

of financial intermediation is produced by rising interest rates in the upswing of the cycle. Since commercial banks are limited by law from paying an explicit rate on demand deposits and by Regulation Q from exceeding a maximum on time deposits, a rise in interest rates in a cyclical upswing provides the means for nonregulated intermediaries to raise the rates they pay on their deposits, attracting the hitherto idle bank deposits. These they lend out, raising the velocity of conventional money.[53] For the Radcliffe Committee this ability to activate idle balances appears unlimited. Many are not willing to go so far and examine the central propositions of this description of the procyclical movements in velocity. First, the description of the lengthening of book or trade credit seldom proceeds beyond the initial statement that it can be lengthened. The description does not inquire how the granter of the more generous terms is able to do so. If payment is due but postponed, someone in the system must have a decreased ability to purchase. It is this decrease which must be offset against the increased ability of others to buy in calculating whether a lengthening of trade credit is an effective offset to a continued policy of monetary stringency.

Second, by examining the balance sheet of a typical nonbank intermediary, their ability to activate idle bank balances can be assessed. In a simple case, all their deposit liabilities are paid the same rate, and if we assume that a long period of interest rate stability has preceded the present moment, all the assets owned by the intermediary should also be earning a common interest rate (if maturity and risk differences are neglected). The difference between the rate paid their depositors and that yielded from their assets is equal to their gross earnings. In the typical portfolio of intermediaries, the maturity structure of their assets is such that they do not all mature on the same day or during a given period—perhaps 25 percent do during a given year.

Thus, if market interest rates are rising during the upswing of a cycle, only a portion of their assets will earn the new higher yields—those that mature during a given period. However, to attract or activate idle bank deposits and to maintain the stock of their current deposits, higher rates will have to be paid to all their creditors, that is, on all their deposits. In this situation, costs tend to rise relative to income and profits tend to fall. This becomes especially acute if short rates rise with long rates and the difference between them lessens, that is, the yield curve flattens. A monumental profit squeeze can develop if short rates

---

[53] Procyclical movements of velocity are quite compatible with the Keynesian model. The rise in income increases the quantity of money needed for transactions, putting upward pressure on the interest rate which induces holders of speculative or idle balances to surrender them in exchange for bonds. In this explanation, money is swapped for nonbank intermediary claims and, secondarily, for bonds.

rise and exceed long rates, that is, the yield curve becomes negative. This pinch on profits frustrates the ability of nonbank intermediaries to offset a restrictive monetary policy. In fact, if the term structure of interest rates slopes negatively, the nonbank intermediaries are likely to be hit by massive disintermediation. Not only are they then unable to attract idle bank deposits, but lose substantial sums of their own deposits. Such events were characteristic of the late 1960's and early 1970's in the United States.

These two considerations would suggest that the ability of nonbank intermediaries to counteract changes in the money supply is at best very limited.

Nevertheless, suppose nonbank intermediaries do have such power, but it is not unlimited. Need this really hamper countercyclical monetary policy? It has been argued that the monetary authority is aware of such cyclical variations in velocity, for this was implied by the Keynesian model long before Radcliffe–Gurley–Shaw arrived to spread the alarm. Since the monetary authority is aware of this ability of nonbank intermediaries, it can, as in the secular case, compensate for it by appropriate adjustments in the supply of money. However, such a policy must be subject to the caveat that variations in the supply of money, conventionally defined, and not variations in velocity, dominate movements in money spending. If velocity changes explain the major movements in money spending, any slight error in forecasting their value could result in disastrous consequences for the course of economic activity. If its movement is underestimated, one consequence might be serious inflation; if overestimated, a recession might be set in motion.

If, historically, velocity changes explain the major movements in money spending, they might serve as a compelling reason for broadening the definition of money and the scope of action for monetary policy.

While the controversy over the ability of nonbank financial intermediaries to circumvent conventional monetary policy has receded into the background, there are many influential economists who believe that regulation of the money supply, narrowly defined, is not the appropriate goal of monetary policy. In 1969, Warren Smith stated:

> Although I have used the term "money" in my discussion above, I am not sure that the term is a very useful or meaningful one. . . . There is no apparent reason why "money"—whether in the form of currency or demand deposits—is more or less important than any of the myriad other financial assets that exist.[54]

[54] Warren L. Smith, "A Neo-Keynesian View of Monetary Policy," in Controlling Monetary Aggregates (Boston: Federal Reserve Bank of Boston, 1969), p. 114.

Robert Eisner, expressing his views in 1971, sounds as though he were composing a chapter for an updated Radcliffe *Report:*

> What is so sacred about money? Money . . . is just one narrow line in the broad spectrum of monetary assets. We really do not have to have money. We can use credit cards. . . . And, of course, what happens in this liquidity crunch is that large businesses, in effect, use money substitutes. They get their cash balances lower and lower, they use more trade credit, they borrow from the market and, I would submit that ultimately, if the Fed keeps selling securities in the open market, they can dispense with money entirely. . . . What really happens as you keep reducing the quantity of "money" or bank money is that money substitutes slip into the system . . . .[55]

Nicholas Kaldor's description of the inability of the monetary authorities to prevent Christmas buying by refusing to issue notes, written in 1970, is evidence that on the other side of the Atlantic the Radcliffe view on the unimportance of money is still far from dead.[56]

The ultimate resolution of the issue on cyclical grounds remains an empirical one. The evidence is largely on the side of those who hold that nonbank intermediaries do not cause cyclical problems for monetary policy.[57]

THE AVAILABILITY DOCTRINE

The availability doctrine was formally presented by Roosa in the postwar period of skepticism over the potency of monetary policy and used by the Radcliffe Committee as a part of its new mechanism for explaining the way monetary policy affects the pace of economic activity. The time is now at hand for a more rigorous examination of the doctrine.[58]

For simplicity, assume a world in which only government and private securities exist, and that the supply of loanable funds from all inter-

---

[55] Robert Eisner, "What Went Wrong: Further Thoughts on Fiscal and Monetary Policy" in James Diamond, ed., *Issues in Fiscal and Monetary Policy: The Eclectic Economist Views the Controversy* (Chicago: DePaul University, 1971), pp. 83–84.

[56] Nicholas Kaldor, "The New Monetarism," *Lloyds Bank Review*, No. 97 (July 1970), pp. 6–7.

[57] See David Fand, "Intermediary Claims and the Adequacy of Our Monetary Controls" in *Banking and Monetary Studies*, pp. 234–53; and A. A. Walters, "The Radcliffe Report—Ten Years After: A Survey of Empirical Evidence" in Croome and Johnson, ed., *Money in Britain, 1959–1969* (London: Oxford University Press, 1970), pp. 39–68.

[58] Neither Roosa nor Radcliffe ever present their doctrine in diagrammatic form. For such a treatment, see D. C. Rowan, "Radcliffe Monetary Theory," *The Economic Record* (Dec. 1961), pp. 420–41; and Victoria Chick, *The Theory of Monetary Policy* (London: Gray-Mills, 1973), pp. 58–74.

mediaries to the private sector depends upon the reserves available to them, consisting of their holding of government securities[59] and the relative yield on private securities. For further simplicity, assume that the demand for loanable funds is totally unresponsive (inelastic) to the yield on private securities, r_p. This situation is shown in Figure 10:1. The supply schedule of loanable funds is drawn assuming that the yield on government securities, r_g, is constant.

FIGURE 10:1. Market For Loanable Funds

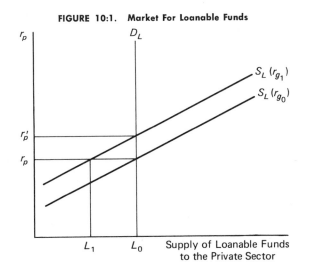

Given the yield on private securities r_p, let the monetary authority now believe that the economy has too much liquidity and through open-market operations sell a sufficient quantity of government securities to raise their yield to r_g. The effect, according to Roosa and the Radcliffe Committee, is to shift upward the supply of loanable funds from S_L to S'_L. They give two reasons to explain this effect. First, given the rise in r_g relative to r_p, the intermediaries obviously desire to hold more government securities and fewer private ones. This is a substitution effect of the rise in yield, r_g. Second, the rise in the yield on government securities reduces their capitalized value and the potential lending ability of the intermediaries. This is the wealth effect of the rise in yield, r_g.

However, the upward shift in the supply schedule to $S_L(r_{g_1})$ does nothing to reduce the demand for loanable funds. If the Roosa and Radcliffe theory on the behavior of intermediaries under circumstances of rising yields on government securities has any meaning, for some reason the yield on private securities, r_p, does not rise to r'_p to clear the market. If private yields did instantaneously adjust, firms or borrowers

---

[59] These must consist principally of long-maturity securities or else changes in interest rates will produce only a minimal change in their capital values.

would still be in possession of the same quantity of loanable funds, OL_0. Thus, Roosa and Radcliffe believe that for some institutional reason private yields are "sticky," or that the degree of imperfection in the market for loanable funds must increase in the face of rising yields on government securities.

Since the yield on private securities remains at r_p, the intermediaries adopt various devices to ration the available supply of loanable funds, OL_1, over the quantity demanded, OL_0.[60] Thus it is through credit rationing that the power of monetary policy is achieved, or, in the words of the Radcliffe *Report*, ". . . if the money for financing the project cannot be got on any tolerable terms at all, that is the end of the matter."[61]

The credit availability doctrine has been subject to both theoretical and empirical criticism. It rests on three rather questionable propositions. First, it assumes that imperfections in the money market exist which prevent the yields on private securities from adjusting to compensate for the rise in yields on government securities. Second, the portfolio decisions of financial intermediaries are made to depend partially on irrational behavior: The reluctance to realize a capital loss by selling a security whose yield has risen. Third, the rise in yields on government securities is supposed to increase the anxieties and uncertainties which make both borrowers and lenders appraise the future with more caution.

To the extent that these propositions are true and private security yields are prevented from rising, the credit availability theory uncovers important potentials for monetary policy neglected by older approaches. However, if private security yields adjust relatively promptly, the claims of Roosa and the Radcliffe Committee are more modest, confined essentially to a disequilibrium period. This is not to say that such transitory effects cannot be important. It may well be that the central bank wishes to curtail inflationary pressures which it regards as only transitory in nature.

Despite the views of the critics, a vast theoretical literature soon appeared to show that under a variety of assumptions and conditions, for example, altering the variable maximized by banks (profits and risks), or imposing constraints upon the profit-maximization condition, credit rationing was a rational response on the part of the lender. Others sought to test empirically alternative models of lender behavior which had differing implications for credit rationing.[62] These tests have been largely

[60] *Rationing* refers to nonprice means of allocation, and includes such devices as requiring large compensating balances, higher collateral, basing loans on past levels of borrowing from the intermediaries, and so forth.

[61] ¶387, p. 131.

[62] For a summary and appraisal of this literature, see Benjamin Friedman, *Credit Rationing: A Review*, Staff Study, Board of Governors, Federal Reserve System (Washington, D.C.: U.S. Government Printing Office, 1972).

inconclusive and do not lend strong support to the credit-rationing thesis.

Regardless of the outcome of this discussion on the rationality of credit rationing, it has helped to popularize once again the central banker view that monetary policy wields its main effect through the availability of credit.

THE NOMINAL SUPPLY OF MONEY

Historically, analysis related to the supply of money has occupied a distinctly second place relative to analysis of the demand for money in terms of time devoted to its study and varieties of theories advanced to explain its behavior over time. In order to appreciate what has been accomplished, this section will survey the literature, with particular emphasis on the theoretical development of a clearly defined supply function of money which relates supply to behavioral variables, much as the demand function relates demand to such variables. Once the supply relationship has been explained, the question of whether the money supply is an exogenous variable shall be considered.

EARLY NOTIONS OF THE MONEY SUPPLY

The neglect in formulating an explicit supply function for money has no doubt occurred because throughout much of the modern history of the developed world, a gold standard with full-bodied money was the prevailing monetary system. Under these institutional arrangements, the supply of money came to depend upon the activities of miners, the explorations of individuals seeking a shorter passage to the Orient, technological developments facilitating the extraction of precious metals, and the use of the monetary metal in alternative endeavors. Unexpected debasements of the coinage could, from time to time, augment the available supply. So long as this type of monetary system was in effect, a theory of the supply of money was unnecessary.

With the growth of demand-deposit exchange, fractional-reserve banking, and the development of central banks with the power to regulate the amount of money a given banking system could create, theories concerning the supply of money were forthcoming.

In order to unify the discussion to follow, we shall employ an identity developed by Friedman and Cagan[63] which decomposes all

[63] Selections, some in paraphrased form, from Milton Friedman and Anna Jacobson Schwartz, *A Monetary History of the United States 1867–1960* (copyright © 1963 by National Bureau of Economic Research, published by Princeton University Press), pp. 336–796. Reprinted by permission of Princeton University Press.

changes in the supply of money to changes in the monetary base of the
system, its currency/money ratio and its reserve/deposit ratio. This will
permit us to see that most modern theories share the belief that the
money supply is jointly determined by the central bank, the commercial
banks, and the public.

AN IDENTITY AS A FRAMEWORK FOR
NOMINAL MONEY SUPPLY ANALYSIS

In most elementary courses in money and banking, it is explained that
the supply of money depends ultimately on the assets which commercial
banks can use as reserves for their demand-deposit liabilities. These
assets in turn represent the liabilities of the central bank and, in part,
of the Treasury. In particular, these liabilities are equal to the actual
reserves of the commercial banks and the paper currency and coin held
by the nonbank public, the latter because these serve as potential reserves
for the banking system. It is customary to designate the sum of commercial bank reserves and the paper currency and coin issued by the
central bank and the Treasury as *high-powered money* in recognition
of its capability of serving as the base upon which the commercial banks
can expand their demand-deposit liabilities. In recognition of this fact,
high-powered money is often called the *monetary base*.

However, it is not the monetary base alone which determines the
supply of money at any moment. As elementary textbooks point out,
the commercial banks and the public (through their portfolio behavior)
and the central bank (through its power to change reserve requirements
and the discount rate) jointly determine the actual supply of money. In
the case of the commercial banks, their portfolio choice governs the extent to which they hold reserves in excess of those set by the central
bank. Similarly, the portfolio decision of the public relates to the relative proportion of its money holding that will take the form of currency
and coin.

These basic determinants of the money supply can all be combined
in an identity which provides a convenient device for explaining various
theories of the money supply. The identity itself does not explain what
causes the money supply to change—it merely identifies the variables
associated with the changes in the supply of money which have taken
place. To explain the changes in the supply, the determinants of the
identity would have to be related to specific hypotheses about their behavior; examples of this are provided below.

To construct the identity, two definitions are required.

First, the money supply is defined to consist of currency and coin
held by the nonbank public, C, and demand deposits, D, or

$$MS = C + D \qquad (10{:}1)$$

Second, as discussed above, the monetary base, or stock of high-powered money, is equal to the sum of actual bank reserves, R, plus paper currency and coin in the hands of the public, C, which can serve as potential reserves, or

$$B = R + C \qquad (10{:}2)$$

If Equation (10:2) is divided by the money supply or MS, it yields

$$\frac{B}{MS} = \frac{R}{MS} + \frac{C}{MS} \qquad (10{:}3)$$

Then, the variable $\dfrac{R}{MS}$ is taken from Equation (10:3) and subjected to several operations. First, it is multiplied by a value equal to unity, or $\dfrac{MS - C}{D}$ (which is, of course, equal to $\dfrac{D}{D}$)

$$\frac{R}{MS} = \frac{R}{MS} \cdot \frac{MS - C}{D}$$
$$= \frac{R(MS - C)}{MSD} \qquad (10{:}4)$$

Second, the indicated multiplication is performed yielding

$$\frac{R}{MS} = \frac{RMS}{DMS} - \frac{RC}{DMS} \qquad (10{:}5)$$

Since MS/MS is unity, (10:5) simplifies to

$$\frac{R}{MS} = \frac{R}{D} - \frac{RC}{DMS} \qquad (10{:}6)$$

Substituting (10:6) into (10:3) results in

$$\frac{B}{MS} = \frac{R}{D} - \frac{RC}{DMS} + \frac{C}{MS} \qquad (10{:}7)$$

If both sides of (10:7) are divided by B and its reciprocal taken, the result is

$$MS = \frac{B}{\dfrac{R}{D} + \dfrac{C}{MS} - \dfrac{RC}{DMS}} \qquad (10{:}8)$$

Equation (10:8) specifies that the money supply, defined to consist of demand deposits and paper currency and coin, varies directly with the monetary base, B, and inversely with the reserve/deposit ratio, $\frac{R}{D}$, and the currency/money-supply ratio.[64] It also draws attention to the

[64] The variable $\frac{RC}{DMS}$ is generally neglected, since it will be much smaller than the other variables in the denominator.

fact that the supply of money is the joint outcome of the behavior of the central bank, the Treasury, the commercial banks, and the public.

In terms of magnitude, $\frac{C}{MS}$ can never exceed unity and empirical work shows that its value varies seasonally, cyclically, and secularly. The reserve/deposit ratio, $\frac{R}{D}$, consisting of both legally required and excess reserves, could be greater than one, but historically has been less than unity.

In order to clarify more sharply the determinants of the money supply, the reserve ratio, $\frac{R}{D}$, is often broken down into its two components, or

$$\frac{R}{D} = \frac{ER}{D} + \frac{LR}{D} \tag{10:9}$$

where ER indicates excess reserves and LR indicates those legally imposed by the central bank. When this finer subdivision is made, Equation (10:8) becomes

$$MS = \frac{B}{\dfrac{ER}{D} + \dfrac{LR}{D} + \dfrac{C}{MS} - \dfrac{C(ER + LR)}{DMS}} \tag{10:10}$$

Equation (10:10) is often stated in a different form in which the reciprocal of the denominator is called the *money multiplier, m,* and is shown in the form

$$MS = B(m) \tag{10:11}$$

Utilizing either Equation (10:8) or Equation (10:10) it will be possible to present a survey of the literature on the money supply.

An identity such as Equation (10:10) can be converted into a money-supply function if the variables determining $\frac{ER}{D}$ and $\frac{C}{MS}$ can be isolated. For example, if $\dfrac{ER}{D}$ is thought to depend on the net profitability of holding the reserves (measured as the difference of the market interest rate and the discount rate), or r, and $\dfrac{C}{MS}$ on per-capita real income, $\dfrac{Y}{N}$, the following money-supply function can be written as Equation (10:12)

$$MS = \int(B, r, \frac{Y}{N}) \tag{10:12}$$

This permits the accuracy of the function to be tested and the relative importance of each argument to be measured.

Utilizing an identity such as Equation (10:8) or Equation (10:10) permits a survey of the literature or the supply of money to be presented in a consistent framework. Before this survey is undertaken, the subject of the exogeneity of money will be discussed.

THE EXOGENEITY OF MONEY

We have previously defined the exogeneity of money in terms of the ability of the central bank to control the supply of money. If the central bank could control the supply, it was called exogenous; if not, the supply was called endogenous. However, the terms *exogenous* and *endogenous* also have well-defined meanings in econometrics. To say that a variable is *exogenous* is to say that it is regarded as independent of the influence of the variable whose value it seeks to explain. The latter variable is called the *dependent,* or *endogenous,* variable. For example, in terms of Equation (10:12), the variables in the parentheses are regarded as independent, or exogenous, and serve to explain the behavior of the money supply. Only if B, r, and $\dfrac{Y}{N}$ are truly independent of any influence of the money supply would they be called exogenous by the econometrician.

One can see immediately the difficulty which emerges, for the money supply, according to the control definition, is an exogenous variable, whereas to the econometrician, it is endogenous.

Unfortunately, the context in which the terms exogenous and endogenous are used is seldom described explicitly and as a consequence there has been a great deal of misunderstanding among economists. The controversy surrounding this subject is detailed in Chapter 12.

THE COMMERCIAL LOAN AND
FISHERIAN THEORIES OF THE MONEY SUPPLY

In the early chapters of this text, the commercial-loan theory of banking was discussed and the Fisherian theory of the business cycle presented in great detail. Each can be stated as a theory of the supply of money.

The commercial-loan theory says that as long as commercial banks create deposits against bills of exchange secured by real goods, the resulting expansion of the money supply will be noninflationary. This (demand-determined) theory of the supply of money holds that given the monetary base, B, the banks will stand ready to create deposits at given interest rates by drawing down their excess reserves until they reach the level legally or traditionally imposed upon them. At that point, the supply schedule becomes vertical. In terms of Equation (10:10), MS rises because the denominator decreases, as $\dfrac{ER}{D}$ is drawn down in response to increases in the demand for loanable funds.

The commercial-loan theory is a mechanistic one, for the variation in $\dfrac{ER}{D}$ is related to no specific behavioral variable.

The Fisherian analysis is both more complicated and more analytical, because the movement of the variables in the multiplier of Equation (10:11) are related to behavior.

Remember that the cycle in Fisher's model is initiated by an increase in gold money, which causes the commodity price level to rise. In terms of Equation (10:10), the initiation of the cycle is prompted by a rise in the monetary base, B.

The inflation leads to a rise in the demand for loanable funds which increases the money rate of interest. The rise in prices is unanticipated by all lenders including commercial banks, and according to Fisher,

> . . . banks are led to become more enterprising. Beguiled by the higher nominal rates into a belief that fairly high interest is being realized, they extend their loans, and with the resulting expansion of loans, deposit currency [demand deposits in contemporary language] . . . expands [relative to gold money].[65]

Fisher tells us that the reserve/deposit ratio, $\dfrac{R}{D}$, in Equation (10:8)

[65] Irving Fisher, The Purchasing Power of Money (New York: MacMillan, 1911), p. 60.

declines, causing the money multiplier to rise and the supply of money to expand, which serves to raise commodity prices further. In Fisher's verbal explanation we have a behavioral hypothesis about the supply of money. According to his account, the reserve/deposit ratio depends upon the perceived real interest rate of the banker. The higher the perceived rate, the smaller becomes the ratio $\frac{R}{D}$, and consequently the larger the money multiplier.

As the reserve/deposit ratio of the commercial banks declines to a level regarded by tradition as unnaturally low, the banks are forced to cease lending and the money supply ceases to expand.

In the later phases of the cycle, as expected inflation rises and overtakes the actual inflation rate, the money rate of interest will cease to rise. With a fairly constant money rate and a rising level of inflationary expectations, the real rate of interest perceived by lenders will decline. At this point in the cycle, banks, believing the yields on their assets to be low in real terms, will seek to restore their reserve/deposit ratio, $\frac{R}{D}$, from its abnormally low level to one consistent with the perceived low yield on assets. The restoration of the ratio is accomplished by calling some loans and failing to renew others, actions which contract the supply of money. The contraction of the money supply precipitates business failures, which weaken confidence in the banking system and lead to a mass effort to convert bank deposits into gold.

In terms of Equation (10:8), the conversion of bank deposits to gold is equivalent to a rise in the currency/money-supply ratio, $\frac{C}{MS}$, decreasing the money multiplier and thus contracting the money supply.

In Fisher's theory of the money supply, apart from the increase in the monetary base which initiates the cycle, it is the change in the money multiplier which alters the money supply. The change in the multiplier results from a perceived change in the real interest rate, which alters the portfolio choice of banks, causing them initially to expand and then to contract the demand-deposit component of the money stock. In the downswing of the cycle, it is the portfolio behavior of the public, which seeks to increase the portion of its money holdings composed of gold, which further aggravates the overall contraction of the money stock and plunges the economy into an even deeper recession.

Since Fisher's theory predates the advent of the Federal Reserve System, his money supply was a purely endogenous variable determined by the portfolio choices of the commercial banks and the public. The econometrician would also regard it as such.

THE RIEFLER–BURGESS MONEY-SUPPLY HYPOTHESIS

With the establishment of the Federal Reserve System, two individuals who were to be long associated with its research activities advanced a theory of the supply of money. While related to explaining the flow of bank credit and its relationship to the level of market interest rates, and not well articulated, their view appears to have served as the basis for subsequent Federal Reserve policy and interpretation of events. Earlier, when alternative definitions of money were discussed, the Riefler–Burgess view, concentrating on bank credit, was called the Federal Reserve definition and note was made that it was concerned with the flow of credit used to finance purchases.

This early formulation of the money supply was set forth in 1927 by W. Randolph Burgess,[66] and in 1930 by Winfield W. Riefler.[67] Burgess appears to be the first person to use the phrase *high-powered money* to describe the monetary base, and the Riefler was among the very first to spell out in detail the implications of Federal Reserve open-market operations.

Their theory of the money supply, as deduced from their works, is based upon their observation that throughout the formative years of the Federal Reserve System (up to 1930) the member banks sought to maintain their total reserve holdings close to the statutory requirements, that is, they sought to avoid any net indebtedness to the central bank. In terms of Equation (10:10), the value of $\frac{ER}{D}$ was always close to zero. They attributed this avoidance of net indebtedness to historic tradition (prior to the Federal Reserve System, banks did not borrow continuously from their larger correspondents) and to the fact that the official position of the Federal Reserve was that continuous borrowing by member banks was a sign of unsound banking and inconsistent with the Federal Reserve Act.[68]

Given this peculiar restraint on commercial bank portfolio behavior, the money-supply function depended upon the base of high-powered money which could be influenced either by open-market operations or international gold flows. All their analysis was presented in a verbal form supported with some statistical data. No equation such as (10:8) or (10:10), supported by mathematical analysis, is presented and

[66] W. Randolph Burgess, *The Reserve Banks and the Money Market.*

[67] Winfield W. Riefler, *Money Rates and Money Markets in the United States* (New York: Harper and Brothers, 1930).

[68] See Burgess, *The Reserve Banks,* pp. 220–21.

there is very little explanation of the reasons for the gold flows or the open-market operations.

The Burgess–Riefler hypothesis on the supply of money has difficulties explaining the holding of positive excess reserves by the banking system. When this occurs, as it did in the 1930's, they generally attribute it to an absence of qualified borrowers, which shows their confusion between supply in the functional, or scheduled, sense, and the actual stock of money. In the words of Burgess:

> The effects of [open market] operations when member banks . . . are out of debt are more direct. At such times, Federal Reserve purchases of securities increase bank reserves. Whether or not the increase in bank reserves forms the base for a multiple expansion of bank credit depends on many attendant circumstances. In 1922 and 1924 such an expansion took place; but in the recent depression years much larger surplus reserves have had only a limited effect in expanding bank credit.
>
> At other times a central bank, in order to try to bring about an expansion of money, finds it necessary to push its funds into the market by buying government securities and so forcing its high-powered money into use. Expansion is dependent not on the banks alone, but on the users of money—their willingness to borrow and their soundness.[69]

In addition, Burgess and Riefler are much more concerned with the flow of bank credit than with the supply of money, which they generally identify with bank loans and investments, although it is sometimes used confusingly and synonymously for demand deposits. As is well known, bank credit and demand deposits do not often vary in a 1:1 relationship. Again, in the words of Burgess:

> . . . the problem is to aid in the adjustment of the volume of credit to the volume of business. Maladjustments in this relationship tend toward inflation, rising prices, and speculation on the one hand, or deflation, falling prices, and depression on the other.[70]

From the Burgess–Riefler viewpoint, the money supply must be regarded as a generally endogenous variable. This conclusion emerges from their discussion of the ability of the central bank to control the supply of money. During the late 1920's, the limited portfolio of the Federal Reserve System made the impact of open-market operations to curb the stock market speculation of limited importance. During the

[69] *The Reserve Banks.* The first paragraph is from pp. 239–40 and the second from p. 8.

[70] *Ibid.,* p. 208. In the context of the discussion, *credit* refers to loans and investments by banks.

1930's, the volume of excess reserves held by the commercial banking system became so large that Burgess thought the banks ". . . independent of the Federal Reserve Banks."[71]

THE ACADEMIC VIEW ON THE MONEY SUPPLY

Quite independent of, and apparently having a limited impact on, the Federal Reserve view of the money supply were developments by various academic economists who were formulating a supply schedule of money.

Among the very early contributors was Professor Chester A. Phillips of Dartmouth College, who was concerned with the question of how many dollars' worth of demand deposits a bank could create given various changes in its reserve base.[72]

Phillips' work is noteworthy in that he is the first to publish a text which correctly distinguishes the amount of deposits an individual bank can create versus the amount the banking system can create on the basis of a given addition of reserves. His banking system deposit multiplier is, however, very elementary containing only the reserve to deposit ratio.

In the early 1930's, two papers appeared which developed formulas for the amount of demand deposits an individual bank and the banking system could create for a given change in its reserves.[73] These formulas became a standard part of most subsequent texts dealing with the banking system and are of a form somewhat similar to (10:8):

$$\frac{\text{Monetary Base}}{\dfrac{\text{Reserve}}{\text{Demand Deposits}} + \dfrac{\text{Currency}}{\text{Demand Deposit}}} = \frac{\text{Demand}}{\text{Deposits}} \qquad (10:13)$$

However, despite the extensive discussion presented in these two papers, they do not contain a supply function of money *per se*. The two ratios in the denominator are given values based apparently on historical experience; they are not related to any behavioral determinants. Thus, this treatment of the money supply rests on a very mechanical analysis somewhat similar to the Fisherian treatment of velocity. Nevertheless, this approach by academic economists ought to be regarded as a major step toward the formulation of a supply function of money.

These mechanical formulations of the money supply give rise to

[71] *Ibid.*, p. 193.

[72] Chester Arthur Phillips, *Bank Credit* (New York: MacMillan, 1920).

[73] See James Harvey Rogers, "The Absorption of Bank Credit," *Econometrica*, Vol. 1 (1933), pp. 63–70; and James W. Angell and Karel F. Ficek, "The Expansion of Bank Credit," *Journal of Political Economy*, Vol. 41, No. 1 (Feb. 1933), pp. 1–32 and No. 2 (April 1933), pp. 152–93. Professor Rogers was at Yale, Professor Angell at Columbia, and Professor Ficek at Villanova.

the inference that the central bank can control the supply of money, rendering that variable exogenous according to the control criterion.

A notable book by Lauchlin Currie of Harvard University[74] appeared in 1934, devoted specifically to an explanation of the supply of money and the degree to which it could be controlled by the central bank.

Currie rejected completely the commercial loan theory of banking, as well as other views which specified that the stock of money depended upon the demand for it or upon the availability of suitable lending opportunities even when the economy was in a deep depression. In addition, Currie drew a clear distinction between money and bank credit, something which he claimed the Federal Reserve failed to understand and which he thought caused them to make very bad policy decisions.

However, the central part of Currie's work is an extension of the analysis of Phillips, Rogers, Angell, and Ficek. It starts by expressing doubt whether the answer concerning the expansion of demand deposits from a given change in bank reserves, derived from an application of their mechanical formula, is even remotely representative of reality. He discusses various reasons why the ratios and the numerator of Equation (10:13) may be subject to change over time and includes an interesting analysis of the cyclical variations in the supply of money due to cyclical changes in bank reserves and in the two ratios in the denominator of Equation (10:13).

The work is largely devoid of any measurement of the relative significance of the various factors causing cyclical variations in the supply of bank money, because an adequate data base was unavailable. To Currie's credit, his work represents an early attempt to formulate behavioral hypotheses about the variables whose change affects the supply of money even though no functional form was specified.

Currie was not optimistic about the ability of the central bank to control the supply of money:

> Indeed, it will be found that so many and diverse are the forces causing variations in the reserve ratio against demand deposits that it is quite impossible to predict the magnitude of a change in the volume of money that will result from any given change in the volume of reserves of commercial banks.[75]

Other references indicate that until the Federal Reserve acquired the power to alter reserve requirements, its ability to control the money-creating capability of commercial banks was limited, especially in expansion, by its meager holding of government securities.

---

[74] Lauchlin Currie, *The Supply and Control of Money in the United States* (Cambridge, Mass.: Harvard University Press, 1934). Quotations are from the 1935 revised edition.

[75] *The Supply and Control of Money*, p. 71.

RECENT ACADEMIC CONTRIBUTIONS

After the contribution by Currie, work on the supply of money entered a relative hiatus. Keynes himself, in *The General Theory,* assumed the supply of money to be given and controllable by the central bank, thus rendering it an exogenous variable. This assumption was refined in an early paper by Kragh, in which he makes the holding of reserves by banks sensitive to the market rate of interest.[76] Thus, even if the demand for money were completely inelastic with regard to the interest rate, so long as supply was responsive the *LM* schedule would slope upward and to the right.[77]

Starting in the late 1950's and early 1960's, work was again directed toward the subject of the money supply from two quite different quarters. Representing the quantity theory tradition were Cagan, Friedman and Schwartz, Brunner and Meltzer, and the Federal Reserve Bank of St. Louis. Formulating the identity of Equation (10:8), Cagan, and Friedman and Schwartz, sought to partition the changes in the money supply from approximately the mid-nineteenth to the mid-twentieth century among the variables in the identity (that is, to attribute movements in the supply to changes in either the monetary base or the elements comprising the multiplier). This was done on both a cyclical and a secular basis. However, the authors go beyond this mechanical exercise and attempt to relate the movement in the denominator ratios, for example, to behavior. Cagan believes that the secular decline in the currency/money-supply ratio can be attributed to the rise in real per-capita income, the net cost of holding currency, and the desire to avoid income taxation. Others have advanced hypotheses to explain the reserve-holding behavior of banks.[78] Emerging from the initial effort by this group is the conclusion that they are applying portfolio, or capital, theory to the supply of money, thereby putting it on the same ground as the theory underlying the demand for money. This makes it possible to formulate a specific supply function for money similar to Equation (10:11).

[76] B. Kragh, "Two Liquidity Functions and the Rate of Interest: A Simple Dynamic Model," *Review of Economic Studies,* Vol. 17, No. 1 (Feb. 1950), pp. 98–106. For some elasticity measurement of both demand and supply when measured simultaneously, see Ronald Teigen, "Demand and Supply Functions for Money in the United States: Some Structural Estimates," *Econometrica,* Vol. 32, No. 4 (Oct. 1964), pp. 476–509.

[77] Kragh's view requires that the *LM* schedule be redefined to specify that it is drawn relative to a given monetary base rather than to a given money supply.

[78] See A. J. Meigs, *Free Reserves and the Money Supply* (Chicago: University of Chicago Press, 1962); and Peter A. Frost, "Banks' Demand for Excess Reserves," *Journal of Political Economy,* Vol. 79, No. 4 (July/August 1971), pp. 805–25.

From the opposite extreme comes the New View on money, developed largely by James Tobin of Yale University.[79] The New View treats a commercial bank as traditional micro theory treats the firm. Its product becomes money—deposits—which it produces guided by the traditional desire to maximize profits. Thus it produces deposits up to the point at which the marginal gain from asset acquisition is equal to the marginal cost of attracting and maintaining deposit liabilities. This desired maximization is subject, in the American institutional framework, to a constraint imposed by legal reserve requirements. This constraint may force the banks to restrict their growth and hence, their relative size, that is, it may force an equilibrium on the banking system short of that dictated by considerations of profit maximization alone.[80]

An interesting conclusion of the Tobin analysis is that if the commercial banks are in an unconstrained profit-maximizing position (that is, have maximized profits before the reserve requirement constraint becomes binding on the system), and if an excess supply of bank money exists, it is the money supply which contracts rather than the economy which expands, contrary to the predictions of the quantity theory approach. Tobin reaches this conclusion even though he shares with modern quantity theory the view that the money supply is the joint outcome of the behavior of the central bank, the commercial banks, and the public.

Tobin reaches his conclusion that the money supply, rather than the economy, reacts to excess supply conditions, by assuming that the banking system is in a state of profit-maximizing equilibrium and then for some reason the tastes of the public change as to the desirability of holding money assets, so that they prefer the deposits of nonbank intermediaries. The public, as a result of this change in tastes, transfers its bank deposits to the nonbank intermediaries, providing these institutions with the means for purchasing assets. These transfers do not in themselves alter the supply of money; rather, they only transfer the ownership of the demand deposits. Subsequent asset acquisition by the nonbank intermediaries bids up asset prices and reduces the interest rate structure. These purchases still have no direct effect on the supply of money. However, because they cause the rate of interest to decline, they reduce the marginal yield on bank assets relative to the marginal cost of maintaining bank deposits. This induces the banks to decrease their asset holdings and with this decrease the supply of money is contracted.

[79] See "Commercial Banks as Creators of Money."

[80] This treatment of commercial banks in the New View is part of its assertion that banks and other financial intermediaries are each merely providers of a differentiated product. Considerations such as maximizing profits, which limit the size of other intermediaries, are shown to effectively limit the size of commercial banks, thus reinforcing the conjecture that banks are like all other intermediaries.

Thus, a change in the tastes of the public, which leads to an excess supply of bank money, finally results in a contraction in that supply through reduced market interest rates.[81]

In terms of Equation (10:10), the fall in the interest rate subsequent to nonbank intermediary purchases of assets raises the desired reserve/deposit ratio, thus producing a contraction of the money supply. In more familiar terms, the disparity between actual and desired money balances is restored through a movement in the money multiplier, not through a movement of output, employment, or the price level. The Tobin analysis reveals that he has in mind a general money-supply function which contains as an argument the relative profitability of lending.

It is important to note that Tobin's result of a contraction in the money supply follows from the assumption that commercial banks are able to maximize profits before the reserve requirement constraint is binding. So long as the world we live in is one in which the constraint is operative before profits are maximized, the Tobin conclusion will not be relevant.

Nevertheless, from his analysis Tobin draws some interesting implications related primarily to his belief that the holding of reserves by banks is related to profitability calculations. First, such calculations can serve to explain the holding of huge excess reserve balances, which happened in the United States during the late 1930's and early 1940's. Second, a given increase in excess reserves may not always generate a multiple amount of deposits, because by changing the rate of interest it changes the desired level of the reserves held by banks.

Because public preferences for various types of assets are thought to change, and because interest rates change as a result, the money supply at any given time is held by Tobin to be an endogenous variable—from the econometric criterion. It may, however, be exogenous from the viewpoint of central bank control, but should not be treated as such for econometric purposes. Thus, Tobin's view is similar to that of Smith and Eisner noted above, and is generally associated with the Keynesian view (that is, while the central bank may well be able to control the supply of money if it desires, the actual supply at any given moment is the outcome of the actions of the public, commercial banks, and the central bank), and for econometric purposes the money supply should be regarded as an endogenous variable.

---

[81] An explicit application of the New View was made by Gramley and Chase. Similar to the proposition advanced by Tobin, economic activity does not react to a disparity between actual and desired cash balances. In fact, an increase in actual cash balances will generate an increase in desired balances. Economic activity reacts to changes in the yield on the security in which the central bank conducts open-market operations. See Lyle Gramley and Samuel B. Chase, Jr., "Time Deposits in Monetary Analysis," *Federal Reserve Bulletin*, Vol. 51, No. 10 (Oct. 1965), pp. 1380–1406.

CONCLUSION

Two quite different topics have been presented in this chapter. The first has involved a discussion of a very old problem and concerns the unique attributes of a small group of assets, such that they among all other assets should be called *money*. However, the discussion went far beyond this subject and included analysis of financial intermediaries in general and their effects on a monetary policy which concentrates on the regulation of commercial bank deposits.

The second topic concerned some fundamental advances in theory. The portfolio approach to monetary demand was presented in detail by examining both a monetary and a fiscal act, separating initial from ultimate effects.

Last, a survey of the development of a supply function for money was attempted. A general conclusion emerging from that discussion was that both those in the quantity theory tradition and those adhering to the New View are applying portfolio-type analysis to the supply of money in an attempt to explain commercial bank holding of excess reserves and the distribution of money holdings by individuals between currency and demand deposits. A great deal of work remains to be done in money supply theory and we should expect valuable contributions in the next few decades.

Selected References and Readings

ALHADEFF, D. A., "Credit Controls and Financial Intermediaries," *American Economic Review*, Vol. 50 (Sept. 1960).

ANDREWS, P. W. S., "A Further Inquiry into the Effects of Rates of Interest," *Oxford Economic Papers*, No. 3 (Feb. 1940).

ANGELL, JAMES W., AND FICEK, KAREL F., "The Expansion of Bank Credit," *Journal of Political Economy*, Vol. 41, No. 1 (Feb. 1933) and No. 2 (April 1933).

ASCHHEIM, JOSEPH, *Techniques of Monetary Control* (Baltimore: Johns Hopkins University Press, 1961).

————, "Commercial Banks and Financial Intermediaries: Fallacies and Policy Implications," *Journal of Political Economy*, Vol. 67, No. 5 (Sept./Oct. 1960).

BECHER, WILLIAM E., "Determinants of the United States Currency–Demand Deposit Ratio," *Journal of Finance*, Vol. 30, No. 1 (March 1975).

BURGER, ALBERT, "Revision of the Money Supply Series," *Review—Federal Reserve Bank of St. Louis* (Oct. 1969).

BRUNNER, KARL, "A Schema for the Supply Theory of Money," *International Economic Review*, Vol. 1, No. 1 (Jan. 1961).

————, AND MELTZER, ALLAN H., "A Credit-Market Theory of the Money Supply and an Explanation of Two Puzzles in U.S. Monetary Policy," *Essays in Honor of Mario Fanno* (Padova, Italy, 1961).

————, "Some Further Investigations of Demand and Supply Functions for Money," *Journal of Finance*, Vol. 19 (May 1964).

————, "Liquidity Traps for Money, Bank Credit and Interest Rates," *Journal of Political Economy*, Vol. 76, No. 1 (Jan./Feb. 1968).

————, "The Use of Money: Money in the Theory of an Exchange Economy," *American Economic Review*, Vol. 61, No. 5 (Dec. 1971).

BURGESS, W. R., *The Reserve Banks and the Money Market* (New York: Harper & Bros., 1927).

CAGAN, PHILLIP, "The Demand for Currency Relative to the Total Money Supply," *Journal of Political Economy*, Vol. 66 (Aug. 1958).

————, *Determinants and Effects of Changes in the Stock of Money, 1875–1960* (New York: Columbia University Press, 1965).

CHASE, SAM B., JR., "Bank Reactions to Security Losses," Federal Reserve Bank of Kansas City, *Monthly Review* (June 1960).

CHICK, VICTORIA, *The Theory of Monetary Policy* (London: Gray Mills Publishing, 1973).

CHETTY, V. K., "On Measuring the Nearness of Near-Money," *American Economic Review*, Vol. 59, No. 3 (June 1969).

Committee on the Working of the Monetary System (Chairman: The Rt. Hon. The Lord Radcliffe, G.B.E.), *Report* (London, 1959).

CRAMP, A. B., "Two Views on Money," *Lloyds Bank Review*, No. 65 (July 1962).

CULBERTSON, J. M., "Intermediaries and Monetary Theory: A Criticism of the Gurley–Shaw Theory," *American Economic Review*, Vol. 48 (March 1958).

CURRIE, LAUCHLIN, *The Supply and Control of Money in the United States* (Cambridge, Mass.: Harvard University Press, 1934).

DUESENBERRY, J., M. FRIEDMAN, A. SCHWARTZ, *et. al.*, "The State of Monetary Economics," *Review of Economics and Statistics*, Vol. 45, No. 1, Part 2: Supplement (Feb. 1963).

EBERSOLE, JOHN, "The Influence of Interest Rates Upon Entrepreneurial Decisions in Business: A Case Study," *Harvard Business Review*, Vol. 17 (1938).

EISNER, ROBERT, "What Went Wrong: Further Thoughts on Fiscal and Monetary Policy," in James Diamond, ed., *Issues in Fiscal and Monetary Policy: The Eclectic Economist Views the Controversy* (Chicago: DePaul University, 1971).

FAND, DAVID, "Intermediary Claims and the Adequacy of our Monetary Controls," in Deane Carson, ed., *Banking and Monetary Studies* (Homewood, Ill.: Richard D. Irwin, 1963).

FREIMER, MARSHALL AND GORDON, MYRON J., "Why Banks Ration Credit," *Quarterly Journal of Economics,* Vol. 79 (Aug. 1965).

FRIEDMAN, BENJAMIN, *Credit Rationing: A Review,* Staff Study, Board of Governors, Federal Reserve System (Washington, D.C.: U.S. Government Printing Office).

FROST, PETER A., "Banks' Demand for Excess Reserves," *Journal of Political Economy,* Vol. 79, No. 4 (July/Aug. 1971).

GOLDSMITH, R. W., *The Share of Financial Intermediaries in National Wealth and National Assets, 1900–1949,* Occasional Paper 42 (New York: National Bureau of Economic Research, 1954).

———, *A Study of Saving in the United States* (Princeton, N.J.: Princeton University Press, 1955).

———, *Financial Intermediaries in the American Economy Since 1900* (Princeton, N.J.: Princeton University Press, 1958).

GRAMLEY, LYLE E., "Interest Rates and Credit Availability at Commercial Banks," Federal Reserve Bank of Kansas City, *Monthly Review* (Feb. 1957).

GURLEY, J. G., *Liquidity and Financial Institutions in the Postwar Economy,* Study Paper 14, Joint Economic Committee, 86th Congress, 2nd Session (Washington, D.C.: U.S. Government Printing Office, 1960).

———, "The Radcliffe Report and Evidence: A Review Article," *American Economic Review,* Vol. 50, No. 4 (Sept. 1960).

———, AND SHAW, E. S., "Financial Aspects of Economic Development," *American Economic Review,* Vol. 45, No. 4 (Sept. 1955).

———, "Financial Intermediaries and the Saving–Investment Process," *Journal of Finance,* Vol. 11, No. 2 (May 1956).

———, "The Growth of Debt and Money in the United States, 1800–1950: A Suggested Interpretation," *Review of Economics and Statistics,* Vol. 39, No. 3 (Aug. 1957).

———, *Money in a Theory of Finance* (Washington, D.C.: Brookings Institution, 1960).

GUTTENTAG, JACK, "Credit Availability, Interest Rates, and Monetary Policy," *Southern Economic Journal,* Vol. 26 (Jan. 1960).

———, AND LINDSEY, ROBERT, "The Uniqueness of Commercial Banks," *Journal of Political Economy,* Vol. 76, No. 5 (Sept./Oct. 1968).

HICKS, J. R., "A Suggestion for Simplifying the Theory of Money," *Economica,* New Series, Vol. 2 (1935).

HODGMAN, DONALD R., "Credit Risk and Credit Rationing," *Quarterly Journal of Economics,* Vol. 74 (May 1960).

JAFFEE, DWIGHT M., AND MODIGLIANI, FRANCO, "A Theory and Test of Credit Rationing," *American Economic Review,* Vol. 59 (Dec. 1969).

JOHNSON, HARRY G., "Monetary Theory and Policy," reprinted as Chapter 1 in *Essays in Monetary Economics* (London: Allen & Unwin, 1967).

KALDOR, NICHOLAS, "The Radcliffe Report," *Review of Economics and Statistics*, Vol. 42, No. 1 (Feb. 1960).

KALISH, LIONEL, "A Study of Money Stock Control, *Journal of Finance*, Vol. 25 (Sept. 1970).

KANE, E. J., AND MALKIEL, BURTON G., "Bank Portfolio Allocation, Deposit Variability, and the Availability Doctrine," *Quarterly Journal of Economics*, Vol. 79 (Feb. 1965).

KAREKEN, J. H., "Lenders' Preferences, Credit Rationing and the Effectiveness of Monetary Policy," *Review of Economics and Statistics*, Vol. 39 (Aug. 1957).

KRAGH, B., "Two Liquidity Functions and the Rate of Interest: A Simple Dynamic Model," *Review of Economic Studies*, Vol. 17, No. 1 (Feb. 1950).

LEE, T. H., "Substitutability of non-Bank Intermediary Liabilities for Money: The Empirical Evidence," *Journal of Finance*, Vol. 21, No. 4 (Sept. 1966).

LAUMAS, G. S., "The Degree of Moneyness of Savings Deposits," *American Economic Review*, Vol. 58, No. 3 (June 1968).

————, "Savings Deposits in the Definition of Money," *Journal of Political Economy*, Vol. 77, No. 6 (Nov./Dec. 1969).

MAKOWER, HELEN, AND MARSCHAK, JACOB, "Assets, Prices and Monetary Theory," *Economica*, New Series, Vol. 5 (1938).

MARKOWITZ, HARRY, "Portfolio Selection," *Journal of Finance*, Vol. 7, No. 1 (March 1952).

————, *Portfolio Selection: Efficient Diversification of Investments* (New York: John Wiley, 1959).

MARTY, ALVIN L., "Gurley and Shaw on Money in a Theory of Finance," *Journal of Political Economy*, Vol. 69, No. 1 (Feb. 1961).

MEADE, J. E., AND ANDREWS, P. W. S., "A Summary of Replies to Questions on Effects of Interest Rates," *Oxford Economic Papers*, No. 1 (Oct. 1958).

MEIGS, A. J., *Free Reserves and the Money Supply* (Chicago: University of Chicago Press, 1962).

MELTZER, ALLAN, "The Demand for Money: The Evidence From the Time Series," *Journal of Political Economy*, Vol. 71, No. 3 (May/June 1963).

————, AND BRUNNER, KARL, "Predicting Velocity: Implications for Theory and Policy," *Journal of Finance*, Vol. 18, No. 2 (May 1963).

MILLER, MERTON, "Credit Risk and Credit Rationing: Further Comment," *Quarterly Journal of Economics*, Vol. 76 (Aug. 1962).

MUSGRAVE, R. A., "Money, Liquidity and the Valuation of Assets," in *Money, Trade and Economic Growth: Essays in Honor of John Henry Williams* (New York: Macmillan, 1951).

ORR, D., AND MELLON, W. J., "Stochastic Reserve Losses and Expansion of Bank Credit," *American Economic Review*, Vol. 51 (Sept. 1961).

PATINKIN, D., "Financial Intermediaries and the Logical Structure of Monetary Theory," *American Economic Review*, Vol. 51 (March 1961).

Poindexter, Carl J., "The Currency-Holding Behavior of the Public and the Strength of Monetary Controls," *The Bulletin,* New York University Graduate School of Business Administration, No. 67 (Nov. 1970).

Riefler, Winfield W., *Money Rates and Money Markets in the United States* (New York: Harper and Brothers, 1930).

Rogers, James Harvey, "The Absorption of Bank Credit," *Econometrica,* Vol. 1 (1933).

Roosa, R. V., "Interest Rates and the Central Bank," in *Money, Trade and Economic Growth: Essays in Honor of John H. Williams* (New York: Macmillan, 1951).

Rowan, D. C., "Radcliffe Monetary Theory," *The Economic Record* (Dec. 1961).

Ryder, Carl E., "Credit Risk and Credit Rationing: Comment," *Quarterly Journal of Economics,* Vol. 76 (Aug. 1962).

Sayers, Richard S., "Monetary Thought and Monetary Policies in England," *Economic Journal,* Vol. 70, No. 4 (Dec. 1960).

Scott, I. O., "The Availability Doctrine: Theoretical Underpinnings," *Review of Economics and Statistics,* Vol. 25 (Oct. 1957).

Shackle, G. L. S., *The Years of High Theory* (London: Cambridge University Press, 1967).

Shelby, D., "Some Implications of the Growth of Financial Intermediaries," *Journal of Finance,* Vol. 13 (Dec. 1958).

Smith, Paul, "Concepts of Money and Commercial Banks," *Journal of Finance,* Vol. 21 (Dec. 1966).

Smith, W. L., "On the Effectiveness of Monetary Policy," *American Economic Review,* Vol. 46, No. 4 (Sept. 1956).

————, "Financial Intermediaries and Monetary Controls," *Quarterly Journal of Economics,* Vol. 73 (Nov. 1959).

————, "A Neo-Keynesian View of Monetary Policy," in *Controlling Monetary Aggregates* (Boston: Federal Reserve Bank of Boston, 1969).

Teigen, Ronald, "Demand and Supply Functions for Money in the United States: Some Structural Estimates," *Econometrica,* Vol. 32, No. 4 (Oct. 1964).

Timberlake, R. H., and Fortsen, James, "Time Deposits in the Definition of Money," *American Economic Review,* Vol. 57, No. 1 (March 1967).

Tobin, James, "Money, Capital and Other Stores of Value," *American Economic Review,* Vol. 51, No. 2 (May 1961).

————, "An Essay in the Principles of Debt Management," in Commission on Money and Credit, *Fiscal and Debt Management Policies* (Englewood Cliffs, N.J.: Prentice-Hall, 1963).

————, "Commercial Banks as Creators of Money," in Deane Carson, ed., *Banking and Monetary Studies* (Homewood, Ill.: Richard D. Irwin, 1963).

————, "Deposit Interest Ceilings as a Monetary Control," *Journal of Money, Credit and Banking,* Vol. 2 (Feb. 1970).

————, AND BRAINARD, WILLIAM, "Financial Intermediaries and the Effectiveness of Monetary Controls," *American Economic Review*, Vol. 53 (May 1963).

TOLLEY, G. S., "Providing for Growth in the Money Supply," *Journal of Political Economy*, Vol. 65 (Dec. 1957).

WALTERS, A. A., "The Radcliffe Report—Ten Years After: A Survey of Empirical Evidence," in Croome and Johnson, ed., *Money in Britain, 1959–1969* (London: Oxford University Press, 1970).

chapter 11

Inflation

Since man was first drawn to the study of economic phenomena, the two great problems of unemployment and inflation have received a disproportionate amount of attention. It was easy for him to regard them as opposite events: The former is due to a deficiency of aggregate demand, whereas the latter results from excessive aggregate demand. In our contemporary society, "fine-tuning the economy" by policymakers has meant the avoidance of either extreme.

But for an equally long time many individuals, perhaps drawing their inspiration from the determination of individual commodity prices, have looked to the supply side for the cause of inflation. They have attributed the observed rise in prices to wars, famines, acts of God, profiteers, trade unions, monopolists, hoarders, speculators, Arab oil sheiks, and so forth. Common to their explanations is the idea that the villain either directly controls the supply of commodities or can influence substantially the cost at which goods and services are produced.

The implication of their analyses or conjectures is that unemployment and inflation need not be mutually exclusive events but may occur simultaneously, that is, an economy can experience both unemployment and inflation.

During the late 1950's empirical work by the British economist

A. W. Phillips[1] supported the idea of the nonexclusivity of inflation and unemployment without at the same time endorsing the concept of cost-push inflation. He envisioned a permanent long-run trade-off which implied that less inflation meant more unemployment, and less unemployment would coexist with a higher rate of inflation. Fine-tuning the economy then implied that policymakers had to choose a socially desirable combination of inflation and unemployment. Once this decision had been made, monetary and fiscal policy could be set in motion to achieve the desired results.

However, in the late 1960's, hardly a decade after the original work by Phillips, the neo-Fisherian, or Monetarist, analysis began to question both the permanence of the trade-off envisioned by the Phillips curve and the common distinction made between demand-induced inflations and those caused by supply or cost factors. This recent analysis views inflation as a unified whole in which demand and cost elements appear as a part of one integrated cycle and in which expectations of future price level movements play a prominent role.

Explaining all these theories and their implications could be a complicated process. In order to simplify it as much as possible, this chapter will first define inflation, discuss its economic costs, investigate the underlying causes of the phenomenon, and finally discuss its possible cures.[2]

INFLATION DEFINED

Inflation is usually defined as a sustained rise in a broadly based index of commodity prices over some period of time. The essential ingredients of the definition are that the rise in prices takes place in a broad group of goods and services, not in one or two commodities, and that the in-

[1] A. W. Phillips, "The Relation Between Unemployment and the Rate of Change of Money Wages in the United Kingdom, 1862–1957," *Economica*, Vol. 25, No. 100 (Dec. 1958), pp. 283–99. In a subsequent section of this chapter Phillips' relationship will be discussed at great length. Those unfamiliar with the concept will benefit from reading Thomas Humphrey, "Changing Views of the Phillips Curve," *Economic Review*, Federal Reserve Bank of Richmond (July 1973), pp. 2–13.

[2] Three rather exhaustive survey articles exist on inflation. The first was commissioned by the American Economic Association; the second was the effort of Harry Johnson. See Martin Bronfenbrenner and Franklyn Holzman, "Survey of Inflation Theory," *American Economic Review*, Vol. 53, No. 4 (Sept. 1963), pp. 593–661; and H. G. Johnson, "A Survey of Theories of Inflation" in *Essays in Monetary Economics* (London: Unwin University Books, 1967), pp. 104–42. Unfortunately, both surveys were completed before the neo-Fisherian approach was reformulated. The third survey, by Laidler and Parkin, embodies most heavily the neo-Fisherian distinction between anticipated and unanticipated inflation. See David Laidler and Michael Parkin, "Inflation: A Survey," *The Economic Journal*, Vol. 85, No. 4 (Dec. 1975), pp. 741–809. All three works have been invaluable reference sources for this chapter.

crease continues for a rather lengthy period of time rather than for one or two quarters. Depending upon the rapidity of the price rise, various authors distinguish between *creeping, trotting, galloping,* or *runaway* inflation but do not define these terms numerically.

Like most definitions, the one used here has problems associated with it; they will be appreciated especially by those interested in em-pirical work.

TABLE 11:1 Consumer Price Index, Wholesale Price Index, and the GNP Deflator, 1939–1975

Year	CPI 1967 = 100		WPI 1967 = 100		GNP Deflator 1958 = 100	
	Index	% Change	Index	% Change	Index	% Change
1939	41.6		39.8		43.2	
1940	42.0	.9	40.5	1.8	43.9	1.6
1941	44.1	2.4	45.1	11.4	47.2	7.5
1942	48.8	10.7	50.9	12.9	53.0	12.3
1943	51.8	6.1	53.3	4.7	56.8	7.2
1944	52.7	1.7	53.6	.6	58.2	2.5
1945	53.9	2.2	54.6	1.9	59.7	2.6
1946	58.5	8.5	62.3	14.1	66.7	11.7
1947	66.9	14.4	76.5	22.8	74.6	11.8
1948	72.1	7.7	82.8	8.2	79.6	6.7
1949	71.4	—1.2	78.7	9.5	79.1	—.6
1950	72.1	1.0	81.8	3.9	80.2	1.4
1951	77.8	7.9	91.1	11.1	85.6	6.7
1952	79.5	2.2	88.6	—2.7	87.5	2.2
1953	80.1	.8	87.4	—1.4	88.3	.9
1954	80.5	.5	87.6	.2	89.6	1.5
1955	80.2	—.4	87.6	0.0	90.9	1.5
1956	81.4	1.1	90.7	3.5	94.0	3.4
1957	84.3	3.6	93.3	2.9	97.5	3.7
1958	86.6	2.7	94.6	1.4	100.0	2.6
1959	87.3	.8	94.8	.2	101.6	1.6
1960	88.7	1.6	94.9	.1	103.3	1.7
1961	89.6	1.0	94.5	—.4	104.6	1.3
1962	90.6	1.1	94.8	.3	105.7	1.1
1963	91.7	1.2	94.5	—.3	107.1	1.3
1964	92.9	1.3	94.7	.2	108.8	1.6
1965	94.5	1.7	96.6	2.0	110.9	1.9
1966	97.2	2.9	99.8	3.3	113.8	2.6
1967	100.0	2.8	100.0	.2	117.3	3.1
1968	104.2	4.2	102.5	2.5	121.8	3.8
1969	109.8	5.4	106.5	3.9	128.2	5.3
1970	116.3	5.9	110.4	3.7	135.3	5.5
1971	121.3	4.3	113.9	3.2	141.6	4.7
1972	125.3	3.3	119.1	4.6	145.9	3.0
1973	133.1	6.2	134.7	13.1	154.3	5.8
1974	147.7	11.0	160.1	18.9	170.2	10.3
1975	161.3	9.2	174.9	9.2	—	—

Source: *Survey of Current Business,* Department of Commerce (Washington, D.C.: United States Government Printing Office).

The first problem concerns the selection of the appropriate price index with which to measure the degree of inflation. Generally, different indices contain different combinations of goods and services or use different weighting schemes, so it should come as no surprise that they measure differently the degree of inflation over time. In the United States three different indices are generally used—Table 11:1 shows the rate of increase in each for the period 1939–1975. As an example of this problem, how should we characterize the period 1958–1965?

Second, over long periods of time or during periods of rapid inflation the weights used to derive an index may become increasingly unrepresentative of the way individuals allocate their income, so that the index no longer measures the inflation accurately.

Third, periods of price stability may be achieved only through the imposition of rigid controls and rationing such as characterized the United States during World War II. Ought we to characterize such periods as noninflationary?

Fourth, in many countries of the world governments attempt to deceive the population by subsidizing commodities which are important in the makeup of a price index, thereby suppressing the true nature of the inflation. Such deceit ought to be recognized and adjusted for in empirical work.

Fifth, very few price indices are adjusted for qualitative changes in the products or services which enter their composition. Thus some authorities believe that creeping inflation is really no inflation at all, but merely reflects qualitative changes.

The list of potential problems could be extended—the five mentioned above are only illustrations.[3] Nevertheless, they demonstrate that care and concern should be exercised in any attempt to apply a definition for measurement purposes. As a rough approximation, however, inflation in this text will continue to be defined as a sustained rise in the general level of commodity prices over some period of time.

THE ECONOMIC COSTS OF INFLATION

Since ancient times inflation has been regarded as an evil. In the fourth, century A.D., the Roman Emperor Diocletian issued an edict imposing extensive wage and price controls to deal with rampant inflation; his most severe measure was to impose the death penalty on those violating the law. Four years after announcing the edict, Diocletian abdicated.[4]

[3] For a comprehensive list see Bronfenbrenner and Holzman, "Survey of Inflation Theory," pp. 597–600; and Johnson, "A Survey of Theories of Inflation," pp. 104–8.

[4] See Anna J. Schwartz, "Secular Price Change in Historical Perspective," *The Journal of Money, Credit and Banking*, Vol. 5, No. 1, Part II (Feb. 1973), pp. 243–69. In this paper Mrs. Schwartz summarizes and explains 2500 years of price history in but 40 pages—no mean feat!

Sixteen centuries later, contemporary political leaders and their advisers are warning that the United States cannot stand double-digit inflation for long.

What is it that men in different centuries find so burdensome about inflation that they impose the death penalty on those violating laws designed to contain it and warn of the impending collapse of society?

Before its cause can be diagnosed and its cure suggested, the nature of the cost of inflation to a society ought to be examined, for the cure may do more harm than the disease.

It is imperative in this discussion to distinguish inflation's cost to a society from its cost to the individual members of society. Our analysis will suggest that under certain circumstances various individuals in the society may lose both income and wealth as a result of inflation, but for the society as a whole, nothing is lost or gained. This implies that the principal effect of inflation is redistributive.

To have both an example of an economic or social loss and a standard against which to measure the social cost of inflation, if a trade-off of the type envisioned by the Phillips curve exists, let the social loss caused by unemployment be noted.

The loss to an economy caused by unemployment consists of the goods and services which could have been produced, but which were not produced because men and machines available for employment were not used. During the 1930's, when unemployment was seldom below 12 percent, the magnitude of this loss was tremendous.

While Milton Friedman cannot claim originality in recognizing the social cost of inflation, it was his rigorous restatement of the quantity theory which drew professional attention to it. Economists had long recognized that inflation constituted a form of taxation on cash balances, and professional attention focused on the redistributive aspects of the tax. However, when Friedman included the expected rate of inflation as an argument in the demand function for money balances, Martin Bailey[5] was among the first to note the loss to society which occurs when individuals, expecting inflation, begin to hold smaller amounts of real cash balances.

To see the nature of the loss, we must recall from the discussion in Chapter 9 that individuals, both ultimate wealth holders and productive enterprise, hold cash balances because they yield utility to the former and can be regarded as a productive factor for the latter. Thus, at any given level of expected inflation—which can, for sake of argument, be assumed to be zero—the balances held by households permit them to

---

[5] Martin Bailey, "The Welfare Cost of Inflationary Finance," *Journal of Political Economy,* Vol. 64, No. 2 (March/April 1956), pp. 93–110. Among earlier work noting that inflation is similar to a tax on cash balances which accrues to the government, see J. M. Keynes, *A Tract on Monetary Reform* (New York: Harcourt, Brace and Co., 1924), pp. 46–70. An analysis of the way inflation acts as a tax on cash balances follows below.

arrange their transactions patterns and provide security against an uncertain future in a way which maximizes the utility from a given income. Similarly, for business enterprise such equilibrium money holdings permit a certain optimum arrangement of its transactions patterns (paying employees, holding a given level of inventories, scheduling production flows, billing customers, maintaining a certain level of working capital balances, and so forth).

In this world of optimum cash holdings, let us assume that individuals suddenly come to expect a higher rate of inflation. What is their response? First, they realize that holding cash balances involves a higher opportunity cost—the now higher rate at which money's purchasing power is diminishing.

Realizing that money balances are losing purchasing power, they discover that the existing system of transactions, requiring a certain amount of real money balances, is now more costly than before. They therefore seek to alter the existing system of transactions or payments to accommodate it to a smaller stock of real money holdings.[6] For business, the adjustment may involve going to the bank more often with deposits, increasing the frequency of ordering inventories, paying employees more frequently, or devoting more time and attention to converting money into inventories or other financial or real assets.

For ultimate wealth holders or households, it may mean rushing more frequently to the markets to exchange money for goods, foreign currencies, or precious metals. It may also mean an increase in barter transactions which are, on average, more time-consuming than similar monetary transactions.

This alteration of payment patterns by business and individuals means that time and energy are diverted from the production of goods and services or from leisure to economizing on money balances as well as to using some resources wastefully—the gathering of information, maintaining excessive inventories of producer and consumer goods, and so forth. In addition, since money balances are held against unexpected contingencies, smaller real money holdings reduce peace of mind and therefore the utility of ultimate wealth owners.

Before we demonstrate how this social cost can be measured, two very important points should be noted carefully.

First, this analysis applies only to noninterest-bearing money, that is, government fiat money and bank money such as demand deposits. To the extent that the interest rate paid on deposits regarded as money re-

---

[6] The analogy between inflation and a tax on cash balances can be made exact insofar as predictive behavior is concerned if inflation is regarded as an excise tax levied only on a commodity called money. In these circumstances, micro theory tells us that if we raise the price of one commodity, all others constant, the quantity demanded of that commodity will fall. Hence, inflation which acts as an excise tax on money will decrease the real quantity demanded—provided, of course, that money is a normal good.

flects fully anticipated inflation, the opportunity cost of holding such money does not rise in an inflation. Thus, the analysis is relevant only to a portion of the money stock—that on which no interest is paid.

Second, the only evidence accumulated thus far of altered payment practices during periods of rising prices is gathered from hyperinflations of the type studied in Europe by Cagan and in China by Babcock and Makinen.[7] In mild inflations of the United States variety, little evidence has been forthcoming to indicate any social cost, suggesting that the social cost from this source for U.S.-type inflations is minimal.

The importance of the second point should be emphasized, for it implies that if a long-run trade-off suggested by the Phillips curve exists, a little more inflation is to be preferred to a little less unemployment, for the former involves less cost to society than does the latter; whereas, the larger output from the latter contains the possibility of making some individuals better off.

Among latter-day Keynesians, the view of James Tobin draws attention to the relative unimportance he attaches to the cost of inflation and his preference for more employment. He writes:

> According to economic theory, the ultimate social cost of anticipated inflation is the wasteful use of resources to economize holdings of currency and other noninterest-bearing means of payment. I suspect that intelligent laymen would be utterly astounded if they realized that *this* is the great evil economists are talking about. They have imagined a much more devastating cataclysm, with Vesuvius vengefully punishing the sinners below. Extra trips between savings banks and commercial banks? What an anti-climax![8]

MEASURING THE SOCIAL COST OF INFLATION

To measure the social loss attributed to inflation, use is made of a Keynesian liquidity preference diagram such as Figure 11:1. Let the analysis begin by assuming a zero rate of inflation and an interest rate of i_0 determined by the demand for real balances at full employment. The area under the demand schedule, then, measures the social value of holding real balances equal to $(M/P)_0$.

---

[7] Phillip Cagan, "The Monetary Dynamics of Hyperinflation," Chapter 2 of Milton Friedman, ed., *Studies in the Quantity Theory of Money* (Chicago: University of Chicago Press, 1956). J. M. Babcock and G. E. Makinen, "The Chinese Hyperinflation Revisited," *Journal of Political Economy*, Vol. 83, No. 6 (Dec. 1975), pp. 1259–68.

[8] James Tobin, "Inflation and Unemployment," *The American Economic Review*, Vol. 62, No. 1 (March 1972), p. 15. Tobin computes for the United States the cost of an extra percentage point of anticipated inflation to be $2/10$ of 1 percent of GNP per year. Italics in the original.

For an alternative computation of the social cost of inflation as well as an excellent discussion of the issues associated with inflation, see Edward Foster, *Costs and Benefits of Inflation, Studies in Monetary Economics*, Federal Reserve Bank of Minneapolis (March 1972).

FIGURE 11:1.

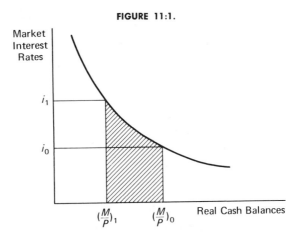

Let inflation now occur which is recognized and anticipated by everyone in the society. The money rate of interest now rises to i_1 ($i_1 - i_0$ = the expected rate of inflation), and the quantity of real balances held declines from $(M/P)_0 - (M/P)_1$. Since the area under the demand schedule is a money measure of the social value of real balances, the shaded area measures the monetary value of the real loss to society resulting from inflation-induced reductions in the holding of real cash balances.

This conclusion is clarified when it is realized that in equilibrium i_0 measures the yield foregone on holding \$1 in cash balances. Thus, i_0 measures the marginal productivity of money in its role as a provider of the services of convenience and security to individuals, a service which cannot be provided by nonmoney alternatives. Because of inflation, the public is induced to hold smaller real balances, and i_1 now measures their marginal product. In giving up balances equal to $(M/P)_0 - (M/P)_1$, the public gains nothing (so long as we assume full employment), since the services of money cannot be provided by the alternatives to money. The shaded area provides a monetary measure of the lost benefits. If price index, P_0, is used as the base of measure, the loss will be stated in dollars of base-year purchasing power.

A SECOND COST OF INFLATION

While a comprehensive discussion of this second social cost of inflation will be given later when an analysis of the Phillips curve is made and objections raised to it, the basic idea is that once an inflation gets underway and is expected to continue, restoring price stability or reducing its rate of increase may create a prolonged period of above-normal unemployment while individuals reformulate their expectations about future price changes. While this is technically not a cost of inflation, it is a cost associated with varying the rate of price change about its long-run trend. It is the unemployment created in attempts to stabilize prices that makes the costs of stopping an ongoing inflation possibly greater than allowing it to continue at its current rate.

The two social costs of inflation discussed above have been advanced primarily by economists in the quantity theory tradition, now called Monetarists. It is doubtful that either the Emperor Diocletian or contemporary American politicians had these costs in mind when they spoke of the evils of inflation. Rather they, like most individuals, probably considered the costs of inflation to be what have been called the *redistributive* effects of inflation, which involve no social cost.[9]

THE REDISTRIBUTIVE EFFECTS OF INFLATION

In addition to causing a misallocation of resources, inflation can have an effect on both the income and the wealth of the individuals in a society. It may redistribute both the flow and the stock from one segment of society to another, and the redistribution occurs either because individuals do not anticipate the inflation, or if they do, some force impedes the right of free contract (for example, wage-and-price controls, usury laws, and so forth) or their ability to adjust their economic behavior. If everyone had equal ability to predict and adjust to inflation, it could have no redistributive effects. It is only because abilities to predict and adjust differ that inflation can redistribute the flow of income and the stock of wealth.

The redistributive question is important, for if it can be shown that inflation comes to be fully and quickly anticipated and adjusted to, we have an absence of money illusion in the economy; members of society think in essentially real terms with regard to wages, rents, and interest rates. If this is the case, money is much less powerful as a stimulus to employment, and the classical world with its assumption of perfect knowledge prevails, in which money is a mere veil. This issue will be discussed in greater detail when the neo-Fisherian, or Monetarist, theory of inflation is considered.

The conventional wisdom of economics holds that inflation redistributes income from wage earners to profit recipients, away from old-age pensioners and other fixed-income recipients, and from creditors to debtors. It is to the validity of these conjectures that our analysis now turns.

---

[9] For some unknown reason, Bronfenbrenner and Holzman discuss only the redistributive effects of inflation. They fail to mention the cost of inflation as analyzed by Monetarists, even though this analysis predates their survey. This is not true of the survey by H. G. Johnson written at approximately the same time.

Income Redistributions

At least two ways exist to measure whether inflation redistributes the income of a society. First, the real value of factor income such as wages, salaries, rents, interest, dividends, and profits can be examined to see if they have changed. However, since any given individual will probably receive income from a variety of sources, a second way to measure any inflation-induced redistributions is to look at the size distribution of income over time. That is, does inflation add to the incomes of the wealthy or the very poor, or does it largely victimize the middle classes?

It has long been part of the conventional wisdom that wage and salary earners are particularly hard-hit victims of inflation. The origin of this wisdom may be hard to find, but in the present century Wesley Mitchell,[10] Irving Fisher,[11] and Earl Hamilton[12] advanced the view with particular vigor and supported their studies by empirical evidence.

The wage-lag hypothesis is based upon the belief that wages are more subject to inertia, or sluggishness, than other prices because of custom, weak bargaining power of labor, or lack of foresight on the part of workers.[13]

Hamilton's support of the wage-lag hypothesis was drawn from an extensive study of the great inflation in Spain from 1350 to 1800 which was partly due to the introduction of gold and silver from the New World in the sixteenth century, and from evidence gathered from the early days of the industrial revolution in England.

Mitchell's conclusions rest on an examination of data recorded in the North during the United States Civil War. Other studies supporting the wage-lag hypothesis utilize data drawn from the South in the Civil War, the German hyperinflation, and the inflation in the United States associated with World War I.

---

[10] W. C. Mitchell, *A History of Greenbacks* (Chicago: University of Chicago Press, 1903).

[11] Irving Fisher, *The Purchasing Power of Money*, Rev. ed. (New York: 1926).

[12] E. J. Hamilton, "American Treasure and the Rise of Capitalism (1500–1700)," *Economica*, Vol. 9 (Nov. 1929), pp. 338–57; *American Treasure and the Price Revolution in Spain, 1501–1650* (Cambridge, Mass.: Harvard University Press, 1934); *Money, Prices, and Wages in Valencia, Aragon, and Navarre, 1351–1500* (Cambridge, Mass.: Harvard University Press, 1936). "Profit Inflation and the Industrial Revolution. 1751–1800," *Quarterly Journal of Economics*, Vol. 56 (Feb. 1942), pp. 256–73. *War and Prices in Spain, 1651–1800* (Cambridge, Mass.: Harvard University Press, 1947).

[13] This view follows from the Keynesian model as presented in Chapter 5. There it was shown that for employment to rise in the short run, the real wage must fall, because an increase in per-unit labor cost occurred as labor's productivity diminished and output expanded in response to a rise in aggregate demand. This analysis was qualified, however, for at high levels of unemployment, labor can be regarded as producing under conditions of constant marginal productivity.

In what must be regarded as a major intellectual *tour de force,* Alchian and Kessel[14] and Felix[15] have shown that the conclusion of these early studies that wages lag behind prices in inflations is incorrect, either because of faulty methodology (Alchian and Kessel show that the supposed 30 percent decline in real wages in Spain from 1520 to 1600 can be turned into a 4 percent rise if one uses as dates of reference 1522–1602), or because the authors neglect real factors (population growth or migration, destruction of capital, depreciation of foreign exchange rates, and so forth) which means that one cannot necessarily infer that because real wages fall during an inflation that the former was caused by the latter.

Alchian and Kessel conclude their rebuttal of the evidence cited above by suggesting that the wage-lag hypothesis remains essentially untested by the available evidence. Thus, it cannot be said that profit recipients gain at the expense of wage earners during inflations.

Even if the relatively long-run evidence shows no wage lag, it should not be assumed that in the short run (during which inflation is unanticipated) there may not be some redistribution in favor of the profit recipient. Nor should the possibility be precluded of shifts among classes of wage and salary earners.

More recent work using United States data for the period subsequent to 1939 shows that the share of national income going to rents and dividends declined, while the share accruing to wage and salary recipients rose. Interest recipients fared poorly during the 1939–1952 period, but received a rising share of national income during the 1950–1957 period.[16]

Other recent evidence gathered by Brimmer[17] and reproduced below suggests wage and salary income as a percentage of personal income rose, as did property income from interest, whereas income from rents and proprietors' income declined. Dividends remained almost rigidly constant over the period 1947–1968.

The Brimmer and Bach–Ando–Stephenson studies ought to be interpreted with great care, for they cover relatively long time periods over which many real factors affecting the distribution of income might

[14] A. A. Alchian and R. A. Kessel, "The Meaning and Validity of the Inflation-Induced Lag of Wages Behind Prices," *American Economic Review,* Vol. 50, No. 1 (March 1960), pp. 43–66.

[15] D. Felix, "Profit Inflation and Industrial Growth: The Historic Record and Contemporary Analogies," *Quarterly Journal of Economics,* Vol. 70 (Aug. 1956), pp. 441–63.

[16] G. L. Bach and A. Ando, "The Redistributional Effects of Inflation," *Review of Economics and Statistics,* Vol. 34, No. 1 (Feb. 1957), pp. 1–13; and G. L. Bach and James B. Stephenson, "Inflation and the Redistribution of Wealth," *The Review of Economics and Statistics,* Vol. 61, No. 1 (Feb. 1974), pp. 1–13.

[17] A. Brimmer, "Inflation and Income Distribution in the United States," *Review of Economics and Statistics,* Vol. 52, No. 1 (Feb. 1971), pp. 37–48.

have changed, thereby accounting for the altered distribution of relative income shares. Indeed, the authors recognize this as a qualification to their conclusions.

TABLE 11:2   Level and Percentage Distribution of Personal Income, by Major Category of Income Recipients, 1947–1968

Type of income	1947	1961	1965	1968
Total personal income				
Amount (billions of dollars)	191.3	416.8	538.9	685.8
Percentage distribution	100.0	100.0	100.0	100.0
Agricultural income	9.6	4.0	3.6	2.9
Nonagricultural income	90.4	96.0	96.4	97.1
Labor income				
Wages and salaries	64.3	66.7	66.6	68.3
Commodity producing	28.4	27.1	26.8	26.5
Manufacturing	22.2	21.5	21.5	21.1
Other industries	6.2	5.6	5.3	5.4
Distributive industries	18.4	16.6	16.1	16.0
Service industries	8.4	10.6	10.8	11.7
Government	9.1	12.5	12.9	14.1
Civilian	—	10.1	10.5	11.4
Military	—	2.4	2.3	2.6
Other labor income	1.2	3.0	3.5	3.5
Property incomes	10.9	13.1	14.4	14.1
Rental income	3.7	3.8	3.5	2.9
Personal interest	3.9	6.0	7.2	7.9
Dividends	3.3	3.3	3.7	3.3
Proprietors' income	18.5	11.6	10.6	8.9
Business and professional	10.6	8.5	7.9	6.7
Farm	7.9	3.1	2.7	2.2
Transfer payments: total	6.1	7.8	7.4	8.7
Less: Personal contributions for social insurance	1.1	2.3	2.5	3.5
Net transfer payments	5.0	5.5	4.9	5.2

Source: Brimmer, "Inflation and Income Distribution," p. 44.

Concerning the size distribution of income, *a priori* considerations would suggest that the individuals most likely injured by inflation would be those living on relatively fixed incomes: The recipients of transfer payments such as unemployment compensation, family assistance allotments (welfare), social security, veterans' benefits, and so forth; and those individuals receiving income in the form of rents and interest. The latter two payments are fixed by contract and unlikely to rapidly adjust to inflation. We might also suppose that the recipients of transfer payments would comprise the lower income classes, whereas those who receive their income from rents and interest would be in the upper portion of the income distribution. Inflation might then be regarded as redistributing income from these two portions of the income scale toward the middle. However, evidence gathered by Brimmer and updated (as shown in Table 11:3) suggests that major redistribution has not occurred to any extent. No doubt this is partly because of periodic revisions in the nominal value of transfer payments which have taken place in the inflationary period of the late 1960's and early 1970's.[18]

Both measures by which the effect of inflation on income redistributions are judged, then, suggest very tentatively that the conventional wisdom on the subject is of doubtful validity. Perhaps its applicability is limited to the very short run.

TABLE 11:3. Trends in the Income of Families and Persons in the United States: 1950–1972

Income rank	1972	1968	1967	1965	1961	1950
Families						
Percent	100.0	100.0	100.0	100.0	100.0	100.0
Lowest fifth	5.1	5.7	5.4	5.3	4.8	4.5
Second fifth	11.8	12.4	12.2	12.1	11.7	12.0
Middle fifth	16.7	17.7	17.5	17.7	17.4	17.4
Fourth fifth	23.2	23.7	23.7	23.7	23.6	23.5
Highest fifth	43.3	40.6	41.2	41.3	42.6	42.6
Top 5 percent	19.5	14.0	15.3	15.8	17.1	17.0
Unrelated individuals						
Percent		100.0	100.0	100.0	100.0	100.0
Lowest fifth		3.0	3.0	2.6	2.6	2.3
Second fifth		7.8	7.5	7.6	7.0	7.0
Middle fifth		13.8	13.3	13.5	13.0	13.8
Fourth fifth		24.4	24.4	25.1	24.2	26.5
Highest fifth		50.8	51.8	51.2	53.3	50.4
Top 5 percent		20.4	22.0	20.2	22.7	19.7

Source: Brimmer, "Inflation and Income Distribution"; Council of Economic Advisers, *Annual Report 1974* (Washington, D.C.: U.S. Government Printing Office, 1974).

Wealth Redistributions

Concerning wealth redistributions, the conventional wisdom holds that inflation favors debtors over creditors and that deflation does the opposite—a belief to which the long struggle of the free-silver advocates in

---

[18] The familiar permanent-income or life-cycle theories of consumption would contradict the a priori view of inflation-induced income redistributions, for they suggest that the rational active producer of national income will eventually retire or has some probability during his active life of falling victim to some accident impairing his earning capability. Thus in his political behavior he ought to have regard for the economic position of the ailing and the retired and ensure that their real income position does not fall victim to the inroads of inflation. Recent work also suggests that the poor gain from inflation. See R. G. Hollister and J. L. Palmer, "The Impact of Inflation on the Poor," Discussion Paper No. 40–69, Institute for Research on Poverty, University of Wisconsin (1969).

United States monetary history stands as a testament. If this belief has any validity whatsoever, it rests on the assumption that when loans are made, the interest rate reflects an underestimate of the future change in prices. This is the only way that price changes can redistribute wealth. Evidence cited above in the discussion of Gibson's Paradox is unclear as to whether interest rates adjust rapidly or slowly to changes in the rate of price inflation.

The evidence gathered on wealth redistributions comes largely from the era after 1939, and it tends to support the conventional view. However, that the one principal debtor, government (federal, state and local), gained at the expense of a principal creditor, households, may have resulted in part from the monetary-debt policy pursued by the Federal government during and for some years after World War II. At the beginning of our participation in World War II, the structure of interest rates on government securities was frozen, and the central bank was directed to support them at that level, which by historic standards was relatively low. This support persisted into the early 1950's, and the interest rate, the normal channel for adjusting debtor–creditor relationships to offset expected change in prices, was rendered inoperative. Once the support was removed in 1953, the structure of interest rates rose to reflect any changes in real conditions as well as changes in inflationary expectations. Thus during the postwar inflation, a major wealth transfer from creditor to debtor occurred. This redistribution of wealth in favor of the government accrues as a benefit to the taxpayer and is reflected in the reduced real value of taxes needed to service and retire the debt. To the extent that the largest creditors of the government are also the largest taxpayers, the reduction in the real value of their assets may be matched by a reduction in the real value of their liabilities. Exact measures of the redistribution from creditors to debtors, when one considers the tax side, may be a very complicated calculation.[19]

INFLATION AS A METHOD OF TAXATION

Among early twentieth-century economists, Keynes provided a lucid exposition of the use of inflation as a means of taxation to raise revenue for a government. He writes:

[19] Bach and Ando, "The Redistributional Effects of Inflation"; Bach and Stephenson, "Inflation and the Redistribution of Wealth"; and Kessel and Alchian, "The Meaning and Validity of the Inflation-Induced Lag." Bach and Stephenson conclude that insofar as wealth redistributions are concerned, the very poor and the very rich are more likely to lose than middle income groups. This is because the poor hold what little wealth they have in monetary forms and have few debts, whereas the very rich hold a substantial part of their wealth in bonds and have relatively few debts. On the other hand, middle-income families are likely to be heavily in debt and hold some wealth in common stock as well as in real assets.

A government can live by this means when it can live by no other. It is the form of taxation which the public finds hardest to evade and even the weakest Government can enforce, when it can enforce nothing else. . . .

The burden of the tax is well spread, cannot be evaded, costs nothing to collect, and falls, in a rough sort of way, in proportion to the wealth of the victim. No wonder its superficial advantages have attracted Ministers of Finance.[20]

Using inflation, either consciously or unconsciously, as a method of government finance is explained by Figure 11:1. The rate of the tax will be seen to be the rate of inflation and the base against which it is levied, the stock of money balances. By decreasing the purchasing power of the stock of money balances, inflationary issues of money serve to transfer the lost purchasing power to the government.

For simplicity, the analysis which supports the above conjectures will assume that only the government issues money, that the initial price level is stable, that the level of real income is constant, that the interest rate in Figure 11:1 is i_0 and therefore equal to a real rate, r_0, and that real balances $(M/P)_0$ are equal to \$50,000,000 at price level $P_0 = 1.00$.

So long as real income is constant, each issue of currency to finance a government budget deficit will serve to raise prices proportionally. If the government should issue \$10,000,000 to finance its deficit, the nominal supply of money will rise to \$60,000,000. However, the 20 percent rise in prices it induces will cause the real value of the money stock to fall back to \$50,000,000 and the original stock of money, $(M/P)_0$, will now only purchase \$40,000,000 worth of goods and services. Thus the issue by the government of \$10,000,000 worth of new currency served to take away an equivalent amount of purchasing power from the existing stock. It was as though the government had confiscated 20 percent of the existing stock of money, $(M/P)_0$. The fraction of national income transferred to the government depends upon the relative size of money balances. If the inflation rate is 20 percent and money balances are equal to 20 percent of national income, 4 percent of national income is transferred to the government through inflationary issues of money.[21]

---

[20] J. M. Keynes, *A Tract on Monetary Reform,* pp. 46–80. See also Phillip Cagan, "The Monetary Dynamics of Hyperinflation," pp. 77–86.

[21] This is not to suggest that it is only through unanticipated inflation that government issues of money serve to transfer resources from the private to the public sector. For example, if real income grows at 10 percent per year and individuals desire to increase their money holdings proportionately, that is, velocity is constant, a 10 percent increase in the supply of government currency will serve to transmit an equivalent value of resources to the government without the necessity for inflation. Likewise, if individuals desire to increase their money holdings by more than the growth in real income, that is, velocity is falling, an increase in the

The unfortunate aspect of this tax is that its incidence falls only on those who hold their wealth in a money form. It is levied without regard to its equity.

However, the above is not the end of the matter. For if the public comes to anticipate a 20 percent rise in the price level, market interest rates will rise accordingly as described by Irving Fisher. If they do come to anticipate the rise in prices, the interest rate will rise to a rate such as i_1 in Figure 11:1. When this occurs, desired money balances will fall from $(M/P)_0$ to $(M/P)_1$, or, let us say, from \$50,000,000 to \$40,000,000. The subsequent rise in velocity will reduce the nominal note issue of \$60,000,000 from a real value of \$50,000,000 to a real value of \$40,000,000 and the price level will now be 50 percent above its initial equilibrium value.

Given that rise in the price level, if the government desires to raise an additional \$10,000,000 in base-year purchasing power, it must increase the nominal supply of money by \$15,000,000 and the rate of taxation now accelerates to \$15,000,000/\$40,000,000, or from 20 percent to 37.5 percent. If the interest rate rises still higher, the desired level of real balances, which serves as the base of the tax, will decline, forcing prices to rise. If the government desires to raise still another \$10,000,000 valued in base-year prices, it will have to accelerate the rate of increase in the nominal money supply to something above \$15,000,000.

These conclusions follow when the change in the money supply (ΔMS) is divided into the change in government notes or currency (ΔN) and the change in bank money or deposits (ΔD). Thus,

$$\Delta MS = \Delta N + \Delta D \qquad (11:1)$$

It has already been explained how ΔN may be viewed as an inflationary tax revenue of the government. It remains to be shown how ΔD, or deposits given to borrowers, may be viewed as an inflationary tax revenue accruing to banks. This can be done when it is realized that the increase in the earnings of the banking system per year is equal to the expansion in bank earning assets multiplied by the rate of interest charged borrowers. Since the increase in the earning assets of the banking system is equal to their newly created deposits, the increase in their annual income becomes

$$i\Delta D \qquad (11:2)$$

---

supply of money equal to the sum of the percentage rise in real output and the fall in velocity will transfer an equivalent amount of resources to the public sector again without any inflation. For a more extensive discussion, see Milton Friedman, *Money and Economic Development: The Horowitz Lectures of 1972* (New York: Praeger, 1973), pp. 48–50.

As this additional income will be earned as long as the additional loans remain outstanding, which can be assumed to be forever, its present value can be expressed as

$$\frac{i\Delta D}{i} \qquad (11\!:\!3)$$

which is simply equal to the value of their newly created deposits or ΔD, provided the interest rate in the numerator, which represents the rate paid by borrowers, is equal to the rate in denominator, or that used by the owners of the bank to discount to the present their future income.

If the rate of interest paid by borrowers does not adequately reflect the rate of inflation, the banks are in effect subsidizing their borrowers' loans. Thus a portion of the inflationary revenue will be transferred from the banks to their customers.

If carried far enough, the rate of taxation becomes prohibitive and the public will abandon money both as a means of exchange and as a store of wealth.[22] When this occurs, the system of exchange and distribution then reverts to barter. Keynes estimated that during its final days one German government, several months before the hyperinflation reached its end in December of 1923, managed to raise the equivalent of $15,000,000 in inflationary taxes on a note issue whose real value was but $20,000,000. To accomplish this required that the nominal issue of German marks be doubled in a week! This only demonstrates that even in the final stages of hyperinflation, additional issues of notes may still be able to effect a substantial resource transfer to the government despite the fact that the base against which the tax is levied is quite small.

When the analysis is expanded to include the money-creating activities of commercial banks, various complications are introduced. Unlike the government, the banks do not directly enter the market to purchase goods and services. Rather, they enable others to do so by extending new loans, earning an additional income which accrues to their owners. Nevertheless, it can be shown that the nominal revenue from the inflationary tax will be shared by the government and the banks in proportion to their respective creations of money. However, if the interest rate charged by the banks to borrowers does not adequately reflect the inflation rate, some of their inflationary revenue may be distributed to their borrowers rather than to their owners.

[22] Keynes provides an interesting example where the inflation tax is converted to a transactions tax by dividing the decline in the purchasing power of money by the turnover rate of the money supply. For example, if the decline in the real value of money is 50 percent per year and the money stock turns over 100 times per year, the rate of tax is ½ of 1 percent per transaction. At high rates of inflation, the transactions tax can increase. A point can be reached when the tax becomes so oppressive that individuals will suffer the trouble and inconvenience of barter. When this occurs, monetary exchange ceases. See J. M. Keynes, A Tract on Monetary Reform, p. 55.

An additional way in which a government can gain from inflation arises from its tax system. This arises if it uses a progressive income tax whose marginal rates are applied against nominal income and if allowable deductions and exemptions are expressed and fixed in nominal terms. As inflation pushes individuals into higher marginal tax brackets, a greater proportion of their nominal income must be surrendered in taxes. In addition, the real value offset afforded by exemptions and deductions fixed in nominal terms diminishes. Both factors serve to increase the real burden of taxation even if nominal income increases as rapidly as the rate of inflation. The same conclusion is forthcoming for taxes levied on nominal capital gains and business profits.

OTHER PROBLEMS RELATED TO INFLATION

Diocletian's concern with inflation and that voiced by American political leaders may be related to the distributional problems summarized above, but it is most likely related to a host of other problems that inflation is alleged to cause or aggravate: Balance-of-payments difficulties, labor unrest, political divisiveness as groups struggle to maintain their real incomes, loss of confidence, a rise in uncertainty about the future, hyperinflation, the collapse of the monetary system, and so forth.

The history of the world would show that most of these concerns are unfounded, in the sense that inflation once commenced does not lead inevitably to these consequences. Be that as it may, it might be of interest to explore several of these problems at greater length.

First, to the extent that labor and management view differently the future expected course of price changes, the collective bargaining process might become more complicated and drawn out, resulting in a rise in the frequency and duration of strikes. Some evidence supporting this conclusion can be drawn from the inflationary period of the early 1970's in the United States.

Second, the balance of payments ought to be mentioned, for it is frequently alleged that inflation has especially serious consequences in this area, involving the possible sacrificing of the advantages of international specialization and division of labor. The only reason inflation causes balance-of-payments difficulties is because governments insist on adhering to a fixed exchange rate, a policy which Harry Johnson contends, "dishonestly pretends that the purchasing power of a currency is stable when in reality it is being eroded by the governmentally-tolerated inflation."[23] If the exchange rate system were truly flexible, inflation would have no distorting impact on the balance of payments.

---

[23] H. G. Johnson, *Inflation and the Monetarist Controversy* (Amsterdam: North-Holland, 1972), pp. 24–25.

Having defined inflation and discussed its economic costs and re-distributive effects, the time is now at hand to examine the various causes of the phenomenon.

CAUSES OF INFLATION

Since the determination of individual prices is based on demand-and-supply conditions, it should not be surprising that when economists have attempted to explain movements in the general level of the index of commodity prices, they have emphasized either demand or supply factors. The aggregate headings *demand-pull* and *cost-push* have generally been used as catchalls for various theories explaining changes in the price level.

Several theories of demand-pull and cost-push will be examined as will one hybrid theory usually called *sectoral-shift*. The discussion will conclude with an in-depth presentation of the neo-Fisherian, or Monetarist, approach, in which demand-pull and cost-push occur as one integrated theory. At the conclusion of each presentation, the appropriate policy suggested for stabilization of the price level will be summarized.

Demand-Pull Inflation

the early quantity theory approach

For the pre-Keynesian quantity theorists, the simple Equation of Exchange provided the means for analyzing inflation. As was emphasized in the discussion of Fisher in Chapter 3, output and velocity were fairly independent of the stock of money and prices, especially in the longer run. The former depended upon such real factors as the size of the labor force, the stock of capital, the state of technology, and so forth, whereas the latter depended upon certain institutional practices. Given this independence, the general level of prices bore a direct relationship to the stock of money. In this framework, inflation must primarily be caused by variations in the stock of money about its trend rate of growth, and secondarily by variations in the level of output about its trend growth.

The cure for inflation was obvious: Reduce the rate of growth of the money stock to its trend level. It was to be accomplished through monetary policy: Raise reserve requirements, sell securities in the open market, or raise the discount rate.

As the discussion in Chapter 3 revealed, you would consider this policy to be effective whether you were a follower of Thornton, Keynes–Wicksell, or Fisher.

the Keynesian approach

Early critics of the Keynesian approach claimed that it was applicable only to the special case of depression and not relevant to what was regarded as the opposite case of inflation. However, Keynes was soon to show that this criticism was unfounded.

In November 1939, shortly after Britain entered World War II, Keynes published three articles in the *London Times* under the title *How to Pay for the War*. The theory of inflation set forth in this tract was remarkably similar to the quantity theory approach in that it directed attention to the upward pull on prices exercised by aggregate demand as the cause of inflation. However, it differed notably in focusing attention not on the stock of money, but on the spending flow of total expenditures. Indeed, the only way the stock of money enters the Keynesian analysis is through its influence on interest-sensitive expenditures and perhaps through the influence of real balances on spending. The principal flaw of this approach may be in relegating the stock of money to such a minor role.

The so-called *inflationary gap* is shown diagrammatically in Figure 11:2. The gap occurs because at full employment[24] the desired level of real expenditures for consumption, investment, and government outlays exceeds the output which the economy is capable of producing. Or, in other words, at the existing level of commodity prices, the value of aggregate demand exceeds the value of aggregate supply.

FIGURE 11:2.   The Inflationary Gap

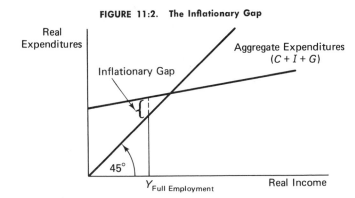

Keynes realized that a mere rise in prices would only temporarily close the gap, for a higher price level would bring higher factor incomes all around, and the gap would then be reopened on a continuous basis. While the mechanics of this process were not spelled out, they might be

[24] Defined to be a situation in which all individuals seeking employment at the going money wage find it.

explained as follows. As businessmen note an increase in orders, they attempt to fill them by expanding output. To do this they seek to hire more labor, but all who desire work at the going money wage are already employed. In order to induce more employees to work for them, businessmen offer higher money wages, but to no avail, for in the aggregate they cannot hire any more workers. The increase in money wages leads to proportionate price increases and the restoration of the real wage. This process can be repeated continually.

It is important to note that the increases in the money wage are designed to be equilibrating; that is, they are designed to remove excess demand in the labor market. Shortly, another type of wage increase will be introduced to which inflation may be attributed. Such wage increases, by themselves, are disequilibrating in the sense of causing excess supply or unemployment in the labor market.

Ultimately, the gap is closed by the continued decrease in real balances (assuming a constant money stock), the operation of a progressive income-tax system, and income distributions away from individuals with high consumption propensities. However, the level to which prices will rise during the adjustment period is unclear without first specifying various assumptions.

Rather than wait for "natural forces" to close the gap, fiscal policy could be used to increase taxes and reduce expenditures, and monetary policy could be directed toward decreasing the money stock. However, subsequent developments in the Keynesian analysis tended to downplay the role of money, so that closing the gap became a job for fiscal policy.

The Keynesian concentration on the flow of expenditures as the cause of the pull of demand on prices leads to the conclusion that a society can have nonmonetary inflations; their cause must obviously be too high a level of $C + I + G$. Yet the history of most inflations would lead to quite an opposite conclusion, for inflations are almost inevitably associated with a growth rate of the money stock above its trend. In the Keynesian scheme of affairs, however, this excessive growth of money may be regarded as inconsequential, because the aggregate spending categories, C, I, and G are insensitive to changes in the rate of interest, whose determination is money's major role in that model.

Cost-Push Inflation

As noted in the introduction to this chapter, observers throughout recorded history have attributed inflation to events which operate essentially on the supply side of the output of goods and services. A revival of interest in cost-push inflations occurred in the late 1950's, when fairly high rates of unemployment coincided with rates of inflation that some observers felt incompatible with the state of aggregate demand. Pre-

sumably, they believed that with rates of unemployment approaching
6 percent and 7 percent, society ought to have had either price stability
or deflation. Table 11:4 records the history of this period.

TABLE 11:4.   Rates of Unemployment and Price Change

	1950	1951	1952	1953	1954	1955	1956	1957	1958	1959	1960	1961
% Unemployed	5.3	3.3	3.0	2.9	5.5	4.4	4.1	4.3	6.8	5.5	5.5	6.7
% Change in consumer prices	1.0	7.9	2.2	.8	.5	—.4	1.1	3.6	2.7	.8	1.6	1.0

Source: *Survey of Current Business*, U. S. Department of Commerce (Washington, D.C.: U.S.
Government Printing Office).

The revival of interest in supply-induced inflation centered attention on two groups as villains: Trade unions and large corporations
operating in oligopolistic markets who have "power over prices—the
plenary power to set them within a considerable range. . . ."[25] The
terms *wage-push* and *profit-push* were coined to center attention on who
was at fault.

Before the several models of cost-push are examined, it may be
worth noting why economists have made a distinction between the forces
causing inflation. The basic reason has to do with public policy. It has
been shown that for demand-pull, a combination of monetary and fiscal
restraint is needed. For cost-push inflations, Harry Johnson spelled out
its policy implication and rendered judgment about its theoretical substance: "with respect to 'cost push' inflation, the obvious policy recommendation for people naive enough to accept the concept in the first
place is the equally naive proposal to stop the pushing, either by appeal-
ing to the pushers' sense of decency or if necessary, by subjecting them
to social discipline . . . an incomes policy."[26]

Why does Johnson brand as naive such luminaries as Walter
Heller, Gardner Ackley, Abba Lerner, Arthur Okun, John Kenneth
Galbraith, Fritz Machlup, and a host of others? As we shall see below,
they make one of the following mistakes: They fail to make an elementary distinction between a monetary and a real adjustment; the micro
theory underlying their work is based essentially on *ad hoc*ry; they fail
to appreciate that monetary expansion is ultimately necessary if the
inflation is to be sustained unless the demand for money can be infinitely
compressed; or a misconception about the definition of full employment

[25] J. K. Galbraith, "Administered Prices and Monetary–Fiscal Policy," reprinted in L.
Ritter, ed., *Money and Economic Activity*, 3rd ed. (New York: Houghton Mifflin, 1967), p. 318.

[26] Harry G. Johnson, *Inflation and the Monetarist Controversy* (Amsterdam: North-
Holland, 1972), p. 56.

causes them to draw inappropriate conclusions from the historical experience of the late 1950's.

FULL EMPLOYMENT RECONSIDERED

Crucial to the inference that the inflation of the late 1950's was due to cost-push forces was the definition of full employment. Several have appeared in the literature and are not at all consistent. Following from the Keynesian supply of labor schedule, full employment may be defined as a situation where everyone seeking employment at the going money wage finds it; this definition implies nothing relating to the price level. A second definition of full employment is that employment level is compatible with stable prices. Or it might be said rather arbitrarily that full employment is achieved when unemployment is reduced to 3 percent or 4 percent, a figure regarded as the level of frictional or structural unemployment.[27] A fourth definition based on a Phillips-curve trade-off is indeterminant. Another to be encountered in the neo-Fisherian analysis states that full employment is achieved whenever actual price-level changes are fully anticipated by labor.

Apparently, the cost-push advocates of the late 1950's accepted a definition based upon the period following the Korean War which implied that price stability ought to be achievable with an unemployment rate around 3 percent to 4 percent, and that higher rates of unemployment should produce deflation. Therefore, the experience of the late 1950's had to be produced by something pushing up labor costs or profit margins. Had one of the alternative definitions of full employment been widely accepted, such conclusions might not have been drawn. Nevertheless, they *were* drawn, so several of the cost-push models which were in vogue in the early 1960's will be analyzed.

A MODEL FOR ANALYSIS

To discuss the several cost-push models as well as to provide a framework for the neo-Fisherian explanation of inflation, a model utilizing aggregate demand-and-supply schedules will be used. A brief discussion is in order concerning its derivation.

Figure 11:3 is a typical construct with real output measured on the horizontal axis and the aggregate price level on the vertical axis.

[27] For the origins of 4.0 percent unemployment as a policy goal, see R. A. McMillan, "A Reexamination of the 'Full Employment' Goal," *Economic Review*, Federal Reserve Bank of Cleveland (March/April 1973), pp. 3–17.

FIGURE 11:3.   A Model for Aggregate Analysis

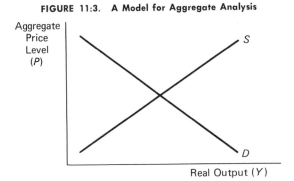

The aggregate supply schedule slopes upward and to the right, based on the assumption that with given money wages diminishing productivity of labor as output expands will cause per-unit labor costs to rise. Thus, increases in output are only forthcoming at higher prices. This supply schedule is sometimes considered appropriate only for the short run, for it implies that labor suffers a declining real wage as output expands.

If labor knew that in the short run, with no productivity increases, every increase in output would cause prices to increase and the real wage to fall, it would demand compensatory money wage increases. In this world of perfect foresight, the aggregate supply curve would have zero price elasticity. Later, this distinction between the supply schedules based upon the foresight of labor will be used; however, for our present analysis we will assume it to have an upward slope and, for any given schedule, the level of money wages to be fixed. Higher wages produce aggregate supply schedules which lie above one another.

The aggregate demand schedule represents all combinations of the price level and real output which clear both the commodity and money markets for a given money supply, fiscal variables and parameters in private spending functions. It slopes downward and to the left for at least three reasons. First, given the stock of financial assets, particularly money and bonds, previous analysis shows that an increase in the price level reduces their real value. If consumption or investment expenditures are in any way affected by the level of real balances, their decrease ought also to decrease aggregate demand. Second, a higher price level, by reducing the level of real balances, tends to increase the rate of interest. This action will reduce the level of interest-sensitive expenditures. Third, higher price levels may have income redistribution effects, and in a society with a progressive income tax the tax may reduce disposable income and consumption expenditures. Of course, this analysis abstracts from some interesting expectational aspects of price-level changes, and for this reason it ought to be regarded as a rough approximation.

WAGE-PUSH INFLATION

In general, the wage-push theories of inflation begin by assuming that trade unions suddenly want more for their members, that is, they desire higher real wages. What motivates this sudden desire for more is usually left unspecified, though the ghost of Samuel Gompers may be resurrected in order to shout "more," a desire to emulate some neighboring wage regarded as strategic may be cited, general conditions of demand might be regarded as more favorable, and so forth. In general, writers resort to some *ad hoc* argument that the prevailing explanation is close to reality.

The effect of the rise in money wages is to shift upward the aggregate supply schedule shown in Figure 11:3. Consequently, real output and the volume of employment fall. In this case the increase in money wages is disequilibrating, for it raises the real wage, thereby creating or increasing excess supply in the labor market. In order to distinguish these disequilibrating wage increases from those equilibrating wage increases in the demand-pull case, words like *spontaneous* are applied to the former, *induced* to the latter.

Following this general description, authors advancing wage-push then specify the conditions which must be present in the labor and product markets for it to be successful, that is, for labor to be able to push up money wages.

Concerning demand for labor: For wage-push to be successful, union labor must be able to prevent substitution for itself either by capital or by nonunion labor. Various authors stress the degree to which labor is essential or critical to the final product, the inelasticity of demand for labor, the ratio of wages to total costs, and the inelasticity of the supply of cooperating factors.

In the absence of some or more of these criteria, labor must be organized to reduce the substitutability between itself and nonunion labor or other factors.

Their analysis further implies that if labor deals with an individual enterprise, that firm cannot be selling its produce in a competitive market, for the rise in its costs relative to the market price would drive the firm from the industry. If the trade unions act in concert and bargain simultaneously on an industry-wide basis, the competitive framework of the industry is inconsequential, for individual firms need not fear loss of sales to rivals when all face the same increase in costs.

As to the supply of labor, the goals of the union and its ability to exercise control over its factor services are considered important in cost-push. If the labor market were perfectly competitive, wage-push could not exist; therefore, the tighter the control exercised by trade unions over the supply of labor, and the less substitutability between it and other factors, the more successful will be the union's attempt to push up wages.

One union bargaining goal which appears to enhance the wage-push argument is making the wage demands of individual trade unions depend on some strategic wage received by a neighboring occupation. The attempt to reach that wage is often thought a basic factor in the propagation of wage-push.

Writers on this subject also point out that unions must be more concerned with higher wages than with the unemployment which the higher wage level may cause.

PROFIT-PUSH INFLATION

The industrial–manufacturing sector of many developed economies, including our own, is characterized by many markets in which a very few firms are found. Generally, this type of market structure is known as *oligopoly,* and it is claimed that since each firm faces a downward-sloping demand schedule, it thereby possesses market power, or the discretionary control over price—in Galbraith's words, "the plenary power to set them within a considerable range."

Since the modern corporation has this power over price, many writers think that prices, rather than being determined by the impersonal forces of the market, are "administered."

The notion of administered prices appears to have gained a foothold in the academic mind because of experience with relative downward rigidity of industrial prices during the Great Depression. The work of Gardner Means and Adolf A. Berle, Jr., and the studies published by the Temporary National Economics Committee in the late 1930's, help propagate the idea in the academic mind, while the various books by J. K. Galbraith spread the word to the general public. Whatever the validity of these ideas, they provided the basis for the belief that industrial prices are set by oligopolists. The profit margin, or markup, then becomes a possible element in the inflationary process: When the markup is increased, prices will rise initially. Whether this price increase is sustainable in the longer run without any increase in aggregate demand is a debatable point.

Some economists believe that if such discretion over prices or wages existed, it would be exercised with great caution if the parties involved realized that unemployment and falling sales would follow whenever the power was used. They therefore blame actions of Congress, such as the Full Employment Act of 1946, for encouraging the exercise of such dis-

FIGURE 11:4. The Exercise of Market Power

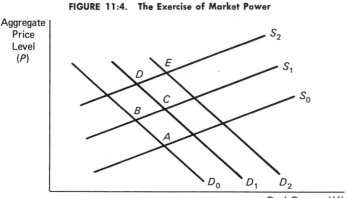

cretion, for both management and labor expect expansions in demand to reduce the unemployment and restore the sales volume which their disequilibrating wage-and-price increases have caused. Figure 11:4 presents graphically the wage-price spiral they envision, where points B and D result from the upward shift of the supply schedule due to increases in either wages or profit margins, and points C and E from compensatory expansions in aggregate demand to restore employment and output. The expansions in demand will require an increase in the supply of money unless the demand for money can be compressed indefinitely.

From their viewpoint it follows that unemployment is necessary to curb the exercise of this market power, whereas for other economists some form of wage-price guidelines or an incomes policy is the appropriate policy tool to curb the exercise of this plenary power.

DEMAND-PULL AND COST-PUSH DISCERNED

It would be very interesting from the policy viewpoint to be able to discern demand-pull from cost-push inflation, for in the discussion of each, it was noted that some combination of monetary and fiscal policy should be effective in the former, while to combat the latter, an incomes policy might be more effective than would a policy of restraining aggregate demand.

Emerging from the discussion of inflation in the late 1950's was the supposed hallmark for discerning the type of inflation facing an economy. In the demand-pull case, rising prices and falling unemployment were supposed to go together, while in the cost-push case, because the wage increases were disequilibrating, rising prices and rising unemployment were supposed to occur simultaneously. These relationships can be seen by a simple manipulation of the aggregate supply-and-demand schedules of Figure 11:3.

Substantial doubt was cast on this method of discerning the cause of inflation when models were developed which combined elements of both demand-pull and cost-push and which have been called the *income inflation,* or *markup inflation* models. One constructed by Gardner Ackley[28] is perhaps the most complete statement of this view. Because this model may have some relevance to the inflation of the late 1960's, it will be examined briefly.

INCOME, OR MARKUP, INFLATION

This model is similar to the cost-push models in that both wages and prices are assumed to be "administered," that is, prices are set by a seller or buyer and maintained unchanged for a considerable period, rather than being determined by continuous bid and offer. In setting its administered price, management adds to its material and labor costs some average markup to represent the contemporary notion of profit. In seeking wages, labor adds to any perceived productivity gains a markup to cover increases in the cost of living. The markup can be based on either historic experience or anticipations of future costs and prices. The criterion used is left uncertain and is made to depend upon conditions of aggregate demand, for the magnitude of the markup applied by labor and management is a function of the pressure of demand felt in the economy. When demand is moderate (some unemployment exists), the markups may be applied to historically experienced costs and prices. When demand is strong and the pace of price increases accelerates, Ackley believes there is an increasing tendency to project labor and materials cost and the cost of living into the future and apply markups to these anticipations or expectations.

Stable price equilibrium occurs in this model when the demand by management for its share of total output or income (based upon its costs plus markups) and that of labor for its share of total output or income add up to exactly 100 percent of the total market value of output or income produced by both valued at current prices.

Even though no inflation can begin in this model without some change in the rate of markup, two ways can be specified in which the disequilibrium process of inflation can start. These two origins can fit either the cost-push or demand-pull doctrine.

If for some reason either labor or management believes that its subjective markup is insufficient, regardless of the state of aggregate de-

---

[28] G. Ackley, "A Third Approach to the Analysis and Control of Inflation," Joint Economic Committee, *The Relationship of Prices to Economic Stability and Growth* (Washington, D.C.: U.S. Government Printing Office, 1958), pp. 619–36.

mand, and seeks to increase its rate, inflation which fits the cost-push explanation begins. In this situation, the increase in markups now means that labor and management together seek more than 100 percent of income valued at the existing price level. There can be no equilibrium state, and the price level is forced to give way in an attempt to arbitrate the claims.

On the other hand, if the decision on the part of labor or management to raise the markup is due to demand pressure, markup pricing becomes the instrument of demand-pull inflation. Here again the increase in markups implies that labor and management seek to increase their real income by raising their monetary income. Unfortunately, if output cannot be expanded, the price level will rise in an attempt to allocate the limited real income among the contending parties.

Ackley's theory suffers from two apparent weaknesses: The origin of the inflation and the implication that once begun it continues forever.

First, a very limited description of the origin of the inflationary process is given, especially of the motives which suddenly inspire management and labor in the absence of demand conditions to ask for "more." It is as though all micro principles based upon maximization are cast aside because the so-called "real world" does not agree with the idealized competitive model.

Second, once the inflation gets underway it appears to be possible for it to continue forever. Each frustration by a power bloc in raising its real income is supposedly met by another attempt with a larger increase in markup, and the process continues indefinitely.

However, the model's emphasis on the possibility that labor and management anticipate the future in setting markups as well as look to the past strikes a common bond with aspects of the neo-Fisherian approach to be explored below.

As a means of controlling inflation, which results only when the markups are inconsistent (that is, if one or both are too high), Ackley proposes a form of wage-and-price guidelines or an incomes policy to be administered by a national wage-and-price commission established by Congress.

SECTORAL-SHIFT INFLATION

Like the Ackley model, the sectoral-shift explanation for inflation arose out of the experience of the late 1950's; it was the creative output of Charles Schultze,[29] sometime Director of the Bureau of the Budget and economic consultant to Presidents Kennedy and Johnson.

[29] C. Schultze, "Recent Inflation in the United States," Joint Economic Committee, *Study Paper No. 1* (Washington, D.C.: U.S. Government Printing Office, 1959).

The idea introduced by Schultze is that inflation can occur in a society in which we have no excess demand overall. It is produced in a dynamic society by a shift in the sectoral composition of demand. That is, the composition of demand may suddenly shift from one mix of goods and services to another, putting pressure on certain sectors of the economy. These sectors then feel substantial demand pressures, to which price-and-wage increases are the response. In the sectors from which demand has shifted, prices and wages do not fall in response to excess capacity because of the alleged downward rigidities in a modern industrial society. As a matter of fact, they may even increase for any of several reasons. First, wages in the sectors with excess capacity may be linked to wages in the sector faced with excess demand, according to the concept of strategic wage or wage contour. Second, the sectors with excess capacity may use as an input the now more costly output of the excess-demand sectors. Third, general increases in the price index may raise wages and other prices throughout the economy, especially if nominal wages are linked to a cost-of-living index.

While this theory has a certain ring of plausibility, there is not a great deal of empirical evidence to support it. Except for the period from mid-1955 to mid-1957, which the theory was designed to explain, there has never been a significant rise in prices in the United States not associated with war-stimulated excess demand or with the reflation of prices following depression depths. Nevertheless, one logically ought to find demand shifting continuously and prices rising as a result.

In addition, Schultze's explanation suffers from the same defects as the prevailing polar case theories of inflation it sought to supplant: Its failure to discuss or specify the monetary preconditions for inflation (it implies either some gratuitous expansions in the supply of money or an indefinite increase in velocity), and imprecision in defining full employment and general excess demand.

THE PHILLIPS' CURVE

In the late 1950's, while much intellectual effort was being spent on demand-pull vs. cost-push theories, a study was published by A. W. Phillips[30] of the London School of Economics. Rarely has a relationship so totally caught the attention and interest of economists as the one Phillips demonstrated. In a very short time it became a centerpiece of macro theory and was used as a major policy device. It took some 10 years for a concerted attack to be mounted against the concept of the trade-off Phillips purported to show and the macro policy to which it

[30] "The Relation Between Unemployment and the Rate of Change of Money Wages."

FIGURE 11:5.   A Hypothetical Phillips Curve

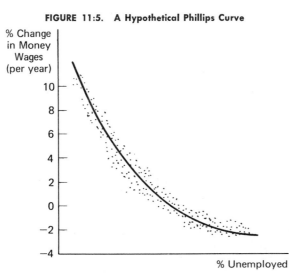

% Unemployed

gave rise: It occurred in December, 1967, in Friedman's presidential address before the American Economic Association.[31]

Since the Phillips relationship plays a central role in the neo-Fisherian, or Monetarist, attack on the Keynesian approach to economic stabilization, it will be introduced and discussed now in order to use it more fully in a subsequent presentation of its critics.

Utilizing annual data for Great Britain from 1861 to 1913, Phillips' original work suggested that an apparently stable and permanent relationship existed between changes in money wages and changes in unemployment. The stability of the relationship was inferred from the fact that, with minor exceptions, the relationship that fits for the data for 1861–1913 also seems to fit about as well for the data covering 1913–48 and 1948–57.

A hypothetical Phillips relationship is shown in Figure 11:5, where each dot represents a paired relationship between wage changes in a given year and the average unemployment of that year. Phillips rationalized his findings by concluding that when labor markets were tight (unemployment low), demand pressures would lead to larger wage increases than when unemployment was high and demand slack. Other explanations have also been forthcoming; they need not be of concern.

Subsequently, the original Phillips wage-change–unemployment relationship was transformed into a rate-of-price-change–unemployment relationship by assuming that prices would change whenever wages rose more rapidly than labor productivity.

[31] M. Friedman, "The Role of Monetary Policy," *The American Economic Review*, Vol. 58, No. 1 (March 1968), pp. 1–17.

FIGURE 11:6.   Revised Phillips Curve

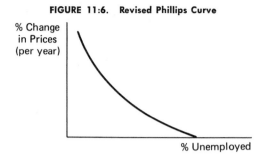

For example, if productivity rose an average of 2 percent per year, a wage increase of 2 percent would be noninflationary, for it would leave per-unit labor costs constant. Thus, the point on the original Phillips curve corresponding to a percentage wage change of 2 percent and, say, unemployment of 8 percent could be transformed into a new point corresponding to 0 percent inflation and 8 percent unemployment. Each point on the original Phillips curve could then be mapped into the new schedule. Figure 11:6 graphs such a hypothetical revised Phillips curve.[32]

The surprising aspect of this revised Phillips curve is that it shows that inflation and unemployment can coexist and that they are not polar cases as had been thought for some time. Moreover, since the Phillips curve no longer permits a unique definition for full employment, it renders much of the cost-push demand-pull debate of the late 1950's meaningless.

Before proceeding further, we ought to note several other aspects of the Phillips relationship in both its revised and original form.

First, to the extent that a stable and permanent relationship exists, it demonstrates that a *permanent* decrease in unemployment can be purchased for a *permanent* increase in the rate of inflation. In light of the inflationary environment prevailing since the mid-1960's, it seems incredible that many believed that such a simple trade-off did exist, for it implies that individuals in the economy suffer from permanent money illusion. Surely the Fisherian would deny this proposition. Nevertheless, it was believed that such a trade-off did in fact exist and was open to the policymaker. Given the Keynesian view that inflation was a mere distributor of wealth and income, while unemployment caused a permanent loss of output to the society, there is little doubt about which policies were favored by economists schooled in that approach.

[32] The revised Phillips curve has been used by various Keynesians to supplement the Keynesian theory of price level determination. In Keynes' original presentation the price level depended upon the historically and institutionally given level of money wages, making it somewhat difficult to explain inflation. To remedy this defect, the Phillips curve has been used to tell us that the rate of change of prices is a function of the unemployment rate. Thus, as the unemployment rate is decreased, the rate of change of prices, or inflation, increases.

The expansionary policies recommended by the Council of Economic Advisers led by Heller, Ackley, and Okun are testimony to their belief in the permanency of the trade-off shown by the revised Phillips curve.

However, beginning in the late 1960's, increasing doubt about the Phillips curve originated from several sources. First, the experience of the late 1960's and early 1970's—rising rates of inflation and rising unemployment rates—is clearly inconsistent with the notion of a stable permanent Phillips curve. These convictions have been reinforced by an examination of the United States data to which a Phillips curve can be fitted. The dispersion of those data is far greater than that of similar British data, which suggests that rather than a stable permanent Phillips curve the United States possesses one which is subject to periodic shifts, with the direction of the shifts indicating a worsening trade-off relationship (that is, higher inflation rates consistent with given unemployment rates or, given the inflation rate, higher unemployment rates).

Various shift parameters have been introduced, among them the expected rate of inflation. Because of the belief that for the United States the Phillips curve is subject to shifts, a distinction is usually made between the short-run and the long-run Phillips curves, with continuing controversy surrounding the degree to which a permanent trade-off exists in the long run. This subject shall subsequently be explored at greater length in this chapter.

However, when the Phillips curve was used for policy formulation purposes, its slope and position were of vital concern—its slope yields the rate at which unemployment can be traded-off against inflation; its position gives us the initial magnitude of the unemployment–inflation relationship. Figure 11:7 shows the importance of the slope property. If schedule A is contrasted with B, it can be seen that by using A, for any given increase in prices a larger reduction in unemployment is possible. Similarly, a schedule whose position was closer to the origin of the

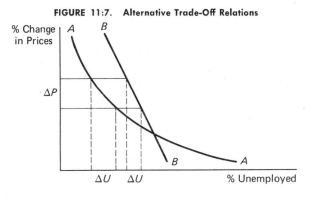

FIGURE 11:7. Alternative Trade-Off Relations

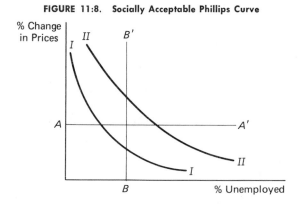

FIGURE 11:8. Socially Acceptable Phillips Curve

diagram was to be preferred to one whose position was farther away, even if their slopes were the same.

In Figure 11:8, two Phillips curves are imposed on lines AA' and BB', which depict the socially tolerable levels of unemployment and inflation as specified by the preferences of the policymaker. Any Phillips curve which passes within rectangle $OACB$ represents an obtainable combination of unemployment and inflation within the socially tolerable level. If the applicable Phillips curve passes outside the rectangle, the so-called *dilemma model* is present—in which none of the available combinations of inflation and unemployment is socially acceptable; one must therefore choose between them.

Such was the derivation and use of the Phillips curve until the late 1960's, when the neo-Fisherian, Monetarist, or Accelerationist theory of inflation was proposed as a substantial challenge to the prevailing Keynesian orthodoxy, which featured the Phillips curve as a centerpiece of both theory and policy. To this alternative view of the inflationary process our analysis now turns.

THE NEO-FISHERIAN VIEW OF INFLATION

While several individuals have contributed to the formulation of the neo-Fisherian view of inflation, substantial efforts have been forthcoming from Friedman, Leijonhufvud, Arman Alchian,[33] Charles Holt,[34] and

---

[33] A. A. Alchian, "Information Costs, Pricing, and Resource Unemployment," in E. Phelps, ed., *Microeconomic Foundations of Employment and Inflation Theory* (New York: Norton, 1970), pp. 27–52.

[34] C. Holt, "Job Search, Phillips' Wage Relation, and Union Influence: Theory and Evidence," *ibid.*, pp. 53–123.

Edmond Phelps.[35] The presentation below may bear little resemblance to the efforts of any one of these individuals.

Not only is this a theory of the inflationary process which combines demand-pull and cost-push as one integrated whole, but it has a central conclusion which should be emphasized again. This conclusion is the same as that emerging from Fisher's view of the business cycle: There is no long-run trade-off between unemployment and inflation. That is, the long-run level of employment and output is independent of the level of prices. What trade-off exists is only short-run, or transitory, in nature and arises because labor, like savers, does not accurately forecast or anticipate inflation. Caught unaware, labor works temporarily for a lower real wage. Once anticipated inflation is equal to actual inflation, the trade-off ceases to exist and the economy is in long-run equilibrium. In other words, money which causes inflation in this explanation is nonneutral in the short run because of lack of perception on the part of labor. In the long run, however, money is completely neutral.

The neo-Fisherian view of inflation, then, has important implications. It denies the existence of a Phillips curve in the long run and the ability of the government to use fiscal and monetary measures to reduce unemployment.

The presentation of this approach to inflation will parallel in many respects the earlier analysis of Fisher's view of the business cycle. However, it will concentrate on the labor and commodity markets, with the latter being represented by aggregate demand-and-supply schedules. The earlier analysis confined attention only to the saving–investment, loanable funds sector. A complete neo-Fisherian theory must combine both sectors.

The Labor Market

Paralleling previous discussions of the labor market in the classical and Keynesian models, this presentation will first discuss the demand for labor and then the supply.

Similar to the findings in previous models, the demand for labor in the neo-Fisherian approach is assumed to be a function of the real wage, which is composed of the actual money wage paid to labor deflated by the actual level of prices prevailing in the economy, designated as P^A.

It is on the supply side of the labor market that a unique aspect of this model becomes evident: The unemployment which exists in equilibrium is not involuntary (that is, caused by a lack of aggregate demand

---

[35] E. Phelps, "Money Wage Dynamics and Labor Market Equilibrium," *ibid.*, pp. 124–66.

as in the Keynesian model) but voluntary—composed of individuals who, on their own volition, leave their present jobs to devote full time to seeking a better alternative. This type of unemployment is usually called *frictional,* and it will be a characteristic distinguishing this model from the Keynesian.[36] How long these people remain unemployed depends upon the opportunity cost of seeking a job in a market in which the acquisition of information is costly. It involves balancing the income foregone from quitting a job against the discounted value of the differential one expects to earn in the sought-after job. The longer one remains unemployed, the greater the likelihood that one will accept a lower-paying position than was originally contemplated.

In order to show frictional unemployment, two concepts of labor supply must be distinguished. The first, called the *labor force,* measures the total number of individuals available for work. The measurement of the total labor force is conceptually difficult, since individuals are subject to both the income and substitution effects of higher real wages. Thus a higher real wage may induce individuals to offer more labor time, retired individuals to re-enter the labor force, and those contemplating retirement to postpone their decisions. However, it may also induce a *decrease* in labor time offered (working wives withdraw from the labor force, and so forth). Because of these conflicting forces set in motion by higher real wages we will, for simplicity, assume that the size of the labor force is a constant, although historic experience contradicts that assumption. In Figure 11:9, the total labor force is represented by the vertical schedule *SS.*

A second supply schedule, designated as $S_L = \int\left(\dfrac{W}{P^e}\right)$, indicates the willingness of the members of the labor force to accept employment. This willingness depends upon the real wage. However, in the case of the supply of labor, the real wage is composed of the money wage deflated by the price level individuals expect to prevail over the term of their employment, which is designated as P^e. In order to induce the frictionally unemployed to accept positions, they must be given a higher real wage, which if constant price expectations are assumed, means paying them a higher money wage.

Before the functioning of the labor sector in an inflationary environment is explained, the concept of labor market equilibrium should be examined. If the actual level of prices, P^A, is equal to the expected level of prices, P^e, stationary equilibrium prevails, where those willing to accept employment at the going real wage, $\dfrac{W}{P^e}$, are equal to the quantity

---

[36] In the early presentation of the classical model, this type of unemployment did not arise, because it was assumed that labor knew with perfect certainty all conditions of the labor market. See Page 12 of this text.

FIGURE 11:9. Supply-and-Demand for Labor Schedules

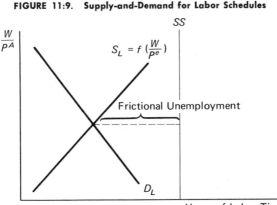

Hours of Labor Time

of those demanded at the going real wage, $\dfrac{W}{P^A}$. Stationary equilibrium is quite compatible with people being hired and people quitting their jobs —it only requires that quittings and hirings be equal.

However, in this state of stationary equilibrium, those willing to accept employment are fewer than the total available for employment, as shown by the SS schedule. The difference between the two represents the frictionally unemployed—those seeking a better job—and the reason for their unemployment is that they do not have perfect information on the alternatives open to them. One way to acquire such information is to seek it out while unemployed. To the extent that such information can be made available at minimal costs, the amount of frictional unemployment at each real wage $\left(\dfrac{W}{P^e}\right)$ would be lower.

The volume of unemployment present in this state of stationary equilibrium, at which $\dfrac{W}{P^A} = \dfrac{W}{P^e}$ is called by the neo-Fisherians the *natural rate of unemployment*. Their analysis shows that neither fiscal nor monetary policy measures can reduce this level in the long run. It can only be lowered by reducing frictions in the labor market and making available information about job opportunities at low cost.

The Effect of Inflation in the Labor Market

As a preface to the presentation of the inflationary cycle, the effects of inflation on the labor market will be reviewed. Three cases will be considered: (1) unanticipated inflation $(\Delta P^A > \Delta P^e)$; (2) fully anticipated inflation $(\Delta P^A = \Delta P^e)$; and (3) expected inflation greater than actual in-

FIGURE 11:10. Impact of Inflation on the Labor Market

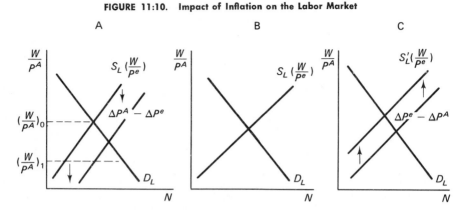

flation ($\Delta P^e > \Delta P^A$). These three cases are shown as parts A, B, and C, respectively, of Figure 11:10.

In case A, where labor does not anticipate inflation, the supply schedule shifts down by the amount by which actual inflation exceeds anticipated inflation. As the real wage falls from $\left(\frac{W}{P^A}\right)_0$ to $\left(\frac{W}{P^A}\right)_1$, excess demand is created in the labor market, leading to a rise in money wages and an increase in the quantity of employment (that is, new hirings exceed quittings until equilibrium is reached). In essence, the frictionally unemployed are deceived into accepting employment because the rise in money wages is, given their assumption of prices, P^e, regarded as a rise in the real wage. Once P^e adjusts to the higher rate of inflation, those induced to accept employment will realize the deception and demand a higher money wage. If it is not forthcoming, they will again start the search for a better job.

In the meantime, the unemployment rate has been reduced, and more individuals are working. The economy appears to be moving along a Phillips curve, but only because workers are subject to short-run money illusion.

In case B, if labor anticipates with perfect certainty the rise in prices, it will demand money wage increases to compensate for the expected fall in real wages. Management will be willing to grant these wage increases because it will be receiving higher prices for its merchandise. In this situation, the position of S_L does not change, and the natural rate of unemployment remains unchanged. Therefore, in a world where anticipations are perfect, the level of employment and output is independent of changes in the level of prices and the stock of money, if changes in the latter lead to price changes (that is, if money is neutral). In addition, there has been no movement along a Phillips curve.

In case C, labor overanticipates the price rise. Because it expects prices to rise, it will demand money wage increases in excess of the actual rise in prices, thereby leading to an increase in the real wage, $\frac{W}{P^A}$. In this situation, S_L will shift up by the difference between ΔP^e and ΔP^A. However, the real wage will not rise by as much as the expected rise in prices, leading some workers to conclude that the real wage has declined. They therefore withdraw their labor time from the marketplace and unemployment rises (that is, quittings start to exceed new hirings until equilibrium is reached). The rise in the unemployment rate over the natural rate might be termed *voluntary unemployment,* for it results from individuals withdrawing their labor time because they perceive a fall in their real wage. Later, this upward shift in S_L will be referred to as the *cost-push phase* of the inflationary cycle. Additionally, in terms of a Phillips curve, the economy has a higher unemployment rate and a higher inflation rate. This is obviously not a movement along a curve, but a shift in the schedule.

The reason for the shifts in the S_L schedule whenever P^e differs from P^A is exactly the same as the Fisherian cycle with savers and investors who had different perceptions of inflation. It arises because S_L is a function of P^e, while P^A is the variable used on the vertical axis of the graph.

Before proceeding, an organizational aspect of the labor market ought to be noted carefully. Labor has been seen as demanding a rise in money wages in the face of inflationary expectations. This does not necessarily imply that labor is organized into trade unions. These demands on the part of labor are compatible with an economy in which labor is completely unorganized. It merely suggests that individuals, in evaluating the subjective worth of their labor time, will not provide the same level of services at the margin unless their money wage is increased to cover the expected rise in the cost of living.

The Commodity Market

In order to complete the preliminary discussion of the neo-Fisherian approach, we will repeat a previous discussion of the commodity market (see Figure 11:3). The short-run aggregate supply schedule slopes upward and to the right to reflect the fact that, because of diminishing returns to labor, more output is forthcoming only at a higher price. Thus, each movement along a short-run aggregate supply schedule also implies a shift of the supply-of-labor schedule along the demand curve for labor, for it is only by employing more labor at a reduced real wage $\left(\frac{W}{P^A}\right)$, that output can be expanded in the short run. This implies that labor does not have perfect foresight and can be deceived into work-ing for a lower real wage.

If, however, labor has perfect foresight, the aggregate supply schedule must be vertical, for no change in prices will induce any change in employment and real output. Thus, to the extent that $\Delta P^e = \Delta P^A$, the economy will be on what the neo-Fisherians call the *long-run supply schedule* of output.[37] Short-run increases in output are only possible be-cause of a temporary money illusion on the part of labor. Thus, unan-ticipated change in prices will induce increases in employment and output, and the economy will move along a short-run aggregate supply schedule. Any wage adjustments to compensate for unanticipated infla-tion will increase production costs and shift upward the short-run aggre-gate supply schedule. Therefore a family of short-run schedules at a corresponding series of money wages can be conceived, with each sched-ule showing the amount of output forthcoming, assuming that money wages are fixed and that labor does not anticipate the change in prices, P^A. Such a construct is shown as Figure 11:11.

FIGURE 11:11.   Aggregate Supply Schedules at Various Levels of Money Wages

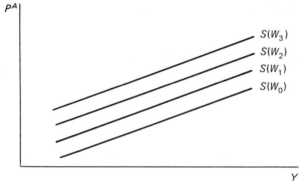

The Inflationary Cycle

Our discussion of the neo-Fisherian view of the inflationary cycle can begin by assuming that the economy is in a state of stable equilibrium in which actual changes in prices are equal to those expected by labor. The prevailing unemployment rate is then at its natural level.[38]

For any of a number of reasons, aggregate demand can increase

[37] This so-called perfect foresight, or long-run aggregate supply schedule, is not stationary—it ought to shift outward over time in response to productivity increases by labor and capital.

[38] The state of equilibrium can be associated with any rate of inflation—positive, negative, or zero. The only condition is that the expected rate and the actual rate must coincide.

(for example, rising animal spirits on the part of business, the necessity to finance foreign wars, or perhaps a program designed to reduce unemployment to a level the political leadership is convinced is normal—their definition of full employment). In Figure 11:12, this increase is shown by an outward shift in the aggregate demand schedule from D_0 to D_1.

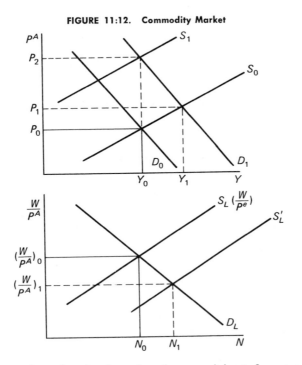

FIGURE 11:12. Commodity Market

To the extent that the rise in prices is unanticipated, output and employment will increase. However, if the rise in prices is fully anticipated, labor will ask for a compensatory rise in money wages, leaving the real wage unchanged at $\left(\frac{W}{P^A}\right)_0$, and the S_L schedule will not shift (case B, above). Nevertheless, the rise in money wages will increase production costs, shifting the aggregate supply schedule to S_1; this shift leaves unchanged the level of output and employment, but increases the price level in proportion to the change in aggregate demand, that is, from P_0 to P_2.

In order to explain the inflationary cycle, let us assume that labor does not initially perceive the inflation and regards the raise in its nominal wage as an equivalent rise in its real wage. (The rise in nominal wages is explained in case A above.) It thereby offers an increased quantity of labor services, $N_1 - N_0$, and output (in Figure 11:12) expands from Y_0 to Y_1.

FIGURE 11:13.   Demand and Supply Shifts in the Commodity Market

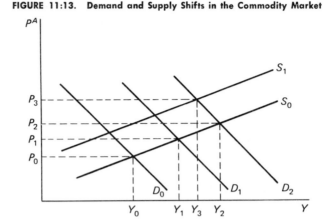

Further increases in demand shift D_1 to D_2, as shown in Figure 11:13, increasing output, employment, and the level of prices. In the labor market, S_L continues to shift down by the amount of unanticipated inflation. The economy appears to be moving along a Phillips curve, such as that in Figure 11:5. If productivity changes are neglected, a unique relationship is present between the commodity and labor markets. To the extent that the real wage, $\dfrac{W}{P^A}$, is below $\left(\dfrac{W}{P^A}\right)_0$, output will be above its long-run level, and unemployment will be below its natural rate. Whenever the real wage is at $\left(\dfrac{W}{P^A}\right)_0$, output and employment will be at their long-run natural levels.

A time must come when labor ultimately realizes that its real wage has been depressed because of unanticipated inflation. When this occurs, labor seeks to recover what has been lost in the past, that is, it wants money wages raised by $P_1 - P_0$. In the labor market S_L will initially shift upward by an amount equal to ΔP^A. However, this action will also increase costs of production and push prices up in the absence of any additional demand stimulation. The schedule of aggregate supply will shift up to reflect the increase in costs arising from the increase in money wages. Because actual prices rise, labor will be unsuccessful in re-establishing its former real wage $\left(\dfrac{W}{P^A}\right)_0$, and unemployment will remain below its natural level. In terms of the Phillips curve, both unemployment and prices increase, which is obviously a movement off the schedule in the upper-right direction.

However, in the absence of any additional increase in aggregate demand, output will fall below the level attained before the rise in wages; the real wage then must be above the level which prevailed when output was at Y_2. The economy is then confronted with rising prices and falling output—the classic symptoms of a cost-push inflation. But as the presentation demonstrates, this cost-push phase of the inflationary cycle comes not from unions wanting "more," but from a delayed adjustment in monetary magnitudes designed to re-establish a real wage relationship which had prevailed earlier.

Output level Y_3 and price level P_3 (in Figure 11:13) represent the momentary equilibrium which prevails after labor attempts to recover its lost real wage.

Having been frustrated once, labor will likely seek another round of money wage increases which, after allowing for future price rises, will restore its real wage to that which prevailed before the inflationary cycle started, that is, $\left(\dfrac{W}{P^A}\right)_0$. Labor can now be said to have positive inflationary expectations, that is, $\Delta P^e > 0$. This and the remaining part of the cycle are shown in Figure 11:14.

FIGURE 11:14. Demand and Supply Shifts in the Commodity Market (Cont'd.)

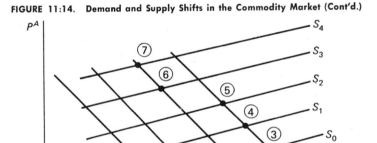

If the government, intervening in the situation, suddenly decides to implement an anti-inflation policy designed to restore price stability and does so with restrictive monetary and fiscal policy, aggregate demand may shift leftward from D_2 to an intermediate position such as D_3.

Output and prices ought to fall, given such a restrictive policy. Whether the data will record such an event depends upon the policies of labor. To the extent that its inflationary expectations are positive or that it continues to seek to recover from past unanticipated inflation, the aggregate supply schedule will continue to shift upward, reflecting increases in money wages. Since output continues to fall under the assumed circumstances, money wages must be rising faster than prices, pushing upward the real wage. Moreover, the movement of the price level and unemployment will bear no relationship to the concept of a stationary Phillips' curve.

If, in formulating its expectations of future price increases, labor uses the past as a reference, then for an anti-inflationary program to be successful, government must moderate price increases, that is, see that they trend in a downward direction. Thus, upward shifts in the aggregate supply schedule must be countered by leftward shifts in aggregate demand so that each succeeding price increase is smaller. Quite clearly, the process of restoring price stability might be very costly after inflationary expectations have gripped labor. It is quite possible that, in order to restore price stability, unemployment will have to be held above its natural rate long enough for labor to expect price stability and act accordingly in its wage demands. It bears emphasizing that "labor" need not belong to trade unions and need not be castigated as a villain, for it is merely interested in preserving a real wage level and hence is acting in its own best interest—labor is truly Adam Smith's economic man.

If the piece needs a villain, it may in fact be the government, which (accepting advice from other than neo-Fisherians) desires to reduce unemployment to some arbitrarily defined full-employment level and which, using monetary and fiscal means, reduces it below its natural level, thereby setting in motion the entire inflationary cycle.

In examining this cycle, attention is again drawn to the fact that it contains both a demand-pull and cost-push phase. Clearly, the increase in demand is the motivating factor, for it increases prices as output expands, thereby catching labor off guard, reducing the real wage, and expanding employment. The cost-push phase merely represents the attempt by labor, acting in its own best interest, to restore a real wage which prevailed prior to the expansion in demand. In this respect, it should be differentiated from the earlier concept of cost-push in which either trade unions or management suddenly wanted "more." Here, they only want to preserve what they had once achieved. However, since it is impossible to discern what is in fact causing the aggregate supply-of-output schedule to shift upward, it is little wonder that different economists can interpret the sequence of events differently; some attribute the cost-push to powerful unions or corporations, while others view it as an attempt to re-establish the previously prevailing real relationships.

The two phases of the neo-Fisherian inflationary cycle can be seen graphically if the points of momentary equilibrium (shown in Figure 11:14) are connected. This is accomplished in Figure 11:15.

Points (1), (2), and (3) represent demand-pull expansion and the short-run departure of output from its long-run level, SS. At such, the expansion phase of the cycle can be said to reflect the nonneutrality of

FIGURE 11:15. Positions of Momentary Equilibria

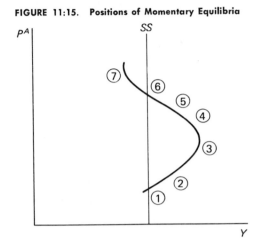

money if changes in the growth rate of the money supply initiate the expansion in demand. Points (4), (5), (6), and (7) represent the cost-push phase and labor's attempt to recover a lost real wage. So long as the points of momentary equilibria do not fall on SS, the real wage and the rate of unemployment are different from their stationary equilibrium and natural values. Output levels to the left of SS, such as point (7), represent unemployment rates above their natural values. This incremental unemployment might be referred to as involuntary and is associated with positive inflationary expectations on the part of labor, in particular, that $\Delta P^e > \Delta P^A$ and that the real wage is above $\left(\dfrac{W}{P^A}\right)_0$.[39]

If the neo-Fisherian explanation is correct, it is easy to see why economists analyzing the period of the late 1950's, when prices and unemployment both rose, could misinterpret events. They did not see that the rise in wages causing the unemployment was a belated monetary adjustment designed to restore a real wage level which had prevailed a few years earlier. Rather, it was interpreted as an evil and irresponsible act by economic power blocs which called for the implementation of wage-and-price guidelines to compel them to act in a socially responsible way.

---

[39] So long as labor perfectly anticipates the future and productivity changes are neglected, the economy will always operate on the long-run supply schedule, SS. In this situation, all changes in demand, MV, will automatically be reflected in proportional changes in the level of prices. This is the same result obtained in chapters 1 and 2, which explained the simple classical model. In the classical world perfect foresight and information ensured that the economy was always on the SS schedule. The neo-Fisherian explanation, which does not make that assumption, presents a vastly more complicated world and one in which adjustments may be protracted.

PUBLIC POLICY IN A NEO-FISHERIAN FRAMEWORK

Throughout the discussion to follow, it should be borne in mind that the neo-Fisherian is as concerned about the economic losses from unemployment as is the Keynesian. However, drawing his conclusions from a different frame of reference, his means of reducing this social evil are decidedly different.

The basic conclusion which emerges from the neo-Fisherian analysis is that the level of output and employment is independent of the level of prices.[40] Thus, no trade-off of the type envisioned by the Phillips curve supposedly exists in the longer run. It then follows that any activist policy on the part of the government to reduce unemployment to some arbitrary level, if this is below its natural rate, is doomed to failure. It will appear successful only as long as the government is able to fool labor by maintaining an actual inflation rate greater than that expected by labor.

The obvious public policy in this framework is to attempt to reduce frictions in the labor market, which among other things reduces the time and costs involved in obtaining information about employment opportunities. This can be done by making available at low cost the best information possible on jobs, including a description of the position, its geographical location, and its salary range. In addition, a number of artificial barriers exist which either limit entry into a profession or maintain wages at artificially high rates (for example, minimum wage laws); these restrictions ought to be eliminated. This is the type of public policy that a neo-Fisherian would recommend, even if he could not define with precision the natural rate of unemployment.

What role would an incomes policy, or wage-and-price guidelines, play in the neo-Fisherian analysis? None. It would represent an unfortunate and misdirected exercise of government power. To see why, assume that having expanded demand to reduce unemployment, the government succeeds in raising output to a level such as that shown by (3) in Figure 11:14. Now, in the face of growing pressure by labor for wage increases, the government decides to curb this economic bloc's "unjustified" exercise of power by imposing wage guidelines which seek to limit money wage increases to some national productivity average. The government does this because it does not want the gain in output and employment to

---

[40] This conclusion is qualified to the extent that real balances are a productive factor for business and a provider of utility to individual wealth owners. Inflation will then induce business to combine factors in inferior combination, reducing real output. It will also cause individual wealth owners to hold small balances, reducing their income to the extent that a broad measure of the latter is adopted.

be dissipated by cost increases, and it may be motivated in its policy recommendation by an Ackley-type analysis, which claims that labor's markup is a function of demand pressure. To the neo-Fisherian this is nonsense, for he realizes that labor is merely seeking to restore a real wage relationship which existed before the ill-conceived government program to reduce unemployment was implemented.

Under an incomes policy, what will labor's reaction be? It will be to seek restoration of the real wage by means other than through direct money increases (for example, by having jobs upgraded, more rapid promotion of employees, more free time at the same wages; by getting increases in fringe benefits; by reducing hours worked at regular rates and increasing those for which overtime is paid; and so forth.) The mind of man is fertile when it comes to circumventing illogical laws.[41]

One of the great difficulties with accepting the neo-Fisherian analysis, especially for those schooled in the Keynesian tradition and the conditions of the 1930's, is the supposition that unemployment in the United States is voluntary and consists of individuals going about gathering information on job opportunities—it seems inconsistent with reality!

THE PHILLIPS' CURVE IN THE NEO-FISHERIAN ANALYSIS

Earlier we noted that substantial doubt was expressed in the late 1960's about whether a stable and permanent Phillips curve was a reality for the United States. Throughout the neo-Fisherian analysis, it was suggested that certain variables caused the Phillips curve to shift over time. One of these shift parameters emphasized by the neo-Fisherian's was the expected rate of inflation; to the extent that labor correctly forecasts inflation and can adjust wages to its forecasts, it can be shown that no long-run trade-off exists.

The neo-Fisherian argument can be more formally presented by starting from a position such as point A in Figure 11:16. This can be assumed to be a point of stable equilibrium (that is, actual inflation is

[41] Sir John Hicks has recently presented an argument questioning whether the demand-pull and induced cost-push inflationary cycle envisioned by the neo-Fisherians, and their related policy prescriptions, are correct. Drawing upon the supposed effects of the pricing policy of the Arab oil cartel, he argues that the aggregate supply schedule in Figure 11:11 for Britain would be shifted upward, which would serve to decrease the real wage. This decrease was strongly resisted by the British trade unions, whose efforts to seek compensatory wage adjustments would lead to further upward shifts as described by the cost-push phase of the neo-Fisherian cycle. These, of course, would cause additional increases in the price index. The crux of Sir John's position is that a change in demand did not initiate the cycle; consequently restriction of demand is not the proper policy prescription. The "social contract" approach of the Labor government, he believes, ought therefore to be viewed more charitably than neo-Fisherian critics have been willing to concede. See Sir John Hicks, "What is Wrong with Monetarism," Lloyds Bank Review, No. 118 (Oct. 1975), pp. 1–13.

FIGURE 11:16. The Neo-Fisherian View of the Phillips Curve

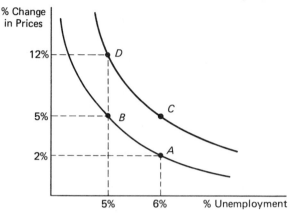

fully anticipated by labor), and so 6 percent unemployment represents its natural rate.

Into this state of affairs the government enters with a monetary–fiscal program designed to close the gap between actual output and its full-employment potential, where the latter is measured for a 3 percent unemployment rate. Success is achieved and the economy moves from point *A* to point *B*. However, to reduce unemployment a higher permanent rate of inflation, 5 percent, must be accepted. According to the neo-Fisherian analysis presented above, this was accomplished because labor was deceived—it expected 2 percent inflation and based its wage demands on that rate. However, it experienced a 5 percent rate and its real wage declined. Now, what happens when labor adjusts fully to the 5 percent inflation rate? Its wage demands will incorporate this figure, and its real wage will be restored to the previous level. When this occurs, the economy will be back with a 6 percent unemployment rate, but with a permanent rate of inflation of 5 percent, not 2 percent, and a point such as *C* will characterize the new equilibrium. In this state of affairs, let the government worry about the high unemployment rate and again expand aggregate demand. To reduce unemployment will necessitate a still higher inflation rate—one above 5 percent. If successful, a point such as *D* is achieved, at which unemployment is 3 percent but inflation is 12 percent. Just to stand still at the 3 percent unemployment rate requires an acceleration in the inflation rate above the 5 percent rate—in this case to 12 percent.[42] If points *C* and *D* are connected, they will trace out

---

[42] Whether the rate of inflation is 12 percent or some other rate is immaterial. It must be a rate which labor does not anticipate. Thus, many believe that the inflation rate must be an accelerating one, for if the rate goes up by equal increments, the pattern will be anticipated by labor and changes in the inflation rate will be ineffectual in reducing unemployment.

a second short-run Phillips curve. In effect, the Phillips curve has shifted with each short-run schedule related to a given state of expectations on the part of labor. Thus, the lower schedule is applicable to a 2 percent expected inflation rate and the upper to a 5 percent inflation rate. A third schedule could be constructed and, given the example, would be applicable to a 12 percent expected rate of inflation.

Thus, according to the neo-Fisherian analysis, a long-run Phillips curve does not exist, that is, there is no long-run trade-off between inflation and unemployment. This is compatible with the view that money is neutral in the long run. Rather, a trade-off exists (due to money illusion) between short-run transitory gains in output and employment, and an accelerating rate of inflation, when previous price increases are adjusted for and come to be anticipated. Whether the neo-Fisherian analysis is correct is an empirical question. Empirical evidence produced by Solow,[43] Eckstein and Brinner,[44] and Cukierman[45] indicates that a long-run trade-off does emerge, but it is worse than that implied by short-run considerations.[46] This means to the neo-Fisherians that in the long run labor suffers from money illusion.

By reversing the process explained above, it can be seen how the Fisherian would decrease the rate of inflation and why stabilization can be such a long, painful, and costly process that some governments prefer

[43] R. M. Solow, *Price Expectations and the Behavior of the Price Level* (Manchester: Manchester University Press, 1969).

[44] The work of Eckstein and Brinner, utilizing data from 1955–1970, suggests that a long-run conventional Phillips-curve trade-off exists up to the point at which the employment rate is 4.5 percent and the inflation rate is 2.5 percent. Beyond this combination (that is, unemployment below 4.25 percent and inflation above 3 percent) no further trade-off is possible. Thus, the Phillips' curve is vertical and corresponds in shape to that postulated by Friedman. See Otto Eckstein and Roger Brinner, *The Inflationary Process in the United States,* Joint Economic Committee, Congress of the United States (Washington, D.C.: U.S. Government Printing Office, 1972).

[45] Alex Cukierman, "A Test of the 'No Trade Off in the Long Run' Hypothesis," *Econometrica,* Vol. 42, No. 6 (Nov. 1974), pp. 1069–80. Utilizing data for the United States for the period 1949–1970, a permanent long-run trade-off is shown to exist. It should be noted that Cukierman was a dissertation student of Robert Solow.

[46] Of both theoretical and empirical merit as an attack on the neo-Fisherian position is the work contained in James Tobin's presidential address before the American Economic Association in December 1971. It may be taken as the neo-Keynesian reply to a similar address by Friedman in 1967. Building on sectoral-shift–type analysis of the Schultze variety, Tobin mounts a substantial theoretical attack on the natural-rate-of-unemployment thesis. In addition, Tobin claims that the available data do not lend support to that thesis. In particular, individuals who lined up a new job before quitting their old position had more improved positions over those who quit and then searched for a new position. Second, using data on quit rates as an index of voluntary search activity, Tobin states that they do not diminish when unemployment is low and wage rates are rapidly rising. Rather they increase, contradicting the inflation illusion aspect of the neo-Fisherian analysis. Last, if the so-called natural unemployment rate is between 5 percent and 6 percent, the characteristics of the unemployment fail to correspond with those suggested by the neo-Fisherian analysis. See Tobin, "Inflation and Unemployment," pp. 6–9.

to let inflation, once started, continue indefinitely and become institutionalized. After all, if the 12 percent inflation rate becomes fully anticipated, the economy can be described as being in a moving stable equilibrium with unemployment at its natural rate. It is deviations in the rate of inflation that cause the problems.

CONCLUSION

This chapter has been an ambitious undertaking. It started out by defining inflation and the problems related to any definition. It then discussed the costs of inflation, differentiating the costs to society from the costs to the individual, which were largely distributional. Next, the various causes of inflation were discussed in terms of a traditional distinction between demand-pull and cost-push. Several variants of the cost-push approach were also examined as was a model called sectoral-shift, all of which were an outgrowth of experience in the late 1950's, when inflation coexisted with a rather high level of unemployment.

The derivation of and the uses to which the Phillips curve was put in the Keynesian analysis were then explained in great detail.

The last task undertaken was to examine the neo-Fisherian, Monetarist, or Accelerationist view of the inflationary process, in which the distinction between demand-pull and cost-push is blurred. This analysis is quite different from its predecessors, and its policy conclusions are radically different. First, it finds that the government may often be the cause of the inflation, with its nobly motivated efforts to cure unemployment by reducing that rate below its natural level. Second, it implies that an incomes policy is not only useless, but easily evaded. Last, it implies that attempts to hold unemployment below its natural rate will only result in an ever-accelerating rate of inflation.

Selected References and Readings

ACKLEY, GARDNER, "A Third Approach to the Analysis and Control of Inflation," Joint Economic Committee, *The Relationship of Prices to Economic Stability* (Washington, D.C.: U.S. Government Printing Office, 1958).

ALCHIAN, ARMAN, "Information Costs, Pricing, and Resource Unemployment," in E. Phelps, ed., *Microeconomic Foundations of Employment and Inflation Theory* (New York: Norton, 1970).

————, AND KESSEL, RUBEN, "The Meaning and Validity of the Inflation-Induced Lag of Wages Behind Prices," *American Economic Review,* Vol. 50, No. 1 (March 1960).

————, "Effects of Inflation," *Journal of Political Economy,* Vol. 70, No. 6 (Dec. 1962).

BACH, GEORGE, AND ANDO, ALBERT, "The Redistribution Effects of Inflation," *Review of Economics and Statistics,* Vol. 34, No. 1 (Feb. 1957).

BAILEY, MARTIN, "The Welfare Cost of Inflationary Finance," *Journal of Political Economy,* Vol. 64, No. 2 (March/April 1956).

BRIMMER, ANDREW, "Inflation and Income Distribution in the United States," *Review of Economics and Statistics,* Vol. 52, No. 1 (Feb. 1971).

BRONFENBRENNER, MARTIN, AND HOLZMAN, FRANKLYN, "Survey of Inflation Theory," *American Economic Review,* Vol. 53, No. 4 (Sept. 1963).

CAGAN, PHILLIP, "The Monetary Dynamics of Hyperinflation," in M. Friedman, ed., *Studies in the Quantity Theory of Money* (Chicago: University of Chicago Press, 1956).

————, *Recent Monetary Policy and the Inflation* (Washington, D.C.: American Enterprise Institute, 1971).

COREY, BERNARD, AND LAIDLER, DAVID, "The Phillips Relation: A Theoretical Explanation," *Economica,* Vol. 34, No. 134 (May 1967).

ECKSTEIN, OTTO, AND BRINNER, ROGER, *The Inflationary Process in the United States,* Joint Economic Committee (Washington, D.C.: U.S. Government Printing Office, 1972).

FOSTER, EDWARD, *Costs and Benefits of Inflation, Studies in Monetary Economics,* Federal Reserve Bank of Minneapolis (March 1972).

FRIEDMAN, MILTON, "The Role of Monetary Policy," *The American Economic Review,* Vol. 58, No. 1 (March 1968).

HANSEN, BENT, *A Study in the Theory of Inflation* (New York: Macmillan, 1951).

HARBERGER, ARNOLD, "The Dynamics of Inflation in Chile," in C. F. Christ, et al., *Measurement in Economics* (Stanford, Calif.: Stanford University Press, 1963).

HINES, A. G., "Unemployment and the Rate of Change of Money Wages in the United Kingdom, 1862–1963: A Reappraisal," *Review of Economics and Statistics,* Vol. 50, No. 1 (Feb. 1968).

HOLT, CHARLES, "Job Search, Phillips' Wage Relation, and Union Influence: Theory and Evidence," in E. Phelps, ed., *Microeconomic Foundations of Employment and Inflation Theory* (New York: Norton, 1970).

HUMPHREY, THOMAS, "Changing Views of the Phillips' Curve," *Economic Review,* Federal Reserve Bank of Richmond (July 1973).

JOHNSON, HARRY, "A Survey of Theories of Inflation," in *Essays in Monetary Economics* (London: Unwin University Books, 1967).

————, *Inflation and the Monetarist Controversy* (Amsterdam: North-Holland, 1972).

KEYNES, J. M., *A Tract on Monetary Reform* (New York: Harcourt, Brace and Co., 1924).

LAIDLER, DAVID, AND PARKIN, MICHAEL, "Inflation: A Survey," *The Economic Journal,* Vol. 85, No. 340 (Dec. 1975).

LIPSEY, RICHARD, "The Relation Between Unemployment and the Rate of Change of Money Wages in the United Kingdom, 1862–1957: A Further Analysis," *Economica,* Vol. 27, No. 1 (1960).

MACHLUP, FRITZ, "Another View of Cost-Push and Demand-Pull Inflation," *Review of Economics and Statistics,* Vol. 42 (1960).

MCMILLAN, R. A., "A Reexamination of the 'Full Employment' Goal," *Economic Review,* Federal Reserve Bank of Cleveland (March/April 1973).

MORLEY, SAMUEL, *The Economics of Inflation* (Hinsdale, Ill.: Dryden Press, 1971).

MORTON, WALTER, "Trade Unionism, Full Employment and Inflation," *American Economic Review,* Vol. 40, No. 1 (1950).

———, Keynesianism and Inflation, *Journal of Political Economy,* Vol. 59 (1951).

PHELPS, EDMUND, "Anticipated Inflation and Economic Welfare," *Journal of Political Economy,* Vol. 73, No. 1 (Feb. 1965).

———, "Phillips' Curves, Expectations of Inflation and Optimal Unemployment Over Time," *Economica,* Vol. 34, No. 135 (Aug. 1967).

———, "Money Wage Dynamics and Labor Market Equilibrium," *Microeconomic Foundations of Employment and Inflation Theory* (New York: Norton, 1970).

PHILLIPS, A. W., "The Relationship Between Unemployment and the Rate of Change of Money Wages in the United Kingdom, 1862–1957, *Economica,* Vol. 25, No. 100 (Dec. 1958).

SAMUELSON, PAUL, AND SOLOW, ROBERT, "Analytical Aspects of Anti-Inflationary Policy," *American Economic Review,* Vol. 50 (1960).

SCHULTZE, CHARLES, "Recent Inflation in the United States," in *Employment, Growth and Price Levels,* Joint Economic Committee, 86th Congress, 1st Session (Washington, D.C.: U.S. Government Printing Office, 1959).

SCHWARTZ, ANNA, "Secular Price Change in Historical Perspective," *The Journal of Money, Credit and Banking,* Vol. 5, No. 1, Part II (Feb. 1973).

SOLOW, ROBERT, *Price Expectations and the Behavior of the Price Level* (Manchester: Manchester University Press, 1969).

chapter 12

The Great Debate

INTRODUCTION

For at least 200 years English-speaking economists have debated the validity of the five key propositions constituting the hypothesis of the quantity theory of money. The essence of what is called the Keynesian Revolution can be found in the denial of the validity of several of these propositions.

In the years immediately following the appearance of *The General Theory,* the debate became relatively dormant as the Keynesian analysis was generally accepted by both academic and policy-oriented circles. The debate might be said to have reached its nadir in the United States when Walter Heller became Chairman of the Council of Economic Advisers and implemented the new economics.

However, despite Professor Pigou's remarkable recantation of his earlier views,[1] those who were adherents to the pre-Keynesian approach to theory and policy were never cast completely into oblivion. From time to time during the period of Keynesian despotism, they raised various issues about both the theoretical completeness of the Keynesian model and what they believed to be an absence of concordance between actual events and those the model predicted.

---

[1] A. C. Pigou, *Keynes's General Theory: A Retrospective View* (London: MacMillan, 1959).

The light which flickered in Chicago to summon the faithful did not fail, but continued to burn with increasing brightness as the decade of the 1960's progressed. From being dismissed as an obscure sect with headquarters at the University of Chicago or as a collection of mildly amusing but not quite respectable eccentrics, those advocating an alternative to the Keynesian view became increasingly highly regarded. The words "counter-revolution" came into vogue to describe their ideas and Harry G. Johnson brought his considerable analytical powers to bear on the essence of their theories in his Richard Ely Lecture at the 1970 Meetings of the American Economic Association.[2] However, he concluded that their success would likely be transitory because their analysis was applicable to but one subject: Inflation. The discussion to follow will show that Johnson clearly misread their contributions, for they are applicable to both inflation and unemployment. Being applicable to both problems, their work has altered irrevocably the state of monetary theory and policy.

Several rather serious problems have had to be faced in writing this summary chapter. A discussion of each is offered and we hope will serve as a qualification for the conclusions reached.

The first problem was a semantic one, namely, the selection of an appropriate chapter title. While *Monetarism vs. Fiscalism* was an original choice, it implies a certain asymmetry in the views of each side. That is, it suggests that for one side only money matters, while for the other it is unimportant. Nothing could be further from the truth, for in both frameworks monetary *and* fiscal policies play a considerable role. Since the current discussion is but part of a continuing dialogue, now some 200 years old, which involves more than merely the role of monetary and fiscal policies, a more inclusive title was selected.

Second, neither contending side in the great debate is monolithic; rather, great diversity is often to be found. In such a case, whose views shall be chosen to represent the respective sides? The resolution of this problem has been accomplished by conveying the ideas of diversity in explaining the range of respective positions, for no exhaustive systematic discussion of the entire literature can be undertaken.

The selection of appropriate economists to include in each camp has not been a simple matter, for some are more eclectic in their views than others. Nevertheless, for the neo-Fisherians, Milton Friedman is the obvious choice for leader, although the major responsibility for developing their view has increasingly been carried by Karl Brunner and his former student and present collaborator, Allan Meltzer. Others whose work is cited are Phillip Cagan, Don Patinkin, David Fand, Anna

[2] Harry G. Johnson, "The Keynesian Revolution and the Monetarist Counter-Revolution," *The American Economic Review*, Vol. 61, No. 2 (May 1971), pp. 1–14.

Schwartz, and a lively group at the St. Louis Federal Reserve Bank under the guidance of Leonall Anderson, Jerry Jordan, and Keith Carlson.

In the neo-Keynesian ranks, it is tempting to include everyone else. However, most noteworthy are James Tobin, Paul Samuelson, Ronald Teigen, Warren Smith, Gardner Ackley, Walter Heller, Arthur Okun, Otto Eckstein, John Kenneth Galbraith, Franco Modigliani, and Lawrence Klein.

A third problem, related to the second, is the difficulty of describing the neo-Fisherian position, for it is one of evolution and change and has yet to be rigorously stated in terms of a model. It was long characterized as a "black box," that is, one into which money was inserted at one end and out of which certain results emerged without any explanation as to cause. In an attempt to remedy this situation, Friedman has set forth in two recent papers[3] an outline of a Monetarist model. However, he has cautioned that this effort is ". . . not . . . a fully developed theory," but the outline of ". . . a general approach that could suggest what empirical issues required study . . ."[4] for he believes ". . . that the basic difference among economists are empirical not theoretical. . . ."[5] Among other Monetarists, Brunner, and Brunner and Meltzer,[6] have been developing an alternative model in which the stocks of existing bonds and real capital play a leading role.

Despite the problems enumerated above, we shall attempt to convey the essence of the debate which has been carried on with renewed vigor for the past two decades and which has, to a sharper degree than perhaps any other recent controversy, polarized the profession.

THE ESSENTIAL NATURE OF THE DEBATE

The basic contention of this chapter is that the current debate is but an extension and renewal of one which has been going on for the past 200 years.

[3] Milton Friedman, "A Theoretical Framework for Monetary Analysis," *Journal of Political Economy*, Vol. 78, No. 2 (March/April 1970), pp. 193–238 and "A Monetary Theory of National Income," *Journal of Political Economy*, Vol. 79, No. 2 (March/April 1971), pp. 323–37. Both papers are combined and slightly extended in *National Bureau of Economic Research Occasional Paper 112* (1971).

[4] Milton Friedman, "Comments on the Critics," *Journal of Political Economy*, Vol. 80, No. 5 (Sept./Oct. 1972), p. 907.

[5] NBER Occasional Paper 112, p. 61.

[6] Karl Brunner, "A Survey of Selected Issues in Monetary Theory," *Schweizerische Zeitschrift Für Volkswirtschaft Und Statistik*, Vol. 107 (Winter 1971), pp. 1–146; Karl Brunner and Allan Meltzer, "The Role of Financial Intermediaries in the Transmission of Monetary Policy," *American Economic Review*, Vol. 53 (May 1963), pp. 372–82; Karl Brunner and Allan Meltzer "Money, Debt, and Economic Activity," *Journal of Political Economy*, Vol. 80, No. 5 (Sept./Oct. 1972), pp. 951–77.

After reviewing a great deal of the literature,[7] one is tempted to state that, in terms of the *conclusions* reached by pre-Keynesians on the five key propositions of the quantity theory, their latter-day Monetarist counterparts have said very little which is either new or original. However, the *means* by which they reach those same conclusions constitutes the basis of the neo-Fisherian contribution to monetary theory and policy. Through the reintroduction of expectations[8] about commodity price changes and through the introduction of costs to acquire information, to search for new opportunities, and to adjust portfolios, it is now possible for the quantity theorists to develop a theoretical explanation for the problem of short-run disturbances which has long been the special preserve of the neo-Keynesians. It also makes it possible for them to formulate an aggregative model employing micro theory, thereby making the micro–macro distinction no longer necessary (although their efforts in this direction are in an embryonic state). A fully developed theory of this type would permit an explanation of the division of changes in aggregate demand between an output and a price component without recourse to *ad hoc* arguments (for example, the institutional rigidities caused by trade unions or oligopolistic industries). Finally, their work has reinstated the Fisherian distinction between real and nominal interest rates, which has a significant implication for the central bank's conduct of monetary policy.

It is more than a platitude to say that the science will never again be the same and that Monetarism has made a lasting contribution.

Thus far, no mention has been made of empirical studies designed to support the propositions advanced by either side. In the evaluation to follow, reference must be made to some of these, for linear regression results have played an important role in the neo-Fisherian revival. However, as far as possible the points of theoretical dissent will be kept separate from the empirical evidence.

Since the first pages of this text, in which the great contribution of the classical economists to monetary theory was stated, subsequent development of economic theory has been carried on in terms of the five core propositions constituting the quantity theory of money:

(1) Proportionality of money and prices

(2) Neutrality of money

---

[7] Much of this literature suffers from a lack of professionalism. Once-faultless theories are reduced to atrophied caricatures to be pushed over like straw men. Equally, it seems incredible that individuals who have known each other personally for long periods of time could have such mistaken views as to the scope and purpose of each other's work.

[8] Expectations alone do not distinguish the Monetarist position, for they play a prominent role in the liquidity preference theory of interest and in the Keynesian view of the origin of the business cycle.

(3) Monetary theory of the price level

(4) Causal role of money

(5) Exogeneity of the nominal stock of money

The great debate will now be examined in terms of these ancient and long-argued propositions.

PROPORTIONALITY OF MONEY AND PRICES

In the classical view, the proportionality of the money stock and the price level was regarded as a long-run relationship, one which followed from the assumptions that the ratio of real balances to the volume of transactions was relatively constant, and from the absence of any meaningful link between the interest rate and the demand for money. Thus, changes in the money supply (from whatever sources) would ultimately produce a proportional change in the general level of commodity prices. This conclusion was subject to the Fisherian caveat that the institutional determinants of velocity change over time, thereby altering strict proportionality.

In addition, proportionality was unlikely to characterize the short run, or period of transition, for changes in the money supply could produce temporary changes in both output and velocity. This has been documented in the discussion of Fisher's view of the business cycle.[9]

Since the Keynesian model is applicable to the short run and generally assumes the initial equilibrium to be characterized by unemployment, changes in the supply of money ought to affect real output, prices, and velocity through its ability to change the money rate of interest (the *LM* schedule is slid along a fixed *IS* curve). The extent to which commodity prices will change in this situation will depend upon what happens to per-unit labor costs. They tend to rise at an increasing rate the closer we get to full employment, as it takes increasingly larger reductions in real wages to induce a given decrease in unemployment because of the sharply diminishing productivity of labor. The ultimate influence

[9] The pre-Keynesian view is summarized by Fand as: "The pre-Keynesian quantity theory assumed that the demand for money was stable, that substantial changes in velocity did not occur unless they were induced by prior changes in M [the money stock] and that changes in the monetary sector did not permanently influence interest rates determined in the real sector, except for possible velocity changes during transition periods. Although they were aware that interest rates and prices often moved together, they nevertheless abstracted from short run changes in employment and output and from independent changes in velocity. The pre-Keynesian quantity theory assumed a given level of output, concluded that changes in prices were related to changes in money, and used the demand for money to predict *changes* in price levels." See David Fand, "Keynesian Monetary Theories, Stabilization Policy, and the Recent Inflation," *Journal of Money, Credit and Banking*, Vol. 1, No. 3 (Aug. 1969), p. 563.

of changes in the supply of money may also depend on how it is introduced into the system (via gold sales, open-market operations, and so forth) and on which sectors experience the monetary-induced change in demand.

Thus the price level, while initially fixed because the money wage rate in the Keynesian model is determined by institutional and historical forces, becomes an endogenous variable determined by the interacting of the elements of the system once any initial state of equilibrium is disturbed. Thus, the nature of the production function and the state of the labor market are important determinants of the price level in a dynamic-type Keynesian analysis. However, if the initial position is one of Keynesian full employment, the increase in the money supply must ultimately produce a proportional increase in commodity prices.

Thus, in the Keynesian system, if one were to compare two states of static equilibria differing only in that the latter had a larger money stock, one would probably not find the price level varying in strict proportionality to the money stock. The latter state would have a higher level of real output, a lower value of velocity, and both a larger nominal and real money stock. This is the view of present neo-Keynesians.[10] They do not, as a rule, discuss the long-run relationship even though Keynes himself presented an intriguing argument for why one ought to expect to find a rough long-run proportionality between the money supply and nominal income.[11]

Notwithstanding the richness of the neo-Keynesian analysis, Friedman continues to imply that for the Keynesians the price level is treated as a constant. In explaining the reversal of the Marshallian ordering of price level and output responses to a change in money demand, Friedman states: "Keynes explored this penetrating insight by carrying it to the extreme: All adjustment in quantity, none in price . . . and his disciples have done the same."[12] Several neo-Keynesians have objected to this treatment.[13]

[10] For evidence that neo-Keynesian static analysis assumes the price level to be an endogenous variable, see Gardner Ackley, *Macreconomic Theory* (New York: MacMillan, 1961), Ch. 9; R. G. D. Allen, *Macro Economic Theory* (London: MacMillan, 1967), Ch. 7; Martin Bailey, *National Income and the Price Level*, 2nd ed. (New York: McGraw-Hill, 1971), Ch. 3; Robert Holbrook, "The Interest Rate, the Price Level and Aggregate Output," in W. L. Smith and R. L. Teigen, eds., *Readings in Money, National Income, and Stabilization Policy*, rev. ed. (Homewood, Ill.: Richard D. Irwin, 1970); and Warren L. Smith, "A Graphical Exposition of the Complete Keynesian System," *Southern Economic Journal* (Oct. 1956).

[11] J. M. Keynes, *The General Theory*, op. cit., pp. 306–7.

[12] "NBER Occasional Paper 112," p. 19. Moreover, in discussing alternative ways to close his so-called "common model," Friedman states that the income–expenditure theory adds the equation $P = P_0$ or that the price level is determined outside the system. See p. 32.

[13] Tobin is especially critical of this misstatement by Friedman: "Between the first and second articles, Friedman learned that Keynes could at worst be charged with assuming a constant value of the money wage rate. . . . Since Keynes also assumed increasing marginal labor and user cost, a constant money wage implies a price level that rises with nominal income."

In the neo-Fisherian view, proportionality is not a characteristic of the short run for two reasons. First, in his restatement of the quantity theory as a theory of the demand for money, Friedman introduced the interest rate and expectations of commodity price changes as determinants of velocity. Thus, deviations in the short-run growth rate of the money stock about its long-run trend can, by affecting interest rates or price expectations, produce variations in velocity. However, the low elasticity assigned by Friedman to the demand for money with respect to the interest rate ($-.15$) implies a minimal effect on velocity from this variable.

Second, the discussion of the neo-Fisherian view of the Phillips' curve indicated that short-run deviations in the growth rate of the money stock could, to the extent that labor failed to perceive or act upon the associated price rise, produce transitory variations in real output. Thus, in the short run, variations in velocity and output alter strict proportionality in the neo-Fisherian framework.[14]

Thus, like the neo-Keynesian analysis, Monetarists hold that short-run changes in velocity and real output will temper the short-run effect of changes in the money supply on the general level of prices. This semblance of agreement is only superficial, for from the neo-Keynesian viewpoint, such changes in the money supply produce permanent changes in velocity and output, whereas from the Monetarist viewpoint, such changes only exist while the actual course of prices differs from that expected by labor and lenders.

It should be noted in this connection that regardless of whether

---

James Tobin, "Friedman's Theoretical Framework," *Journal of Political Economy*, Vol. 80, No. 5 (Sept./Oct. 1972), p. 855. Don Patinkin is equally critical of this view by Friedman. See "Friedman on the Quantity Theory and Keynesian Economics," *Journal of Political Economy*, Vol. 80, No. 5 (Sept./Oct. 1972), pp. 892–900. It should be noted that in most Keynesian macro texts, any rise in prices does not appear to have any effect on expectations of future price changes.

[14] In sharply defining the Monetarist position on proportionality, Brunner writes: "The growth rate dm/m [the money supply] exerts relatively little influence on the growth rate dy/y of output. Monetary growth affects dominantly the price-level. Monetary accelerations or decelerations, on the other hand, operate essentially on output and employment" and that "The impact of monetary accelerations (or decelerations) on output and employment is essentially temporary." See his, "The 'Monetarist Revolution' in Monetary Theory," *Weltwirtschaftliches Archiv*, No. 1 (1970). In addition, he has stated: "This emphasis on the central role of *accelerations* of the money stock, irrespective of the growth rate itself, forms probably the most important implication of the monetarist analysis of economic fluctuations." See "A Survey of Selected Issues in Monetary Theory," p. 89. Expressions in italics are found in original.

In a similar vein, Friedman and Schwartz state: ". . . our survey of experience leads us to conjecture that the longer-period changes in money income produced by a changed secular rate of growth of the money stock are reflected mainly in different price behavior rather than in different rates of growth of output; whereas the shorter-period changes in the rate of growth of the money stock are capable of exerting a sizable influence on the rate of growth of output as well." See their "Money and Business Cycles," *The Review of Economics and Statistics*, Vol. 45, No. 1, Part 2 (Feb. 1963), p. 53. See also footnote 16.

the effects are permanent or transitory, neither side can predict the exact division of a change in aggregate demand between a price-level component and real output component.[15]

In the longer run, the two viewpoints on proportionality differ fundamentally. The neo-Fisherian view is that once the actual course of prices becomes fully anticipated, the transitory effect on real output and velocity vanishes and the short-run increase in the rate of growth of the money supply serves only to raise commodity prices.[16]

The above analysis has considered only the question of a short-run deviation from the long-run growth path of the money supply. Suppose, instead, the question had been considered of whether proportionality must necessarily be characterized by a situation in which the money stock grows only at its long-run trend rate. In this case, the neo-Fisherians, speaking through Friedman, would assert nonproportionality, for his empirical work with Anna Schwartz implies a long-run secular decline in the velocity of money. In terms of his velocity function, the secular decline would be explained by an evolutionary change in the institutional practices enumerated by Fisher as governing the turnover rate of money.[17]

[15] This is clearly acknowledged by Friedman: "The general subject of the division of changes in money income between prices and quantity badly needs more investigation. None of our leading economic theories has much to say about it." See "The Monetary Studies of the National Bureau," reprinted in W. Gibson and G. Kaufman, *Monetary Economics, Readings on Current Issues* (New York: McGraw-Hill, 1971), pp. 5–22.

[16] In a fairly recent paper, Friedman lists the key propositions of Monetarism. Seven of them bear on the subject of proportionality and attach a time dimension to the terms *transitory* and *longer run*. These propositions are;

(1) "There is a consistent though not precise relation between the rate of growth of the quantity of money and the rate of growth of nominal income.

(2) This relationship is not obvious to the naked eye largely because it takes time for changes in monetary growth to affect income and how long it takes is itself variable.

(3) On the average, a change in the rate of monetary growth produces a change in the rate of growth of nominal income about six to nine months later. This is an average and does not hold in every individual case.

(4) The changed rate of growth of nominal income typically shows up first in output and hardly at all in prices.

(5) On the average, the effect on prices comes about six to nine months after the effect on income and output, so the total delay between a change in monetary growth and a change in the rate of inflation averages something like 12–18 months.

(6) Even after allowance for the delay in the effect of monetary growth, the relation is far from perfect. There's many a slip 'twixt the monetary change and the income change.'

(7) In the short run, which may be as much as five or ten years, monetary changes affect primarily output, over decades, on the other hand, the rate of monetary growth affects primarily prices."

See Milton Friedman, *The Counter-Revolution in Monetary Theory, First Wincott Memorial Lecture,* The Institute of Economic Affairs (1970), pp. 22–24. Reproduced by and with permission of The Institute of Economic Affairs and The Wincott Foundation.

[17] For an alternative explanation of the secular decline in velocity in which the interest rate is an important explanatory variable, see Henry Latané, "Cash Balances and The Rate of Interest—A Pragmatic Approach," *Review of Economics and Statistics*, Vol. 36 (Nov. 1954), pp. 456–60.

MONETARY THEORY OF THE PRICE LEVEL

The necessity for adding this proposition to the quantity theory arose because the proportionality proposition by itself was insufficient to preclude nonmonetary forces from exerting an impact on the general level of prices. Hence, a monetary theory of the price level was set forth explicitly by the classical economists. Thus, changes in government spending or taxation, changes in the rate of business investment or private spending in general, in and of themselves, unaccompanied by changes in the money stock, would exert no influence on the general level of prices.

This proposition implies that for these early pre-Keynesians, inflations and deflations were always monetary phenomena.

The earlier discussion of the Keynesian theory presented in various sections of this text has emphasized that the only way the price level can be changed is by changing either per-unit labor costs or the profit markup. Through problems it was demonstrated that changes in the money supply, government spending and taxation, private expenditures, and personal savings could all exert an influence on the price level. Thus, for the neo-Keynesians, the price level need not be a monetary phenomenon.[18] Moreover, the predominance of Keynesian-inspired cost-push inflation models,[19] the possibility that demand inflation can occur without increases in the money supply,[20] and the neo-Keynesian emphasis on guidelines and wage-and-price controls are additional evidence that for that school, inflations and deflations may be nonmonetary in

---

[18] Paul Samuelson has identified the following three propositions as both post-Keynesian and quite incompatible with the Monetarist hypothesis:
  (1) "Even when the money supply is held constant, any significant changes in thriftiness and the propensity to consume can be expected to have systematic independent effects on the money value of current output, affecting average prices or aggregate production or both.
  (2) Even when the money supply is held constant, an exogenous burst of investment opportunities or animal spirits on the part of business can be expected to have systematic effects on total GNP.
  (3) Even when the money supply is held constant, increases in public expenditures or reductions in tax rates—and even increases in public expenditures balanced by increases in taxation—can be expected to have systematic effects upon aggregate GNP."
See his "Reflections on the Merits and Demerits of Monetarism," in *Issues in Fiscal and Monetary Policy: The Eclectic Economist Views the Controversy*, James J. Diamond, ed., Chicago, Ill.: DePaul University, 1971), p. 7.

[19] For an excellent discussion of the nonmonetary theories of inflation put forth by Keynesians, see David Fand, "Some Issues in Monetary Economics," *Review—Federal Reserve Bank of St. Louis* (Jan. 1970), pp. 20–23.

[20] This can occur if the demand for money depends upon the interest rate. A rise in the interest rate because of the pressure of aggregate demand can increase velocity, thereby providing the wherewithal to accommodate the inflationary pressure.

nature depending on oligopolistic corporations, powerful trade unions, and private investment spending.

The modern neo-Fisherian view appears to contain some inconsistencies, for while Friedman postulates a velocity function in which the rate of interest appears as an argument, and which therefore implies a conclusion akin to the neo-Keynesian view, he boldly asserts ". . . That *inflation is always and everywhere a monetary phenomenon* in the sense that it is and can be produced only by a more rapid increase in the quantity of money than in output."[21] Fand also states: "The Monetarists have a monetary theory of price level . . . while the Fiscalists tend to have . . . a nonmonetary theory of the price level."[22]

Elsewhere, Friedman has taken a more temperate tone:

Long period changes in the quantity of money relative to output determine the secular behavior of prices. Substantial expansions in the quantity of money over shorter periods has been a major proximate source of the accompanying inflation in prices.[23]

Much of the work by Friedman and Schwartz, by Cagan on hyperinflations, by Harberger on inflation in Chile, and in papers gathered by Meiselman, is intended to substantiate Friedman's claims. In his most recent declaration, Friedman states:

We accept the quantity theory presumption, and have thought it supported by the evidence we examined, that changes in the quantity of money as such *in the long run* have a negligible effect on real income, so that nonmonetary forces are "all that matter" for changes in real income over decades and money "does not matter." On the other hand, we have regarded the quantity of money, plus other variables (including real income itself) that effect *k* [the reciprocal of velocity] as essentially "all that matters" for the long-run determination of nominal income. The price level is then a joint outcome of the monetary forces determining nominal income and the real forces determining real income. . . .[24]

From their statements, one might conclude that the neo-Fisherians have a largely monetary theory of the price level, for so long as they admit the interest rate as a determinant of velocity (albeit weakly in Friedman's work), changes in real variables by themselves will be able to exert a lasting influence on aggregate demand and the price level.

[21] Milton Friedman, *The Counter-Revolution in Monetary Theory*, p. 24. Italics in the original.

[22] David Fand, "Monetarism and Fiscalism," *Banca Nazionale del Lavoro Quarterly Review*, No. 94 (Sept. 1970), p. 8.

[23] Milton Friedman, "The Monetary Studies of the National Bureau," p. 16.

[24] Milton Friedman, *NBER Occasional Paper 112*, p. 27.

Keynesian-type cost-push inflations are rejected completely by the neo-Fisherians. They hold that:

. . . "cost-push" is merely an institutional manifestation of the natural tendency to restore equilibrium to real relative price relationships whose expression in monetary terms has been disrupted by the erosion of the real value of money through inflation. . . .[25]

This conclusion was evident from our earlier presentation of the neo-Fisherian view of inflation. In that presentation, the purpose of cost-push pressure was to restore the relationship between aggregate demand and the long-run supply schedule of output.

NEUTRALITY OF MONEY

For the pre-Keynesian quantity theorists, the neutrality of money meant that changes in the money stock or its rate of growth could not produce changes in the equilibrium value of real variables: The real rate of interest, the volume of employment, the rate of economic growth, the rate of capital formation, and the relative structure of prices (the composition of final output). The only lasting influence of money was on the general level of prices. However, since at least the time of Cantillon and Hume, classical economists expressed the notion that money could be nonneutral in the short run. This view received much attention and refinement in the work of Irving Fisher.

As the Keynesian model is confined to the short run, little work has been done by the Fiscalists on the longer-run effects of changes in the money stock. For that investigation growth models are required, which are beyond the scope of this text. However, in the short-run context, if the initial position is one of Keynesian unemployment, changes in the money supply will produce permanent nonneutral effects—that is, will permanently change the rate of interest, the level of employment, the rate of capital formation, and so on.

This ability of changes in the money stock to alter the rate of flow of real output has been treated by some neo-Fisherians as *the* contribution by Keynes to understanding the functioning of the real world, for it reversed the usual Marshallian ordering in which prices adjusted more rapidly than output to a monetary change. It is this theme of Keynes that latter-day Monetarists have expanded upon in formulating their theory of nonneutral adjustment following a change in the growth rate of the money supply.[26]

[25] Harry G. Johnson, *Inflation and the Monetarist Controversy* (Amsterdam: North-Holland, 1972), p. 57.
[26] See Brunner, "The 'Monetarist Revolution' in Monetary Theory." This forms the basis

The formulation and acceptance of the Phillips-curve relationship, which implies permanent tradeoffs, is a clear indication of the neo-Keynesian belief in nonneutrality.[27] This belief, derived either from the Phillips curve or from the formal structure of the model (which permits monetary changes to alter the value of real variables), implies either the presence of money illusion or the existence of very long lags in forming expectations of price changes. This often leads the neo-Keynesians to fail to distinguish between changes in monetary and in real variables; a change in the former is taken to be an equivalent change in the latter. To the extent that this assumption is contradicted by actual behavior, it can lead to serious policy errors. As noted several times above, high or rising interest rates may be taken as resulting from tight monetary conditions when in fact they may only represent the operation of expectations of rising prices induced by a prior period of monetary expansion.[28]

It is the neo-Fisherian view on the issue of neutrality that must be taken to represent a substantial contribution to monetary economics, for it returns the focus of the quantity theory to an analysis of short-run disturbances. It is this return to a study of the period of transition that is creating the viable Monetarist alternative to the orthodox Keynesian theory.

Friedman's views on neutrality are set forth in his 1967 presidential address before the American Economic Association. There he asserted that monetary policy ". . . cannot peg interest rates for more than very limited periods and it cannot peg the rate of unemployment for more than very limited periods."[29]

From the discussion in Chapter 11 on the neo-Fisherian view of

---

for the claims by some Monetarists that they are the real disciples of Keynes and that the so-called "Keynesians" have really misread the Master.

[27] That the neo-Keynesians believed in a long-run trade-off can be seen from the work of a former Chairman of the Council of Economic Advisers, Arthur Okun. We are told: "Over the long run, the big question will be what the middle of the road looks like. On an optimistic–realistic view, the best hope is that a 4 percent rate of unemployment and a 2 percent annual rate of price increase will prove compatible and such a combination will be regarded as a satisfactory compromise by the American Public." See The Political Economy of Prosperity (Washington, D.C.: The Brookings Institution, 1970), p. 102.

[28] We are told by Okun that price expectations do have an impact on interest rates. Yet he asserts that the Phillips' curve gives a long-run trade-off. Holding both opinions appears inconsistent. As to the influence of price-level changes on interest rates, he states: "But the lofty levels of market interest rates—which also reflected price expectations— . . ." and "In time of inflation, market interest rates are very hard to interpret because the price expectations built into the security markets are unknown." Arthur Okun, The Political Economy of Prosperity, pp. 94, 115–16.

[29] Milton Friedman, "The Role of Monetary Policy," p. 5. This quotation is a partial paraphrase. The exact time dimension attached to the phrase "very limited periods" is not given by Friedman. In other sources he expresses the opinion that the short run may be as long as five or ten years (see footnote 16 for source). Fisher expressed the view that the period of transition may last for a decade or more.

the Phillips' curve and the natural rate of unemployment, it is quite clear why monetary policy cannot peg the unemployment rate. A similar analysis is applied by Friedman to the determination of the interest rate; it is essentially the same argument made by Irving Fisher many years before. It is repeated below because it allows the representation to be made in an *IS–LM* framework and also allows the evaluation of the neo-Keynesian response. If desired, the student may bypass it.

As with the Keynesians, Friedman believes that a more rapid rate of growth of the money stock engineered by the central bank will drive down the interest rate—both nominal and real. This he calls the *liquidity effect* and he asserts that it is transitory. In terms of Figure 12:1, the liquidity effect is shown as a rightward shift in the *LM* schedule and a decline in the interest rate from point (1) to (2). However, two forces are set in motion which tend to push the rate of interest back in the direction of its initial equilibrium, point (1)—these are the income and price expectation effects. The former represents the rise in interest rates due to the expansion in aggregate demand set in motion when the liquidity effect has reduced the real and nominal rate. All else being constant, the market rate will rise toward point (3), real income will expand beyond Y_0, and unemployment will fall below its natural rate.

FIGURE 12:1. The Effects of Money on Interest Rates

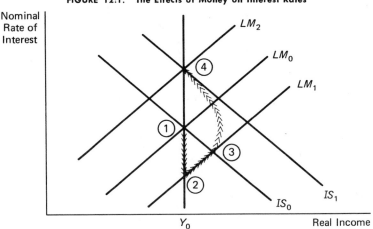

However, in order to lower unemployment and expand real income, the price level must rise. This will set in motion two forces. First, the *LM* schedule will shift to the left as real money balances decline. In addition, to the extent that lenders perceive the inflation, the *IS* schedule will shift upward by the amount of that perception as they demand a higher money interest rate to compensate them for the loss in purchasing power. This *price expectation effect* will move the market interest rate toward a position such as point (4), above (1) by the amount of the expected inflation. If no expectations of inflation develop, the economy will move back to (1), once the real wage relationship is restored.

In order for equilibrium to prevail at the natural rate of unemployment associated with real income Y_0, the real value of money balances must continue to fall until the LM schedule shifts leftward to coincide with the IS curve at point (4).[30]

The movement from (1) to (2) to (3) to (4) traces out the period of transition, or short run, which Friedman's analysis of United States data suggests "may be as much as five or ten years."[31] This analysis clearly implies that interest rates cannot be used as a guide to monetary policy and that an acceleration in the rate of growth of the money supply produces not lower interest rates but higher ones, if the entire cycle of events is considered. Thus, monetary policy cannot peg interest rates except for limited periods. Any attempt to do so will only produce sustained inflation, just as would a similar attempt to use monetary policy to hold unemployment below its natural rate.[32]

Friedman's views are in substantial accord with those of Brunner, who describes the exploration of short-run nonneutrality as: "probably the most important implication of the monetarist analysis of economic fluctuations."

[30] The discussion embodied in Figure 12:1 can be used to explain the argument of Thomas Sargent (see Chapter 3, footnote 28) that attempts to measure the time it takes for expectations of inflation to be incorporated into nominal interest rates may overstate the time lag because they, in effect, measure two time lags. The shift of the IS schedule from IS_0 to IS_1 is due to the incorporation of a given rate of expected inflation in the investing and saving behavior of individuals. However the movement of nominal interest rates from point (1) to (4) also depends upon the speed with which actual prices change when real income departs from its full employment level, Y_0. It is this rise in actual prices which shifts the LM schedule to its equilibrium position, LM_2.

[31] In his response to Friedman, Teigen is only partially correct and may reveal a lack of understanding of Friedman's analysis. First, Teigen is quite correct in asserting that Keynesians do not neglect the income effect, as Friedman implied when he said they only recognize the liquidity effect of monetary expansion. However, Teigen's claim that the income effect will produce rising interest rates does not follow from his diagrammatic analysis, which is similar to Figure 12:1. If one were to plot a time series of interest rates from the data generated by his example, they would always be below the initial equilibrium rate (i_0 in Figure 12:1). Thus, a monetary expansion would produce lower interest rates, not higher ones. His error is to be found in not shifting up the IS curve due to price expectations. See Ronald Teigen, "A Critical Look at Monetarist Economics," Review—Federal Reserve Bank of St. Louis (Jan. 1972).

[32] This is not to imply that the Monetarists believe that no expansions in the money stock will produce permanent effects on output and employment. We are told by Fand, for example: ". . . a change in nominal M, or a change in its rate of growth, is not assumed to have a significant, and permanent, effect on real balances or interest rates, except possibly when dealing with an economy that has substantial unemployed resources." See his "Keynesian Monetary Theories, Stabilization Policy and the Recent Inflation," p. 564, footnote 24. He leaves undefined the forces which produce substantial unemployed resources—presumably in excess of the natural rate. Compatible with the Monetarist position, he must have in mind something akin to the massive monetary contraction during the period 1929–1933.

In order to explain nonneutrality, Brunner emphasizes a distinction between the growth rate of the money stock and accelerations or decelerations in that rate of growth. The distinction is important in order to explain why nonneutrality can occur at vastly different rates of money growth. Thus, even in the midst of hyperinflations, by further accelerating the growth rate of the money stock, additional output and employment can be induced. Conversely, a deceleration in the rate can produce an inflationary recession.[33] This analysis is, of course, quite consistent with the neo-Fisherian view of the relevant trade-off given by the Phillips curve. Brunner's special twist to to emphasize the costs of acquiring information and of making adjustments in light of such information. The speed with which an economic agent can absorb such information depends on its cost of production or acquisition. This emphasis on the costs of search, adjustment, and information acquisition is an important part of the theoretical model of Monetarism which Brunner and Meltzer are currently evolving.[34]

The work of Friedman, Brunner, and Meltzer leads to the conclusion that the neo-Fisherians believe that money is nonneutral in the short run—which may be a considerable time span. However, such nonneutrality is essentially transitory depending on the time it takes labor and lenders to perceive inflation and adjust to it.

Given the preceding discussion of natural rates of unemployment, and distinctions between real and nominal interest rates and money balances, it might be concluded that Monetarists believe that money is neutral in the long run. However, this is not the case and we find Friedman attacking Patinkin in a disconcerting fashion:

> I conjecture that Patinkin's insistence on labeling my analytical framework Keynesian ultimately reflects his concentration on "neutrality." For if he interprets my framework as in the "quantity-theory" tradition, he cannot continue to regard "the quantity theory" as synonymous with the long run neutrality of money, since my framework is clearly and obviously not about that. . . .[35]

---

[33] In this regard, Brunner states, "Monetarist analysis thus attributes stagflation not to the wickedness of trade unions or of assorted speculators, but to the rational response of the information system to the uncertainties imposed by volatile and unreliable government policies." See his "The Monetarist View of Keynesian Ideas," *Lloyds Bank Review*, No. 102 (Oct. 1971), p. 41.

[34] This model was developed in response to Brunner and Meltzer's view that Friedman's restatement of the quantity theory, in terms of a stable demand function for money, does not permit a discrimination between quantity theories and nonquantity theories. It is compatible with both. See their "Friedman's Monetary Theory," *Journal of Political Economy*, Vol. 80, No. 5 (Sept./Oct. 1972), p. 841.

[35] "Comments on the Critics," p. 945.

Why does Friedman believe that money may be nonneutral in the long run? To answer this question, we must draw on two previous pieces of analysis. First, Friedman regards real money balances as both a productive factor to business enterprise and a provider of utility to the ultimate wealthholder. Second, inflation will reduce the desired level of real balances which business and the ultimate wealth owner will hold. Given these two suppositions, a permanent acceleration in the growth rate of the money supply (for example, from 3 percent to 8 percent will produce nonneutrality, for it will permanently alter the level of real income. However, this depends on the way in which real income is measured

. . . in particular whether it includes or excludes the nonpecuniary services of money. If it includes them, as in principle it should, then the level of real output will be lower after the monetary change than before. It will be lower for two reasons: first, the higher cost of holding cash balances will lead producers to substitute other resources for cash, which will lower productive efficiency; second, the flow of nonpecuniary services from money will be reduced.[36]

---

[36] Milton Friedman, *NBER Occasional Paper 112*, pp. 56–57; and "The Optimum Quantity of Money" in *The Optimum Quantity of Money and Other Essays* (Chicago: Aldine, 1970), pp. 14–15. Among Monetarists, Phillip Cagan, drawing on the literature of monetary growth models, identifies and discusses two reasons why money could be nonneutral in the long run.

The first pertains to the effect of changing price levels on the demand for real money balances and is quite similar to the discussion given by Friedman. Cagan notes first that real money holding will decline only if the explicit or implicit interest payable on money fails to adjust adequately for the higher inflation rate. If such a failure occurs, then, as both a store of value and medium of exchange, smaller money balances will be held.

In place of money as a store of value, individuals are likely to hold substitutes whose income stream is not subject to depreciation, for example, equities, real capital goods, inventories, real estate, and so forth. The attempt to substitute should bid up the prices of these assets and, to the extent possible, induce an increase in their supply. An increase in supply will expand the existing capital stock, raising the existing capital/labor ratio and requiring a larger flow of investment per period of time to maintain the capital stock.

As to the use of money as a medium of exchange, a higher inflation rate will cause business to substitute labor and machinery whose function is to see that smaller transactions balances are held. Individuals can achieve the same end by surrendering leisure time.

So long as the new higher inflation rate is maintained, the economy will gradually achieve a new desired relation between capital stock, real money balances, and labor supply. The new relationship is likely to feature a higher capital/labor ratio, manifesting the long-run nonneutrality of money. However, for inflations of the magnitude experienced by the United States, Cagan believes the nonneutrality to be unimportant.

A second method for achieving long-run nonneutrality comes through the interest rate. A faster rate of monetary growth supposedly expands the supply of loanable funds. This lowers the market rate of interest, encouraging a higher rate of capital formation and discouraging saving. To the extent that the interest elasticity of investment exceeds that of consumption, more real resources will be diverted to the construction of capital goods even though consumption, in nominal dollars, may rise. The additional capital formation is supposed to continue as long as banks continue to create additional loanable funds.

For a more complete discussion of these issues, see Phillip Cagan, "The Non-Neutrality of Money in the Long Run," *Journal of Money, Credit and Banking*, Vol. 1, No. 2 (May 1969), pp. 207–27.

Both of these can be called the income effect of inflation, for inefficient production ought to reduce real output and the convenience and security provided by money holding ought to fall, thereby reducing the utility, or income, of the ultimate wealth owner. For U.S.-type inflations, the sum of these two factors decreasing income must be quite insignificant, so that one might reasonably conclude that Friedman is about as far from Patinkin on the issue of long-run neutrality as Ivory Soap is from being pure.

James Tobin has offered a compelling analysis of why any model of the type usually associated with Friedman's restatement of the quantity theory in which the wealth holder may select money, bonds, real and human capital, and commodities, ought to produce long-run nonneutrality, given the usual way in which monetary policy is conducted.[37]

Suppose, says Tobin, we start from a position of a balanced Federal budget and allow the central bank to expand the supply of money along some long-run growth path by buying government securities. The effect will be to alter the long-run composition of private sector wealth: Individuals now have more money and fewer bonds. This changed composition of wealth ought to alter the income stream of its recipients, raising the relative portion accounted for by human labor income. Other things being equal, the variance of that income stream should increase because labor income is more variable than that accruing from interest on government bonds, thereby altering the behavior of the wealth holder. Moreover, this is not a once-and-for-all occurrence. The removal of the bonds and their interest liability ought to swing the Federal budget into surplus. If taxes are not reduced to offset the surplus, a continual destruction of the Federal debt will occur, with long-run alteration in the composition of wealth. If taxes are cut, however, neutrality is produced only if the tax burden on human and nonhuman income is reduced proportionately, risk and portfolio considerations aside. A nonproportional reduction will raise the relative yield on one or the other forms of capital, thereby inducing a further compositional change in wealth.

Finally, the removal of bonds may have additional wealth-altering effects even if both the income and the liability aspects of those debt instruments are fully recognized. These wealth-altering effects can occur if the discount rates applicable to both streams (interest and taxes) are not equal. This might occur, for example, if the variance or uncertainty attached to the total income stream of an individual were less than that applicable to his tax liability. Under these circumstances the discount rate appropriate for the income stream would be less than that appropriate to his tax liability. Thus, the removal of bonds can either raise or lower aggregate wealth.

37 "Friedman's Theoretical Framework," pp. 860–63.

It is for these reasons that Tobin believes a multiasset model will produce long-run nonneutrality. It also tells us the list of assets which must have been employed in the pre-Keynesian classical quantity theory model to have produced long-run neutrality.

In summary, for both the neo-Keynesians and the Monetarists, money may be nonneutral in the short run. Thus, changing the growth rate of the money stock can lead to changes in real variables. The main difference is that the neo-Fisherians argue that all such changes are essentially transitory in nature. In their analysis, one must distinguish carefully between real and nominal magnitudes and pay close attention to price expectations, which link the two.

It is of great interest that the Monetarist analysis which bears on these periods of transition, like the Keynesian Theory it seeks to supplant, reverses the Marshallian ordering of price–output responses to a change in money supply.

This difference between the two schools in the degree to which nonneutrality is regarded as permanent has an effect upon their respective policy prescriptions. For the neo-Keynesians monetary policy becomes one of the two instruments for stabilizing the economy, whereas for the neo-Fisherians a stable growth rate in the money stock is preferred, since according to their theories variations in the growth rate must be rectified ultimately at the cost of painful readjustments.[38]

THE CAUSALITY OF MONEY

This has been the most difficult part of the great debate to disentangle, for interwoven in the arguments emanating from each side are questions involving the channels through which money exercises its influence, the causes of cyclical disturbances, the effectiveness of fiscal policy, the empirical substantiation of the respective positions, and the validity of the methodology used by each side. After a summary of pre–great-debate positions on the causality of money, the remainder of the discussion deals with each issue separately.

In saying that money played a causal role, the pre-Keynesian quantity theorists meant that changes in the money stock caused subsequent changes in the price level and in nominal income. To explain how this occurred, they specified two means or channels through which monetary impulses were transmitted to the real sector, the price level and nominal income. The first channel, the direct mechanism, specified that

[38] Henry Wallich argues that adopting such a stable growth rate is no guarantee of price stability; it may be inflationary or deflationary. See his "Comment," *Journal of Money, Credit and Banking*, Vol. 1, No. 3 (Aug. 1969), pp. 597–99.

the rate of money spending would change whenever there was a disparity between the actual cash-balance holdings of the public and the level of money balances it desired to hold given its income and expenditure patterns. This lack of equilibrium would lead ultimately to proportional changes in the price level and the restoration of equality between the actual and desired levels of real cash holdings.

The second channel (the more common one for advanced societies) they called the indirect mechanism, because it involved the money rate of interest. Increases in the money stock would, by depressing the money rate of interest relative to the real rate, create a disparity between the actual and desired stock of real capital, leading to a higher rate of investment. Thus, a balance sheet or stock adjustment would give rise to a higher flow rate of money expenditures to restore the equilibrium. In an economy with full employment, the higher flow rate would act simply to drive up the price level in proportion to the rise in the money stock.

Thus, both direct and indirect means were set forth as the channels through which monetary impulses would exert a transitory effect on real variables and a permanent effect only on the general level of prices.

The cause of the business cycle was also attributed to variations in the rate of growth of the money stock about its long-run trend. Thus, any changes in the flow of investment expenditures unaccompanied by a change in the money stock would merely alter the composition of final output between consumption and capital goods.

Since the economy postulated in classical theory was one ever-tending toward full employment, the role of fiscal policy was purely allocative, that is, it was used to decide how the available resources would be divided between the public and private sectors.

In *The General Theory*, Keynes incorporated in his presentation the totality of the indirect mechanism. Thus we find in liquidity preference a balance sheet, portfolio, or stock adjustment mechanism—that is, changes in the supply of money induce, via interest rate movements, a disparity between the actual and desired capital stocks, setting in motion variations in the flow of investment expenditures amplified subsequently by the multiplier.

With the generalization of Keynes by Hicks, the potency of monetary policy came to depend upon the slope properties of the *IS* and *LM* schedules. The more elastic the former and inelastic the latter, the more effective monetary policy. Thus the elasticity of each schedule became an important empirical question. Samuelson provides a vivid account of how early investigations by Keynesian economists lost sight of money:

In 1939 Oxford questionnaires were sent to businessmen and investors asking whether interest rates were of any importance to them. To a man they all answered: "No, no importance whatsoever!" So, this is coffin nail No. 1 on the importance of money. At the Harvard Business School, the late Professor Ebersole did case studies on finance, and what do you think they all showed, every one of them? They showed that money and finance were of no importance. If that doesn't convince you, let's turn to econometrics. Professor Tinbergen of Rotterdam did the first econometric studies—giant computer models for an economy. He tried regression coefficients, and no matter how he regressed investment on the interest rate, he always got a zero coefficient.

Finally, if more is necessary, economic theory came to the rescue of this view and people like Sir John Hicks said that as far as short-term investment is concerned, interest is of no consequence as a cost, and as far as long-term investment is concerned, uncertainty is so great that it completely swamps interest which leaves you with only a minuscule of intermediate investment that is interest elastic. Well, that was the 1939 view. Unfortunately, some people get frozen into what they learned in their youth, and those views still prevail in some circles. Still these fellows are dying out in this country.[39]

In addition to this initial de-emphasis of monetary policy, two other themes from *The General Theory* were important in the subsequent debate. The first concerned the cause of cyclical instability. Keynes attributed these to the variability of investor expectations about the future. Swept by alternate waves of optimism and pessimism, business investment expanded or contracted, thereby producing the cycle.

In the late 1930's, Alvin Hansen, using a variation on this theme, developed the theory of secular stagnation, attributing it to a lack of profitable investment opportunities regardless of the rate of interest.

The stagnation thesis and the belief that investor expectations caused the cycle gave rise to the distinctive Keynesian emphasis on the stabilization role of fiscal policy. Compensatory alterations in government spending and taxation were to be used to offset the cyclical fluctuations caused by fickle investor behavior as well as to ensure secular full employment of resources. Both of these themes, combined with the early empirical evidence gathered in the late 1930's, suggest that to the Keynesians "money doesn't matter." This has become a rallying cry of

[39] Paul Samuelson, "Money, Interest Rates, and Economic Activity," in *Proceedings of A Symposium on Money, Interest Rates and Economic Activity* (New York: American Bankers Association 1967).

Elsewhere Samuelson adds that experience during the 1930's contributed to the view that money doesn't matter. This involves the inflow into the United States of billions of dollars resulting from the distrust of Hitler's Europe, producing, in the eyes of at least Alvin Hansen, a controlled experiment in which the reserves of the banking system were vastly expanded and yet no commensurate expansion in business activity or even in the total money supply was achieved. See his "Reflections on the Merits and Demerits of Monetarism," pp. 11–12.

the Monetarists and a major point of contention in the Monetarist counter-revolution.[40]

During the decades of the 1950's and 60's, the neo-Keynesian view on the transmission mechanism of money received extensive theoretical refinement as more asset categories were added to the primitive money–bond portfolio model of Keynes. In addition, the construction of large-scale econometric models contributed additional insight into how money affects the real sector. Nevertheless, the original balance sheet or stock adjustment mechanism has been retained.

We now turn to a brief description of the transmission mechanism and its neo-Fisherian counterpart. This discussion will partly overlap that presented in preceding chapters; however, the nature of the difference in the two approaches can only be fully understood by describing both models of the monetary adjustment mechanism.

The Transmission Mechanism

neo-Keynesian view

In the neo-Keynesian approach, the effect of changes in the supply of money is transmitted to the real sector of the economy via a portfolio or stock adjustment process in which substitution, wealth, and often credit availability effects are clearly distinguished.

Substitution Effects. The neo-Keynesian view of the substitution effect is well described by the work of the late Warren Smith:

A purchase of, say, Treasury bills by the Federal Reserve will directly lower the yield on bills and, by a process of arbitrage involving a chain of portfolio substitutions, will exert downward pressure on interest rates of financial assets generally. Moreover—and more important—the expansion of bank reserves will enable the banking system to expand its assets. . . . But the bulk of the addition to reserves will ordinarily be used to make loan accommodation available on more favorable terms, and to buy securities, thereby exerting a further downward effect on security yields.

With the expected yield on a unit of real capital initially unchanged, the decline in the yield on financial assets, and the more favorable terms on which new debt can be issued, the balance sheet of households and businesses will be thrown out of equilibrium. The adjustment toward a new equilibrium will take the form of a sale of existing financial assets and the issuance of new debt to acquire real capital and claims thereto. This will raise the

---

[40] In the most elementary sense, this rallying cry of the Monetarists is patently absurd, for the analysis by Keynes represented the integration of the monetary and real sectors. This had not been formally achieved by the classical economists.

price of existing units of real capital—or equity claims against these units—
relative to the (initially unchanged) cost of producing new units, thereby open-
ing up a gap between desired and actual stocks, a gap that will be closed
by production of new capital goods. This stock adjustment approach is
readily applicable, with some variations to suit the circumstances, to the
demands for a wide variety of both business and consumer capital—including
plant and equipment, inventories, residential construction, and consumer
durable goods.[41]

Wealth Effects.   From the Keynesian viewpoint, no direct wealth
effect is involved in this purchase of Treasury bills, for an open-market
operation merely swaps one asset (money) for another (bonds), the latter
being regarded as wealth because, while it is an asset to its holder, the
taxpayer, in the neo-Keynesian view, does not perceive its tax liability.[42]
However, this is not the case when gold money is introduced into the
system, for it is regarded as a clear addition to wealth as well as giving
rise to substitution effects.

The open-market operation does cause market interest rates to
decline and this produces a wealth effect in the neo-Keynesian framework. This wealth effect results from the fact that at a lower interest rate
the present or capitalized value of the expected income stream, repre-

[41] Warren L. Smith, "A Neo-Keynesian View of Monetary Policy," *Controlling Monetary
Aggregates* (Boston: Federal Reserve Bank of Boston, 1969), pp. 106–10. See also Paul
Samuelson, "Reflections on the Merits and Demerits of Monetarism," pp. 8–10.

[42] As to the general neo-Keynesian position, we are told by Samuelson that "all men
are mortal. Most men do not concern themselves with the well-being of their remote posterity.
Hence, government bonds as an asset are not completely offset in their minds by the recognition of the liability of paying taxes in perpetuity to carry the interest on those bonds. Only if
people live forever, foreseeing correctly the tax payments they (or the posterity as dear to
them in the most remote future as in their own lifetime well-being) must make on account of
the perpetual future interest payments on government bonds—only then would it be true to
say that retirement of public debt would have no substantive effects upon the reckoning of
wealth, the level of spending, and the level of prices generally." See his "Reflections on the
Merits and Demerits of Monetarism," p. 9.

Another prominent neo-Keynesian, James Tobin, admits that over the years he has
vacillated on the wealth potential of government bonds. In 1952 he asked: "How is it possible
that society merely by the device of incurring a debt to itself can deceive itself into believing
that it is wealthier? Do not the additional taxes, which are necessary to carry the interest
charges, reduce the value of other components of private wealth? There certainly must be
effects in this direction." See "Asset Holdings and Spending Decisions," *American Economic
Review, Papers and Proceedings,* Vol. 42 (May 1952), pp. 109–23. Reprinted in *Essays in Economics,
Vol. 1, Macro Economics,* p. 91. In 1963, in demonstrating that the issuance of long-term government securities can be expansionary, he assumes they increase, dollar for dollar, net private
wealth. See his "An Essay on the Principles of Debt Management," pp. 378–98. In 1971 he
believes that government bond issues do, to a degree, increase private wealth because future
tax liabilities are probably discounted at a higher rate than future interest claims against the
government.

For a recent and complex argument as to why government bonds should not comprise
part of net wealth, see Robert J. Barro, "Are Government Bonds Net Wealth?" *Journal of
Political Economy,* Vol. 82, No. 6 (Nov./Dec. 1974), pp. 1095–1117.

sented either by government bonds and real capital assets or by their equity claim equivalents, ought to rise. Feeling wealthier, individuals are led to buy more of all assets in their portfolios. Additionally, certain formulations of the consumption function contain wealth variables. Thus, increases in wealth can also affect the purchase of consumer nondurables.

Credit Availability Effects. Again, we quote from Warren Smith in order to describe the operation of this channel:

> The portfolio and wealth effects appear to constitute the basic channels through which monetary policy has its initial impact on economic activity. In addition, however, the institutional arrangements for providing financing to certain sectors of the economy may be such as to give monetary policy a special leverage over the availability of credit to these sectors, thereby affecting their ability to spend.[43]

The housing industry is a special example of the operation of credit availability and often gives rise to the Keynesian complaint that monetary policy is discriminatory.

The above three effects can be labeled *initial*, to be followed by *secondary* effects:

> Working through portfolio effects, wealth effects, and credit availability effects, the initial impacts of monetary policy will generate additional income, and this will further increase the demand for consumer nondurable goods and services. It will also expand the demand for services of durable goods, thereby giving a further boost to the desired stocks of these goods. Thus, the familiar magnification of demand through multiplier and accelerator effects comes into play.[44]

neo-Fisherian view

As the following quotation from Friedman and Meiselman[45] shows, as far as the substitution effect is concerned, absolutely no difference exists between the two schools. Preceding the quotation, Friedman and Meiselman have supposed that the Federal Reserve has purchased Treasury bills:

> In order to persuade holders of Government bills to sell them, the monetary authorities had to make it attractive for them to do so. This means

---

[43] "A Neo-Keynesian View of Monetary Policy," pp. 107–9.

[44] *Ibid.*, p. 109.

[45] Milton Friedman and David Meiselman, "The Relative Stability of Monetary Velocity," pp. 219–21. Reprinted by Permission of Prentice-Hall, Inc., Englewood Cliffs, New Jersey.

that the initial effect of the open-market operation is twofold: it made prices of bills higher (i.e., yields on them lower) than they otherwise would have been; it changed the structure of assets held by the community—excluding of course the monetary authorities. The community now holds a larger nominal amount of Government bills yielding less on the market than prior to the open-market operation.

If money and bills (or perfect substitutes for bills) were the only form in which the community held assets . . . this would be the end of effects on existing balance sheets. For any further effects we would have to look for the effect of the changed bill yield on expenditures financed by borrowing in the form of bills or of the changed income from bills on expenditures.

Given other assets, this is far from the end of the matter. Since the community voluntarily exchanged bills for money under the inducement of a higher price, there is a sense in which its new balance sheet is a "desired" or "equilibrium" balance sheet. But the sense is a highly restricted one. The balance sheet is in momentary but not longer-run equilibrium. The major function of money and the basic source of its social utility is to enable individuals to avoid barter by separating the purchase of particular goods from the sale of particular goods. Money is a temporary abode of purchasing power to which the proceeds from attractive selling opportunities can be added pending decisions what to buy and from which attractive buying opportunities can be financed pending the finding of attractive selling opportunities. Money performs this function no less in the market for assets than in the market for current services. In our example, individuals parted with bills for money because they saw an attractive selling opportunity. But this does not mean that they want to hold the new amount of money indefinitely or even for any very long period. The shift to money is more likely to be a temporary shift which is simply an intermediate step in the rearrangement of the balance sheet in light of the altered circumstances.

The initial change in the structure of assets therefore introduces a deviation between the structure of assets desired under the new circumstances and the actual structure; the community holds more money and fewer assets other than bills than it desires. It will seek to correct this discrepancy by converting money into other assets. Let us suppose that the community first turns to marketable securities. In the process of trying to acquire more of them, it will of course bid up their prices (i.e., lower the yield on them), since the amount available at any point of time is fixed. But this will again introduce a disequilibrium in the balance sheet and induce the community to continue the process further, say, by trying to shift to nonmarketable securities and to real assets. In this way, the process of readjusting the portfolio leads to a bidding up of the prices not only of fixed money claims but also of equities and such real assets as houses, land, and the like. The rises in the prices of such assets raises "the" price level and so contributes to reducing the apparent "excess" money stock by reducing its real value, thereby moderating the changes in interest rates needed to achieve equilibrium.

The rise in the nominal price of real assets (i.e., the fall in rates of interest) has further effects. On the supply side, it makes it more profitable to produce such assets and hence leads to an increase in the demand for resources employed in their production, and perhaps a bidding up of the prices of such resources. On the demand side, the rise in prices will temper the rise in amount demanded because it means a rise in the prices of assets relative to the current prices of services. It now becomes cheaper, for example, to acquire housing services by renting a house instead of buying one, to acquire the services of automobiles by renting the use of an automobile rather than buying one, and so on down the line. The readjustment of the portfolio, whose first impact we have assumed to be directed towards the acquisition of additional assets, therefore produces a partly offsetting shift toward direct acquisition of services, in the process widening the range of goods for which the money demand increases. This is equivalent to saying that lower interest rates lead to an increase in what is generally termed consumption expenditures relative to what is generally termed saving or investment.

Of course, we describe the process in this particular order only for expositional purposes. The first impact may be on goods rather than securities. And more generally, the readjustment will take place simultaneously in all areas, though perhaps at a faster rate in some than in others. An initial increase in the stock of money will tend, via its impact on the demand for other assets, to produce an increase in money expenditures on all varieties of them and hence on both what is termed investment and what is termed consumption; it will tend, *via* its impact on the relative prices of assets and flows of services, to produce an increase in money expenditures for consumer services and hence a further increase in what are termed consumption expenditures. Whether the reaction is manifested sooner in investment expenditures or in consumption expenditures, whether the major quantitative effect is on the one or the other, whether the effect is mostly in prices or quantities, what the initial and subsequent impacts are on interest rates—these are all matters that depend on the speed with which the economic participants react, on the technical problems involved in readjusting various categories of expenditures, on the state of supply conditions and employment at the time in question, and the like.

Notwithstanding that the above quotation is virtually identical in substance with the quote from Smith, an attempt is made to make it appear different, to differentiate the product so to speak. This is done in several ways by both Friedman and Brunner.

For example, we are told by Brunner:

At present, a broad consensus accepts the relevance of money and monetary policy with respect to economic activity. But this consensus concerning the relevance of money emerges from *two substantially different* views about the nature of the transmission mechanism. One view is the Keynesian conception . . . [in which] the interest rate is the main link between money and economic activity. According to this other view, output and employment are explained by a suitable application of relative price theory.[46]

However, three paragraphs later, Brunner says:

The operation of relative prices between money, financial assets, and real assets may be equivalently interpreted as the working of an interest rate mechanism (prices and yield of assets are inversely related). Monetary impulses are thus transmitted by the play of interest rates. . . .

In a similar vein, Friedman states:

The Keynesians regard a change in the quantity of money as affecting, in the first instance, "the" interest rate, interpreted as a market rate on a fairly narrow class of financial liabilities. They regard spending as affected only "indirectly" as the changed interest rate alters the profitability of investment spending, again interpreted fairly narrowly, and investment spending, through the multiplier affects total spending.[47]

Surely, given the statement of the neo-Keynesian position on the substitution effect by Smith, these statements by Brunner and Friedman are designed to create a distinction where none exists.

A possible difference between the two schools related to the substitution effect has to do with the purchase of consumer nondurables. Consistent with the Keynesian approach is the view that new investment spending (on either producer or consumer durables) following a reduction in interest rates produces (via the multiplier) a rise in disposable income. This in turn leads to an increase in spending on consumer nondurable goods. In the Monetarist approach, no mention is made of the multiplier, and consumer spending on nondurable goods could, in fact,

---

[46] Karl Brunner, "The Role of Money and Monetary Policy," *Review, Federal Reserve Bank of St. Louis* (July 1968), p. 18. Italics added.

[47] *NBER Occasional Paper No. 112*, p. 28. In their final summations, both Brunner and Friedman have expressed the view that "the difference in this area [the transmission mechanism] between the Monetarists and the Keynesians is not in the nature of the process, but in the range of assets considered." If the statement by Smith is taken to be the neo-Keynesian view, this opinion is quite misleading. Quote taken from Friedman, *The Counter-Revolution in Monetary Theory*, p. 25. For a similar opinion by Brunner, see "A Survey of Selected Issues in Monetary Theory," p. 56.

precede spending on producer and consumer durables depending on how the money supply is increased.

But because the Monetarists in general do not regard government interest-bearing debt as wealth, any open-market operation which exchanges money for such interest-bearing debt produces a wealth effect. Friedman's description of the operation of this wealth adjustment process is reminiscent of a description of the classical direct mechanism:

> We, on the other hand, stress a much broader and more "direct" impact on spending. Saying that individuals seeking to dispose of what they regard as their excess money balances . . . will try to pay out a larger sum for the purchase of securities, goods and services, for the repayment of debts, and as gifts than they are receiving from the corresponding sources.[48]

Since variations in the money stock always produce a wealth effect, Friedman is unconcerned with how money gets into the system and in a recent essay has supposed it to be dropped on households from a helicopter.[49] This wealth effect of the Monetarists is clearly inconsistent with the neo-Keynesian approach and differentiates them from the latter.[50] Thus, in the Monetarist approach, when an individual sells his government securities for cash, he is as likely to purchase pantry and boudoir stocks for his household as to purchase a substitute financial asset for that given up; such is the effect produced by the adjustment to an increase in net wealth.

Moreover, the change in the interest rate following an open-market operation would probably not, in the Monetarist framework, generate a wealth effect via private or government bonds unless different interest rates were used to discount the asset and liability streams each bond represents.

Unlike the neo-Keynesians, the Monetarists would regard open-market operations *per se* as producing a wealth effect, for a bond (both

---

[48] *Ibid*. While this quotation is taken to be an explanation of the wealth effect, it may, however, merely be Friedman's shorthand description of a complicated substitution adjustment process. This can be seen if it is remembered that in the portfolios are consumer durable goods, which because they yield a stream of services are regarded as wealth. However, no identifiable or market quoted yield corresponds to these assets. Nevertheless, if the Treasury bill rate falls, it can have a potential demand effect on these durables through a portfolio substitution process. But since the yield on these units of wealth is implicit and does not appear in any financial market, it may appear as though excess money balances (those received in exchange for the bills) were exchanged directly for goods even though a relative interest rate mechanism actually explains the adjustment.

[49] "The Optimum Quantity of Money," p. 11.

[50] However, in a recent statement by the Monetarists, recognition is given to the fact that some portion of government bonds may be regarded as wealth. See Roger W. Spencer, "Channels of Monetary Influence, A Survey," *Review—Federal Reserve Bank of St. Louis* (Nov. 1974), pp. 22–23.

an asset and a liability) is taken from the system and a pure asset, money (both inside and outside), is its replacement. Thus, the nominal wealth of society rises.

However, as with the neo-Keynesians, a fall in interest rates ought to raise the market value of the existing capital stock or its equity equivalent, thereby raising the nominal wealth of society. Both wealth effects ought to lead to the purchase of all portfolio assets including consumer durables.

As for the credit-rationing channel, it is totally rejected by Brunner:

> The relative price theory rejects emphatically the idea that the housing industry forms a focal locus of monetary policy, through which the major force of monetary impulses must be channeled in order to swing the whole economy in the desired direction.[51]

His rejection is based upon several grounds. First, he believes that the credit-rationing argument, which views monetary policy as discriminatory, is wrong because the effects of money are not limited to one or a few channels. Second, the credit-rationing argument is used to rationalize the use of fiscal policy, which he believes to have a limited and uncertain impact. Third, he believes that the acknowledged instability in housing results from variability in monetary and fiscal policy combined with rigid price-fixing in the form of ceiling rates on time deposits and share accounts of savings-and-loan associations. Thus rising interest rates, due to either expansionary monetary policy or heavy Treasury borrowing, lead to disintermediation and a decrease in the availability of mortgage funds whenever the ceiling rates are exceeded.[52]

summary—transmission mechanism

Given that each side uses a similar portfolio or stock adjustment mechanism to explain the transmission of monetary impulses to the real sector, it can be concluded that as far as the neo-Keynesians are concerned, money matters. How much it matters is, however, an empirical, not a theoretical, question.[53] We do find the two sides differing somewhat on the nature of the wealth effects generated by money.

One additional point ought to be made about the neo-Keynesians. For them the portfolio adjustment process can be set in motion by a

[51] "A Survey of Selected Issues in Monetary Theory," pp. 53–55.

[52] Ibid.

[53] Since Brunner calls the portfolio adjustment mechanism the "weak Monetarist thesis," we are all Monetarists now; some, no doubt, weak ones.

change in the relative supply of any asset in the portfolio, not only money (for example, the supply of equities). So long as velocity is sensitive to the money rate of interest, an effect on the real sector can be expected. While such a view is consistent with the neo-Fisherian approach, it is not emphasized in their literature.

Despite the fact that both sides employ a similar approach to explain how money influences the real sector, they exhibit markedly different preferences in the construction of econometric models to explain the influence of money. The neo-Keynesian approach has been to construct elaborated structural relationships which spell out in relatively great detail how money is supposed to work its influence. The Monetarists, on the other hand, believing the process to be so complicated as to make adequate description impossible, prefer simple single-equation models of the type introduced by the St. Louis Federal Reserve Bank (which are examined below).

The *IS–LM* Framework and Monetary Theory

How has consideration of the portfolio adjustment mechanism affected the ability of the *IS–LM* apparatus to explain monetary theory? In the neo-Keynesian analysis, so long as only the substitution effect is considered, the slopes of the two schedules provide a relatively simple means to describe the adjustment process. However, once wealth effects are acknowledged, then the schedules themselves must shift to reflect the effect of wealth on consumption, investment, and money demand. Thus, *IS* and *LM* schedules are no longer independent of each other, and shifts in the *LM* schedule may induce shifts in the *IS* curve. To that extent, the explanation process becomes much more complicated and is often omitted from standard textbooks.

Brunner objects to the theoretical approach embodied in the *IS–LM* apparatus, or as he calls it, "the ruling paradigm," because he believes that constraining the theory to these two schedules has implied that only their slope properties are relevant in judging the usefulness of monetary and fiscal policies, whereas:

The relative price process involving the whole spectrum of assets and liabilities, connecting the production of new assets and liabilities with the existing assets and liabilities, introduced substitution and wealth adjustment channels which operate independently of the slope of the two curves and occur as shifts of the *IS* and *LM* curves. These shift properties supplement the slope properties in the transmission of monetary impulses. The relative price theory thus describes important channels of monetary influences which could not be subsumed under a Keynesian analysis. The heavy emphasis on the shift properties . . . converts the traditional *IS–LM* diagram into a rather inconvenient description.[54]

From this we can conclude that if one takes the simple *IS–LM* framework as a sophisticated statement of the Keynesian view, the neo-Fisherians have made a valid point that their slope properties do not summarize all the relevant channels of monetary influence. On the other hand, when regarded in a reasonable way as a relatively simple abstraction of a more complicated process, Brunner's criticism appears to be much ado about nothing.[55]

Later, in discussing fiscal policy, a further omission in the usual *IS–LM* analysis will be explored.

The Cause of Cyclical Disturbances

The issue involved here concerns the source of the periodic business cycles experienced in most market economies. The prior discussion of Gibson's Paradox revealed the two fundamentally differing views. One side holds that variations in the growth rate of the money stock are the cause, whereas the other side finds the source in the real-sector–investor expectations.

As viewed by Harry Johnson,

This . . . is . . . the crux of the issue prevailing between Keynesians and Monetarists: the Keynesian position is that the real economy is highly unstable and that monetary management has both little relevance to it and little control over it; the Monetarist position, on the contrary, is that the real economy is inherently fairly stable, but can be destabilized by monetary developments, which therefore, need to be controlled as far as possible by intelligent monetary policy. The monetarist position . . . seems to me the only alternative consistent with the facts . . . of historical experience.[56]

The choice of the word *unstable* to characterize the real sector was unfortunate, for in commenting on a similar Monetarist assertion,

[54] "The 'Monetarist Revolution' in Monetary Theory," pp. 4–5. Despite frequent attacks upon the paradigm, Brunner and Meltzer say in a recent paper: "If we were willing to assume that changes in the stock of government securities held by the public have no effect on wealth . . . our model could be pressed into the standard *IS–LM* framework." See their "Money, Debt and Economic Activity", p. 953.

[55] This is not to imply that the *IS–LM* framework does not suffer other shortcomings, especially its difficulty in handling the effects of price expectations. His criticism also means that any description of the aftermath of an increase in the money supply is likely to be complicated, involving both the slopes of the schedules as well as shifts in them.

[56] *Inflation and the Monetarist Controversy*, pp. 6–7.

Lawrence Klein objected to this as a characteristic of the neo-Keynesian position:

> I don't think it is correct to say that Post-Keynesians contend that the economy is inherently unstable. They may contend that it is oscillatory or subject to fluctuations and it has a tendency to move about a position of underemployment equilibrium, but this is far different from saying that the economy is unstable.[57]

Klein apparently interprets *unstable* to mean that if an economy is pushed from a point of equilibrium, its oscillations diverge in larger and larger swings rather than converging toward a new equilibrium. However, the Monetarists appear to mean that the Keynesian analysis implies that the *IS* schedule is more variable than the *LM,* due either to exogenous changes in the business community's long-run profit anticipations or to animal spirits; and moreover, that small changes in investment, through the multiplier and accelerator process, produce rather large changes in output.

If we accept the neo-Fisherian definition of *unstable,* it accords well with both Keynes and the neo-Keynesian view of the business cycle. For example, Arthur Okun states:

> Recessions did not just happen; they reflect the vulnerability of an industrial economy to cumulative movements upward and downward. While they have diverse specific causes, cyclical fluctuations can usually be viewed as the result of imbalances between the growth of productive capacity and the growth of final demand for its output. . . . If the growth of final demand . . . keeps pace . . . the increase in fixed and working capital normally turns out to be profitable. The expansionary decisions of businessmen are thus validated, and further expansion is encouraged. . . . If . . . final demand fails to grow sufficiently to make use of growing capacity, businessmen have an incentive to slow down the expansion. . . .
>
> Two recessions emerged in the 1957–60 period because expansions had not enough vigor to be self-sustaining. The slow advance failed to make use of existing capital; hence, incentives to invest deteriorated and the economy turned down.[58]

The neo-Fisherian view is diametrically opposite to the above. The real sector is regarded as fundamentally stable and they:

> . . . argue . . . that the major *instabilities* and *uncertainties* of the

[57] Lawrence Klein, "The State of the Monetarist Debate," Review—*Federal Reserve Bank of St. Louis* (Sept. 1973), p. 11.

[58] *The Political Economy of Prosperity,* pp. 34, 43.

economic process result from the behavior of the government sector. The uncertainties pertain, in particular, to the tax and expenditure programs to be
pursued and the actions of regulatory agencies. The instability refers mostly
to monetary, credit and fiscal policy.[59]

Thus, as viewed by the Monetarists:

Large changes in the growth rate of money become a main source of
instability . . . the Federal Reserve permits or forces the stock of money to
grow at too high or too low a rate for too long a time. Excessive expansions
and contractions of money become the main cause of the fluctuations in output and of inflations or deflations. Inappropriate public policies, not changes
in private expenditures, become the main cause of instability.[60]

Neo-Fisherians do not deny that variations in private spending may
affect the growth rate of nominal GNP, but these variations are largely
caused by the uncertainties attached to various government programs.
For example, Friedman and Schwartz note with approval the analysis of
Kenneth Roose attributing to government policy the very low level of
private investment during the period 1933–1941.[61]

This belief in the inherent stability of the private sector has
recognizable counterparts in the theoretical work of both Friedman and
Brunner and Meltzer. Friedman's views on stability are to be found in
his *Restatement*. There the hypothesis was set forth that the demand for
money or velocity was fundamentally stable and changed slowly and
gradually over time. Thus, major short-run changes in nominal income
must be due to changes in the supply of money, over which the central
bank has control, so that cyclical fluctuations can be attributed to the
monetary authorities.

The belief in private sector stability is to be found in the Brunner–
Meltzer money supply hypothesis.[62] With reference to Equation (10:11),

[59] Karl Brunner, "The 'Monetarist Revolution' in Monetary Theory," p. 6.

[60] Allan Meltzer, "The Role of Money: Comment," *Controlling Monetary Aggregates*, p. 29.

[61] *A Monetary History of the United States, 1867–1960*. Among government programs
reducing the incentive to invest, Roose mentions the NIRA, National Labor Relations Act,
minimum wage laws, social security taxes, Federal provision for unemployment compensation,
the Undistributed Profits Tax Law, Securities Act of 1933 and the Securities Exchange Act of
1934, restrictions on public utility holding companies, the TVA, the Home Owners Loan
Corporation, the Federal Farm Mortgage Corporation, the nationalization of gold, unbalanced
budgets, Roosevelt's attacks on monopoly and "economic royalists," the attempt to reorganize
the Supreme Court, the rise of the CIO–AFL and the Sit-Down Strike, etc. The effect of all of
these proposals: (1) reduced profitability of business, (2) weakened business confidence, (3)
expanded government into areas traditionally reserved for businessmen and (4) threatened the
sanctity of private contracts and property.

[62] This hypothesis is analyzed in great detail below.

$MS = B(m)$, the stability thesis requires that the dominant cause of changes in the money supply must be changes in the base, B, over which the central bank has control. If changes in the multiplier, m, dominate, the dynamics of the private sector (business expectations, portfolio decisions by banks and private citizens) may be the principal cause of economic fluctuations—to the extent that these decisions are not induced by uncertainties attached to various government policies.

In summary, our discussion of this issue reveals that the Thornton–Fisher versus Keynes–Wicksell debate as to the cause of the cycle is still alive and well in the last third of the twentieth century.

The Role of Fiscal Policy

A discussion of fiscal policy must first distinguish its ability to allocate resources from its ability to stabilize economic activity. In the former role, fiscal policy affects the allocation of resources between the private and public sectors. Higher rates of government expenditures and taxation together serve to allocate an increasing share of GNP to the public sector.

Concerning its ability to stabilize economic activity, variations in government spending and taxation are designed to be compensatory or to offset variations in private expenditures which, left to themselves, would produce a business cycle.

For the pre-Keynesian classical writers, fiscal policy was accorded an allocation role, but as their theory implied that the economy always tended toward full employment, a stabilization role was deemed unnecessary. Thus, the resources used by the public sector were obtained by voluntarily "crowding out" an equivalent use of those resources by the private sector.

For Keynes and the neo-Keynesians, the ability of fiscal policy to stabilize an economy became the *pièce de résistance* for achieving and maintaining full employment in a world which, they believed, tended toward an unemployment equilibrium. For two reasons fiscal policy was preferred to monetary policy. First, in the case of an inelastic *IS* schedule or a perfectly elastic *LM* schedule, money did not matter. Second, fiscal policy, by directly and immediately altering the disposable income of consumers and profitability of investors, had a faster impact than monetary policy, which acted through an indirect interest-rate process.

For many neo-Keynesians fiscal policy continues to be of the first importance. During the era of the "New Economics" the calibration of fiscal policy was refined in terms of a relative full-employment measure rather than an absolute sum. The supremacy of fiscal policy was supposedly achieved in 1964, when a major tax cut and rate revision was engineered by the New Economists to get America moving again.[63]

Warren Smith provides a brief description of the neo-Keynesian view of fiscal policy which is worth repeating because it brings out what many in that school appear to believe is the principal point at issue between them and the Monetarists: The slope of the LM schedule.

An increase in government purchases of goods and services, with tax rates constant, would affect the economy by three different routes. First, there would be a direct expansionary *income effect* resulting from the purchase of output by the government. Second, there would be an expansionary *wealth effect* as the private sector, experiencing an increment to its wealth entirely in the form of net claims against the government, increased its demand for real capital in an effort to diversify its portfolios. These income and wealth effects would set off a multiplier—accelerator process of economic expansion. The expansion, in turn, would activate a partially offsetting monetary effect as the rise in income increased the demand for money. If the dial settings of the monetary instruments remained unchanged, this would drive up interest rates. The rise in interest rates would cause some reductions in those types of expenditures that were sensitive to interest rates through portfolio, wealth and availability effects.[64]

The wealth effect of fiscal policy may be quite powerful, particularly because it is cumulative—that is, it continues to operate until the budget has been brought back into balance, thereby shutting off the increase in net claims against the government. . . .

If we neglect the wealth effect . . . we are left with the income effect and the offsetting monetary effect. The monetary effect will be greater (a) the greater the proportion of expenditures in GNP that are affected by interest rates, (b) the greater (in absolute value) is the average interest elasticity of these expenditures, (c) the greater is the income elasticity of demand for

[63] According to Arthur Okun, the same stimulus could have been achieved by monetary policy, but the fiscal route was chosen because the balance of payments could not stand the low interest rates the necessary monetary expansion would have entailed. See *The Political Economy of Prosperity*, pp. 57–58.

[64] In this first paragraph Smith defines and distinguishes a fiscal from a monetary act. The former involves changes in government spending or taxation, holding the money stock constant. The Monetarists have always contended that the Keynesians never clearly distinguish between the two. In particular, when Walter Heller and Arthur Okun computed the GNP impact of the 1964 tax cut they defined a neutral monetary policy in terms of maintaining a constant interest rate. Thus, since the Federal Reserve maintained such a neutral policy, all the rise in GNP subsequent to the tax cut was attributed to fiscal policy. However, Friedman was quick to point out that to keep the rate constant, the Fed was forced to increase the rate of money creation. It was because of this higher growth rate that the GNP grew as it did. Thus, the tax cut was really the device used to implement monetary policy and a majority of the GNP growth ought to be attributed to money, not to the fiscal act of cutting taxes. Because of this exchange between Friedman and Heller, the neo-Keynesians and Monetarists now agree that a pure fiscal policy act must be defined as Smith defines it.

money, (d) the smaller (in absolute value) is the interest elasticity of demand for money and (e) the smaller is the interest elasticity of the supply of money.

Only if the interest elasticity of both the demand for and supply of money are zero will the monetary effect completely cancel out the income effect. . . . Since the empirical evidence is overwhelming that both money demand and money supply possess some degree of interest elasticity, it seems clear that fiscal policy is capable of exerting an independent effect on income.[65]

Unmentioned by Smith, the neo-Keynesian analysis of the effectiveness of temporary changes in taxes had undergone searching reassessment with the formulation of the life-cycle theory of the consumption function by Modigliani–Ando–Brumberg and the permanent income theory formulated by Friedman. Both theories imply that transitory changes in taxes will have little effect on consumption and, hence, economic activity.

The neo-Fisherian assessment of fiscal policy is aimed at showing that it does not have a direct and immediate effect on economic activity. Rather, in Friedman's words, the effect of discretionary fiscal policy ". . . is certain to be temporary and likely to be minor,"[66] with any sustainable effect depending upon how the government operations are financed. Friedman's words would suggest that a crucial issue between the Monetarists and the neo-Keynesians is not so much the effectiveness of monetary policy, but the effectiveness of fiscal policy. Thus the slope, or interest elasticity, of the *LM* schedule should be of critical importance. The more inelastic it becomes the less effective is fiscal policy, for inelasticity causes a large crowd-out effect from changes in government expenditures (that is, they merely displace an equal amount of private expenditures).

It is for this reason that among Keynesians, at least Smith and Tobin believe that the main issue between them and Friedman is "the shape of the *LM* locus."[67] Not so, says Friedman: ". . . the main issue between us clearly is not and never has been whether the *LM* curve is vertical or has a positive slope"[68] . . . for:

. . . both Monetarists and neo-Keynesians accept the *LM* curve as positively sloped and, nevertheless, come out with very different conclusions on many issues, particularly the effects of fiscal and monetary policy.[69]

[65] "A Neo-Keynesian View of Monetary Policy," pp. 111–12.
[66] "Comments on the Critics," p. 915.
[67] James Tobin, "Friedman's Theoretical Framework," p. 853.
[68] "Comments on the Critics," p. 917.
[69] Ibid., p. 915.

How is it that both sides can accept the *LM* schedule as positively sloped, but Friedman can conclude that discretionary fiscal policy will have an effect which is "certain to be temporary and likely to be minor?"

To answer this question, he has conveniently analyzed a tax increase in terms of *IS* and *LM* schedules. The effect of the tax hike is certain to be temporary:

> Because the leftward shift in the *IS* curve is a once-for-all shift, even though the reduced deficit or increased surplus produced by the tax rise with no change in government spending were to continue indefinitely.[70]

However, if a budget surplus produced by the tax hike did emerge, it would recur each year and would be used to retire the interest-bearing debt of the government. If this debt were purchased from the central bank, the money supply would contract sliding the LM schedule continuously leftward. Such a slide would, in the longer run, be the dominant force reducing income. Hence, the once-for-all influence of the shift in the *IS* schedule is thought by Friedman to exert a temporary influence. It is likely to be minor:

> Because the Monetarists view is that "saving" and "investment" have to be interpreted much more broadly than neo-Keynesians tend to interpret it, that the categories of spending affected by the change in interest rates are far broader than business capital formation, housing construction, and inventory accumulation to which the neo-Keynesians tend to restrict "investment."[71] Hence, even a fairly substantial tax increase will produce only a minor shift in the *IS* curve. Further, while the *LM* curve slopes positively, it is very far from being horizontal, so that the reduction in income associated with a "minor" shift in the *IS* curve will also be minor.[72]

However, despite his disclaimer, the slope of the *LM* locus is far

---

[70] *Ibid.*

[71] Apparently in Friedman's concept of affairs, boudoir and pantry supplies are to carry the main burden of adjustment.

[72] *Ibid.*, p. 915. In another source, Friedman has said of fiscal policy: "I believe that the state of the government budget matters; matters a great deal—for some things. The state of the government budget determines what fraction of the nation's income is spent through the government and what fraction is spent by individuals privately. The state of the government budget determines what the level of our taxes is, how much of our income we turn over to the government. The state of the government budget has a considerable effect on interest rates. If the Federal Government runs a large deficit, this means the government has to borrow in the markets, which raises the demand for loanable funds and so tends to raise interest rates. . . . But—and I come to my main point—in my opinion, the state of the budget itself has no significant effect on the course of nominal income, on inflation, on deflation, or on cyclical fluctuations." See *Monetary vs. Fiscal Policy* (New York: Norton, 1969), pp. 50–51.

from being insignificant in terms of his conclusion as to the temporary and minor effects of fiscal policy.

Friedman's analysis of a tax reduction brings out his belief that the method of financing a deficit is of crucial importance. The tax reduction will result in a once-for-all shift in the *IS* schedule to the right, a higher interest rate and a higher level of spending.[73] But if the deficit is financed by creating money, the *LM* curve shifts to the right at a more rapid rate.

> But this is not a once-for-all shift. So long as the deficit continues, and continues to be financed by creating money, the nominal money stock continues to grow and the *LM* curve (at initial prices) continues to move to the right. Is there any doubt that this effect must swamp the effect of the once-for-all shift in the *IS* curve?[74]

As in the case of the tax hike analyzed above, in the short run the effect of the shift in the *IS* curve will clearly dominate the movement in income. When a longer-run view is taken, the *LM* schedule will exert the dominant influence on subsequent changes in income. When it comes to a bond-financed deficit, Friedman is a little ambiguous. He asserts that some crowd-out will occur:

> The total nominal volume of debt grows by less—and I believe much less—than the size of the deficit. Moreover, even this growth is offset by two other factors: the increase expected in future tax liabilities accompanying the growth of the government debt . . . and the reduction in the physical volume of assets created because of lowered private productive investment.[75]

However, as long as the deficit continues, even with perfect crowd-out, the stock of bonds will accumulate relative to the stock of money, which must, if reasonable portfolio balance is to be maintained, increase the

---

[73] Consistent with his previous analysis would be the view that the tax cut would not shift the *IS* schedule out very far because the tendency for interest rates to rise would reduce a myriad of other durable expenditures, which would work to offset the rise in disposable income available to consumers. Friedman appears to claim that a broadened interpretation of saving and investment results in smaller shifts in the *IS* schedule in response to either tax increases or reductions. This is clearly incorrect. The broadened interpretation of saving and investment will produce a more elastic *IS* schedule than that acknowledged by Keynesians; however, the degree to which the *IS* schedule shifts in response to a tax change is independent of its slope. Nevertheless, a flatter *IS* schedule shifted along any *LM* schedule with positive slope will result in a smaller change in real income than would a similar shift in a more inelastic *IS* schedule. Thus, Friedman may be correct, but his analysis is faulty. For proof of this, see T. Norman Van Cott, and Gary Santoni, "Friedman versus Tobin: A Comment," *Journal of Political Economy*, Vol. 82, No. 4 (July/Aug. 1974), pp. 883–85.

[74] "Comments on the Critics," p. 916.

[75] "Comments on the Critics," p. 917.

demand for money, shifting the *LM* schedule leftward at a more rapid rate and exerting a contracting influence on the economy. Blinder and Solow have shown that in this case where fiscal policy is impotent in a longer-run context, the economy is unstable, that is, once an initial equilibrium with a balanced budget is disturbed to produce a deficit in the budget, we get cumulative decreases in income.[76]

Karl Brunner is in general agreement with the view that fiscal policy does not have a direct and immediate impact:

> Changes in government expenditures or tax parameters operate on economic activity via the same relative price mechanism which conveys monetary impulses. The Keynesian notion of a "direct influence" exerted by fiscal variables, as against an "indirect effect" of money working through a complex chain, loses all meaning in the context of a relative price analysis of the transmission mechanism.[77]

In judging the probable effect of fiscal policy, Brunner analyzes government purchases of existing real assets, current output of goods, and the current services of labor. Each type of purchase sets in motion various wealth and substitution effects which may be mutually reinforcing or work at cross purposes. Like Friedman, he and Meltzer conclude:

> . . . the analysis provides a foundation for the proposition that changes in budgetary variables (government expenditures or taxes) exert by themselves relatively little effect on economic activity or price levels. The crucial effect depends on the manner of financing.[78]

To the extent that government spending and tax policies are by themselves expansionary on balance, the Monetarists are conceding points to the Keynesians. In Tobin's words: "The camel's nose is in the tent."

[76] Alan Blinder and Robert Solow, "Does Fiscal Policy Matter?" *Journal of Public Economics*, No. 2 (1973), pp. 319–37. However, Blinder and Solow assert that Friedman's conclusions on the impotency of fiscal policy follow from his belief that a wealth effect on the demand for money produces a leftward shift in the *LM* curve and that this wealth effect follows from an imperfect discounting of the tax liability attached to the bond. This conclusion is absolutely at variance with Friedman's oft-stated position. However, the same effect can be produced by assuming that government bonds accumulate relative to money even if they do not add to net wealth.

[77] "A Survey of Selected Issues in Monetary Theory," pp. 47–48.

[78] Karl Brunner and Allan Meltzer, "Fiscal and Monetary Policy in a non-Keynesian World," unpublished, p. 57. In "A Survey of Selected Issues," Brunner notes that money-creation financing has "substantial expansionary repercussions," whereas bond financing has "ambiguous repercussions" on aggregate demand and economic activity. Brunner is aware that results of empirical studies by the St. Louis Federal Reserve Bank show pure fiscal policy to have some effect on economic activity. These results cannot be neglected—hence, they have "ambiguous repercussions" rather than no repercussions. The St. Louis results are reported in a subsequent section.

Perhaps the Monetarist view of discretionary fiscal policy is best summarized by David Fand:

> To the monetarist, the impact of fiscal action will depend crucially on *how the government deficit is financed:* expenditures financed either by taxing or borrowing involve a transfer of resources (from the public to the government), with both interest rate and wealth effects in private portfolios, but the net effect of a temporary change in fiscal policy on spending may be ambiguous. Similarly, the effect of a reduction in taxes on private demand, financed through borrowing, will depend on (1) the extent to which it is viewed as a permanent or temporary, tax cut, and (2) its effect on market interest rates. Accordingly, the direct income-generating effect of a deficit— the pure fiscal effect—may be quite small and uncertain. On the other hand, if the deficit is financed through money creation by the banking system—if the deficit is monetized—the effect is unambiguously expansionary.[79]

Whether this unambiguously expansionary effect is permanent or not returns us to the Monetarist position on the Phillip's curve and the neutrality of money. Accordingly, a monetized deficit will likely be transitory and, in the longer run, merely serve to inflate the price level.

While most of the preceding discussion of fiscal policy has centered on its stabilization, or short-run, role, both sides also recognize its longer-run, or allocative, role. The neo-Keynesian view is discussed extensively in various texts on public finance and will not be repeated here. The neo-Fisherian position is best stated by Fand:

> If we move away from short run stabilization problems and focus on the longer run allocative effects of alternative policies, there appears to be a reversal of positions. Thus, suppose it was necessary for the Government to select a policy to effect a permanent change in the rate of capital formation. Monetarists would have to find some fiscal policy while (some) Fiscalists would seek to achieve this result with monetary policy. Although Monetarists believe that control of the money stock is the appropriate and preferred instrument for dealing with stabilization problems, they also believe that monetary actions have their permanent effects on prices. As a consequence, it follows that fiscal policy may be the only instrument to bring about permanent

---

[79] "Some Issues in Monetary Economics," p. 24. Italics in the original. In a companion piece Fand states: "The Monetarists' view is that the *ceteris paribus* fiscal effects on aggregate demand may be uncertain and subject to lags, that these effects are not entirely dependable or easily predictable, and that the important long-run allocation effects implicit in the budget decision should not be sacrificed for the alleged short-run stabilization gains. For all these reasons, they do not view budget policy as an efficient stabilization instrument. Moreover, they also hold that the need for such discretionary fiscal action may be less urgent, to the extent that a stabilizing monetary policy is itself a powerful factor in eliminating the very forces that generate instability in the private economy." See his "Monetarism and Fiscalism," pp. 22–23.

changes in interest rates, capital formation (and possibly the long term rate of growth) as well as permanently changing the resource flow from the private to the public sector. . . .

. . . Since Monetarists postulate that in the long run money is essentially a veil (having its permanent effects primarily on prices) they would of necessity have to rely on some kind of fiscal action if public policy required some changes in interest rates and rates of return.[80]

The *IS–LM* Framework and Fiscal Policy

Much of the discussion on fiscal policy has referred explicitly to the *IS–LM* framework and it is popularly used to analyze the operation of fiscal policy. Various shortcomings have been attributed to this analytical framework, basically because of its neglect of the influence of the stock of government securities on the respective schedules.[81]

For example, assume that government spending increases and is bond-financed, and that all or part of the additional bonds used to finance the rise in expenditures are counted as wealth. In addition, assume that both the demand for money and desired consumption are positively related to wealth.

The rise in expenditures will shift IS_0 to IS_1 on a once-for-all basis. The expansion in income, by increasing the quantity of money demanded for transactions, will raise the interest rate. The rise in the deficit will necessitate a continual flow of bonds onto the financial market. To persuade individuals to purchase the bonds, the market interest rate must rise. Hence, point B cannot be one of equilibrium.

FIGURE 12:2.   A Bond-Financed Deficit

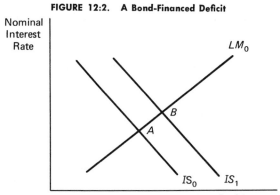

[80] "Monetarism and Fiscalism," pp. 23–24.

[81] See especially William Silber, "Fiscal Policy in *IS–LM* Analysis: A Correction," *Journal of Money, Credit and Banking*, Vol. 2, No. 4 (Nov. 1970), pp. 461–72.

By increasing wealth, the continual flow of government bonds onto the financial markets increases the demand for money, shifting the LM schedule continuously to the left, raising interest rates and contracting income. Ultimately, as the stock of bonds expands, the wealth effect on demand for money must be contractionary (that is, push the LM schedule along IS_1 to the left of point A). It should be noted that in his discussion of the effectiveness of fiscal policy, Warren Smith completely neglects this negative effect of wealth.

However, since the increase in wealth has a positive effect on consumption (and perhaps on the investment function as well), the IS schedule is shifted continuously to the right. Whether the net result of these two conflicting wealth effects is positive or negative depends on the relative wealth elasticities of consumption and money demand. Nevertheless, the interest rate will continue to rise and will probably produce a further negative wealth effect of the type identified in our discussion of the monetary transmission mechanism (that is, the market value of bonds and equities ought to fall).

Similarly, as Friedman noted above, a money-financed deficit will induce a continuous rightward shift in the LM schedule, producing the anomoly, in the Monetarist framework, of a continuous increase in the money supply causing falling interest rates. Quite clearly, a distinction between real and nominal rates would ultimately be called for, as would adjustments to the LM schedule for any changes in price increases.

If the deficit were to be financed by a mixed bond–money arrangement such that the increased money supply exactly offset the rise in money demand, a stable LM schedule would be a possibility.

Empirical Verification of the Causality of Money

While many economists have presented empirical estimates bearing on the causality of money, none have come near the scope and magnitude of Friedman and Schwartz's monumental *Monetary History of the United States*, supplemented in important respects by Phillip Cagan's *Determinants and Effects of Changes in the Money Stock*. These two works, augmented by some recent studies from the St. Louis Federal Reserve Bank, will form the basis for the discussion in this section.

Since it forms the focal point for analysis, it is worth repeating the conclusion which emerges from the work of Friedman and Schwartz:

Stated simply, it is that money does matter and matters very much. Changes in the quantity of money have important, and broadly predictable, economic effects. Long period changes in the quantity of money, relative to output, determine the secular behavior of prices. Substantial expansions in the quantity of money over short periods have been a major proximate source of the accompanying inflation in prices. Substantial contractions in the quantity of money over shorter periods have been a major factor in producing severe economic contractions. And cyclical variations in the quantity of money may well be an important element in the ordinary mild business cycle.[82]

Thus, their analysis is concerned with both the secular and cyclical swings of economic activity, and these are attributed to changes in the supply of money. In a later work, Friedman is somewhat more precise on the importance of money:

I do believe that changes in the supply of money have accounted for more than half the variance of money income for reasonably long periods and for changes measured over intervals of a year or more.[83]

Thus, the key issue which their data are supposed to resolve:

is not whether the direction of influence is wholly from money to business or wholly from business to money; it is whether the influence running from money to business is significant, in the sense that it can account for a substantial fraction of the fluctuations in economic activity.[84]

If it is, then in Fisher's words the cycle is largely a "dance of the dollar" rather than the dollar being largely a dance of the cycle.

To do justice to their work, it must be noted that Friedman and Schwartz caution the reader in many places that their findings are "suggestive of an influence running from money to business but they are by no means decisive" and "in a scientific problem, the final verdict is never in. Any conclusion must always be subject to revision in the light of new evidence." While such caveats are usual in work which is original and somewhat tentative, they also provide a handy screen behind which to hide when criticism is raised, thereby leaving the observer wondering about the substance and worth of their accomplishments.

Nevertheless, their tentative conclusions on the causality of money are based upon five different kinds of evidence, some assembled by themselves, others by their students and fellow practitioners largely associated with the National Bureau of Economic Research. Such evidence consists of: (1) qualitative historical circumstances, (2) the behavior of the determinants of the money stock, (3) consistency of timing on a positive

---

[82] "The Monetary Studies of the National Bureau," p. 49.

[83] Milton Friedman, "Money and Income: Post Hoc Ergo Prompter Hoc? A Comment," Quarterly Journal of Economics, Vol. 84, No. 2 (May 1970), p. 319.

[84] Friedman and Schwartz, "Money and the Business Cycle," p. 49.

and inverted basis, (4) serial correlation of amplitudes of cyclical phases, and (5) evidence from foreign countries. Our examination of the evidence will center on that found in the first three groups.

qualitative historical circumstances

The historical circumstances analyzed encompass both secular and cyclical phenomena, as well as a number of specific instances in which the money stock was changed either by the authorities or by events unrelated to contemporary economy activity. Friedman and Schwartz were interested in seeing whether these monetary changes induced subsequent changes in the same direction in economic activity. Our interest will center on the secular and cyclical evidence, for the latter class of specific instances are too numerous to evaluate in detail.

The secular events are the easier of the two to discuss. Friedman's conclusions are that "secular changes in the quantity of money relative to output determine the secular behavior of prices." Figure 12:3 records this relationship and, indeed, the correlation between the two series is remarkable. However, Friedman is quick to caution that while "there can be little doubt about this statistical connection" it ". . . tells nothing about the direction of influence . . ."—that is, does money cause changes in prices or do price changes cause changes in the money stock? His critics have ever since reminded him that correlation implies only covariability, not cause and effect. It is for this reason that attention

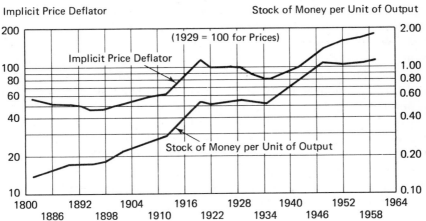

FIGURE 12:3.   Money–Price Level Relationship

Source: Milton Friedman, "The Supply of Money and Changes in Prices and Output," in *The Relationship of Prices to Economic Stability and Growth*, 85th Congress, 2nd Session, Joint Economic Committee (Washington, D.C.: U.S. Government Printing Office, March 31, 1958), p. 247.

has been placed on the cyclical relationship between money and economic activity in an attempt to show that the cycle is largely a "dance of the dollar."

In this endeavor, the approach of Friedman and Schwartz has been to accept the opinion of the NBER concerning the dating of various phases of the business cycle. The usual cycle consists of a contraction phase, in which economic activity declines to the trough of the cycle, followed by expansion and the reaching of the cyclical peak. These cycles are superimposed over a secularly upward trend. These relations between the phases of the cycle and the relation of the cycle to the secular trend are shown in Figure 12:4.

FIGURE 12:4.   Cycle–Secular Relationship

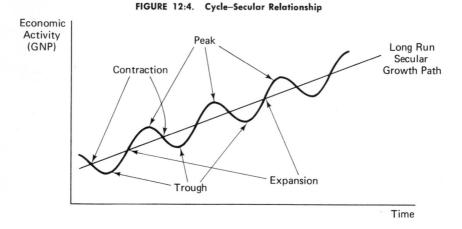

In the period covered by Friedman and Schwartz, 1867–1960, the economy experienced 23 such cycles according to the NBER. Among these, six are noteworthy, for they were especially severe and in each the money supply experienced an absolute contraction. For each of the other 17, the money stock generally rose during both the contractionary and the expansionary phase of the cycle. Thus, much of their attention is devoted to six severe episodes which occurred from: (1) Oct. 1873–March 1876 (4.9 percent contraction in the money stock); (2) Jan. 1893–June 1894 (5.8 percent); (3) May 1907–June 1908 (3.7 percent); (4) Jan. 1920–July 1921 (5.1 percent); (5) Aug. 1929–March 1933 (35.2 percent); and (6) May 1937–June 1938 (2.4 percent).[85] Quite clearly, the great contraction of 1929–1933 has merited the most intensive analysis.

To explain each of the 23 cycles, the determinants of the money supply are subjected to a separate analysis. That is, in terms of Equation (10:8),

---

[85] For a discussion of each of the six periods, refer to either *A Monetary History* or "Money and Business Cycles," pp. 50–55.

$$MS = \frac{B}{\dfrac{R}{D} + \dfrac{C}{MS} - \dfrac{RC}{DMS}}$$

the monetary base, B, the currency/money supply ratio, C/MS, and the reserve/deposit ratio, R/D, are analyzed and rationalized.

It is on the matter of the great contraction and the cause of the Great Depression that the controversy between the Keynesians and Friedman is centered—this being the ultimate test of his basic contention that the cycle is a "dance of the dollar." The issue was raised by Friedman in his AEA presidential address:

The revival of belief in the potency of monetary policy was fostered also by a re-evaluation of the role money played from 1929 to 1933. Keynes and most other economists of the time believed that the Great Contraction in the United States occurred despite aggressive expansionary policies by the monetary authorities—they did their best, but their best was not good enough. Recent studies have demonstrated that the facts are precisely the reverse; the U.S. monetary authorities followed highly deflationary policies. The quantity of money in the United States fell by one-third in the course of the contraction. And it fell, not because there were no willing borrowers—not because the horse would not drink. It fell because the Federal Reserve System forced or permitted a sharp reduction in the monetary base, because it failed to exercise the responsibilities assigned to it in the Federal Reserve Act to provide liquidity to the banking system. The Great Contraction is tragic testimony to the power of monetary policy—not, as Keynes and so many of his contemporaries believed, evidence of its impotence.[86]

Friedman fails to mention the sharp rise in both the currency/money-supply and reserve/deposit ratios during the 1929–1933 period. In *A Monetary History*, the rise in the former is attributed to a lack of confidence in the banking system because of widespread failures, while the rise in the latter reflects the buildup of precautionary reserves against bank runs, because the Federal Reserve failed to assist banks during the period when currency drains were especially heavy.

For a full appreciation of the Keynesian critique, it should be noted that while the currency/money-supply ratio rose a bit in late 1933 and 1934, in July 1960 it was at almost the same level as in July 1932. The reserve/deposit ratio continued to rise throughout the decade of the 1930's. In 1940, almost one-half of all commercial bank reserves were in excess of legal requirements. Moreover, the Treasury bill rate was driven down in the late 1930's to almost zero (from 1938 to 1940 it was about .014 percent).

[86] "The Role of Monetary Policy," p. 3

Friedman interprets this buildup of excess reserves to the continued precautionary demand by banks to guard against bank runs and to be able to offset any changes in their legal reserve requirement which might arise from the exercise by the Federal Reserve of newly acquired power to alter reserve requirements. The low yield on Treasury bills, according to Friedman, had no influence on the holding of bank reserves, for they are regarded by him as insensitive to interest rates.[87]

The neo-Keynesian interpretation of this period is quite the opposite. The cause of the depression was the collapse of the marginal efficiency of capital schedule caused, in part, by the increased uncertainty following the stock market collapse and bank failures. This, in turn, caused a decrease in the demand for loanable funds and a decline in the stock of money (this view assumes that banks supply money passively in response to a demand for it). Their denial of Friedman's interpretation is based upon several pieces of evidence. First, contrary to Friedman's assertion in his presidential address, his own data reveal that the monetary base did not decline, but rose throughout the period 1929–1933—in July 1932, for example, it was more than 10 percent higher than in July 1929.[88] Thus, the contraction was produced by a decline in the money multiplier—or by the rise in the two ratios.

But if the currency/money-supply ratio rose because of widespread fears of the solvency of the banking system, why was it still at the same level in July 1960 as in July 1932 (its lowest point in the twentieth century)? Surely 30 years of experience ought to have taught the public that banks were safe once again.[89] As to the rise in the reserve/deposit

---

[87] If the reserve holdings by commercial banks in excess of those required by law are extremely insensitive to the interest rate, the supply of money will also be insensitive to the interest rate. This will, when combined with Friedman's contention that the demand for money is insensitive to the interest rate, produce an almost vertical *LM* schedule or one that is highly inelastic and indicative of a potent monetary policy. All data cited in the previous paragraph are from *A Monetary History*, Chart 64 and pp. 336 and 457.

[88] It remains an unanswered mystery how Friedman could have made such an error. In subsequent work he still blames the Federal Reserve for allowing the contraction to take place, but he does not mention a decline in the base as the cause. See his *Counter-Revolution in Monetary Theory*, pp. 15–17. See references in footnote 87 for data on monetary base and the two ratios.

[89] Among neo-Keynesians, Nicholas Kaldor believes the rise to be due to changes in the relative magnitude of expenditures paid for in paper currency (goods and services) and those paid for by check (financial or income expenditures). Among Monetarists, Phillip Cagan has provided an explanation for the rise in the ratio and its subsequent failure to decline. The initial rise during the first half of the 1930's he attributes to bank failures and panic. During the second half of the 1930's, after the failure and panic subsided, the ratio remained high because of the introduction by banks of service charges on checking accounts, which led individuals to economize on the use of demand deposits, and because of a general decline in the rate of interest paid on savings deposits. During World War II the high ratio was sustained because currency transactions were used as a means of tax evasion, as was currency holding. After the war, Cagan believes, the rise in check service charges is the principal reason the ratio fails to decline. See Phillip Cagan, *Determinants and Effects of Changes in the Stock of*

ratio and the decline in the Treasury bill rate, neo-Keynesians interpret this as reflecting mainly a lack of borrowers. Thus, banks invested their surplus funds in Treasury bills to such a degree that they drove their yield to practically zero. Any further additions to those reserves through open-market operations would have resulted in cash holdings by banks. In this situation the bank's demand for excess reserves was in a virtual liquidity trap—money didn't matter and monetary policy was impotent.[90]

As for the remaining 17 minor economic fluctuations, Friedman and Schwartz believe that they are also caused by variations in the money supply. They tell us "if money plays an independent role in major movements, is it likely to be almost passive in minor movements? The minor movements can be interpreted as less virulent members of the same species as the major movements."[91]

Richard G. Davis has contributed important findings on this point.[92] First, for the six severe contractions, the ranking of monetary contractions with business contractions does not correspond exactly. Thus, in some cases larger monetary contractions are associated with smaller business contractions or the same degree of contraction of business activity was associated with vastly different rates of contraction of the money stock. Second, for 12 moderate cycles between 1882 and 1961 there is virtually no correlation whatsoever between the ranking of the declines in the rate of money growth and the declines in business activity.

Nevertheless, Friedman and Schwartz conclude their section on qualitative historical circumstances concerning the relationship between money and income with:

> mutual interaction, but with money rather clearly the senior partner in longer run movements and in major cyclical movements, and more nearly an equal partner with money and income and prices in shorter run and milder movements—this is the generalization suggested by our evidence.[93]

Money, 1875–1960 (New York: NBER, 1965), pp. 132–34. It should be noted that Cagan's conjectures are not supported by any empirical work.

[90] For an extensive discussion of this point, see James Tobin, "A Monetary Interpretation of History: A Review Article," *American Economic Review*, Vol. 55, No. 3 (June 1965), pp. 470–72. Among contemporary observers of the period, Lauchlin Currie, generally regarded as an early follower of Keynes, wrote in 1935 that the buildup of excess reserves in the period 1932–1934 could not be attributed to an alleged lack of loans suitable as bank assets, for a large quantity of government securities were available among other possible outlets for the surplus reserves of banks. See Lauchlin Currie, *The Supply and Control of Money*, pp. 121–23.

[91] Milton Friedman, and Anna Schwartz, "Money and Business Cycles," p. 55. Unlike the six deep contractions cited above, in the minor fluctuations the money stock generally grew during the contraction phase of the cycle. We will deal with this seeming contradiction in part (3) on the timing evidence.

[92] Richard G. Davis, "The Role of the Money Supply in Business Cycles," in *Essays in Domestic and International Finance*, Federal Reserve Bank of New York (1969), pp. 25–36.

[93] Milton Friedman, "The Monetary Studies of the National Bureau," pp. 8–9.

the behavior of the determinants of the money stock

The evidence summarized here comes largely from the work of Phillip Cagan. Both secular and cyclical changes in the money stock are decomposed into changes in the monetary base, and the two ratios. This permits the relative importance of each to be measured and makes possible a more refined explanation of the causes of the change in the money stock.

Cagan believes that 91 percent of the secular movement in the money supply over the period 1875–1955 can be attributed to movements in the monetary base.[94] This growth of high-powered money can be accounted for chiefly by growth of the gold stock and, after 1913, by credit extended by the Federal Reserve System. Cagan believes the secular evidence supports an influence running from money to business activity. If the reverse were true, an autonomous rise in economic activity ought to produce a rise in prices, which in a system of fixed international exchange rates would lead to a gold outflow and a reduction in the base. Thus, increases in the general level of prices should be negatively correlated with the size of the base. This is contrary to his findings, so he concludes that for secular movements, the predominant direction of influence must run from money to income.

For cyclical fluctuations the Cagan evidence is more mixed and may in fact contradict the Friedman–Schwartz hypothesis.

For severe cyclical contractions (the six cases cited above) Cagan believes:

> the evidence is therefore consistent with and, taken as a whole, impressively favors emphasis on the decline in the rate of monetary growth as the main reason some business contractions, regardless of what may have initiated them, become severe.[95]

For the mild cycles, Cagan finds clear evidence of the influence of economic activity on the money stock, because the dominant role in determining the money stock is attributed to the two ratios, and variations in these are explainable in terms of the portfolio decisions of individuals and commercial banks, both of which are determined by movements in the level of economic activity. For the period 1877–1954 the currency/money ratio itself accounted for roughly one-half of the cyclical variation in the rate of change of the money stock.[96] Thus, for the great majority of cyclical fluctuations, money does not seem to play

---

[94] *Determinants and Effects of Changes in the Stock of Money, 1875–1960,* p. 19, Table 2.

[95] *Ibid.,* p. 267.

[96] *Ibid.,* p. 26, Table 4 and p. 29, Addendum to Table 4.

an independent role, but to be the passive determinant resulting from changes in the money multiplier (which reflects changes in economic activity).

consistency of timing on a positive and inverted basis

It is on the evidence marshaled under this point that by far the most controversy has centered. The source for the timing evidence is manipulations in the money stock made necessary because (as noted above) the stock grows during both the contraction and the expansion phase of most mild cycles. The Monetarists attribute this to the strong upward secular trend in the growth of the money stock. Thus, the trend effect swamps what is felt to be the normal tendency for the stock of money to decline absolutely during the contraction phase, producing a statistical time series of the money stock which rises during cyclical contractions.

In order to concentrate on the cyclical aspects of the data on the money stock, Friedman and Schwartz compute its rate of change after converting the data to logarithms. Having constructed a rate-of-change time series, they then match this series to the corresponding NBER business cycle series. In each NBER business cycle, they indicate when the rate of change of money series reaches its peak and trough. This series for 1867–1960 (with the peaks and troughs indicated by dots) appears as Figure 12:5.

Even before the evidence is investigated, the chart reveals an immediate problem. The rate-of-change-of-money series is very erratic, producing a sawtooth graph which makes it difficult to designate any month as a peak or trough. For this reason, Friedman and Schwartz have constructed an alternative measure, suggested by the fact that the rate-of-change series often appears to move about the same level for a time and then shift to a new level. Thus, they have approximated the rate-of-change series by a series of horizontal steps. The step peak is then the month in which a high step ends and is succeeded by a low step, and a step trough becomes the month in which a low step ends and is succeeded by a high step. These steps are also indicated in Figure 12:5.

The most remarkable deduction from Figure 12:5 is that a turning point in the rate-of-change-of-money series comes before the corresponding turning point in the NBER reference cycle for every one of the 45 turning points. That is, if the rate of change of the money stock reaches a trough, it precedes a trough in the level of economic activity, as a peak in the rate-of-change series precedes a peak in the level of economic activity. When the steps are used, their troughs and peaks precede those in the level of economic activity for 30 of 45 turning points.[97]

---

[97] This approach of relating the rate of change of money to the level of economic activity may appear as rather arbitrary. In fact, recent neo-Fisherian theory does not support this

FIGURE 12:5.   Month-to-Month Rate of Change in U.S. Money Stock, 1867–1960

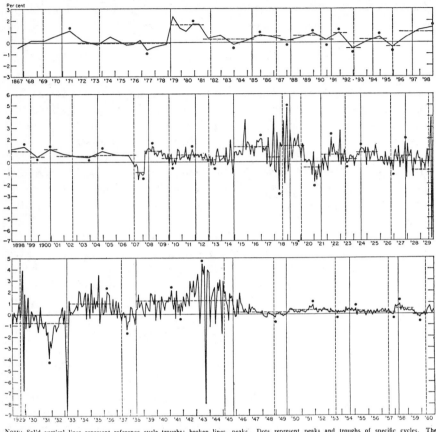

Note: Solid vertical lines represent reference cycle troughs; broken lines, peaks. Dots represent peaks and troughs of specific cycles. The
horizontal broken lines represent high and low steps in the rate of change.
Source: In the annual or semiannual segment, 1867–1907, the change in natural logarithm from one date to the next in the data underlying
Chart 1 was divided by the number of months intervening, and the quotient plotted at the middle of the month halfway between. In
the monthly segment, 1907–60, the month-to-month change in natural logarithm was plotted in the middle of the second month. Reference dates are from the National Bureau (see Table 1).

Source: Friedman and Schwartz, "Money and Business Cycles," p. 35. Reproduced with the
consent of the authors and The North-Holland Publishing Company.

Figure 12:5 also conveys at least one other piece of vital information. The lag in economic activity behind peaks and troughs in the rate
of change of the money stock are by no means uniform. The money
peak, on the average, comes 17.6 months earlier than the reference peak
in economic activity (the step peak averages 7.1 months earlier); the
money trough occurs some 12 months earlier, on the average, than the

method. We are told by Brunner that monetary accelerations or decelerations ought to affect the
growth rate of output. Thus, the *rate of change* of the money stock ought to be related to the
rate of change of economic activity to be consistent with recent Monetarist theorizing.

trough in economic activity (the step trough is some 4.1 months earlier). Moreover, substantial variations are to be found in the lag of business activity behind changes in the rate of growth of the money stock. Using the rate-of-change data, the standard deviation of the lag is 6.9 months at peaks and 5.7 months at troughs. Using the step data, the standard deviation is 7.9 months for peaks and 5.6 months for troughs.[98]

It is from this evidence that Friedman has concluded that monetary policy, involving changes in the growth rate of the money stock, affects the level of economic activity with a lag which is both long and variable. Therefore, discretionary monetary policy should not be used to fine-tune the economy because it is likely to be destabilizing. What we need is a program calculated to yield monetary stability—for example, a fairly constant rate of growth of the money supply. If this program is followed, the social costs of adjustments which arise when the money supply is varied irregularly will be minimized. This evidence produces the famous Friedman rule for the conduct of monetary policy —a steady rate of growth in the money stock.

The neo-Keynesian counterattack on this evidence is both theoretical and statistical, and is designed to show that the turning-point relationship is neither suggestive nor decisive evidence in favor of money causing changes in income. Quite the contrary, it is alleged to be equally compatible with the reverse causation—income changes cause changes in money.

The neo-Keynesian analysis builds on earlier work by Wesley Mitchell and R. G. Hawtrey.[99] Let a rise in investment opportunities be the source for a rise in economic activity. Two relationships then work to correlate the use of paper currency with ups and downs in business activity. First, retail sales (which use more paper currency per dollar of payments than do other transactions) rise relative to total transactions during expansions in economic activity and fall during contractions. Second, the relative income of wage earners (who are the largest users of currency) conforms positively to business activity. Both of these relationships ought to cause the money stock to fall—however, the money stock grows during the expansion for two reasons. First, banks draw down their excess reserves in response to rising interest rates prompted by the expansion in money demand. Second, the central bank, pursuing a countercyclical monetary policy, will be expanding the base in response to the previous downswing. However, as the expansion continues, the central bank reduces the rate of growth of the base, and banks find it

---

[98] See Friedman and Schwartz, "Money and Business Cycles," p. 38, Table 2.

[99] W. C. Mitchell, *Business Cycles and Their Causes* (Berkeley: University of California Press, 1950) and R. G. Hawtrey, "The Trade Cycle," in *Readings in Business Cycle Theory*, American Economic Association (Homewood, Ill.: Richard D. Irwin, 1950), pp. 343–44.

increasingly difficult to continue to lend out their excess reserves. The
continued rise in the amount of paper currency relative to deposits
ultimately causes the rate of growth of the money supply to diminish.
This usually occurs before the absolute peak in the upswing of the level
of economic activity. The opposite chain of events occurs during the
downswing. Thus, the cyclical pattern of the currency ratio and the
strategy typically pursued by central bankers can explain the customary
lead of monetary growth over turning points in economic activity.[100]

An additional major neo-Keynesian attack on the interpretation of
this evidence was a theoretical one mounted by James Tobin.[101] He
produced a Keynesian model in which money reacts only to changes in
economic activity. With this model he was able to produce timing evidence which corresponds exactly with that reported by Friedman,
whereas with a model of the type Friedman would use (in which money
causes changes in income), he could not duplicate Friedman's timing
evidence.

In an earlier piece of economic work, John Kareken and Robert
Solow relate the rate of change of the money stock to the *rate of change*
of economic activity rather than to its level. They conclude:

In summary [our results] overwhelmingly support the conclusion that the
money supply itself and the level of aggregate output move more or less
simultaneously over the business cycle, and that the lead of ΔM over aggregate output is a pure arithmetic artifact.[102]

Figure 12:6, which plots the rates of change of nominal income and
two definitions of the money supply, serves to substantiate the claim of
Kareken and Solow.

Last, and most important, the timing evidence presented by Friedman and Schwartz is inconsistent with the Monetarist doctrine developed by Brunner, which was explained above in the discussion on the

[100] For additional examples, see Nicholas Kaldor, "The New Monetarism," pp. 1–18.

[101] James Tobin, "Money and Income: Post Hoc Ergo Prompter Hoc?" *Quarterly Journal of Economics*, Vol. 84, No. 2 (May 1970), pp. 301–17.

[102] See John Kareken and Robert Solow, "Lags in Monetary Policy," Commission on Money and Credit, *Stabilization Policies: A Series of Research Studies Prepared for the Commission on Money and Credit* (Englewood Cliffs, N.J.: Prentice-Hall, 1963), pp. 14–25. Reprinted by permission of Prentice-Hall.

In addition, it is well known that if the *level* of the money stock and the *level* of GNP move together, with no significant leads or lags, in a cyclical pattern, movements in the rate of change of either series will "lead" movements in the level of the other by one-quarter cycle. This is due to the mathematical relationship between a variable moving in a sine curve and the variable's rate of change—the rate of change will lead the variable by one-quarter cycle. No economic relationships are necessarily involved. For this, see Ronald Teigen, "The Keynesian–Monetarist Debate in the U.S.: A Summary and Evaluation," *Saertrykk au Statsøkonomist Tidsskrift*, No. 1 (1970), pp. 5–6.

FIGURE 12:6.   The Relationship between the Rate of Change in Nominal Income and the
Money Stock, 1870–1961, Excluding Intracyclical Effects

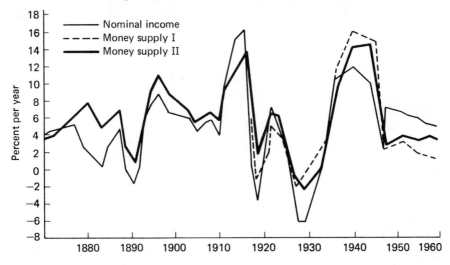

Source: Milton Friedman, *Dollars and Deficits: Inflation, Monetary Policy and the Balance of Payments,* © 1968, p. 128. Reprinted by permission of Prentice-Hall, Inc., Englewood Cliffs, New Jersey.
Note: Money Supply I consists of currency and demand deposits. Money Supply II adds time deposits of commercial banks.

nonneutrality of money. There, Brunner explained the neo-Fisherian position as one which relates the rate of change of the money stock (accelerations) to the rate of change of economic activity (accelerations). Brunner's theoretical position implies that the type of test performed by Kareken and Solow is the relevant one rather than that of Friedman and Schwartz.

Friedman's rejoinder was to draw attention to the caveat that the timing evidence was suggestive but not decisive about causation. If one were to expunge this evidence, as unimportant, from that which he has assembled, he would still not ". . . be led to change to any major extent the confidence attached to our basic conclusion."[103] The evidence was really assembled, not for its implications about causality, but in order to calculate lags, or so we are now told. "These studies popularized and introduced the concept of a long and variable lag between changes in monetary growth on the one hand and changes in economic activity on the other."[104] If this evidence is purged, we are left with that examined in (1) and (2) above.

[103] "Money and Income: Post Hoc Ergo Prompter Hoc: A Comment," p. 301.
[104] *Money and Economic Development,* p. 8.

Karl Brunner quite rightly realizes:

. . . that Tobin's argument effectively shows that timing relations observed are *per se* irrelevant observations. They yield no discriminating evidence, they are consistent with the Monetarist hypothesis and its denial.[105]

He then proposes a number of tests designed to substantiate the Monetarist hypothesis. They yield inconclusive results and will be examined below in the section on the exogeneity of money.

Accepting their method of relating rate of change of money to level of economic activity, Thomas Mayer[106] has suggested that, for at least five reasons, the Friedman–Schwartz estimates of the variability of the lag impart to it a substantial upward bias. His work is not meant to deny that the lag itself may be highly variable, only that the standard deviations found by Friedman and Schwartz are not good estimates of the variability of the lag.

After examining, in an admittedly brief fashion, the evidence gathered by one of the leading Monetarists and his associates, and considering the neo-Keynesian critique of some of it, what might we conclude to be the neo-Keynesian view on the causality of money? James Tobin summarizes their view:

Consider the following three propositions: Money does not matter. It does too matter. Money is all that matters. It is all too easy to step from the second proposition to the third, to use reasoning and evidence which supports the second to claim the third. In this book, F & S [Friedman and Schwartz] have ably and convincingly marshalled evidence for the proposition that money matters. They have put to rout the neo-Keynesian, if he exists, who regards monetary events as mere epiphenomena, postscripts added as afterthoughts to the nonmonetary factors that completely determine income, employment and even prices. But in their goal and exuberance, Friedman and his followers often seem to go—though perhaps less in this book than elsewhere—beyond their own logic and statistics to the other extreme, where the stock of money becomes the necessary and sufficient determinant of money income. Much as I admire their work, I cannot follow them there.[107]

It should be noted that even though the evidence is controversial and in

[105] "A Survey of Selected Issues in Monetary Theory," p. 98. As noted above, Brunner's theory of Monetarism implies that the rate of change of the money stock should be related to the rate of change of economic activity. When this is done, little or no lag of economic activity behind the money stock is found. See the work of Kareken and Solow, cited in footnote 102.

[106] Thomas Mayer, "The Lag in the Effect of Monetary Policy: Some Criticisms," *Western Economic Journal*, Vol. 7, No. 3 (1965), pp. 324–42.

[107] "Monetary Interpretation of History," p. 481.

some cases does not support the neo-Fisherian position, it must not be taken to mean that money cannot act in the way they hypothesize. It is still quite possible that the business cycle is "a dance of the dollar."

the St. Louis studies

In November 1968, Anderson and Jordan published the results of an empirical investigation designed to test the propositions that "the response of economic activity to fiscal actions, relative to that of monetary actions, is (I) greater, (II) more predictable, and (III) faster."[108] Using quarterly data for the period 1952–1968 and a single so-called *reduced-form* equation based on an unspecified structural model of the economy, they were able to reject all three propositions.

In fact, over the period studied, monetary policy measured either by the money supply or the monetary base had a considerably larger and faster impact on GNP than did changes in the budget surplus or deficit measured at full-employment income. This suggests that monetary policy is a very powerful tool for stabilization, whereas fiscal policy is fairly weak, because any change in government expenditures quickly crowds out an equivalent amount of private outlays.[109] Table 12:1 summarizes the Anderson–Jordan results.

TABLE 12:1   **Cumulative Impact on GNP of Monetary and Fiscal Policy**
(Billions of Current Dollars)

Cumulative effect on GNP after	Money supply change	Expenditure change	Tax change
1 Quarter	$1.51	$0.36	0.16
2 Quarters	3.10	0.89	0.15
3 Quarters	4.57	0.84	0.12
4 Quarters & beyond	5.84	0.06	0.23

Source: Anderson and Jordan, "Monetary and Fiscal Actions," Equation 1.2, Table 1, p. 17.

[108] Leonall Anderson and Jerry Jordan, "Monetary and Fiscal Actions: A Test of Their Relative Importance in Economic Stabilization," *Review—Federal Reserve Bank of St. Louis* (Nov. 1968), pp. 11–24. Quotation taken from p. 11.

[109] Because we do not know the structure of the model from which this reduced-form equation emerges, we are unable to explain how the crowd-out occurs. To the extent that these results are true, they clearly imply that fiscal expenditures quickly displace an equivalent amount of private outlays. However, how this occurs is left unspecified by the model. Other St. Louis Bank economists have presented some theoretical and historical analysis of the crowd-out. See Roger W. Spencer and William P. Yohe, "The 'Crowding-Out' of Private Expenditures by Fiscal Policy Actions," *Review—St. Louis Federal Reserve Bank*, Vol. 52, No. 10 (Oct. 1970), pp. 12–24, and their "Historical Analysis of the 'Crowding-Out' of Private Expenditures by Fiscal Policy Actions," *Working Paper No. 13*, Federal Reserve Bank of St. Louis (Jan. 31, 1971), and Keith M. Carlson and Roger W. Spencer, "Crowding Out and Its Critics," *Review —St. Louis Federal Reserve Bank*, Vol. 57, No. 12 (Dec. 1975), pp. 2–18.

Thus, a $1 billion increase in the money supply will raise GNP by $1.51 billion in the same quarter, and after one year and thereafter, GNP will be higher by $5.84 billion. On the other hand, a $1 billion increase in full-employment expenditures will never raise GNP by more than $900 million; and the effect is largely transitory, for after 4 quarters most of the effect will disappear. The tax variable has no effect whatsoever, for none of its coefficients in the regression were significant. Had they been, they would imply that to raise GNP one need only raise taxes!

In response to this paper, De Leeuw and Kalchbrenner make one essential and damaging point. The dependent variable (GNP in the Anderson–Jordan regression) is not independent from its explanatory variable (the money stock, or the monetary base). This lack of statistical independence implies that the monetary coefficients are biased. Anderson and Jordan in their reply neglect this point.[110]

In addition, the methodology underlying the Anderson–Jordan approach has been subject to attack, as has the neo-Fisherian methodology in general. We turn now to a discussion of methodology, for it forms a last area of dispute between the two schools and is often interwoven in the discussion on the causality of money.

Methodology

Very early in his academic career, Milton Friedman set forth the methodology which was to guide his approach to both research on the causality of money and acceptance or rejection of theory. This approach has been followed subsequently by many who are in the neo-Fisherian tradition. His approach can be summarized as:

> Viewed as a body of substantive hypotheses, theory is to be judged by its predictive power for the class of phenomena which it is intended to "explain." Only factual evidence can show whether it is "right" or "wrong" or, better, tentatively "accepted" as valid or "rejected." As I shall argue at

---

[110] Frank De Leeuw and John Kalchbrenner, "Monetary and Fiscal Actions: A Test of Their Relative Importance in Economic Stabilization—Comment," *Review—Federal Reserve Bank of St. Louis* (April 1969), pp. 6–11, and *Reply* by Anderson and Jordan, same issue. De Leeuw and Kalchbrenner attempt to purge the fiscal variable and the base of various components that they believe are related to GNP. Regressions are then computed, and using a base purged of paper currency and other minor variables they obtain highly favorable results to fiscal policy. However, such regressions are again unrelated to any specific structural model and may be consistent with any number of them.

It should also be noted that the Anderson–Jordan results are quite inconsistent with those obtained by Friedman. Rather than money influence being distributed over a long and variable period, Anderson and Jordan show that it has an immediate and strong impact which is exhausted after four quarters!

greater length below, the only relevant test of the *validity* of a hypothesis is comparison of its predictions with experience. . . .[111]

As to the attributes which the theory's assumptions should have, Friedman notes:

> In so far as a theory can be said to have "assumptions" at all, and in so far as their "realism" can be judged independently of the validity of predictions, the relation between the significance of a theory and the "realism" of its "assumptions" is almost the opposite of that suggested by the view under criticism. Truly important and significant hypotheses will be found to have "assumptions" that are wildly inaccurate descriptive representations of reality, and, in general, the more significant the theory, the more unrealistic the assumptions. . . .
>
>   . . . the relevant question to ask about the "assumptions" of a theory is not whether they are descriptively "realistic," for they never are, but whether they are sufficiently good approximations for the purpose in hand. And this question can be answered only by seeing whether the theory works, which means whether it yields sufficiently accurate predictions. . . .[112]

Insofar as Friedman's approach to methodology can be summarized, it appears to say that if I have a theory whose predictions are empirically valid to a useful degree of approximation, then it is a good theory regardless of whether its assumptions are empirically valid. He goes so far as to suggest that it may be a merit for a theory to have unrealistic assumptions, for only in that way can it be made applicable to a wide variety of empirical situations. Unless complex situations can be explained by simpler ones, theory has achieved little.

Much of Friedman's empirical work has been based on such a methodology. Its essence has been that "much" ought to be explained by "little" and it focuses on "crucial relationships" by which rival theories are tested.

In a now well-known test which has been much commented upon, the quantity theory was pitted against its rival, which is called by Chicago economists the income–expenditure approach. The crucial relationship in the former was the velocity function connecting the money supply with nominal income, whereas in the latter the multiplier stands between autonomous expenditures and nominal income. The quantity theory was of course vindicated, because velocity outperformed the mul-

111 Milton Friedman, "The Methodology of Positive Economics," in *Essays in Positive Economics* (Chicago: University of Chicago Press, 1953), pp. 8–9.
    112 *Ibid.*, pp. 14–15.

tiplier in the sense that its predictions compared more favorably with experience.[113]

The neo-Keynesian response to this methodological approach, while it agrees with Friedman's dictum that the ultimate acceptability of a theory or hypothesis must rest on its ability to predict, has been twofold. Most people responding to the empirical work of Friedman and his followers have accepted this research strategy and tried to argue that if the variables used in these simple single-equation regressions were specified in an alternative fashion (rate of change vs. levels) or measured differently (using only part of the monetary base or the money supply or redefining autonomous expenditures, and so forth), they would yield results favoring the Keynesian approach. Having accepted the methodology of Friedman, they guaranteed their own defeat or at least weakened the power and persuasiveness of their criticisms.

The second type of neo-Keynesian response has been to dismiss the methodology lying behind these tests rather than the results themselves. This response until recently has not attracted wide attention, but on the scientific level represents the correct route of criticism. It asserts that Friedman's views about the acceptability of a theory and the nature of its assumptions offend the principles of logic and are therefore invalid; thus it denies his methodology as unscientific. In addition, it raises doubts about the measure used by some neo-Fisherians to test the validity of theories and raises serious criticisms about the legitimacy of the single-equation estimation procedures used by the St. Louis Federal Reserve Bank.

Paul Samuelson,[114] in a neglected paper, was among the first to question the scientific worth of Friedman's statement on methodology. Relying on the canons of formal logic, Samuelson concluded that, as far as economics was concerned, Friedman was wrong in thinking that unrealism in the assumptions of a theory (in the sense of their factual inaccuracy even to a tolerable degree of approximation) is meritorious.

Friedman's conclusions appear to follow from his method of testing theories. He considers what he perceives to be the direct conclusions or implications of a set of assumptions, and if they accord well with ex-

---

[113] It is this same approach to methodology which has guided the research strategy of the St. Louis Federal Reserve Bank. Assumed causes (money, monetary base, high employment expenditures, and so forth) are regressed on assumed effects (the level of GNP or its rate of change). The selection of the cause–effect relationship is guided largely by which equation yields the highest R^2, that is, explains most of the variation in the dependent variable. How the estimating equation was derived, the logic for the structure of lags used in the independent variables, the particular measure used of the variable in question, and so forth, are all left basically unanswered, assumed to be self-evident, or rationalized after the R^2's for the alternative equations have been computed.

[114] Paul Samuelson, "Problems of Methodology—Discussion," American Economic Review, Vol. 53, No. 2 (May 1963), pp. 231–36. See also Eugene Rotwein, "On 'The Methodology of Positive Economics,'" The Quarterly Journal of Economics, Vol. 73, No. 4 (Nov. 1959), pp. 554–75.

perience, however judged, he concludes that the theory is consistent with the evidence and may be better than its rivals. Samuelson objects that one cannot test the merits of a theory in this fashion, for in judging its merits one must look at all the implications—direct and indirect—of a given set of assumptions. The conclusions of a theory consist not only of the direct implications of its assumptions, but of the assumptions themselves—that is, their indirect implications; for according to the principles of formal logic, the assumptions of a theory imply themselves, as well as all things that they themselves imply. Thus, since the assumptions imply themselves, their validity, or factual accuracy to a useful degree of approximation, is quite important in judging the validity of a theory.

That some subset of implications of a theory (its direct conclusions) is shown to be valid does not atone for the possibility that other implications (its assumptions) may be false. If they are, one must revise the theory and replace its false assumptions by others shown to be valid. If this reduces the theory to irrelevance, so be it.

As Samuelson's argument is applied to the Friedman–Meiselman test of the quantity theory vs. the income–expenditure approach, it says that although the former outperformed the latter when velocity was pitted against the multiplier, this does not necessarily establish the "superiority" of the quantity theory *per se* if it can be shown that one or more of the assumptions of that theory are empirically invalid. If that can be done, only some revised version of the quantity theory may be assumed superior to its rivals.

Friedman's contention that the validity of a theory can be judged by the conformability of its predictions with experience has been reduced by some Monetarists to the trivial proposition that if the empirical results obtained from one theory yield a higher value of the R^2 than that from an alternative, the first theory is superior to the second. The value of the R^2 then becomes the final judge of validity or goodness. The neo-Keynesians do not deny the importance of the R^2, but insist on its limitations as an arbitrator of the final acceptability of a theory. Thus, the neo-Keynesians are concerned with how the value of the R^2's are achieved. For example, if any sample period is broken down into subperiods, is there any observed variation in the value of the R^2's over the subperiods? Over time, what is the relationship between actual and predicted variables (do they drift apart, are they consistently over- or underestimated, and so forth)? How well does the model forecast critical turning points in the cycle? What is the rationale for including the variables in the equation yielding the highest R^2?[115] These and other

---

[115] For example, several years ago a model prepared by a young economist at the Office of Management and Budget, one Arthur Laffer, had a sudden but brief impact on the national scene. It predicted that money had a quick, strong, and sustained impact on GNP.

questions are designed to cast doubt on the use of the R^2 as the only judge of the worth of a theory. In addition, the neo-Keynesian approach has been to prepare elaborate structural models of a general equilibrium nature of the United States economy which state clearly the assumed causal relationships and whose forecasting ability is measured by both point estimates and the error attached to those estimates. The neo-Fisherians criticize this approach, arguing that no structural model can accurately capture the myriad ways in which money can affect the real sector. This leads them to a preference for simple single-equation reduced-form models, which do not spell out in detail the structural relationship. It is this approach which has been criticized heavily by James Tobin:

> Much evidence has been presented purporting to show the superior power of monetary variables over fiscal variables and private investment measures in explaining changes in GNP. This evidence comes in what I call pseudo-reduced-forms.
>
> The meaning of the term *reduced-form* is this: If you think of the economy as really a complex set of equations—basic structural relationships describing business investment, demands for loans, demand for money, the consumption function and so on—conceivably you could solve such a system and relate the variables in which you are ultimately interested, such as GNP, to the truly exogenous variables, including the instruments of the monetary and fiscal authorities. Such a solution of a big complicated model, you would call a *reduced-form*. And then one possible way of estimating a model of the system would be not to estimate the structural equations, the building blocks of the system, but to estimate the condensed equations which relate the ultimate outputs like GNP to the ultimate causal factors. That would be reduced-form estimation.
>
> . . . What I mean by pseudo-reduced-form is an equation relating an ulti-

---

The R^2 was .96, which meant that 96 percent of the variation in GNP over the sample period could be explained by variations in the present and lagged values of the money stock and several other variables. However, on closer examination, David Fand was able to show that 91 percent of the variation in GNP could be explained from dummy variables inserted in the regressions to represent seasonal factors.

In addition, the Federal Reserve Board–MIT–Penn model, one of Keynesian persuasion, was made to run off data to which reduced-form equations of the St. Louis Bank type were fitted. The results were that the St. Louis regression equations reported falsely that money was the sole causal agent. See Samuelson, "Reflections on the Merits and Demerits of Monetarism," p. 18.

Finally, those who are addicted to judging the acceptability of a theory by reference to its R^2 would do well to read a piece by Thomas Mayer. Concerned with whether a hypothesis which produces a high R^2 for a sample period also produces an equally good fit beyond the sample period, he concludes that goodness-of-fit statistics are a poor guide by which to choose a hypothesis. See Thomas Mayer, "Selecting Economic Hypotheses by Goodness of Fit," *The Economic Journal*, Vol. 85, No. 4 (Dec. 1975), pp. 877–83.

mate variable of interest, like GNP, to the supposedly causal variables, but one which doesn't come out of any structure at all. Instead, the investigator just says, "Here are the effects and here are the causes, let's just throw them into an equation." The form and content of the equation—the list of variables and the lag structure—are not derived from any structural model. This is what we have had presented to us as the main evidence for the supposed superiority of monetary variables in explaining GNP.[116]

Summary—the Causality of Money

The preceding lengthy discussion of the respective views on the causality of money has involved us in many issues: The nature of the monetary transmission mechanism, the adequacy of the *IS–LM* framework to present monetary and fiscal policy, the source of cyclical economic disturbances, the effectiveness of fiscal policy, the empirical work offered to substantiate various hypotheses, and the methodologies of the respective sides. It is little wonder that the discussion of the subject appears confusing, since so many separate issues bearing on the relationship of money to economic activity are interwoven in the debate.

EXOGENEITY OF MONEY

Few discussions in monetary economics in the past 200 years, and especially in the last two decades, have evoked more words and strong emotions than those of the exogeneity of the *nominal* money stock. Yet surprisingly, any serious review of the literature leads to the conclusion that the word *exogeneity* means vastly different things to different people. Because it does, each definition has a substantial influence on the individual's interpretation of the monetary history of the United States and other countries, and on their choice of instruments to measure the impact of monetary policy. It also leads to rather pointless arguments which can never be resolved until a common definition of the word can be agreed upon.

To the economist who builds formal mathematical models, apply-

---

116 "The Role of Money in National Economic Policy," p. 23. Italics in the original.

Two other criticisms of the direct estimation procedure have been made. First, the implicit structural model from which the reduced form is derived may not itself be consistent internally, that is, it completely ignores a priori restrictions on coefficients of the independent variables in the equation (for example, the restrictions that are built into general equilibrium models through lags, identities, omitted variables, and so forth).

Second, we have a problem of selecting what are really exogenous variables. Depending upon which variables one assumes to be exogenous—monetary base, free reserves, narrow money, broad money—one can conclude that only money matters, or fiscal policy matters most, and so forth. See Yung Chul Park, "Some Current Issues on the Transmission Process of Monetary Policy," *International Monetary Fund Papers*, Vol. 19, No. 1 (1972), pp. 39–40.

ing the term *exogeneity* to a variable means that the variable is used in an explanatory equation to account partially for variations in the dependent, or endogenous, variable. Thus, it must be independent of the disturbance term of the equation or system of equations. If the variable cannot meet this test of independence, but is nevertheless used as an independent, or explanatory, variable, it will bias the results of any computed estimate purporting to show its impact on the endogenous variable.

On the other hand, *exogenous* has been used to describe those variables which can be heavily and directly influenced by policymakers or which can be controlled by them.

An obvious conflict emerges between these two definitions. For example, suppose that in the presence of a central bank, the money supply passively expands or contracts depending on the needs of trade or the financial requirements of the Treasury. The econometrician would consider this a strong case for calling the supply of money endogenous, and it might be represented in any potential model as that kind of variable—one whose behavior is explained by changes in income, interest rates, or the budget deficit of the central government. An econometrician who reads the monetary history of the United States under the circumstances outlined above might describe the money supply as a largely endogenous variable.

However, for the Monetarist who defines exogeneity in terms of control, the money stock would be called exogenous whenever it was shown that the central bank could exercise control over the money stock if it desired to do so, even though it might not choose to. According to their reading of United States monetary history, the money supply is exogenous. Moreover, it would be consistent with the Monetarist view to argue that money causes income to change in the sense that without these accommodations on the part of the central bank, income could not have expanded as it did. Monetarists might further assert, with supporting evidence, that some changes in the money supply were exogenous in the statistical sense. Thus, from their theoretical viewpoint it makes little difference whether money is exogenous in the statistical or the control sense—Money is exogenous, pure and simple, unless it can be shown that the central bank cannot control the nominal money supply.

It is when the Monetarists decide to test for the significance of the influence of money on the level of income that the exact definition of *exogeneity* can be extremely important. The econometrician would certainly disagree if it were asserted that a money stock supplied to finance the needs of trade caused subsequent changes in income; he would object to such an assertion being formalized in an equation with money as an independent variable, or if correlations were run with money as one variable and income the other. The econometrician would quickly point out that the first formalization would produce biased estimates because the money stock is not independent of the endogenous variable, income, which it seeks to explain. In addition, the correlation would in no way indicate causality unless it could be shown that money was statistically exogenous.

It should also be noted that nothing would preclude the econometrician from applying the word *endogenous* to a money supply which the central bank cannot control. He then would conclude that such a money supply is likely to be endogenous statistically as well.

Exogeneity and Causality

To fully appreciate the significance of the argument about exogeneity, the question of causality, or dominant influence, must be separately distinguished. If the nominal money stock is controllable, it does not follow that changes in that stock cause subsequent changes in income. However, from the viewpoint of the quantity theory, both causality and controllability quite clearly go hand in hand. Thus, it is necessary to assert that money causes income change and that the central bank controls the supply of money even though on occasion it permits other forces to determine the supply. The quantity theory approach would be severely weakened if it could be shown that while changes in the money supply were the dominant cause of changes in income, the money stock could not be controlled. But quite simply, the issues of control and causality are very distinct. The issue of statistical exogeneity is important when it becomes an underlying assumption of some of the tests for causality. Then, clearly, controllability is not the relevant test for exogeneity. It must be shown that the supply of money is not allowed to respond passively to the demands for loanable funds.

Contemporary neo-Keynesians, responding to the work of Friedman and Schwartz, have frequently confused the issues of exogeneity and causality, largely because in their empirical work, supporting their interpretation of the quantity theory, the issues of causality and exogeneity are not separated very well by Friedman and Schwartz. They assert that the money supply, at least since 1913, has been controllable by the Federal Reserve, thereby making it exogenous in the control sense. Then, using correlation analysis and the timing evidence (examined above) they assert that money causes income to change. Quite clearly this implies that money is exogenous in the statistical sense. However, as has been pointed out by numerous critics, mentioned by Friedman and Schwartz, and acknowledged by Brunner,[117] the Federal Reserve has at

---

[117] Karl Brunner, "The Monetarist View of Keynesian Ideas," *Lloyds Bank Review*, No. 102 (Oct. 1971), pp. 44–45.

times accommodated the needs of the Treasury and business, maintained orderly conditions in the bond market, and stabilized market interest rates. Thus, the Federal Reserve has allowed the supply of money to accommodate itself to the demand for loanable funds. How then, the neo-Keynesians ask, can the money supply be regarded as exogenous—statistically speaking? Looking at the tests conducted by Friedman and Schwartz, the neo-Keynesians seem to believe (with good reason) that Friedman and Schwartz also mean exogeneity in the statistical sense. Friedman and Schwartz obviously cannot have it both ways—that is, argue that the money supply is determined by changes in income *and* that the Federal Reserve caused the change in income.[118] For the same reason De Leeuw and Kalchbrenner have objected to the Anderson–Jordan study. Because the money supply or monetary base accommodated itself to changes in income, it cannot be argued (statistically speaking) that these two measures of monetary influence are truly independent variables. They have within themselves elements of statistical endogeneity.

In addition to this criticism of Friedman, several neo-Keynesians have proposed hypotheses designed to explain the observed cyclical variations in the money supply and their relationship to variations in the level of income (the so-called *timing evidence*). As noted above, each theory explains the variations by some combination of Federal Reserve policy (support of the Treasury, countercyclical stabilization, maintaining orderly conditions in the bond markets, and so forth) and changes induced in the money multiplier via either changes in the ratio of currency to money or in the ratio of reserves to deposits. Such hypotheses are also embodied in formal econometric models constructed by neo-Keynesian economists. Inevitably, the word *endogenous* is attached to these money-supply theories. Among some Monetarists, a distinguishing characteristic of Keynesianism is its endogenous theory of the supply of money. Clearly, the above money-supply theories and models using them do not necessarily mean that neo-Keynesians deny that the stock of money can be controlled by the central bank. For those who do believe that control is possible, the central question then becomes one of the causality of money.[119] There are, however, some neo-Keynesians who

---

[118] Friedman and Schwartz would no doubt argue that the instances where income changes cause the money supply to change are very few relative to the cases where money-supply changes were independent of income changes.

[119] The degree to which the central bank could control the money supply was not a dominant theme of *The General Theory*. Control was assumed to exist and the central issue became one of the dominant influence of money on economic activity. Even in the case where the liquidity trap in the demand for money exists, control is not denied. The issue in this situation becomes one of dominant influence, or whether money has any causal impact at all. Even when the supply of money is made a function of the interest rate, the neo-Keynesians will not deny that the central bank can control the stock so long as it can alter the monetary base in

argue that the money supply cannot be controlled; Nicholas Kaldor is undoubtedly their leader. He believes that a central bank is much like a constitutional monarch—it can reign, but cannot rule. For him the money supply:

. . . is largely a reflection of the rate of change in money incomes and, therefore, is dependent on, and varies with, all the forces, or factors, which determine this magnitude. . . .[120]

Led by Tobin and Kaldor, some neo-Keynesians even argue that control of the money supply makes little sense, for it is liquidity which governs aggregate demand, and changes in the money supply may induce offsetting changes in velocity because of the availability of money substitutes.[121] However, so long as these offsetting relationships are stable and predictable, they pose no essential problem for the Monetarist approach. It merely means that monetary management must contend with a variable velocity whose value is, however, predictable.

Both the proposition that the central bank cannot control the supply of money and the assertion that liquidity rather than money *per se* is important, lead certain neo-Keynesians to propose the interest rate as a guide to monetary policy rather than the growth rate of the money stock. This concentration on the interest rate can also arise because it serves as the link between the real and monetary sectors in the Keynesian model.

Since the neo-Fisherians have defined exogeneity in terms of the ability of the central bank to control the supply of money (so that control becomes their principal tool to achieve economic stabilization), it becomes essential to their approach to spell out in detail their theory of the supply of money and the role of the central bank. This labor has been willingly assumed by Brunner and Meltzer. Essential to their

---

a compensatory manner, unless the supply of money is infinitely elastic with respect to the interest rate. In that situation, the monetary base can be changed, but it will have no affect on the money supply.

[120] Nicholas Kaldor, "The New Monetarism," p. 16. Quite clearly he means that the money supply is statistically endogenous, for he prefaces these remarks with, "In this country (U.K.) it is even less plausible to argue that the money supply is under the direct control of the monetary authorities, regulated through the rate of creation of bank reserves."

[121] Kaldor poses the question of whether the monetary authorities could stop the Christmas buying spree by refusing to supply money. One way or another, he alleges, money substitutes would appear to permit individuals to do their buying. Consistency would probably cause him to deny that the central bank could cause Christmas in June by standing willing to supply high-powered money. If the public buying habits said "no," the central bank could not persuade them to say "yes."

Paul Samuelson questions the idea that any undesired changes in the money supply will produce offsetting changes in velocity. He refers to this as a remnant of the Radcliffe Committee heresy. See "Reflections on the Merits and Demerits of Monetarism," p. 19.

analysis are two propositions. The first is that the Federal Reserve can control the monetary base; the second, that changes in the base dominate changes in the money multiplier as a determinant of the money supply. If the multiplier were large relative to the base as a determinant of the money supply, it would not preclude Federal Reserve control, but it would then be possible that slight errors in adjusting the base could lead to very large errors in the growth rate of the money stock. Given the Monetarist views on dominant influence, the results (both in theory and in practice) could be catastrophic changes in income, employment, and prices.

There is little doubt that in the United States the Federal Reserve could, if it desired, control the monetary base. The Federal Reserve clearly dominates the sources of the base, with its only rival being the gold stock. Moreover, data on the base are made available on a weekly basis, which ensures that the Federal Reserve can take prompt action to achieve any level of the base it desires.

Control of the money stock (using any of several alternative definitions) is not as easy as it might appear, for standing between the base and the money supply is the money multiplier, whose value is determined by portfolio decisions of commercial banks and private individuals. This is clearly acknowledged by Brunner and Meltzer, and the former tells us that:

> this behavior dominates, in particular, the shortest run (weekly) variations of the money stock, but declines in relative importance beyond the shortest run. Investigations of different periods and countries establish, thus far, that the longer the period or the larger the relative change of the money supply, the greater is the role of the monetary authorities in the behavior of the money stock.[122]

Using evidence from the post–World War II period, Meltzer informs us that:

> . . . 85 percent of the variance of the monthly changes in money— currency and demand deposits—resulted from changes in the monetary base and changes in Treasury deposits at the commercial banks in the current and previous month

and that:

> more than 75 percent of the variance of the monthly changes in this monetary aggregate (money plus time deposits) can be controlled by using

[122] "A Survey of Selected Issues in Monetary Theory," p. 102.

the base . . . and estimating Treasury deposits as accurately as in the past.[123]

Thus, using the narrow definition of money, the Federal Reserve would be able to control an average of more than 85 percent of the monthly changes in money by controlling changes in the base and obtaining estimates of the change in Treasury deposits at commercial banks.

To further substantiate the position that the base, and hence the monetary authorities, dominate the money supply, Brunner computed rank correlations between changes in the base and the money stock and between changes in the multiplier and the money stock. The coefficient of the former, measuring each change for the initial and terminal month for each NBER half-cycle from March 1919 to December 1966, was .537, while for the latter it was only .084.[124]

On the basis of their evidence, it can be concluded that the Monetarists have made a good case for their contention that the central bank can control the supply of money and that it is, therefore, exogenous, as they define the term.[125] The fact that it is not controllable on an hourly, daily, or monthly basis, but probably at best on a quarterly basis, is one of those truths which is largely irrelevant to the central contention that money is exogenous. If more precise information could be made available at more frequent intervals, the Monetarist case for control could be strengthened.

In summary, the controversy over exogeneity can never be resolved until both sides recognize that they define the term differently. However, the Monetarists must realize that because they define the word as "ability to control money," they cannot violate the principles of statistical esti-

[123] Allan Meltzer, "Controlling Money," Review—Federal Reserve Bank of St. Louis (May 1969), pp. 18–19.

[124] Karl Brunner, "The Role of Money and Monetary Policy," p. 16. This evidence is offered by Brunner to support the Monetarist view on the causality of money. Because the base dominates the money stock and the Federal Reserve controls the base, it is asserted that the Federal Reserve caused the base changes. This view is subject to the same objection as the timing evidence—the Federal Reserve may only be passively expanding the base in response to demands for it.

It should also be noted that Brunner's evidence is at variance with that given by Cagan on the cyclical importance of the multiplier relative to the base as a determinant of the money supply. This difference could result from the fact that Brunner used the money stock at various points in the NBER business cycle to make his computations, whereas Cagan used a money cycle matched to a business cycle. In his findings, Cagan observed that the monetary base seldom explained more than 25 percent of the variation in the cyclical rate of change of the money supply. However, as far as the secular evidence is concerned, Cagan agrees with Brunner, for in his computations, variations in the base accounted for 91 percent of the variation in the money supply over the period 1875–1955.

[125] For an excellent additional discussion by a leading Monetarist of the issues involved in the control of the money stock see David Fand, "Some Issues in Monetary Economics," pp. 12–16.

mation if it is known that the central bank has permitted the money stock to accommodate itself to factors which cause income to change.

THE GREAT DEBATE: CONCLUSIONS

Harry G. Johnson tells us that the great challenge of Keynesian theory is to be found in changing the perspective of monetary theory from long-run equilibrium to short-run disequilibrium analysis and that it was this weakness (and in some cases disinterest in, disdain for, or non-comprehension of the problem of short-run disturbances on the part of the quantity theorists, as they existed in the 1920's) that offered the point of attack on orthodoxy and the opportunity for success to the Keynesian Revolution.

Slowly, the anti-Keynesian theoretical position has evolved to center on providing an explanation for short-run disturbances. Concentrating on the costs of search, adjustment, and acquisition of information, the Monetarists have been constructing a theoretical position on the non-neutrality of money which forms the foundation for their explanation of short-run variations in employment and prices. An essential part of this analysis is the distinction between real and nominal magnitudes, which has profound effects on both monetary theory and policy.

It is this concentration on the short run, however, which represents the renewed interest in the quantity theory approach and the success of the Monetarist counter-revolution.

Insofar as policy is concerned, the Monetarists (as their name implies) rely primarily on the effectiveness of monetary policy to stabilize the economy. Their old guard (represented by Milton Friedman) relies primarily on a steady rate of growth of the money stock because of the uncertainty and variability in the lags of economic activity behind monetary growth. The younger, more optimistic members of the group, mesmerized by the research results flowing from the St. Louis Federal Reserve Bank, advocate monetary fine-tuning.

While money occupies a prominent place in their policy prescriptions, both short-run and long-run considerations flowing from their analyses suggest that fiscal policy is not entirely useless.

As the flow of econometric research continues, the validity of the theoretical propositions advocated by the Monetarists will become more apparent.

Perhaps the profession will really believe that the two sides have made an objective examination of their beliefs when Chicago produces a dissertation demonstrating that fiscal policy matters and Yale produces one showing that money matters.

Selected References and Readings

ANDERSON, LEONALL, AND JORDAN, JERRY, "Monetary and Fiscal Actions: A Test of Their Relative Importance in Economic Stabilization," *Review—Federal Reserve Bank of St. Louis* (Nov. 1968).

———, "Reply," *Review—Federal Reserve Bank of St. Louis* (April 1969).

BLINDER, ALAN, AND SOLOW, ROBERT, "Does Fiscal Policy Matter?" *Journal of Public Economics*, No. 2 (1973).

BRUNNER, KARL, "The Role of Money and Monetary Policy, *Review—Federal Reserve Bank of St. Louis* (July 1968).

———, "The 'Monetarist Revolution' in Monetary Theory," *Weltwirtschaftliches Archiv*, No. 1 (1970).

———, "A Survey of Selected Issues in Monetary Theory," *Schweizerische Zeitschrift Für Volkswirtschaft Und Statistik*, Vol. 107 (Winter 1971).

———, "The Monetarist View of Keynesian Ideas," *Lloyds Bank Review*, No. 102 (Oct. 1971).

———, "The State of the Monetarist Debate," *Review—Federal Reserve Bank of St. Louis* (Sept. 1973).

———, AND MELTZER, ALLAN, "The Role of Financial Intermediaries in the Transmission of Monetary Policy," *American Economic Review*, Vol 53 (May 1963).

———, "Fiscal and Monetary Policy in a Non-Keynesian World," unpublished.

———, "Friedman's Monetary Theory," *Journal of Political Economy*, Vol. 80, No. 5 (Sept./Oct. 1972).

———, "Money, Debt, and Economic Activity," *Journal of Political Economy*, Vol. 80, No. 5 (Sept./Oct. 1972).

CAGAN, PHILLIP, *Determinants and Effects of Changes in the Stock of Money, 1875–1960* (New York: NBER, 1965).

DAVIS, RICHARD G., "The Role of the Money Supply in Business Cycles," in *Essays in Domestic and International Finance*, Federal Reserve Bank of New York (1969).

DE LEEUW, FRANK, AND KALCHBRENNER, JOHN, "Monetary and Fiscal Actions: A Test of Their Relative Importance in Economic Stabilization—Comment," *Review—Federal Reserve Bank of St. Louis* (April 1969).

FAND, DAVID, "Keynesian Monetary Theories, Stabilization Policy, and the Recent Inflation," *Journal of Money, Credit and Banking*, Vol. 1, No. 3 (Aug. 1969).

———, "Some Issues in Monetary Economics." *Review—Federal Reserve Bank of St. Louis* (Jan. 1970).

———, "Monetarism and Fiscalism," *Banca Nazionale del Lavoro Quarterly Review*, No. 94 (Sept. 1970).

FRIEDMAN, MILTON, "The Methodology of Positive Economics," in *Essays in Positive Economics* (Chicago: University of Chicago Press, 1953).

————, "The Supply of Money and Changes in Prices and Output," in Edwin Dean, ed., *The Controversy Over the Quantity Theory of Money* (New York: Heath, 1968).

————, *Monetary vs. Fiscal Policy* (New York: Norton, 1969).

————, "Money and Income: Post Hoc Ergo Prompter Hoc? A Comment," *Quarterly Journal of Economics*, Vol. 84, No. 2 (May 1970).

————, *The Counter-Revolution in Monetary Theory, First Wincott Memorial Lecture*, The Institute of Economic Affairs (1970).

————, "The Optimum Quantity of Money," in *The Optimum Quantity of Money and Other Essays* (Chicago: Aldine, 1970).

————, "The Monetary Studies of the National Bureau," reprinted in *Monetary Economics, Readings on Current Issues* (New York: McGraw-Hill, 1971).

————, "A Monetary Theory of National Income," *Journal of Political Economy*, Vol. 79, No. 2 (March/April 1971).

————, "A Theoretical Framework for Monetary Analysis," *Journal of Political Economy*, Vol. 78, No. 2 (March/April 1970). Reprinted in a slightly enlarged form in *National Bureau of Economic Research Occasional Paper 112* (1971).

————, "Comments on the Critics," *Journal of Political Economy*, Vol. 80, No. 5 (Sept./Oct. 1972).

————, AND MEISELMAN, DAVID, "The Relative Stability of Monetary Velocity and the Investment Multiplier in the United States, 1897–1958," *Stabilization Policies: A Series of Research Studies Prepared for the Commission on Money and Credit* (Englewood Cliffs, N.J.: Prentice-Hall, 1963).

————, AND SCHWARTZ, ANNA, "Money and Business Cycles," *The Review of Economics and Statistics*, Vol. 45, No. 1, Part 2 (Feb. 1963).

JOHNSON, HARRY G., "The Keynesian Revolution and the Monetarist Counter-Revolution," *The American Economic Review*, Vol. 61, No. 2 (May 1971).

————, *Inflation and the Monetarist Controversy* (Amsterdam: North-Holland, 1972).

KALDOR, NICHOLAS, "The New Monetarism," *Lloyds Bank Review* (July 1970); and "Reply to Friedman," Vol. 98 (Oct. 1970).

KAREKEN, JOHN, AND SOLOW, ROBERT, "Lags in Monetary Policy," Commission on Money and Credit, *Stabilization Policies: A Series of Research Studies Prepared for the Commission on Money and Credit* (Englewood Cliffs, N.J.: Prentice-Hall, 1963).

KLEIN, LAWRENCE, "The State of the Monetarist Debate," *Review—Federal Reserve Bank of St. Louis* (Sept. 1973).

LATANÉ, HENRY, "Cash Balances and the Rate of Interest—A Pragmatic Approach," *Review of Economics and Statistics*, Vol. 36 (Nov. 1954).

MAYER, THOMAS, "The Lag in the Effect of Monetary Policy: Some Criticisms," *Western Economic Journal*, Vol. 7, No. 3 (1965).

MELTZER, ALLAN, "Controlling Money," *Review—Federal Reserve Bank of St. Louis* (May 1969).

OKUN, ARTHUR, *The Political Economy of Prosperity* (Washington, D.C.: Brookings Institution, 1970).

PARK, YUNG CHUL, "Some Current Issues on the Transmission Process of Monetary Policy," *International Monetary Fund Papers*, Vol. 19, No. 1 (1972).

PATINKIN, DON, "Friedman on the Quantity Theory and Keynesian Economics," *Journal of Political Economy*, Vol. 80, No. 5 (Sept./Oct. 1972).

SAMUELSON, PAUL, "Problems of Methodology—Discussion," *American Economic Review*, Vol. 53, No. 2 (May 1963).

———, "Money, Interest Rates and Economic Activity," in *Proceedings of a Symposium on Money, Interest Rates and Economic Activity* (New York: American Bankers Association, 1967).

———, "Reflections on the Merits and Demerits of Monetarism," in *Issues in Fiscal and Monetary Policy: The Eclectic Economist Views the Controversy*, James J. Diamond, ed. (Chicago: DePaul University, 1971).

SILBER, WILLIAM, "Fiscal Policy in *IS–LM* Analysis: A Correction," *Journal of Money, Credit and Banking*, Vol. 2, No. 4 (Nov. 1970).

SMITH, WARREN L., "A Neo-Keynesian View of Monetary Policy," *Controlling Monetary Aggregates* (Boston: Federal Reserve Bank of Boston, 1969).

———, "Some Current Topics in Monetary Economics," *Journal of Economic Literature*, Vol. 8, No. 3 (Sept. 1970).

SPENCER, ROGER W., "Channels of Monetary Influence, A Survey," *Review—Federal Reserve Bank of St. Louis* (Nov. 1974).

SPENCER, ROGER W., AND YOHE, WILLIAM P., "The 'Crowding-Out' of Private Expenditures by Fiscal Policy Actions," *Review—Federal Reserve Bank of St. Louis*, Vol. 52, No. 10 (Oct. 1970).

———, "Historical Analysis of the 'Crowding-Out' of Private Expenditures by Fiscal Policy Actions," *Working Paper No. 13*, Federal Reserve Bank of St. Louis (Jan. 31, 1971).

TEIGEN, RONALD, "The Keynesian-Monetarist Debate in the U.S.: A Summary and Evaluation," *Saertrykk au Statsøkonomist Tidsskrift*, No. 1 (1970).

———, "A Critical Look at Monetarist Economics," *Review—Federal Reserve Bank of St. Louis* (Jan. 1972).

TOBIN, JAMES, "Asset Holdings and Spending Decisions," *American Economic Review, Papers and Proceedings*, Vol. 42 (May 1952), 109–23. Reprinted in *Essays in Economics, Vol. 1, Macro Economics* (Chicago: Markham Publishing Company, 1971).

———, "A Monetary Interpretation of History: A Review Article," *American Economic Review*, Vol. 55, No. 3 (June 1965).

———, "Money and Income: Post Hoc Ergo Prompter Hoc?", *Quarterly Journal of Economics*, Vol. 84, No. 2 (May 1970).

———, "Friedman's Theoretical Framework," *Journal of Political Economy*, Vol. 80, No. 5 (Sept./Oct. 1972).

Index